D1294178

The Foundations of Program Verification

Wiley-Teubner Series in Computer Science

The Foundations of Program Verification

Jacques Loeckx and Kurt Sieber
Fachrichtung Informatik,
Universität des Saarlandes,
Saarbrücken,
Germany

IN COLLABORATION WITH

Ryan D. Stansifer
Department of Computer Science,
Cornell University,
USA

B. G. TEUBNER
Stuttgart

JOHN WILEY & SONS
Chichester · New York · Brisbane · Toronto · Singapore

Library of Congress Cataloging in Publication Data:

Loeckx, J. J. C. (Jacques J. C.)
  The foundations of program verification.
  (Wiley-Teubner series in computer science)
  Includes index.
  1. Computer programs—Verification.   I. Sieber, Kurt.
II. Stansifer, Ryan D.   III. Title.   IV. Series.
QA76.6.L585   1984   001.64′2   83–16658

ISBN 0 471 90323 X

British Library Cataloguing in Publication Data:

Loeckx, Jacques
  The foundations of program verification.—
  (Wiley-Teubner series in computer science)
  1. Computer programs—Verification
  I. Title   II. Sieber, Kurt
  III. Stansifer, Ryan D.
  001.64′24   QA76.6

ISBN 0 471 90323 X

CIP-Kurztitelaufnahme der Deutschen Bibliothek

Loeckx, Jacques
  The foundations of program verification.
  Jacques Loeckx and Kurt Sieber. In collab.
  with Ryan D. Stansifer. – Stuttgart:
  Teubner; Chichester; New York; Brisbane;
  Toronto; Singapore; Wiley, 1984.
  (Wiley-Teubner series in computer science)

ISBN 3 519 02101 3 (Teubner)
ISBN 0 471 90323 X (Wiley)

NE: Sieber, Kurt:

Filmset by Mid-County Press, London, SW15
Printed by Pitman Press Ltd., Bath, Avon.

Authors' Preface

This is a textbook on program verification. It concentrates on those verification methods that have now become classic such as the inductive assertions method of Floyd, the axiomatic method of Hoare and Scott's fixpoint induction. The aim of the book is to present these different verification methods and to explain their mathematical background. The subject is treated with mathematical precision, and many examples are included. Throughout the book the same examples will reappear to illustrate how the different methods are related. The material is self-contained and accessible without prior knowledge of logic or semantics, but elementary knowledge of programming languages, formal languages and the theory of computation is helpful.

A main concern has been to present the subject in as simple a setting as possible. For this reason three elementary, representative programming languages are introduced: a flowchart programming language, a language of while-programs and a language of recursive programs. For these programming languages the operational and denotational semantics are introduced. Each verification method is then illustrated in the most appropriate of these languages and proved correct with the help of the most appropriate of the semantics.

Part A of the book briefly presents the mathematical background required. It contains a discussion of induction (Chapter 1) and a short introduction to predicate logic (Chapter 2). *Part B* is devoted to the description of the semantics of programming languages. First, operational semantics is illustrated by means of the three elementary programming languages (Chapter 3). After a short, but self-contained, treatment of the theory of fixpoints in complete partial orders (Chapter 4), denotational semantics is introduced and the equivalence to the operational semantics is proved (Chapter 5). *Part C* is devoted to verification methods and constitutes the core of the book. First, the notion of correctness of a program is given a precise definition (Chapter 6). Floyd's inductive assertions method and the well-founded sets method are described and proved to be correct (Chapter 7). Next the Hoare calculus for while-programs is introduced, its soundness and its relative completeness are proved. The notion of expressiveness is also discussed. A generalization of the Hoare calculus for total correctness is sketched (Chapter 8). The applications of the fixpoint induction principle are discussed in some detail. The verification methods of subgoal induction and structural induction are described, and their correctness is proved (Chapter 9). Finally, Milner's Logic for Computable Functions (LCF) is introduced and discussed (Chapter 10). *Part D* presents a short overview of other approaches and further development in the field of program verification.

Each chapter ends with a list of exercises and bibliographic notes. The exercises are arranged by section. More difficult problems are marked with an asterisk '*'. The bibliographic notes do not try to list all the relevant literature on the respective topics. Their only purpose, apart from the historical references, is to list monographs, overview papers and research papers that may help the reader interested in further study.

The organization of the text allows the following deviations from a sequential reading of the book. Section 1.1 contains definitions from everyday mathematics and may be skipped and consulted later if necessary. The same holds for Section 1.2 and Chapter 2, provided the reader is familiar with induction and predicate logic, respectively. Chapters 6 through 8 may be read immediately after Chapter 3, or after even Section 3.2, since the theory of cpo's is not needed until Chapter 9. This sequence allows the reader to see verification methods as soon as possible. More difficult sections are marked with an asterisk '*' and may be skipped if wanted.

The present book has similarities with Manna's well-known book, *Mathematical Theory of Computation*, from which many examples are borrowed. It differs by treating the subject in more detail and with more mathematical rigor. Moreover, it treats a few newer results such as subgoal induction and Cook's completeness theorem. The present book differs from de Bakker's book, *Mathematical Theory of Program Correctness*, by treating the subject in a wider context and avoiding the problems involved in an extensive account of a particular programming language with many different features.

The book grew out of a course held by one of the authors at the University of Saarbrücken. The critical remarks of students and colleagues at Saarbrücken and elsewhere on previous versions of the manuscript are gratefully acknowledged. In particular, Krzysztof Apt, Andrzej Blikle, Robert Constable, Zohar Manna and Robin Milner provided many clarifying discussions. Chapters 2 and 11 profited from critical reading by Wolfgang Thomas and Manfred Broy, respectively. Dieter Gross and Ralf Treinen pointed out several errors. The manuscript was typed with much patience and many typeballs by Margot Günther.

Saarbrücken and Ithaca,

Jacques Loeckx
Kurt Sieber
Ryan Stansifer

Contents _____

List of Symbols

PART A
Preliminaries

1
Mathematical Preliminaries

This chapter has two objectives. First, the basic mathematical concepts and notation used throughout this book are introduced. Secondly, the principle of induction, the indispensable tool in program verification, is presented in two guises and discussed in some detail.

1.1 Basic Concepts and Notation

The reader is assumed to have some familiarity with normal everyday set theoretic apparatus as well as with some elementary notions from formal languages and computation theory. The aim of this section is merely to fix the notation and recall some definitions. It is suggested that the reader, instead of poring over this section at the outset, simply refer to it if and when questions of this nature arise in later sections.

The notation of set theory includes in particular:

$\emptyset$ for the *empty set*;
$S \subseteq T$ for S is a *subset* of T;
$S \subset T$ for S is a *proper subset* of T, that is $S \subseteq T$ but $S \neq T$;
$P(S)$ for the *power set* of S, that is, $P(S)$ is the set of all subsets of S;
$S \backslash T = \{s \in S \mid s \notin T\}$ for the *set difference* of S and T;
$S - T$ for the set difference, when $T \subseteq S$;
$S_1 \times \cdots \times S_n$ for the *Cartesian product* of sets, that is

$$S_1 \times \cdots \times S_n = \{(s_1, \ldots, s_n) \mid s_i \in S_i \text{ for } i = 1, \ldots, n\};$$

if $S_i = S$ for $i = 1, \ldots, n$, then one writes S^n;
S^{Nat} for the set of all *infinite sequences* of S,

$$S^{Nat} = \{(s_1, s_2, \ldots) \mid s_i \in S \text{ for } i = 0, 1, 2, \ldots\}.$$

Particular sets to be used in this book are

$$Nat = \{0, 1, 2, \ldots\}$$

$$Int = \{\ldots, -1, 0, 1, \ldots\}$$

$$Bool = \{\text{true}, \text{false}\}$$

3

1.1.1 Relations

Let S and T be sets. A *relation* (between S and T) is a subset $R \subseteq S \times T$. If $S = T$, then one says R is a relation *on* S.

Let $R \subseteq S \times T$ be a relation. For every subset $A \subseteq S$, the *image* of A (under the relation R) is defined to be:

$$R(A) = \{t \in T \mid (s, t) \in R \text{ for at least one } s \in A\}.$$

For every subset $B \subseteq T$, the *pre-image* of B (under the relation R) is defined to be:

$$R^{-1}(B) = \{s \in S \mid (s, t) \in R \text{ for at least one } t \in B\}.$$

A relation $R \subseteq S \times T$ is called

onto (with respect to S and T) if $R(S) = T$, in other words, if for every $t \in T$ there is at least one $s \in S$ such that $(s, t) \in R$;

total (with respect to S and T) if $R^{-1}(T) = S$, in other words, if for every $s \in S$ there is at least one $t \in T$ such that $(s, t) \in R$;

one-to-one (with respect to S and T) if for every $t \in T$ there is at most one $s \in S$ such that $(s, t) \in R$;

a *(partial) function* (from S to T) if for every $s \in S$ there is at most one $t \in T$ such that $(s, t) \in R$; t is called the *value* of the function for the *argument* s;

a *total function* (from S to T) if R is total with respect to S and T, and R is a function from S to T;

a *predicate* if it is a total function to *Bool*.

A relation R on S is called

reflexive, if $(s, s) \in R$ for all $s \in S$;

irreflexive, if $(s, s) \in R$ for no $s \in S$;

symmetric, if $(s_1, s_2) \in R$ implies $(s_2, s_1) \in R$ for all $s_1, s_2 \in S$;

antisymmetric, if $(s_1, s_2) \in R$ and $(s_2, s_1) \in R$ implies $s_1 = s_2$ for all $s_1, s_2 \in S$;

transitive, if $(s_1, s_2) \in R$ and $(s_2, s_3) \in R$ implies $(s_1, s_3) \in R$ for all $s_1, s_2, s_3 \in S$.

The *closure* of a relation R on S is the smallest reflexive, transitive relation which contains R; it is denoted R^*.

Instead of $(s, t) \in R$ one often uses the infix notation $s\,R\,t$.

1.1.2 Functions

The fact that f is a partial function from S to T is denoted

$$f : S \rightsquigarrow T;$$

in contrast to

$$f : S \longrightarrow T,$$

which is reserved for *total* functions f from S to T. The set of all total functions from S to T is denoted $(S \longrightarrow T)$.

If $f : S \rightsquigarrow T$ and $A \subseteq S$, then the *restriction* of f to A is defined to be the intersection of f (which is a subset of $S \times T$) with $A \times T$ and is denoted $f \mid A$.

A function will not usually be defined with the set theoretic notation used for relations, but instead the 'customary' notation will be used as illustrated by the following example for the definition of subtr: $Nat^2 \rightsquigarrow Nat$:

$$\text{subtr}(m, n) = \begin{cases} m - n & \text{if } m \geq n, \\ \text{undefined} & \text{otherwise.} \end{cases}$$

For any *total* function $f: S \rightarrow T$ the function that differs from f only at $s \in S$ by taking on the value $t \in T$ is denoted $f[s/t]$. In the notation introduced above $f[s/t]: S \rightarrow T$ is defined by

$$f[s/t](r) = \begin{cases} t & \text{if } r = s, \\ f(r) & \text{otherwise.} \end{cases}$$

A *fixpoint* of a (total) function $f: S \rightarrow S$ is an element $s \in S$ for which $f(s) = s$.

Let $f: S \rightarrow T$ and $g: T \rightarrow V$ be total functions. The *composition* of g and f is denoted $g \circ f$ and is defined by

$$g \circ f(s) = g(f(s))$$

for each $s \in S$. Given a total function $f: S \rightarrow S$, composition can be used to define a collection of functions, one for each $i \in Nat$. These functions are denoted f^i and defined by:

f° is the identity function
$f^{i+1} = f \circ f^i$

The function f^i is called the ith *iterate* of f.

In the course of this book nearly all examples make use of *total* functions on *Nat*. Contrasting with the example of the function subtr given above, the subtraction of two numbers m and n is then defined by

$$m - n = \begin{cases} \text{the 'usual' value} & \text{if } m \geq n \\ 0 & \text{otherwise.} \end{cases}$$

The properties of this subtraction should not be confounded with those of the (total) subtraction on *Int*, as illustrated by the following:

$m > m - 1$ iff $m > 0$
$m - n + p = m + p - n$ iff $m \geq n$ or $p = 0$
$m = n - p$ implies $m + p = n$ iff $n \geq p$

1.1.3 *Generalized Cartesian Products

An element of the Cartesian product of the sets $S_1, \ldots, S_n$, $n \geq 1$, may be considered as a (total) function

$$s: \{1, \ldots, n\} \rightarrow S_1 \cup \cdots \cup S_n$$

such that $s(i) \in S_i$ for $i = 1, \ldots, n$. The Cartesian product itself is then the set of all these functions. According to usual mathematical notation one writes s_i instead of $s(i)$; an element of the Cartesian product is written $(s_1, \ldots, s_n)$ instead of s.

The concept of a Cartesian product may now be generalized as follows. Let I be an arbitrary set (not necessarily a finite subset $\{1, \ldots, n\}$ of Nat), the elements of which are called *indices*. Assume that to each index $i \in I$ is associated a set S_i. Then the (*generalized*) *Cartesian product* of the sets S_i—denoted $\prod_{i \in I} S_i$—is the set of all functions

$$s: I \rightarrow \bigcup_{i \in I} S_i$$

with $s(i) \in S_i$ for each $i \in I$. Again one writes s_i instead of $s(i)$. An element of the Cartesian product is often written $(s_i)_{i \in I}$ instead of s and is called the *family* of the elements s_i.

1.1.4 Partial Orders

Let P be a set and '$\sqsubseteq$' a relation on P. The pair $(P, \sqsubseteq)$ is called a (*reflexive*) *partial order* if the relation '$\sqsubseteq$' is reflexive, antisymmetric, and transitive. A partial order $(P, \sqsubseteq)$ is *total*, when for any two elements, $a, b \in P$ either $a \sqsubseteq b$ or $b \sqsubseteq a$.

If $(P, \sqsubseteq)$ is a partial order and S is a subset of P, then an element $m \in S$ is called *minimal* if there is no other element $n \in S$ such that $n \sqsubseteq m$. Should $m \sqsubseteq n$ for all $n \in S$ then m is called the *least* element of S (that there is at most one such element is shown in Exercise 1.1–1); this least element is denoted min S. A *maximal* element of S and its *greatest* element can be analogously defined.

Let $(P_1, \sqsubseteq)$ and $(P_2, \sqsubseteq)$ be two partial orders. (Naturally, two different relations '$\sqsubseteq$' are being considered. In such cases where the relations can be easily inferred from context only one symbol will be used.) A total function $g: P_1 \rightarrow P_2$ is called *monotonic* (with respect to these partial orders) when for all $a, b \in P_1$

$$a \sqsubseteq b \quad \text{implies} \quad g(a) \sqsubseteq g(b).$$

The set of all total monotonic functions from P_1 to P_2 is denoted $(P_1 \overrightarrow{_m} P_2)$.

Now three 'natural' methods will be introduced to construct new partial orders from given ones.

(1) *Restriction of a partial order.* Let $(P, \sqsubseteq)$ be a partial order and S a subset of P. Then $(S, \sqsubseteq)$ is also a partial order. (More precisely, the pair $(S, \sqsubseteq_S)$ is a partial order, where $\sqsubseteq_S$ is the intersection of $\sqsubseteq$ with S^2.)

(2) *Product of partial orders.* Let $(P_1, \sqsubseteq), \ldots, (P_n, \sqsubseteq)$, where $n \geq 2$, be partial orders. One defines the relation '$\sqsubseteq$' on the Cartesian product $P_1 \times \cdots \times P_n$ by

$$(a_1, \ldots, a_n) \sqsubseteq (b_1, \ldots, b_n) \qquad \text{iff } a_i \sqsubseteq b_i \text{ for all } i, 1 \leq i \leq n.$$

Then $(P_1 \times \cdots \times P_n, \sqsubseteq)$ is also a partial order. (This is Exercise 1.1–3.) This process generalizes for infinite products.

(3) *The partial order of functions.* Let $(P, \sqsubseteq)$ be a partial order and S any set. One defines a relation '$\sqsubseteq$' on the set $(S \rightarrow P)$ of all total functions from S to P by

$$f \sqsubseteq g \qquad \text{iff } f(s) \sqsubseteq g(s) \text{ for all } s \in S.$$

Then $((S \rightarrow P), \sqsubseteq)$ is also a partial order. (The proof is left to Exercise 1.1–4.)

These three methods of constructing partial orders are so straightforward that they will often be applied without explicit mention.

Finally, one more notation: let $(P, \sqsubseteq)$ be a partial order. For all $a, b \in P, a \sqsubset b$ is defined to hold whenever $a \sqsubseteq b$ and $a \neq b$. It is shown in Exercise 1.1–5 that '$\sqsubset$' can be viewed as an irreflexive and transitive relation.

1.1.5 Strings

Fix for a moment an arbitrary set S of symbols. A (possibly infinite) sequence of symbols from S is called a *string* (over S). Strings are generally written one symbol after the other without any sort of punctuation. A set of strings over S is called a *formal language* over S.

The number of symbols of a finite string s is called its *length* and is denoted $|s|$. The string with length equal to zero is a sequence of no symbols at all; it is called the *empty string* and is denoted ε. The set of all finite strings over the set S of symbols (including the empty string) is written S^*.

Two strings can be *concatenated* by joining the two sequences of symbols one after the other. A string p is a *prefix* of a string s if there is a string r such that the concatenation of the strings p and r yields the string s; this prefix is called *proper*, if $p \neq \varepsilon$ and $p \neq s$.

1.1.6 Computation Theory

The amount of computation theory which is needed can, if necessary, be understood intuitively without the help of an exact theory of Turing machines and the like. So, for the following definitions the reader may understand under algorithm whatever formal or informal notion is at hand. When a function is said to be *computable*, it is meant that there is an algorithm to compute its values. When a set is said to be *recursive* or *decidable*, it is meant that there is an algorithm which given a potential element says 'yes' or 'no' according to whether it is an element of the set or not. A set is *recursively enumerable* if there is an algorithm which recognizes elements of the set (by saying 'yes') but which may not terminate for elements not in the set.

From time to time elementary results concerning these concepts will be used. These can be found in any book devoted to this topic, for example in those indicated at the end of this chapter.

1.2 Induction

Induction is not only typical for program verification but also common in other parts of computer science and in mathematics. In this book induction will be used in definitions and in proofs.

Inductive definitions are especially suitable for infinite sets. Moreover, sets defined by induction implicitly get a structure which may serve as a basis for the inductive definition of functions on these sets.

Inductive proofs are especially suitable for properties of sets with elements of unbounded 'length'. These proofs play a significant role in the verification of programs, because correctness expresses a property of the results computed by programs and these computations can be unlimitedly 'long'. Two proof principles will be considered here, called structural induction and Noetherian induction respectively. Both proof principles can be viewed as generalizations of the induction principle over the natural numbers. Consider the following two equivalent formulations of this principle:

I. To prove that a property P holds for all numbers $n \in Nat$, it is sufficient to show:

(a) P holds for 0.
(b) If P holds for a number $n \in Nat$, then P also holds for $n + 1$.

II. To prove that a property P holds for all numbers $n \in Nat$, it is sufficient to show:

(a) P holds for 0.
(b) If $n \in Nat$, $n \neq 0$, and P holds for all $m \in Nat$ such that $m < n$, then P also holds for n.

(Exactly what it means that these two formulations are equivalent, is best expressed with the help of predicate logic; therefore, this is deferred to Exercise 2.4–4.)

The first formulation is closely connected to the fact that the natural numbers can be 'constructed' by beginning with the number 0 and repeatedly adding one. By permitting more general 'construction methods', namely those used by inductive definitions, one obtains structural induction.

The second formulation has more to do with the ordering of the natural numbers; more precisely, it is closely connected to the fact that every non-empty subset of Nat contains a minimal element with respect to the relation '$\leq$'. By permitting arbitrary partial orders with this property, one obtains Noetherian induction.

As they are interrelated, the inductive definition of sets and functions and the proof principle of structural induction are treated first; Noetherian induction is examined next.

1.2.1 Inductive Definitions and Structural Induction

The concepts that are introduced in this section are first illustrated by means of an example. This example is taken from mathematical logic but should be understandable to the reader who has no knowledge in this field.

EXAMPLE 1.1   Let B be a set of symbols disjoint from the set $\{\neg, \vee, \wedge, \supset, \equiv, (,)\}$ and let Z denote the union of these two sets.

(1) The set of *propositional formulas* over B (denoted PF_B) is defined as a subset of Z^* by the following inductive definition:

(a) $B \subseteq PF_B$.
(b) If $w \in PF_B$, then $(\neg w) \in PF_B$.
    If $w_1, w_2 \in PF_B$, then $(w_1 \wedge w_2), (w_1 \vee w_2), (w_1 \supset w_2), (w_1 \equiv w_2) \in PF_B$.

(2) Consider the function $f: Z^* \to Nat$ defined by:

$f(x)$ = the number of left parentheses in x minus
        the number of right parentheses in x.

A proof by structural induction that $f(w) = 0$ for all $w \in PF_B$, consists in showing that:

(a) $f(w) = 0$ for all $w \in B$.
(b) If $f(w) = 0$, then $f((\neg w)) = 0$.
    If $f(w_1) = f(w_2) = 0$, then $f((w_1 \wedge w_2)) = f((w_1 \vee w_2)) = f((w_1 \supset w_2)) = f((w_1 \equiv w_2)) = 0$.

That (a) holds, is trivial, since no symbol in B can contain any parenthesis; that (b) holds, is a consequence of the fact that $f((\neg w)) = f(w) + 1 - 1$ for all $w \in PF_B$ and similar arguments for the other cases.

(3) Let $\mathcal{I}_0$ be a predicate $\mathcal{I}_0: B \to Bool$. Then $\mathcal{I}_0$ can be extended to a predicate $\mathcal{I}: PF_B \to Bool$ by the following inductive definition:

(a) $\mathcal{I}(w) = \mathcal{I}_0(w)$ if $w \in B$.

(b) $\mathcal{I}((\neg w)) = \begin{cases} \text{true} & \text{if } \mathcal{I}(w) = \text{false}, \\ \text{false} & \text{if } \mathcal{I}(w) = \text{true}, \end{cases}$

and similarly for $\wedge, \vee, \supset$, and $\equiv$. $\square$

In what follows the three methods illustrated in the above example, namely, the inductive definition method for sets, the proof method of structural induction, and the inductive definition methods for functions will be precisely defined.

DEFINITION 1.2 (Inductive Definition of Sets)   Let U be a set called the *universe*. Let B be a subset of U, called the *basis set*, and let K be a set of relations $r \subseteq U^n \times U$ (where $n \geq 1$ and n depends on r), called the *constructor set*. A set A is called *inductively* (or *recursively*) *defined* by B and K, when A is the smallest (with respect to set inclusion) of all the subsets S of U for which the following two conditions hold:

(a) $B \subseteq S$
(b) $r(S^n) \subseteq S$ for all $r \in K$ (or, expressed another way: if $a_1, \ldots, a_n \in S$ and $((a_1, \ldots, a_n), a) \in r$ for some constructor $r \in K$, then $a \in S$). $\square$

Notice that such a set always exists and is uniquely determined (Exercise 1.2–2). In practice the relations $r \in K$ are often (total) functions $f: U^n \to U$.

EXAMPLE 1.3   The definition of the set of propositional formulas of Example 1.1 can now be rephrased in the terminology of the definition above. The universe is the set Z^*, the basis is the set B of symbols, and the constructor set is the set $\{f_\neg, f_\wedge, f_\vee, f_\supset, f_\equiv\}$ of functions where

$$f_\neg: Z^* \to Z^* \quad \text{is defined by} \quad f_\neg(w) = (\neg w)$$

and so on.   □

The definition given above does not indicate how to construct the new set. Therefore, another equivalent definition will be given. (The proof of equivalence is Exercise 1.2–3.)

DEFINITION 1.4   Let U, B, and K be as in Definition 1.2. A sequence $u_1, \ldots, u_m$ ($m \geq 1$) of elements from U with $u_m = u$ is called a *construction sequence* for u (from B and K), when for every $i = 1, \ldots, m$ either

(a) $u_i \in B$, or
(b) there is a constructor $r \in U^n \times U$ from K and $i_1, \ldots, i_n < i$, such that $((u_{i_1}, \ldots, u_{i_n}), u_i) \in r$.

$A \subseteq U$ is called *inductively defined* by B and K, when A consists of all those elements $u \in U$, for which there exists a construction sequence.   □

From the constructive character of this definition emerge two consequences. First if B, K and the relations in K are all recursively enumerable, then A is also recursively enumerable. Second, since by definition *all* elements of a construction sequence are in A, then for every $a \in A$ either $a \in B$ or there exists a constructor $r \subseteq U^n \times U$ from K and $a_1, \ldots, a_n \in A$ such that $((a_1, \ldots, a_n), a) \in r$. In other words

$$A = B \cup \bigcup_{r \in K} r(A^n)$$

—and not only $A \supseteq B \cup \bigcup_{r \in K} r(A^n)$ as implied by Definition 1.2. Notice that this equation cannot serve as a definition because the set to be defined, namely A, occurs on both sides of the equation.

Of particular interest is the case when this construction process unambiguously describes how to obtain an element of the set.

DEFINITION 1.5 (Free Inductive Definitions)   The inductive definition of a set A by a basis set B and a constructor set K is called *free*, if for every element $a \in A$ either $a \in B$ or there is just one constructor $r \in K$ and just one n-tuple of elements $a_1, \ldots, a_n \in A$ such that $((a_1, \ldots, a_n), a) \in r$ (but not both).   □

In other words: the definition is free, if and only if B and all $r(A^n)$ are pairwise disjoint, and $r \cap (A^n \times A)$ is one-to-one for every $r \in K$. (Examples of definitions which are not free are given in Exercise 1.2–4.) The importance of this definition will become clear when we discuss the inductive definition of functions (Theorem 1.9).

As indicated above the inductive definition of a set constitutes a general construction process. A particular and simple instance of this process is the construction of the natural numbers by the repeated addition of one. The pertinent induction principle over the natural numbers can also be generalized to all inductively defined sets:

THEOREM 1.6 (The Principle of Structural Induction) Let $A \subseteq U$ be inductively defined by the basis set B and the constructor set K. To prove that a property P holds for all $a \in A$, it is sufficient to show:

(a) *Induction basis* P holds for all $a \in B$.
(b) *Induction step* If P holds for $a_1, \ldots, a_n \in A$ (*Induction hypothesis*) and $((a_1, \ldots, a_n), a) \in r$ for some $r \in K$, then P holds for a also.

Proof. Let $C \subseteq A$ be the set of all elements of A for which P holds. It is necessary to show that (a) and (b) imply that P holds for all $a \in A$, in other words that $A \subseteq C$. Since (a) means $B \subseteq C$, and (b) means that if $a_1, \ldots, a_n \in C$ and $((a_1, \ldots, a_n), a) \in r$ for some $r \in K$, then $a \in C$, the set C fulfils exactly the two conditions in Definition 1.2. Since A is by definition the smallest subset of U which satisfies these two conditions, it follows that $A \subseteq C$. $\square$

EXAMPLE 1.7 In Example 1.1 it was shown for all propositional formulas w of PF_B that $f(w)$ (the number of left parentheses in w minus the number of right parentheses) is equal to zero. Now another property of PF_B will be proved which will be needed in a later example, namely:

for all $w \in PF_B$: if u is a proper prefix of w, then $f(u) > 0$ (hence $f(u) \geq 0$ for every prefix u of w).

According to the principle of structural induction one proves:

(a) *Induction basis* If $w \in B$, then there is no proper prefix of w and the property is vacuously true.
(b) *Induction step* According to the structure of w two cases are distinguished:

Case 1: $w = (\neg w_1)$ with $w_1 \in PF_B$. There are only two possibilities for a proper prefix u of w:

  $u = ($, so $f(u) = 1$, or
  $u = (\neg u'$, where u' is a—not necessarily proper—prefix of w_1. By induction hypothesis $f(u') \geq 0$ so $f(u) = f(u') + 1 > 0$.

Case 2: $w = (w_1 \circ w_2)$ with $\circ \in \{\wedge, \vee, \supset, \equiv\}$ and $w_1, w_2 \in PF_B$. There are again only two possibilities for a proper prefix u of w:

$u = (u_1$, where u_1 is a prefix of w_1. Then $f(u) = f(u_1) + 1 > 0$, since $f(u_1) \geq 0$ by induction hypothesis.

$u = (w_1 \circ u_2$, where u_2 is a prefix of w_2. Then $f(u) = f(w_1) + f(u_2) + 1 > 0$, since $f(w_1) = 0$ by Example 1.1 and $f(u_2) \geq 0$ by induction hypotnesis.

□

It should be remarked that a proof by structural induction can always be replaced by a proof with induction over Nat. The trick is to change the proof to be one of induction over the 'depth' of the elements in the following way. When the set A is inductively defined by the basis set B and the constructor set K, then there exists a construction sequence for every $a \in A$. The *depth* $d(a)$ of an element $a \in A$ is defined by:

$$d(a) = \min\{m \in Nat \,|\, u_1, \ldots, u_m \text{ is a construction sequence for } a\} - 1.$$

Let P be any property, and define Q to be the property:

'P holds for all $a \in A$ of depth $d(a) = n$'.

The two assertions 'P holds for all $a \in A$' and 'Q holds for all $n \in Nat$' are equivalent. Moreover, a proof with structural induction of P can easily be translated into a proof of Q using induction over Nat:

(a) $d(a) = 0$ iff $a \in B$; so, both induction bases are equivalent;
(b) $d(a) > d(a_i)$ for $i = 1, \ldots, n$ when $((a_1, \ldots, a_n), a) \in r$ for some $r \in K$; so, the induction step of the structural induction proof can be easily rephrased, too.

This shows that structural induction is not more powerful than induction over Nat. Hence the advantage of structural induction over induction over Nat merely lies in the perspicuity of the proofs.

The structure induced by an inductive definition of a set can also be used to define functions which have this set as their domain. To do this one uses the fact that every function is a relation, hence a set, and therefore can be itself inductively defined.

DEFINITION 1.8 (Inductive Definition of Functions) Let the set $A \subseteq U$ be inductively defined by the basis set B and the constructor set K, and let V be an arbitrary set. Furthermore, associate to every element $a \in B$ an element $h(a) \in V$ and to every constructor $r \subseteq U^n \times U \in K$ $(n \geq 1)$ a function $h(r) \colon V^n \to V$. An inductive definition of a function $g \colon A \to V$ (to begin with one is only sure that it is a relation $g \subseteq A \times V$ according to Definition 1.2) is given by:

(a) $g(a) = h(a)$ (that is, $(a, h(a)) \in g$) for all $a \in B$,
(b) $g(a) = h(r)(g(a_1), \ldots, g(a_n))$ (that is, $(a, h(r)(b_1, \ldots, b_n)) \in g$ if $(a_1, b_1), \ldots, (a_n, b_n) \in g$) for all $r \subseteq U^n \times U \in K, a_1, \ldots, a_n \in A$ and $((a_1, \ldots, a_n), a) \in r$.

□

This definition is consistent only if every $a \in A$ is assigned exactly one value by (a) and (b) (that is, if the relation g is a total function). If this condition is satisfied, it can be said that the function g is *well-defined*. The following theorem gives a sufficient criterion for a function to be well-defined.

THEOREM 1.9 (Recursion Theorem)   If the inductive definition of a set A by the basis set B and the constructor set K is free, then the function $g: A \to V$ defined inductively as in Definition 1.8 is well-defined.

Proof. It is necessary to show that for every element $a \in A$ the inductive definition of g provides exactly one value $g(a)$. This property will be proved by structural induction on A.

(a) *Induction basis*   Suppose $a \in B$. One value for $g(a)$ is given by the definition, namely $h(a)$. On the other hand, no other value can be given, else there would exist $a_1, \ldots, a_n \in A$ such that $((a_1, \ldots, a_n), a) \in r$ for some constructor $r \subseteq U^n \times U \in K$; this is not possible since the inductive definition of A is free. Therefore, the property holds for a.

(b) *Induction step*   Let $a_1, \ldots, a_n \in A$ be such that $((a_1, \ldots, a_n), a) \in r$ for some constructor $r \subseteq U^n \times U \in K$. By induction hypothesis $g(a_1), \ldots, g(a_n)$ are all well-defined, so there is one value for $g(a)$ given by the definition, namely $h(r)(g(a_1), \ldots, g(a_n))$. No other value for $g(a)$ is derivable from the definition, since the inductive definition of A is free: $a \notin B$ and for no other $a'_1, \ldots, a'_m \in A$ and $r' \in U^m \times U \in K$ does $((a'_1, \ldots, a'_m), a) \in r'$.   □

EXAMPLE 1.10   It was shown in Example 1.1 how to extend a predicate $\mathcal{J}_0: B \to Bool$ to a predicate $\mathcal{J}: PF_B \to Bool$. Now it will be shown that this function $\mathcal{J}$ is well-defined since the inductive definition of PF_B is free. That this definition is free means exactly one of the following three cases must hold for every $w \in PF_B$:

(1) $w \in B$
(2) $w = (\neg w')$ for a uniquely defined $w' \in PF_B$
(3) $w = (w_1 \circ w_2)$ for a uniquely defined symbol $\circ \in \{ \wedge, \vee, \supset, \equiv \}$ and uniquely defined formulas $w_1, w_2 \in PF_B$.

Case (1) holds exactly when w consists of one symbol; case (2) holds exactly when the second symbol of w is '$\neg$', and w' is then uniquely determined. It remains to show that w is not representable by two formulas of the form in case (3). Suppose $w = (w_1 \circ w_2) = (w'_1 \square w'_2)$ with $\circ, \square \in \{ \wedge, \vee, \supset, \equiv \}$. Without loss of generality one can assume that w_1 is a prefix of w'_1. Since w_1 is not the empty word and since due to the number of parentheses (see Example 1.7) w_1 cannot be a proper prefix of w'_1, it follows that $w_1 = w'_1$. But then $\circ$ and $\square$ must also be the same, as must w_2 and w'_2.   □

Since inductive definitions are so common, from now on the basis and constructor sets will not always be explicitly given nor will proofs be given that the definitions are free. Moreover, a generalized version of induction, called

14

simultaneous structural induction which is briefly discussed in Exercise 1.2–5, will also be used.

1.2.2 Noetherian Induction

Next the second possibility for generalizing the principle of induction over the natural numbers is taken up. For this purpose the notion of a well-founded set is needed.

Let $(W, \sqsubseteq)$ be a partial order. The pair $(W, \sqsubseteq)$ is called a *well-founded set* (WFS), if every non-empty subset of W contains at least one minimal element with respect to the relation '$\sqsubseteq$'.

An infinite sequence $a_0, a_1, a_2, \ldots$ of elements from W is said to be *descending*, if $a_{i+1} \sqsubset a_i$ for all $i \in Nat$. (Recall $a_{i+1} \sqsubset a_i$ was defined to hold if $a_{i+1} \sqsubseteq a_i$ and $a_{i+1} \neq a_i$.) As the following theorem demonstrates, this concept leads to an equivalent definition of well-founded sets.

THEOREM 1.11 For a partial order $(W, \sqsubseteq)$ the following two statements are equivalent:

(1) $(W, \sqsubseteq)$ is a well-founded set.
(2) There exists *no* infinite descending sequence of elements in W.

Proof. First it is shown that (1) implies (2). Suppose there is an infinite descending sequence $a_0, a_1, \ldots$ of elements in W. Let $S = \{a_0, a_1, \ldots\}$ be the set of these elements. Then for every element $a_i \in S$ there is a smaller element in S, namely a_{i+1}. Hence, S is a non-empty subset of W which has no minimal element; this contradicts (1).

Now it is shown that (2) implies (1). Suppose $(W, \sqsubseteq)$ is not a WFS. Then there is at least one non-empty subset S of W which has no minimal element. One can construct an infinite descending sequence in the following way:

(a) Choose an arbitrary element a_0 from S; such an element exists since S is non-empty.
(b) If $a_0, \ldots, a_i \in S$ $(i \geq 0)$ have already been chosen, then choose an element $a_{i+1} \in S$ such that $a_{i+1} \sqsubset a_i$; such an element exists since a_i is not a minimal element of S.

(This construction actually constitutes an inductive definition of a function $f: Nat \rightarrow S$ with $f(i) = a_i$ for all $i \in Nat$.) Therefore, in contradiction to (2), an infinite descending sequence has been exhibited. □

EXAMPLE 1.12 Examples of well-founded sets are:

(1) The natural numbers under the usual ordering '$\leq$'.
(2) Let A be an inductively defined set. Define the relation '$\sqsubseteq$' on A using the depth function d introduced above:

$$a \sqsubset b \qquad \text{iff } d(a) < d(b) \text{ or } a = b.$$

Then $(A, \sqsubseteq)$ is a well-founded set.

(3) Define the *lexicographic ordering* on Nat^2 by

$$(m_1, m_2) \sqsubseteq (n_1, n_2) \qquad \text{iff } \begin{cases} m_1 < n_1, \text{ or} \\ m_1 = n_1 \text{ and } m_2 \le n_2. \end{cases}$$

Then $(Nat^2, \sqsubseteq)$ is a well-founded set as the following argument shows: let S be an arbitrary non-empty subset of Nat^2. Then S has a least (not just a minimal) element (m_0, n_0) defined as follows:

$$m_0 = \min\{m \in Nat \,|\, \text{there is } n \in Nat \text{ such that } (m, n) \in S\}$$

$$n_0 = \min\{n \in Nat \,|\, (m_0, n) \in S\}$$

Notice that in $(Nat^2, \sqsubseteq)$ there can be infinite *ascending* sequences between two elements, for example, the sequence $(0, 1), (0, 2), \ldots$ between the elements $(0, 0)$ and $(1, 0)$. Therefore, it is not possible in general to define the 'depth' of an element in a well-founded set, as was done for inductively defined sets. Hence, unlike the principle of structural induction, the principle of Noetherian induction (which will be introduced next) cannot be reduced to induction over the natural numbers in the same way. $\qquad \Box$

By generalizing the second formulation of the principle of induction over the natural numbers one arrives at the principle of Noetherian induction.

THEOREM 1.13 (The Principle of Noetherian Induction) Let $(W, \sqsubseteq)$ be a WFS. In order to prove that a property P holds for all $x \in W$, it is sufficient to show:

(a) *Induction basis* P holds for all minimal elements of W.
(b) *Induction step* For each $x \in W$ the following holds: if $x \in W$ is not minimal and P holds for all $y \in W$ such that $y \sqsubset x$, then P holds for x, too.

Remark. These two assertions can be combined to:

for all $x \in W$: if P holds for all $y \sqsubset x$, then P holds for x.

This equivalence is due to the fact that the assertion that P holds for all $y \sqsubset x$ is vacuously true, when x is a minimal element of W.

Proof. It will be shown from this shorter formulation that P holds for all $x \in W$. Suppose to the contrary that the set S of all elements of W for which P does not hold is non-empty. Since $(W, \sqsubseteq)$ is a WFS, S has a minimal element, say m. By the definition of S, for all $y \sqsubset m$, P holds for y. But whenever this happens P must hold for m, contradicting the choice of m. So the assumption that the set S was non-empty is false, hence, P must hold for all $x \in W$. $\qquad \Box$

EXERCISES

1.1–1 Show that for a partial order $(P, \sqsubseteq)$ and a subset S of P:

(1) S can have at most one least element.
(2) The least element of S is a minimal element of S.

1.1–2 Give a partial order $(P, \sqsubseteq)$ and a subset S of P such that

(1) S has at least one minimal element but no least element.
(2) S has exactly one minimal element but no least element.
(3) S has no minimal element.

1.1–3 Let $(P_1, \sqsubseteq), \ldots, (P_n, \sqsubseteq)$, where $n \geq 2$, be partial orders. Show $(P_1 \times \cdots \times P_n, \sqsubseteq)$ is also a partial order.

1.1–4 Let $(P, \sqsubseteq)$ be a partial order and S any set. Show $((S \to P), \sqsubseteq)$ is also a partial order.

1.1–5 (1) Let $(P, \sqsubseteq)$ be a partial order. Show that the relation '$\sqsubset$' on P defined by $a \sqsubset b$ iff $a \sqsubseteq b$ and $a \neq b$ is irreflexive and transitive.

(2) Conversely let '$\sqsubset$' be an irreflexive and transitive relation on a set P. Prove that $(P, \sqsubseteq)$, where '$\sqsubseteq$' is defined by

$$a \sqsubseteq b \qquad \text{iff } a \sqsubset b \text{ or } a = b$$

is a (reflexive) partial order.

1.2–1 Consider PF_B, the set of propositional formulas over the set of symbols B defined in Example 1.1. For $v, w \in PF_B$ and $p \in B$, let w_p^v be the formula obtained by replacing every occurrence of p in w by v. Give an inductive definition of the function that maps every $w \in PF_B$ to w_p^v for fixed v and p.

1.2–2 Prove that the set always exists that fulfils the conditions (a) and (b) of Definition 1.2. (*Hint*: Form the intersection of all the sets that fulfil both conditions.)

1.2–3 Prove that both definitions of an inductively defined set (Definition 1.2 and Definition 1.4) are equivalent.

1.2–4 Explain why the following definitions are not free.

(1) The set E, a subset of the universe *Int* defined by

    (a) $0 \in E$,
    (b) if $n \in E$, then $n + 2 \in E$ and $n - 2 \in E$.

(2) The set Z_n for some $n \geq 1$, a subset of the universe *Int*, defined by

    (a) $0 \in Z_n$,
    (b) if $m \in Z_n$, then $(m + 1) \bmod n \in Z_n$.

1.2–5 Definition 1.2 can be generalized to allow the definition of a finite number of sets by 'simultaneous induction'. Let U be the *universe* of discourse and $B_1, \ldots, B_n \subseteq U$ for $n \geq 1$ be the *basis sets*. For each 'type' $\tau = (\beta_1, \ldots, \beta_k \to \beta_{k+1})$ where the $\beta_i \in \{1, \ldots, n\}$ for $i = 1, \ldots, k + 1$ and $k \geq 1$, let K_τ be a set of relations $r \subseteq U^k \times U$ called the *constructors* of type τ. Furthermore, extend the partial order '$\subseteq$' on the power set $P(U)$ to $P(U)^n$ in the usual way by defining $(S_1, \ldots, S_n) \subseteq (T_1, \ldots, T_n)$ iff $S_i \subseteq T_i$ for all $i = 1, \ldots, n$. One says that the sets $A_1, \ldots, A_n$ are defined by *simultaneous (structural) induction* by the basis sets $B_1, \ldots, B_n$ and the constructor sets K_τ, if $(A_1, \ldots, A_n)$ is the smallest of all n-tuples $(S_1, \ldots, S_n) \subseteq U^n$ for which the following two conditions hold:

(a) $(B_1, \ldots, B_n) \subseteq (S_1, \ldots, S_n)$
(b) $r(S_{\beta_1} \times \cdots \times S_{\beta_k}) \subseteq S_{\beta_{k+1}}$ for every $r \in K_\tau$ with $\tau = (\beta_1, \ldots, \beta_k \to \beta_{k+1})$.

EXAMPLE The sets of even and odd numbers, each a subset of the universe *Nat*, are defined by simultaneous induction by

(a) the basis sets $B_1 = \{0\}$, $B_2 = \varnothing$.

(b) the constructor sets $K_{(1 \to 2)} = \{r\}$, $K_{(2 \to 1)} = \{r\}$, where $r = \{(n, n + 1) \mid n \in Nat\}$

(Coincidentally it is the same relation for both types.)   □

(1) Show that the definition of the sets $A_1, \dots, A_n$ by simultaneous induction can be replaced by a definition of the (single) set

$$A = \{(a, i) \mid a \in A_i\}$$

by (usual) induction.
(2) Show that the set of sentences derivable from each non-terminal of a context-free grammar can be defined by simultaneous induction.
(3) A definition by simultaneous induction is called *free* when the corresponding usual induction given in part (1) is free. What is the connection in part (2) between free inductive definitions and unambiguous grammars?

1.2–6 Which of the following partial orders are well-founded sets?

(1) $(P(Nat), \subseteq)$.
(2) The set of all finite subsets of Nat with '$\subseteq$'.
(3) The set of all non-negative rational numbers with '$\leq$'.
(4) The set of all non-negative numbers with finite decimal expansions with '$\leq$'.

BIBLIOGRAPHICAL REMARKS

There are several good textbooks on computation theory. For the notions used here the reader may consult for instance, Brainerd and Landweber (1974), Cutland (1980), or Loeckx (1976).

Inductive definitions and structural induction have been introduced in this book along the lines of Enderton (1972). Structural induction is discussed at some length in Aubin (1979); illustrative examples may be found in Wand (1980). Noetherian induction is introduced in the frame of universal algebra in Cohn (1965); its application to program verification is discussed in Burstall (1969) and Manna (1974).

2
Predicate Logic

This chapter is a brief introduction to first-order predicate logic. Both the method and content of logic are important in the study of program verification. On the one hand, the development of logic, its syntax, semantics, and calculus, is the prototype for the development of programming logics. On the other, the formalism and results of predicate logic are subsumed by the formalism and results of these programming logics. The aim of this chapter is to present that part of predicate logic essential for studying program verification. Of course, this is not the place for a complete treatment of logic and the reader is referred to the books listed at the end of the chapter or any of the other numerous books in this area for details.

In the next two sections the syntax and semantics of predicate logic are described. Section 2.3 deals with a calculus for predicate logic and the results of soundness and completeness. In the last section theories are introduced and some are examined for completeness, axiomatizability, and decidability.

2.1 The Syntax of Predicate Logic

The symbols used in a language of first-order predicate logic with equality are divided into two types. First, there are the 'logical' symbols which belong to all languages and have a fixed meaning. Second, there are the 'extralogical' symbols which depend on the particular application one has in mind and are subject to changes in meaning.

Once and for all the *logical symbols* are fixed to be the following ones:

the *connectives* $\neg$, $\wedge$, $\vee$, $\supset$, and $\equiv$
the *equality symbol* $=$
the *existential quantifier* $\exists$ and the *universal quantifier* $\forall$
the four punctuation marks ., (,), and ,
the *variables* $x, y, z, x_1, \ldots, x', \ldots$
the *truth symbols true* and *false*.

Exactly what symbols are to be variables does not matter, all that is assumed is that the set of these symbols, denoted V, is infinite but recursively enumerable.

Also, notice that explicit truth *symbols* have been included. These symbols are not to be confused with the truth *values* 'true' and 'false'.

The *extralogical symbols* are taken from two arbitrarily chosen sets, which must be disjoint from one another as well as from the set of all logical symbols. These two sets are called:

F, the set of *function symbols*.
P, the set of *predicate symbols*.

Each of these function and predicate symbols has associated with it a natural number which is called its *arity*. As customary, 0-ary function symbols are called *constants* and 0-ary predicate symbols are called *propositional constants*. Furthermore, both F and P are assumed to be recursively enumerable.

Since the extralogical symbols act as a parameter to a language of predicate logic and often require explicit mention, the following definition is made:

DEFINITION 2.1 A *basis* for predicate logic is a pair $B = (F, P)$ of sets of symbols, where F and P are understood to be the sets of function and predicate symbols as described above. □

2.1.1 Terms and Formulas

The strings of interest in predicate logic come in two types, called terms and well-formed formulas.

DEFINITION 2.2 The set T_B of all *terms* of (first-order) predicate logic over a basis $B = (F, P)$ is inductively defined by:

(a) Every variable from V is a term.
   Every constant from F is a term.
(b) If $t_1, \ldots, t_n$ $(n \geq 1)$ are terms and $f \in F$ is an n-ary function symbol, then $f(t_1, \ldots, t_n)$ is also a term. □

DEFINITION 2.3 (Syntax of Predicate Logic) The set WFF_B of all (*well-formed*) *formulas* of (first-order) predicate logic over a basis $B = (F, P)$ is inductively defined by:

(a) The truth symbols *true* and *false* are formulas.
   Every propositional constant from P is a formula.
   If t_1 and t_2 are terms, then $t_1 = t_2$ is a formula.
   If $t_1, \ldots, t_n$ $(n \geq 1)$ are terms and $p \in P$ is an n-ary predicate symbol, then $p(t_1, \ldots, t_n)$ is a formula.
(b) If w is a formula, then $(\neg w)$ is also a formula.
   If w is a formula and x is a variable, then $(\forall x . w)$ and $(\exists x . w)$ are also formulas.
   If w_1 and w_2 are formulas, then so are $(w_1 \wedge w_2)$, $(w_1 \vee w_2)$, $(w_1 \supset w_2)$, and $(w_1 \equiv w_2)$. □

A well-formed formula which does not have any quantifier is called *quantifier-free*, the set of quantifier-free formulas is denoted QFF_B.

The inductive definitions of the sets T_B, QFF_B, and WFF_B are easily seen to be free. Hence the Recursion Theorem guarantees that functions defined recursively over these sets are well-defined.

2.1.2 Simplification of Notation

Strictly observing the syntax of formulas as prescribed by the definition can lead to formulas which are difficult to read. Hence in the interest of legibility, conventions and abbreviations in accordance with normal mathematical usage are permitted.

(1) The 'operators' of the language are assigned a priority according to the following table:

Operator	Priority
$\neg$, $\exists x.$, $\forall x.$	4 (highest)
$\wedge$	3
$\vee$	2
$\supset$, $\equiv$	1 (lowest)

The operators with higher priority bind more tightly and the parentheses around the operator can be dropped. In addition, parentheses can be left out in the case of right associativity of operators with the same priority. Finally, the outermost pair of parentheses is not necessary.

(2) $\forall x_1 . \forall x_2 . \ldots . \forall x_n .$ can be abbreviated by $\forall x_1, x_2, \ldots, x_n .$; the same holds for the existential quantifier.

(3) Function and predicate symbols (such as $*$, $+$, and $<$) can be written in infix notation where this is customary. Here, too, the usual rules of priority between operators can be used to leave out parentheses.

2.2 The Semantics of Predicate Logic

How meaning is given to the strings of a language, be they strings of predicate logic, programming languages, or natural languages is the task of semantics—the study of meaning. Here the task is relatively easy. Predicate logic will be given, by fiat, an explicit meaning.

In the previous section, by fixing the symbols in a language of predicate logic and selecting certain strings of these symbols, the syntax of this language was specified. The next step is to interpret these strings, the terms and formulas, precisely. Immediately the problem arises concerning the meaning of the individual symbols. The meaning of the logical symbols is somehow foreordained, but the interpretation of function and predicate symbols is lacking. The next definition describes what is needed.

DEFINITION 2.4 (Interpretation) Let $B = (F, P)$ be a basis for predicate logic. An *interpretation* of B is a pair $\mathcal{I} = (D, \mathcal{I}_0)$, where D is a non-empty set (called the *domain* or *universe of discourse* of $\mathcal{I}$) and $\mathcal{I}_0$ is a mapping which assigns

(1) To every constant $c \in F$ an element $\mathcal{I}_0(c) \in D$;
(2) To every function symbol $f \in F$ of arity $n \geq 1$ a total function $\mathcal{I}_0(f): D^n \to D$;
(3) To every propositional constant $a \in P$ an element $\mathcal{I}_0(a) \in Bool$;
(4) To every predicate symbol $p \in P$ of arity $n \geq 1$ a predicate $\mathcal{I}_0(p): D^n \to Bool$.
□

An interpretation alone does not always determine the meaning of a term or formula, which can depend on what elements of the domain the variables have been assigned. A total function $\sigma: V \to D$ mapping variables to the domain D of some interpretation is called an *assignment*; note that in the context of imperative programming languages such a function is generally called a 'state'. The set of all assignments for an interpretation $\mathcal{I}$ is denoted by $\Sigma_{\mathcal{I}}$ or simply by Σ.

Together an interpretation and an assignment induce a mapping from every term to an element of the domain of the interpretation and from every formula to a truth value. This mapping can be described in different ways. Here a functional is defined mapping terms and formulas to functions. The value of a term or formula is then found by applying these functions to a given assignment.

DEFINITION 2.5 (Semantics of Predicate Logic) Let $\mathcal{I} = (D, \mathcal{I}_0)$ be an interpretation for a basis $B = (F, P)$. To $\mathcal{I}$ is associated a functional, also denoted by $\mathcal{I}$, which maps every term $t \in T_B$ to a function $\mathcal{I}(t): \Sigma \to D$ and every formula $w \in WFF_B$ to a function $\mathcal{I}(w): \Sigma \to Bool$; the functions $\mathcal{I}(t)$ and $\mathcal{I}(w)$ are defined inductively over the sets of terms and formulas as follows:

Semantics of terms
(a) If $c \in F$ is a constant, then

$$\mathcal{I}(c)(\sigma) = \mathcal{I}_0(c) \qquad \text{for all assignments } \sigma \in \Sigma.$$

If $x \in V$ is a variable, then

$$\mathcal{I}(x)(\sigma) = \sigma(x) \qquad \text{for all assignments } \sigma \in \Sigma.$$

(b) If $t_1, \ldots, t_n$ $(n \geq 1)$ are terms and $f \in F$ is an n-ary function symbol, then

$$\mathcal{I}(f(t_1, \ldots, t_n))(\sigma)$$
$$= \mathcal{I}_0(f)(\mathcal{I}(t_1)(\sigma), \ldots, \mathcal{I}(t_n)(\sigma)) \qquad \text{for all assignments } \sigma \in \Sigma.$$

Semantics of formulas
(a) $\mathcal{I}(true)(\sigma) = \text{true} \qquad \text{for all } \sigma \in \Sigma.$
$\mathcal{I}(false)(\sigma) = \text{false} \qquad \text{for all } \sigma \in \Sigma.$

If $a \in P$ is a propositional constant, then

$$\mathscr{I}(a)(\sigma) = \mathscr{I}_0(a) \qquad \text{for all } \sigma \in \Sigma.$$

If t_1, t_2 are terms, then

$$\mathscr{I}(t_1 = t_2)(\sigma) = \begin{cases} \text{true} & \text{if } \mathscr{I}(t_1)(\sigma) = \mathscr{I}(t_2)(\sigma) \\ \text{false} & \text{otherwise,} \end{cases} \qquad \text{for all } \sigma \in \Sigma.$$

If $t_1, \ldots, t_n$ $(n \geq 1)$ are terms and $p \in P$ is an n-ary predicate symbol, then

$$\mathscr{I}(p(t_1, \ldots, t_n))(\sigma) = \mathscr{I}_0(p)(\mathscr{I}(t_1)(\sigma), \ldots, \mathscr{I}(t_n)(\sigma)) \qquad \text{for all } \sigma \in \Sigma.$$

(b) If $w \in WFF_B$ is a formula, then

$$\mathscr{I}((\neg w))(\sigma) = \begin{cases} \text{true} & \text{if } \mathscr{I}(w)(\sigma) = \text{false} \\ \text{false} & \text{otherwise,} \end{cases} \qquad \text{for all } \sigma \in \Sigma.$$

Analogously for $(w_1 \wedge w_2)$, $(w_1 \vee w_2)$, $(w_1 \supset w_2)$, and $(w_1 \equiv w_2)$. If $w \in WFF_B$ is a formula and $x \in V$ is a variable, then

$$\mathscr{I}((\exists x . w))(\sigma) = \begin{cases} \text{true} & \text{if there is an element } d \in D \text{ of the domain such} \\ & \text{that } \mathscr{I}(w)(\sigma[x/d]) = \text{true} \\ \text{false} & \text{otherwise,} \end{cases}$$

$$\text{for all } \sigma \in \Sigma.$$

If $w \in WFF_B$ and $x \in V$, then

$$\mathscr{I}((\forall x . w))(\sigma) = \begin{cases} \text{true} & \text{if for all } d \in D \ \mathscr{I}(w)(\sigma[x/d]) = \text{true} \\ \text{false} & \text{otherwise,} \end{cases}$$

$$\text{for all } \sigma \in \Sigma. \qquad \square$$

The semantic functional $\mathscr{I}$ is a complicated gadget and it may be thought of as two functionals of the following types:

$$T_B \rightarrow (\Sigma \rightarrow D)$$

$$WFF_B \rightarrow (\Sigma \rightarrow Bool)$$

where Σ is the set $(V \rightarrow D)$ of all assignments. If the definition of the semantic functional $\mathscr{I}$ is still difficult to understand, then consider the following rendering in 'English' of the beginning of the definition:

(1) The value of $\mathscr{I}$ at any constant c is a constant function, namely the function which regardless of the assignment delivers the value $\mathscr{I}_0(c)$.
(2) The value of $\mathscr{I}$ at any variable x is a function, which for every assignment σ has as its value that element of the domain which σ assigns to x.

Some types of formulas are distinguished by virtue of their semantic properties. A formula w is called *valid* in an interpretation $\mathscr{I}$—briefly $\models_\mathscr{I} w$—if $\mathscr{I}(w)(\sigma) = $ true for all assignments $\sigma \in \Sigma_\mathscr{I}$. The set of all formulas valid in $\mathscr{I}$ is denoted $Th(\mathscr{I})$. A formula w is called *logically valid*—written $\models w$—if it is valid in all interpretations. Two formulas w_1 and w_2 are called *equivalent* in an interpretation

$\mathscr{I}$, if the formula $w_1 \equiv w_2$ is valid in this interpretation; they are called *logically equivalent*, if $w_1 \equiv w_2$ is logically valid.

EXAMPLE 2.6   Let $B = (F, P)$ be a basis with $F = \{0, 1, \ldots, *, +\}$ and $P = \{\leq\}$.

(1) One of many possible interpretations for B is $\mathscr{I} = (Nat, \mathscr{I}_0)$, where $\mathscr{I}_0$ maps the function and predicate symbols to their 'usual' functions and predicates over the natural numbers. In this interpretation the following holds for all assignments σ:

$$\mathscr{I}(\neg z = 1 \wedge \forall x, y . (x * y = z \supset x = 1 \vee y = 1))(\sigma) = \text{true}$$

iff $\mathscr{I}(\neg z = 1)(\sigma) = \text{true}$ and for all $m, n \in Nat$,

$$\mathscr{I}(x * y = z \supset x = 1 \vee y = 1)(\sigma[x/m][y/n]) = \text{true}$$

iff $\sigma(z) \neq 1$ and for all $m, n \in Nat$: $m * n = \sigma(z)$ implies $m = 1$ or $n = 1$
iff $\sigma(z)$ is a prime number.

Thus, for a given interpretation $\mathscr{I} = (D, \mathscr{I}_0)$ a formula can be used to characterize a subset of the domain D (more generally of D^k, $k \geq 1$), as was done above for the set of prime numbers.
(2) The formula $x \leq y \wedge y \leq z \supset x \leq z$ is valid in an interpretation $\mathscr{I} = (D, \mathscr{I}_0)$ exactly when $\mathscr{I}_0(\leq)$ is a transitive relation on D. Thus a formula can also serve to characterize a set of interpretations.
(3) The following formula is an example of a logically valid formula:

$$(\forall x . x + 1 \leq x) \supset (\forall x . (x * x) + 1 \leq x * x)$$

(4) For every variable $x \in V$ and formula $w \in WFF_B$ the following formulas are logically equivalent:

$$\forall x . w \quad \text{and} \quad \neg \exists x . \neg w \qquad \qquad \square$$

2.2.1 Semantic Properties

Now that the semantics has been defined it is necessary to state those properties which are used over and over again in proofs concerning semantics. For that purpose some additional syntactic definitions must first be introduced.

Let w be a formula and x a variable. An occurrence of x in w is called *bound*, when it appears in a substring of w of the form $\exists x . w'$ or $\forall x . w'$ where w' is a formula. Every other occurrence of x in w is called *free*. For example, in the formula $x = y \wedge \forall x . x = x$ the first occurrence of x is free; the other three occurrences are bound.

THEOREM 2.7 (Coincidence Theorem)   Let w be a formula from WFF_B and $\mathscr{I}$ an interpretation of a given basis. If two assignments σ and σ' from $\Sigma_{\mathscr{I}}$ agree on all variables that occur free in w, then $\mathscr{I}(w)(\sigma) = \mathscr{I}(w)(\sigma')$. $\qquad \square$

This theorem says that a formula can be construed to be a statement about its free variables. This was just seen in Example 2.6, where the assertion 'z is a prime number' was expressed by the formula

$$\neg z = 1 \land \forall x, y. (x * y = z \supset x = 1 \lor y = 1)$$

Notice only z occurs free.

Often one wants to transfer an assertion about some variables or terms to others. For example, one may want to obtain a formula expressing the statement '$y + 1$ is a prime number' from the formula given above that expresses 'z is a prime number'. It is clear from this example that it is not always possible to build such a formula by simply replacing $y + 1$ for z. A 'name collision' would take place between the two y's yielding a formula with unexpected meaning. Therefore, the following theorem is helpful:

THEOREM 2.8 (Renaming Theorem) Let w be a formula, x a variable that occurs bound in w, and x' a variable that does not occur in w. Let w' be the formula that is formed when every bound occurrence of x in w is replaced by x'. Then w and w' are logically equivalent. $\qquad\square$

For example, two applications of the Renaming Theorem on the formula expressing the assertion that 'z is a prime number' yield an equivalent formula:

$$\neg z = 1 \land \forall x', y'. (x' * y' = z \supset x' = 1 \lor y' = 1)$$

DEFINITION 2.9 (Substitution) Let w be a formula, x a variable, and t a term. A formula created by *substituting* t for x in w, denoted by w_x^t, is a formula formed by applying the Renaming Theorem until no variable in t occurs bound in w and then replacing all free occurrences of x by t. $\qquad\square$

What variable symbols are chosen to rename the bound variables in w has been left unspecified. Any choice of variables results in a formula which may be shown to be logically equivalent to any other formula created by some other choice.

THEOREM 2.10 (Substitution Theorem) Let w, x, t be a formula, a variable, and a term, respectively. Then, for every interpretation $\mathscr{I}$ and every assignment $\sigma \in \Sigma$:

$$\mathscr{I}(w_x^t)(\sigma) = \mathscr{I}(w)(\sigma[x/\mathscr{I}(t)(\sigma)]). \qquad\square$$

In words, the value of w_x^t is the same as the value of w, where the value of t is used for x. For an example of substitution and the use of the Substitution Theorem, let w stand for the formula expressing 'z is a prime number'; then w_z^{y+1} is the formula:

$$\neg y + 1 = 1 \land \forall x, y'. (x * y' = y + 1 \supset x = 1 \lor y' = 1),$$

where the choice of y' is arbitrary. And as intended:

$$\mathscr{I}(w_z^{y+1})(\sigma) = \text{true} \qquad \text{iff} \quad \mathscr{I}(y + 1)(\sigma) \text{ is a prime number.}$$

The definition of substitution and the Substitution Theorem can easily be generalized to more variables and terms. When the distinct variables $x_1, \ldots, x_n$ are substituted simultaneously by the terms $t_1, \ldots, t_n$, the resulting formula is denoted $w^{t_1, \ldots, t_n}_{x_1, \ldots, x_n}$. It must be pointed out that, in general, the formulas $w^{t_1, t_2}_{x_1, x_2}$ and $(w^{t_1}_{x_1})^{t_2}_{x_2}$ are different. For example, if w is the formula $x = y$, then $w^{y, x}_{x, y}$ is the formula $y = x$ and $(w^{y}_{x})^{x}_{y}$ the formula $x = x$.

2.2.2 Models and Logical Consequence

Now an arbitrary set $W \subseteq WFF_B$ of formulas of predicate logic will be the focus of attention. An interpretation $\mathscr{I}$ is called a *model* of W, if $\models_\mathscr{I} w$ for every formula $w \in W$. A formula $w \in WFF_B$ is called a *logical consequence* of W—denoted $W \models w$—if $\models_\mathscr{I} w$ for every model $\mathscr{I}$ of W. The set of all logical consequences of W is denoted $Cn(W)$.

Clearly every interpretation is a model of the empty set; the logical consequences of the empty set are exactly the logically valid formulas, hence:

$$\models w \qquad \text{iff } \varnothing \models w.$$

EXAMPLE 2.11   Let $B = (F, P)$ be a basis with $F = \{0, +\}$ and $P = \varnothing$. Suppose $W \subseteq WFF_B$ consists of the following formulas:

$$\forall x, y, z \,.\, (x + (y + z) = (x + y) + z)$$

$$\forall x \,.\, (x + 0 = x \wedge 0 + x = x)$$

$$\forall x \,.\, \exists y \,.\, (x + y = 0 \wedge y + x = 0)$$

Then the models of W are exactly those interpretations $\mathscr{I} = (D, \mathscr{I}_0)$ of B in which $(D, \mathscr{I}_0(+))$ is a group with identity element $\mathscr{I}_0(0)$, because W contains exactly the group axioms. An example of a logical consequence of the set W is the formula:

$$\forall x, y \,.\, \exists z, z' \,.\, (x + z = y \wedge z' + x = y). \qquad \square$$

Next the connection between the concept of logical consequence and the logical symbol '$\supset$' will be worked out culminating in the Deduction Theorem. But first the free variables must be brought under control.

A formula is called *closed* when it has no occurrences of free variables. If a formula w is closed, then by the Coincidence Theorem it is seen that either $\models_\mathscr{I} w$ or $\models_\mathscr{I} \neg w$ for every interpretation $\mathscr{I}$. There is a standard way to make a closed formula from any given formula. Let w be any formula and let $x_1, \ldots, x_n$ be all the variables that occur free in w. Then the (closed) formula $\forall x_1, \ldots, x_n \,.\, w$ is called the *generalization* of w and will be denoted by $\bar{w}$. The formula $\bar{w}$ is unique up to logical equivalence (nothing is said about the order of the variables) and the following holds for every interpretation $\mathscr{I}$:

$$\models_\mathscr{I} w \qquad \text{iff } \models_\mathscr{I} \bar{w}.$$

Be careful not to confuse this with the equivalence of formulas. w and $\bar{w}$ are in general not equivalent, because $\mathscr{I}(w)(\sigma)$ depends on σ and $\mathscr{I}(\bar{w})(\sigma)$ does not.

THEOREM 2.12 (Deduction Theorem)   Let W be a set of formulas and let v_1, v_2 be formulas. Then the following two implications hold:

(1) $W \models v_1 \supset v_2$ implies $W \cup \{v_1\} \models v_2$
(2) $W \cup \{v_1\} \models v_2$ implies $W \models \bar{v}_1 \supset v_2$ □

In particular, when $W = \{w_1, \ldots, w_n\}$ is finite, this theorem can be used to reduce the concept of logical consequence to that of logical validity:

$$\{w_1, \ldots, w_n\} \models v \qquad \text{iff} \quad \models \bar{w}_1 \supset \cdots \supset \bar{w}_n \supset v.$$

2.2.3 Reduction of Logical Symbols

It is possible to reduce the number of logical symbols on which the predicate logic is built, without decreasing the power of the logic. Because of their semantic properties, one can consider certain logical symbols as a convenient shorthand for others. It is possible to make do with $\vee$, $\neg$, $\exists$ and the punctuation marks by allowing the following abbreviations:

$w_1 \wedge w_2$	for $\neg(\neg w_1 \vee \neg w_2)$
$w_1 \supset w_2$	for $\neg w_1 \vee w_2$
$w_1 \equiv w_2$	for $(w_1 \supset w_2) \wedge (w_2 \supset w_1)$
$\forall x . w$	for $\neg \exists x . \neg w$
true	for $w \vee \neg w$ |where w is an
false	for $w \wedge \neg w$ |arbitrary formula

(See also Exercise 2.2–4.)

This reduction is of practical use in theoretical considerations of predicate logic because proofs about logic often use structural induction and these are shorter when the structure of logic is built on fewer symbols. For this reason, this approach will be taken for the rest of the chapter.

2.3 Predicate Calculus

The set of logically valid formulas of predicate logic is particularly interesting because it consists of the formulas that 'always' hold; that is, they hold in every 'theory'. In this section a method will be introduced which provides a way of obtaining the logically valid formulas in a purely syntactic manner. In fact, the method is more general, it produces the logical consequences of any set of formulas. That this is possible is fortunate, because the non-constructive definition of the semantic functional provides no clue for a mechanical way to distinguish valid formulas from invalid ones. However, everything is not perfect.

Although the set of logically valid formulas can be generated in a mechanical way, it is not decidable. So there is no algorithm which given a formula of predicate logic decides whether it is logically valid or not. These ideas will now be formulated more precisely.

The starting point is the definition of a calculus in the abstract.

2.3.1 Calculi

DEFINITION 2.13 (Calculi)   Let SO be some set of syntactic objects. A *calculus* (or *axiomatic system*) over SO is a pair $\mathscr{K} = (\mathscr{A}, \mathscr{R})$, where

$\mathscr{A}$ is a finite set of *axiom schemes*, which are decidable subsets of SO; the elements of an axiom scheme are called *axioms*

$\mathscr{R}$ is a finite set of *inference rules*, which are decidable subsets of $SO^n \times SO, n \geq 1$. $\qquad \Box$

EXAMPLE 2.14   For $SO = WFF_B$, the set of formulas of predicate logic, a possible axiom scheme is:

$$\{w \vee \neg w \mid w \in WFF_B\}.$$

An axiom from this scheme is, for instance,

$$x = y \vee \neg x = y. \qquad \Box$$

An inference rule viewed as a relation R can be defined in the standard set theoretic notation by:

$$R = \{((s_1, \ldots, s_n), s) \in SO^n \times SO \mid P \text{ holds for } s_1, \ldots, s_n, s\},$$

where P is a decidable property, usually some simple syntactic property. Instead of this notation, an inference rule is normally presented like this:

$$R: \frac{s_1, \ldots, s_n}{s} \qquad \text{for all } s_1, \ldots, s_n, s \text{ such that P holds.}$$

$s_1, \ldots, s_n$ are called the *premises*, s the *conclusion* of the inference rule R.

EXAMPLE 2.15   With $SO = WFF_B$ as in the previous example

$$R: \frac{w_1}{w_1 \vee w_2} \qquad \text{for all } w_1, w_2 \in WFF_B$$

is an inference rule which stands for the decidable relation:

$$R = \{((w_1), w_1 \vee w_2) \mid w_1, w_2 \in WFF_B\}.$$

According to the definition

$$R: \frac{\neg w_1, \; \neg w_2}{w_1 \wedge w_2} \qquad \text{for all } w_1, w_2 \in WFF_B$$

is also a perfectly good inference rule. However, as a rule of inference for the predicate calculus it would violate its intuitive purpose. $\qquad \Box$

Now let X be a (possibly empty) subset of a set SO of syntactic objects. The set of all syntactic objects which are *derivable* from X in calculus $\mathcal{K} = (\mathcal{A}, \mathcal{R})$ over SO is inductively defined by:

(a) the basis set $X \cup \left(\bigcup_{A \in \mathcal{A}} A \right)$, and

(b) the constructor set $\mathcal{R}$.

If a syntactic object s is derivable from a set of syntactic objects X in a calculus $\mathcal{K}$, one writes $X \vdash_{\mathcal{K}} s$ or, briefly, $X \vdash s$; if X is the empty set, one writes $\vdash s$. A construction sequence of s is called a *deduction* for s from X in $\mathcal{K}$.

An immediate consequence from the remarks about inductive definitions in Chapter 1, is that the set of all syntactic objects derivable from a set X is recursively enumerable whenever X is. In particular for $X = \varnothing$, the set $\{s \in SO \mid \vdash s\}$ is recursively enumerable.

The definition of a calculus was from a completely syntactic point of view. But generally one has some application in mind when setting up a calculus, for instance, the deduction of formulas with certain semantic properties, such as

(1) the logically valid formulas of predicate logic,
(2) the formulas of predicate logic valid in $\mathcal{I}$ for a given interpretation $\mathcal{I}$, or
(3) the logical consequences of a set of predicate logic formulas.

In connection with some such application, a calculus is called 'sound' when all the derivable syntactic objects possess the desired semantic property, and 'complete' when all the syntactic objects with the desired property are derivable. A more precise definition of these two concepts will not be given here; instead 'soundness' and 'completeness' will be defined for each particular application encountered.

2.3.2 The Predicate Calculus

Here a calculus for predicate logic will be introduced, the so-called predicate calculus. Strictly speaking, it is incorrect to refer to *the* predicate calculus, since different (equivalent) calculi for predicate logic are presented by different authors.

For a given basis $B = (F, P)$ the following calculus uses the restricted language of predicate logic discussed earlier; in particular, the symbol ' $\supset$ ' occurring in the axiom schemes and inference rules should be viewed as an abbreviation.

Axiom schemes

(A1)	$\neg w \vee w$	for all $w \in WFF_B$
(A2)	$w_x^t \supset \exists x . w$	for all $w \in WFF_B$, $x \in V$, $t \in T_B$
(A3)	$x = x$	for all $x \in V$
(A4)	$x = y \supset y = x$	for all $x, y \in V$
(A5)	$x = y \wedge y = z \supset x = z$	for all $x, y, z \in V$

(A6) $x_1 = y_1 \supset \ldots \supset x_n = y_n \supset p(x_1, \ldots, x_n) \supset p(y_1, \ldots, y_n)$
for all $x_1, \ldots, x_n, y_1, \ldots, y_n \in V$ $(n \geq 1)$
and all n-ary predicates $p \in P$

(A7) $x_1 = y_1 \supset \cdots \supset x_n = y_n \supset f(x_1, \ldots, x_n) = f(y_1, \ldots, y_n)$
for all $x_1, \ldots, x_n, y_1, \ldots, y_n \in V$ $(n \geq 1)$
and all n-ary function symbols $f \in F$

Inference rules

(R1) $\dfrac{w \vee w}{w}$ for all $w \in WFF_B$

(R2) $\dfrac{w_2}{w_1 \vee w_2}$ for all $w_1, w_2 \in WFF_B$

(R3) $\dfrac{w_1 \vee (w_2 \vee w_3)}{(w_1 \vee w_2) \vee w_3}$ for all $w_1, w_2, w_3 \in WFF_B$

(R4) $\dfrac{w_1 \supset w_2}{(\exists x . w_1) \supset w_2}$ for all $w_1, w_2 \in WFF_B$, $x \in V$, such that x is not free in w_2

(R5) $\dfrac{w_1 \vee w_2, \; \neg w_1 \vee w_3}{w_2 \vee w_3}$ for all $w_1, w_2, w_3 \in WFF_B$

EXAMPLE 2.16   Let $W = \{w_1, \neg w_1 \vee w_2\}$, then $W \vdash w_2$. A possible deduction for w_2 from W is:

(1) w_1 from W
(2) $w_2 \vee w_1$ rule (R2) applied to (1)
(3) $\neg w_2 \vee w_2$ from axiom scheme (A1)
(4) $w_1 \vee w_2$ rule (R5) applied to (2) and (3)
(5) $\neg w_1 \vee w_2$ from W
(6) $w_2 \vee w_2$ rule (R5) applied to (5) and (4)
(7) w_2 rule (R1) applied to (6) $\square$

2.3.3 Soundness and Completeness of the Predicate Calculus

The purpose of the predicate calculus is to derive the logical consequences of a set of formulas; and the following important theorem says that this purpose is fulfilled:

THEOREM 2.17 (Soundness and Completeness of the Predicate Calculus) The predicate calculus is sound and complete, that is, for every set $W \subseteq WFF_B$ and every formula $w \in WFF_B$, the following holds:

$$W \vdash w \qquad \text{iff } W \models w.$$

In particular, for $W = \emptyset$:

$$\vdash w \qquad \text{iff} \vDash w. \qquad \square$$

The proof of the soundness of the calculus is relatively easy, and the method of proof will be used by other calculi—to be introduced in the course of this book—therefore, a brief explanation of the proof is given.

More specifically, it will now be argued that in order to prove the soundness of the calculus it is sufficient to show that:

(1) all the axioms are logically valid, and
(2) for every interpretation $\mathscr{I}$ the application of an inference rule on formulas valid in $\mathscr{I}$ results in a formula valid in $\mathscr{I}$.

Let $W \subseteq WFF_B$ be an arbitrary set of formulas. The set of all formulas derivable from W is—by definition—inductively defined by

(a) the basis set $W \cup \left(\bigcup_{A \in \mathscr{A}} A \right)$, and

(b) the constructor set $\mathscr{R}$,

where $\mathscr{A}$ is the set of axiom schemata and $\mathscr{R}$ the set of inference rules of the predicate calculus. So one can show by structural induction that all the formulas derivable from W are also logical consequences of W as follows:

(a) For every formula $w \in W$, $W \vDash w$ holds by definition, and for every axiom w, $W \vDash w$ holds because of (1).
(b) Let $w_1, \ldots, w_n \in WFF_B$ with $W \vDash w_1, \ldots, W \vDash w_n$. Then by definition, $\vDash_{\mathscr{I}} w_1, \ldots, \vDash_{\mathscr{I}} w_n$ for every model $\mathscr{I}$ of W. Furthermore, let $w \in WFF_B$ be a formula derived from $w_1, \ldots, w_n$ by an application of an inference rule. Then, because of (2), $\vDash_{\mathscr{I}} w$ holds for all models $\mathscr{I}$ of W, hence $W \vDash w$.

Thus, it has been shown that (1) and (2) are sufficient to prove the soundness of the calculus. The proofs of (1) and (2), however, are left to the reader (Exercise 2.3–2).

The proof of the completeness of the calculus is significantly harder and bears no resemblance to the completeness proofs of the other calculi that will be considered here. The proof can be found in the books listed in the bibliographical remarks at the end of this chapter.

The next three theorems are immediate consequences of the soundness and completeness of the predicate calculus.

THEOREM 2.18   For every basis for predicate logic the set of logically valid formulas is recursively enumerable. $\square$

This theorem says that there exists an algorithm that halts (with a positive answer) exactly when a logically valid formula is given as input: it suffices to enumerate the formulas derivable in the calculus and to compare each one with the given formula. A more efficient procedure for accomplishing the same task is the so-called *resolution principle* (see the bibliographical remarks at the end of this chapter). With other methods it can be shown that the set of logically valid formulas is not decidable.

THEOREM 2.19 (Finiteness Principle)   For every set W of formulas of predicate logic, a logical consequence w of W is a logical consequence of a finite subset of W (which depends on the choice of w). □

THEOREM 2.20 (Compactness Theorem)   Let W be a set of formulas of predicate logic such that every finite subset of W has a model. Then W has also a model.
□

*2.4 Theories

It was seen in the last section that there is a sound and complete calculus for the set of all logically valid formulas. Because these formulas are 'universally' valid, they are too general to be revealing about specific applications: so one is often interested in a larger set of formulas, namely those that are valid in a concrete theory, say group theory or number theory. The question is then raised about the existence of a calculus for such a specific theory, and moreover, about the decidability of such a theory. First, the problem must be made precise, and then some examples will be given.

DEFINITION 2.21   Let WFF_B be the set of well-formed formulas of the predicate logic over the basis B. A non-empty subset T of formulas from WFF_B is called a *theory* (over B) when the following two conditions hold:

(1) (Consistency). There exists at least one model for T.
(2) (Closure under logical consequence). All logical consequences of T are already in T. □

Note that, by definition, a theory contains at least all logically valid formulas of predicate logic.

If $W \subseteq WFF_B$ is a set of formulas which has at least one model, then the set $Cn(W)$ of all logical consequences of W is a theory (Exercise 2.4–1). This property provides a convenient way to create a theory: take a set of formulas with a model and form the closure under logical consequence.

EXAMPLE 2.22   Two theories formed by taking all the logical consequences of a set W of formulas are:

(1) the set of all logically valid formulas of predicate logic over any basis (here W is $\varnothing$), and
(2) group theory—the set of all formulas over the basis $B = (\{0, +\}, \varnothing)$ which are logical consequences of the three group axioms (see Example 2.11). □

For every interpretation $\mathscr{I}$, it can be shown (left to Exercise 2.4–2) that the set $Th(\mathscr{I})$ of all formulas valid in $\mathscr{I}$ is a theory. Two important theories, Peano arithmetic and Presburger arithmetic, are formed in this way.

Peano arithmetic (also called *first-order arithmetic*) is the set of all formulas for the basis $B = (\{0, 1, +, *\}, \{<\})$ which are valid in the interpretation $\mathscr{I} = (Nat, \mathscr{I}_0)$ where $\mathscr{I}_0$ gives the usual meaning to the function and predicate symbols. *Presburger arithmetic* is like Peano arithmetic only without multiplication.

2.4.1 Complete Theories

A theory T over a given basis B is called *complete* (with respect to B), if for every closed formula w either w or $\neg w$ appears in T. (The concept 'complete theory' has nothing to do with the concept 'complete calculus'.) Intuitively, a theory is complete if it indicates for every 'statement' whether it is true or not. It is easy to show that every recursively enumerable complete theory is decidable (see Exercise 2.4–3).

THEOREM 2.23   For a theory T over a basis B the following three conditions are equivalent:

(1) T is complete.
(2) There exists an interpretation $\mathscr{I}$ of B with $T = Th(\mathscr{I})$ (this interpretation is a model of T).
(3) For all models $\mathscr{I}$ of T, $T = Th(\mathscr{I})$.

(The proof is left to Exercise 2.4–3.) □

It would be a mistake to conclude from this theorem that a complete theory has only one model. As will gradually become apparent, Peano arithmetic is a complete theory with very different models.

EXAMPLE 2.24   By the first part of Theorem 2.23, both Peano and Presburger arithmetic are complete theories, as are any theories constructed that way.

Predicate logic (or, more precisely, the set of logically valid formulas of predicate logic) and group theory are *not* complete. This is not astonishing: both theories are very general, leaving place for special 'applications'. □

2.4.2 Axiomatizable and Decidable Theories

As already indicated one is interested in calculi for given theories. Usually these calculi are not created from scratch, but instead are created by extending the predicate calculus by additional axioms. This leads to the following definition.

A theory T is said to be *axiomatizable* when there exists a decidable set $W \subseteq T$ such that T is exactly the set of all formulas derivable from W in the predicate calculus. In that case the formulas of W are called the *axioms* of the theory T and it is possible to consider the predicate calculus extended by these axioms to be a calculus for T. Note that because of the soundness and completeness of the predicate calculus the theory T is exactly the set $Cn(W)$ of all logical consequences of W.

Clearly, every axiomatizable theory is recursively enumerable but not necessarily decidable.

EXAMPLE 2.25 Some examples and counter-examples of axiomatizable and decidable theories are now presented without proof.

(1) The predicate logic or, more precisely, the set of its logically valid formulas is itself axiomatizable (one chooses simply $W = \varnothing$); it is, however, not decidable as indicated in Section 2.3.

(2) Let $B = (\{0, S\}, \varnothing)$ and $\mathscr{I} = (Nat, \mathscr{I}_0)$ be the usual interpretation for B, $\mathscr{I}_0(S)$ being the successor function over the natural numbers (adding 1 to its argument). The theory $Th(\mathscr{I})$ is called the *theory of natural numbers with successor function*. $Th(\mathscr{I})$ is axiomatizable because, as one may show, $Th(\mathscr{I}) = Cn(Z)$ for the following infinite but decidable set $Z \subseteq Th(\mathscr{I})$:

$$Z = \{\forall x . \neg S(x) = 0,$$
$$\forall x, y . (S(x) = S(y) \supset x = y),$$
$$\forall x . (\neg x = 0 \supset \exists y . x = S(y)),$$
$$\forall x . \neg (x = S(x)),$$
$$\forall x . \neg (x = S(S(x))), \ldots\}$$

Since $Th(\mathscr{I})$ is also complete, $Th(\mathscr{I})$ is decidable.

(3) Presburger arithmetic is decidable and hence, by definition, axiomatizable (one chooses simply all the valid formulas as axioms).

(4) Peano arithmetic is not decidable and hence—since it is a complete theory—cannot be recursively enumerable nor axiomatizable. □

While Peano arithmetic is not axiomatizable it is necessary to say something of the so-called Peano axioms. The *Peano axioms* consist of the following formulas over the basis $B = (F, P)$ of Peano arithmetic (with $F = \{0, 1, +, *\}$ and $P = \{<\}$):

(S1) $\forall x . ((\neg x = 0) \equiv (\exists y . y + 1 = x))$

(S2) $\forall x, y . (x + 1 = y + 1 \supset x = y)$

(L1) $\forall x, y . ((x < y + 1) \equiv (x < y \vee x = y))$

(L2) $\forall x . \neg (x < 0)$

(L3) $\forall x, y . (x < y \vee x = y \vee y < x)$

(A1) $\forall x . x + 0 = x$

(A2) $\forall x, y . x + (y + 1) = (x + y) + 1$

(M1) $\forall x . x * 0 = 0$

(M2) $\forall x, y . x * (y + 1) = x * y + x$

These axioms *together with* the principle of induction over the natural numbers (see Section 1.2) characterize the natural numbers completely in a sense made precise in Exercise 2.4–4. Less formally, the Peano axioms together with the principle of induction characterize all properties of the natural numbers, including those of the Peano arithmetic or, in other words, including those which may be expressed as formulas of the first-order predicate logic. This is not in contradiction to the fact that Peano arithmetic is not axiomatizable, because the principle of induction cannot be expressed as a formula of the first-order predicate logic (as it involves a quantification over sets).

By the way, one might think that the (first-order) axioms

$$w_x^0 \land (\forall x . (w \supset w_x^{x+1})) \supset \forall x . w$$

for all formulas $w \in WFF_B$ with only x free fully capture the induction principle over the natural numbers. This is not the case since these axioms express the induction principle only for properties which may be expressed by formulas w of the first-order predicate logic.

2.4.3 Non-standard Models

A given theory such as the Peano arithmetic has generally an 'intended' model. It will now be shown that a theory, even if it is complete, may have models—called 'non-standard' models—which are 'intrinsically different'. A particular non-standard model of the Peano arithmetic will be introduced in which the principle of induction is not valid. This model will be used later to show that certain program properties cannot be proved within the frame of (first-order) predicate logic but that their proof requires moreover the power of the principle of induction.

First it must be made clear what two 'intrinsically different' models are.

DEFINITION 2.26   Let a basis $B = (F, P)$ for the predicate logic be given, and let $\mathscr{I} = (D, \mathscr{I}_0)$ and $\mathscr{I}' = (D', \mathscr{I}_0')$ be interpretations of B. A mapping $\Phi \colon D \to D'$ is called a *homomorphism* from $\mathscr{I}$ to $\mathscr{I}'$, if the following four conditions hold:

(1) $\Phi(\mathscr{I}_0(c)) = \mathscr{I}_0'(c)$ for every constant $c \in F$.
(2) $\mathscr{I}_0(a) = \mathscr{I}_0'(a)$ for every propositional constant $a \in P$.
(3) $\Phi(\mathscr{I}_0(f)(d_1, \ldots, d_n)) = \mathscr{I}_0'(f)(\Phi(d_1), \ldots, \Phi(d_n))$ for all n-ary function symbols $f \in F$ ($n \geq 1$), and all $d_1, \ldots, d_n \in D$.
(4) $\mathscr{I}_0(p)(d_1, \ldots, d_n) = \mathscr{I}_0'(p)(\Phi(d_1), \ldots, \Phi(d_n))$ for all n-ary predicate symbols $p \in P$ ($n \geq 1$), and all $d_1, \ldots, d_n \in D$. $\qquad\square$

A one-to-one and onto homomorphism is called an *isomorphism*; two interpretations $\mathscr{I}$ and $\mathscr{I}'$ are called *isomorphic* if there exists an isomorphism from one to the other.

THEOREM 2.27   If $\mathscr{I}$ and $\mathscr{I}'$ are isomorphic interpretations of the same basis for predicate logic, then $Th(\mathscr{I}) = Th(\mathscr{I}')$. $\qquad\square$

The converse of the theorem is false, as shall be seen when two models that are not isomorphic are given for a complete theory (recall that all models of a complete theory have the same set of valid formulas), namely Peano arithmetic.

A *non-standard model* is simply any model which is not isomorphic to the 'intended' model. This is naturally not an exact definition since it is not always clear what is meant by the intended model for a given theory, but it suffices for the purposes here.

There exists in fact (left to Exercise 2.4–5) at least one non-standard model $\mathscr{I}^* = (Nat^*, \mathscr{I}_0^*)$ for Peano arithmetic. In each such model there are 'infinite numbers', that is, elements d of Nat^*, for which

$$\mathscr{I}_0^*(<)(\mathscr{I}_0^*(1) + \cdots + \mathscr{I}_0^*(1), d)$$

holds for every finite sum of $\mathscr{I}_0^*(1)$'s. It is complicated to present a concrete non-standard model for Peano arithmetic. In order to given an idea of what such a model is like, a non-standard model will now be given for a 'subtheory' of Peano arithmetic, namely, for the theory of natural numbers with successor of Example 2.25(2).

Let $\mathscr{I} = (Nat, \mathscr{I}_0)$ be the usual interpretation for the basis $B = (\{0, S\}, \varnothing)$. As already mentioned $Th(\mathscr{I})$ is axiomatizable by a set of axioms denoted by Z in Example 2.25. Now consider the interpretation $\mathscr{I}^* = (Nat^*, \mathscr{I}_0^*)$ with:

$$Nat^* = (\{0\} \times Nat) \cup (\{1\} \times Int)$$

$$\mathscr{I}_0^*(0) = (0, 0)$$

$\mathscr{I}_0^*(S): Nat^* \to Nat^*$ defined by

$$\begin{cases} \mathscr{I}_0^*(S)(0, n) = (0, n + 1) & \text{for all } n \in Nat \\ \mathscr{I}_0^*(S)(1, z) = (1, z + 1) & \text{for all } z \in Int \end{cases}$$

This interpretation can be graphically illustrated by:

$$(0, 0) \to (0, 1) \to (0, 2) \to \cdots$$

$$\cdots \to (1, -2) \to (1, -1) \to (1, 0) \to (1, 1) \to (1, 2) \to \cdots$$

$\mathscr{I}^*$ is a model of the set Z of axioms—as one can easily check—and hence also of $Th(\mathscr{I})$. But it is clearly a non-standard model because it is not isomorphic to the 'usual' model. Moreover, the principle of induction does not hold in this non-standard model. By the principle of induction it is possible to prove a false proposition, namely that the sum of the first and second component of an element of the domain is always equal to the second component. This proposition is true for $\mathscr{I}_0^*(0)$ and when true of any element m of Nat^*, it is true of $\mathscr{I}_0^*(S)(m)$ (by elementary properties of addition); by the principle of induction the proposition is true of all elements of Nat^*.

By the way, as a consequence of the existence of this non-standard model there exists no subset of the Peano arithmetic—whether decidable or not—which expresses the principle of induction. (The fact that Peano arithmetic is not axiomatizable only allows the conclusion that there is no such decidable subset.)

36

EXERCISES

2.2–1 Let $B = (F, P)$ be a basis for predicate logic with $F = \{0, 1, \ldots, +, *, \ldots\}$ and $P = \{<, \leq, \ldots\}$. Furthermore, let $\mathscr{I}$ be the usual interpretation of the function and predicate symbols over the set Nat of natural numbers. Determine for each of the following formulas $w \in WFF_B$ the set of all assignments $\sigma: V \to Nat$ with $\mathscr{I}(w)(\sigma) = \text{true}$:

(a) $\neg \exists y . (x < y \wedge y < z)$
(b) $\exists x . \forall x . y \leq x$
(c) $x = 0 \supset x = 1 \supset x = 2$
(d) $\exists y . x * x = x \supset x \leq x$

Which of these formulas are valid in $\mathscr{I}$?

2.2–2 Let $B = (F, P)$ and $\mathscr{I}$ be as in Exercise 2.2–1. Give a formula $w \in WFF_B$ such that, for each assignment σ, $\mathscr{I}(w)(\sigma) = \text{true}$ exactly when

(a) $\sigma(z)$ divides $\sigma(x)$
(b) $\sigma(x)$ and $\sigma(y)$ are relatively prime
(c) $\sigma(z)$ is the gcd of $\sigma(x)$ and $\sigma(y)$.

2.2–3 For each of the following formulas give the set of all interpretations in which this formula is valid:

(a) $x = y$ (b) $\forall x, y . x = y$
(c) $\forall x . \exists y . x = y$ (d) $\exists y . \forall x . x = y$
(e) $\exists x, y . \forall z (z = x \vee z = y)$ (f) $x = y \wedge y = z \supset x = z$
(g) $f(x) = f(y) \supset x = y$ (h) $x = y \supset f(x) = f(y)$

Which of these formulas are logically valid?

2.2–4 Show that for all formulas w, w_1, w_2 each of the following pairs of formulas are logically equivalent:

(a) $w_1 \supset w_2$ and $\neg w_1 \vee w_2$
(b) $\forall x . w$ and $\neg \exists x . \neg w$
(c) $true$ and $w \vee \neg w$

2.2–5 Let $P(V)$ denote the power set of V, i.e. the set of all subsets of variables.

(a) Give an inductive definition of the function free: $WFF_B \to P(V)$, that maps every formula $w \in WFF_B$ to the set free (w) of all variables occurring free in w.
(b) With the help of part (a) prove the Coincidence Theorem 2.7 by structural induction.

2.2–6 Substitute the variable y by the term $y + z + x$ in the formula $\exists z . y * z = x$.

2.2–7 Prove the Substitution Theorem 2.10 presupposing the Renaming Theorem 2.8. (*Hint*: Use structural induction.)

2.2–8 Is there a set of formulas whose models are those interpretations with (a) exactly one element in the domain, (b) exactly two elements, and (c) finitely many elements?

2.2–9 Let $Z = \{x + x = x, \forall y . y + 0 = y\}$. Which of the following formulas are logical consequences of Z?

(a) $x = 0$ (b) $1 + 0 = 1$ (c) $0 + 1 = 1$ (d) $1 + 1 = 1$

2.2–10 Prove that

$$\models_{\mathscr{I}} w \qquad \text{iff} \qquad \models_{\mathscr{I}} \bar{w}$$

for all formulas $w \in WFF_B$ and all interpretations $\mathscr{I}$.

2.2–11
(a) Prove the Deduction Theorem 2.12.
(b) Find a pair of formulas w_1, w_2 for which $\{w_1\} \models w_2$, but not $\models w_1 \supset w_2$.

2.3–1 Give a deduction of the formula $\forall x . w \supset w_x^t$ from the empty set in the predicate calculus.

2.3–2 Finish the proof of the soundness of the predicate calculus (Theorem 2.17), that is, $W \vdash w$ implies $W \models w$ for all $W \subseteq WFF_B$, $w \in WFF_B$. It remains to show that (1) and (2) hold.

2.3–3 Presupposing the completeness of the predicate calculus, prove the Finiteness Principle and the Compactness Theorem (Theorems 2.19 and 2.20).

2.4–1 Let $W \subseteq WFF_B$ be a set of formulas with at least one model. Show that $Cn(W)$ is a theory.

2.4–2 Prove that for all interpretations $\mathscr{I}$, $Th(\mathscr{I})$ is a theory.

2.4–3

(a) In the definition of a complete theory it was required that for every *closed* formula w, either w or $\neg w$ is in the theory. Why does it not make sense to require this of *all* formulas w?

(b) Prove Theorem 2.23.

(c) Show that every complete recursively enumerable theory is decidable.

2.4–4 Let $B = (F, P)$ be a basis with $F = \{0, 1, +, *\}$ and $P = \{<\}$, and let PA be the set of Peano axioms given in text.

(a) Prove that for a model $\mathscr{I} = (D, \mathscr{I}_0)$ of PA the following two properties are equivalent:
  I. For every subset S of D:
     If $\mathscr{I}_0(0) \in S$
     and if $\mathscr{I}_0(+)(d, \mathscr{I}_0(1)) \in S$ whenever $d \in S$,
     then $S = D$.
  II. For every subset S of D:
     If $\mathscr{I}_0(0) \in S$
     and if $d \in S$ whenever $e \in S$ for all e such that $\mathscr{I}_0(<)(e, d) = \text{true}$
     then $S = D$.

(b) Show that two models of PA which have the property I (or II) are isomorphic.

*2.4–5 Let T be the theory of Peano arithmetic.

(a) Prove that there is a non-standard model of T. (*Hint:* Extend the basis to include a new constant ∞ and add the formulas $0 < \infty, 1 < \infty, 1 + 1 < \infty$, and so on, to T. Then use the Compactness Theorem.)

(b) Show that each non-standard model of T contains infinite elements.

*2.4–6 Let $B = (F, P)$ be a basis with $F = \varnothing$ and $P = \{\leq\}$.

(a) Give a theory $T \subseteq WFF_B$ whose models $\mathscr{I} = (\mathscr{I}_0, D)$ are exactly those for which $(D, \mathscr{I}_0(\leq))$ is a partial order.

(b) Is there a theory whose models $\mathscr{I} = (\mathscr{I}_0, D)$ are exactly those for which $(D, \mathscr{I}_0(\leq))$ is a well-founded set?

BIBLIOGRAPHICAL REMARKS

There are a large number of good textbooks on predicate logic. The reader may, for instance, consult Bell and Machover (1977), Enderton (1972), Kleene (1967), Ebbinghaus, Flum, and Thomas (1983), or Bergmann and Noll (1977).

A detailed description of the resolution principle may be found in Robinson (1979) or Bergmann and Noll (1977).

PART B

Semantics of Programming Languages

3
Three Simple Programming Languages

In this chapter three simple programming languages will be introduced, with which the different methods for program verification will be illustrated. The first two languages are imperative (that is, ALGOL-like) languages, the last is functional (that is, LISP-like). Each of these programming languages will be defined by giving its syntax and operational semantics.

3.1 The Flowchart Programming Language $\mathcal{L}_1$

The flowchart programming language is built up of assignments and (conditional and unconditional) jumps. The language is, therefore, similar to assembly code. Its name comes from the fact that these programs are usually represented as flowcharts.

The following definition of the flowchart programming language builds upon the predicate logic. Somewhat more precisely, a predicate logic with an interpretation $\mathcal{I}$ of a basis B is fixed in advance; B determines the exact syntax of $\mathcal{L}_1$ and $\mathcal{I}$ its semantics; by proceeding in this way the work in defining terms and formulas anew is spared. The flowchart programming language thus defined is denoted $\mathcal{L}_1^{B,\mathcal{I}}$ or $\mathcal{L}_1$ for short.

3.1.1 Syntax

In addition to the symbols of predicate logic, flowchart programs need the following sets of symbols:

the set

$$\{ := , ;, :, goto, \textit{if}, \textit{then}, \textit{else}, \textit{fi} \}$$

a recursively enumerable set *Lab* of *labels* with two distinguished elements denoted 'begin' and 'end' respectively.

Now let B be a basis for predicate logic. A *command* (over B) has one of the following two forms:

(1) *Parallel assignment*

$$l_1 : (x_1, \ldots, x_n) := (t_1, \ldots, t_n); \text{goto } l_2 \qquad (n \geq 1)$$

with $l_1, l_2 \in Lab, l_1 \neq$ end, $x_1, \ldots, x_n$ different variables from V and $t_1, \ldots, t_n$ terms from T_B; for $n = 1$ one writes $x := t$ instead of $(x) := (t)$.

(2) *Conditional jump*

$$l_1 : \textit{if } e \textit{ then goto } l_2 \textit{ else goto } l_3 \; fi$$

where $l_1, l_2, l_3 \in Lab, l_1 \neq$ end, $l_2 \neq l_3, e \in QFF_B$ is a quantifier-free formula.

A label that appears to the left of ':' in a command is said to constitute a *defining occurrence*, a label that appears immediately after a '*goto*' an *applied occurrence*.

DEFINITION 3.1 (Syntax of $\mathscr{L}_1$) A *flowchart program* over the basis B is defined as a finite, non-empty sequence of commands over B, which are separated by the symbol ';' and fulfil the following three conditions:

(1) The labels of the defining occurrences are all different.
(2) Each label of an applied occurrence other than 'end' has also a defining occurrence.
(3) The label 'begin' has a defining occurrence. □

The set of all flowchart programs over B is denoted L_1^B. Notice the difference between L_1^B and $\mathscr{L}_1$: the former is a formal language, the latter is this formal language *together with* an interpretation.

EXAMPLE 3.2 Let $B = \{F, P\}$ be a basis for predicate logic with $F = \{0, 1, \ldots, +\}$ *and* $P = \{\leq\}$. The following is an example of a flowchart program from L_1^B:

begin: $(y_1, y_2, y_3) := (0, 1, 1); \textit{goto } \text{test};$
test: *if* $y_3 \leq x$ *then goto* loop *else goto* end $fi;$
loop: $(y_1, y_2) := (y_1 + 1, y_2 + 2); \textit{goto } \text{upd};$
upd: $y_3 := y_3 + y_2; \textit{goto } \text{test}$ □

A flowchart program is usually represented by a diagram. This diagram is obtained as follows:

(1) An assignment

$$l_1 : (x_1, \ldots, x_n) := (t_1, \ldots, t_n); \textit{goto } l_2$$

is represented as

where the arrow that exits the diagram points to the (defining occurrence of the) label l_2.

(2) A conditional jump

$$l_1 : if \; e \; then \; goto \; l_2 \; else \; goto \; l_3 \; fi$$

is represented as

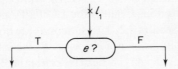

where the arrows marked with 'T' and 'F' point to l_2 and l_3 respectively.

(3) The labels 'begin' and 'end' are represented by

respectively.

EXAMPLE 3.3   The flowchart representation of the program given in Example 3.2 is:

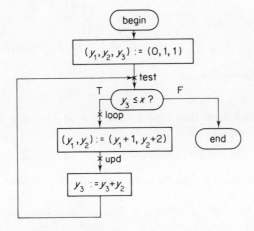

3.1.2 Operational Semantics

Let B be a basis for predicate logic and $\mathscr{I} = (D, \mathscr{I}_0)$ an interpretation of this basis. This interpretation will allow a 'meaning function' $\mathscr{M}_\mathscr{I}(S)$ representing the input–output behaviour of the program S to be associated to each flowchart program S from L_1^B. The description of the semantics of the flowchart programming language $\mathscr{L}_1$ consists in the definition of these meaning functions. According to the principle of 'operational' semantics these functions will now be described constructively (in the sense of computation theory). Non-constructive definitions of such functions will be discussed in Chapter 5 on denotational semantics.

For a precise description of the meaning function of a program it is necessary to first introduce some additional concepts. As in Section 2.2 let $\Sigma_{\mathscr{I}}$ denote the set of all states for the interpretation $\mathscr{I}$, that is the set of all functions $\sigma: V \rightarrow D$. (Note that, in accordance with Section 2.2, these functions are now called 'states' instead of 'assignments'.) A *configuration* (for the basis B, the interpretation $\mathscr{I}$ and the program S) is an element of $\{l \in Lab \,|\, l$ occurs in $S\} \times \Sigma_{\mathscr{I}}$. Informally, a configuration (l, σ) expresses that l is the defining label occurrence of the command currently being executed and that σ defines the current value of the variables. Next a relation is defined on the configurations describing the transitions performed during the execution of the program.

DEFINITION 3.4 (Transition Relation) For every flowchart program $S \in L_1^B$ over the basis B and every interpretation $\mathscr{I}$ of B, the relation $\overset{S}{\Rightarrow}$—or $\Rightarrow$ for short—on the set of configurations is defined by:

$(l_1, \sigma_1) \Rightarrow (l_2, \sigma_2)$ iff one of the following three conditions holds:

(1) There is a command

$$l_1: (x_1, \ldots, x_n) := (t_1, \ldots, t_n); \text{ goto } l_2$$

in the program S such that

$$\sigma_2 = \sigma_1[x_1/\mathscr{I}(t_1)(\sigma_1)] \ldots [x_n/\mathscr{I}(t_n)(\sigma_1)];$$

(2) There is a command

$$l_1: \text{ if } e \text{ then goto } l_2 \text{ else goto } l_3 \text{ } fi$$

in the program S such that $\sigma_1 = \sigma_2$ and $\mathscr{I}(e)(\sigma_1) = \text{true}$;

(3) There is a command

$$l_1: \text{ if } e \text{ then goto } l_3 \text{ else goto } l_2 \text{ } fi$$

in the program S such that $\sigma_1 = \sigma_2$ and $\mathscr{I}(e)(\sigma_1) = \text{false}$. □

Clearly the relation '$\overset{S}{\Rightarrow}$' is always a (partial) function whose value for a configuration (l, σ) is defined whenever l is different from 'end'.

A *computation sequence* (of a flowchart program S) for a state σ (called *input state*) is a—possibly infinite—sequence of configurations

$$(l_0, \sigma_0), (l_1, \sigma_1), \ldots$$

such that $l_0 = \text{begin}$, $\sigma_0 = \sigma$, and for every pair of consecutive configurations in the sequence

$$(l_i, \sigma_i) \Rightarrow (l_{i+1}, \sigma_{i+1}) \qquad (i \geq 1).$$

A computation sequence which is

either infinite
or ends with a configuration (l_k, σ_k) such that $l_k = \text{end}$

is called a *computation*.

A flowchart program is said to *terminate* for an input state σ, if it has a finite computation

$$(l_0, \sigma_0), \ldots, (l_k, \sigma_k)$$

for this input state. The state σ_k is then called the *output state*. In other words, the program terminates for the input state σ with the output state σ' if

$$(\text{begin}, \sigma) \overset{*}{\Rightarrow} (\text{end}, \sigma')$$

where '$\overset{*}{\Rightarrow}$' denotes the reflexive, transitive closure of the relation '$\Rightarrow$'.

The meaning of a flowchart program can now be defined.

DEFINITION 3.5 (Operational Semantics of $\mathscr{L}_1$)   Let S be a flowchart program from L_1^B over the basis B and $\mathscr{I}$ an interpretation of B. The *meaning* of the flowchart program S (in the interpretation $\mathscr{I}$) is the function $\mathscr{M}_\mathscr{I}(S)\colon \Sigma \rightharpoonup \Sigma$—or $\mathscr{M}(S)$ for short—defined by:

$$\mathscr{M}_\mathscr{I}(S)(\sigma) = \begin{cases} \sigma', \text{ if S terminates for the input state } \sigma \\ \quad \text{with the output state } \sigma'; \\[2mm] \text{undefined, if S does not terminate for} \\ \quad \text{the input state } \sigma. \end{cases} \qquad \Box$$

It is easy to prove that the meaning $\mathscr{M}_\mathscr{I}(S)$ is indeed a function, since the relation '$\Rightarrow$' is a function and since whenever the label 'end' is reached the computation sequence cannot be continued (see also Exercise 3.1–1).

Three things must be remarked here.

(1) The meaning of a flowchart program does not in any way depend on the choice of the (denotations used for the) labels (except for 'begin' and 'end'). The proof is left to the reader.

(2) Let $x_1, \ldots, x_n$ be the variables that occur in a given flowchart program S. For every computation sequence of S

$$(l_0, \sigma_0), (l_1, \sigma_1), \ldots$$

two states in the sequence differ at most in $x_1, \ldots, x_n$ by the very definition of the relation '$\Rightarrow$'. In addition, for every state σ_i of the sequence the values of $\sigma_i(x_1), \ldots, \sigma_i(x_n)$ depend only on the values of $\sigma_0(x_1), \ldots, \sigma_0(x_n)$ and *not* on the values of σ_0 for other variables. This follows from the Coincidence Theorem of predicate logic. So, in a computation sequence it is sufficient to keep track of a *state vector* $(\sigma_i(x_1), \ldots, \sigma_i(x_n))$ instead of the whole state σ_i (as in the next example). This property might be used to define the meaning of a program S to be—instead of a function from $\Sigma_{\mathscr{I}}$ to $\Sigma_{\mathscr{I}}$—a function from D^n to D^n, that is, a function from an 'input vector' to an 'output vector'. This approach is not taken here, since the former approach simplifies combining programming languages and predicate logic.

(3) Not a single programming language but a class of programming languages was introduced, namely one for every basis B and for every interpretation $\mathscr{I}$ of B. This generality is no doubt irrelevant in practice (since in practice B and $\mathscr{I}$ are fixed for every programming language), but fixing a particular basis and a particular interpretation does not simplify matters and would only distract from the main issues.

EXAMPLE 3.6   Consider again the flowchart program S in L_1^B given in Example 3.2. In the usual interpretation $\mathscr{I} = (Nat, \mathscr{I}_0)$ of B, this program is intended to compute the square root of x. The result is found in the variable y_1.

Given an input state $\sigma \in \Sigma_{\mathscr{I}}$ with, say $\sigma(x) = 15$, the computation of this program looks like (only the state vector is given for each configuration):

$$
\begin{array}{ll}
 & (\text{begin}, (15, \sigma(y_1), \sigma(y_2), \sigma(y_3))) \\
\Rightarrow & (\text{test}, (15, 0, 1, 1)) \\
\Rightarrow & (\text{loop}, (15, 0, 1, 1)) \\
\Rightarrow & (\text{upd}, (15, 1, 3, 1)) \\
\Rightarrow & (\text{test}, (15, 1, 3, 4)) \\
\vdots & \\
\Rightarrow & (\text{test}, (15, 3, 7, 16)) \\
\Rightarrow & (\text{end}, (15, 3, 7, 16))
\end{array}
$$

Hence

$$
\mathscr{M}_{\mathscr{I}}(S)(\sigma)(z) = \begin{cases} 3 & \text{if } z = y_1 \\ 7 & \text{if } z = y_2 \\ 16 & \text{if } z = y_3 \\ \sigma(z) & \text{else} \end{cases}
$$

The relevant property of this program is that for all states $\sigma \in \Sigma_{\mathscr{I}}$

$$
\mathscr{M}_{\mathscr{I}}(S)(\sigma)(y_1) = \sqrt{\sigma(x)}
$$

where '$\sqrt{}$' is the integer square root function. (In words: the value of y_1 in the output state is the integer square root of the value of x in the input state.) A proof of this property belongs to the realm of program verification and may be found in Chapter 7.   □

3.1.3 Some more Syntax

For later use in Chapter 7 some additional syntactical notions are introduced.

Let l, l' be labels occurring in a flowchart program S. A *path from l to l'* (in S) is a sequence $(l_0, l_1, \ldots, l_k)$ $(k \geq 0)$ of labels such that

(1) $l_0 = l$;
(2) for $i = 0, 1, \ldots, k - 1$ the label l_{i+1} has an applied occurrence in the command in which the label l_i has a defining occurrence;
(3) $l_k = l'$.

The *length* of the path $(l_0, \ldots, l_k)$ is defined to be k. A path from a label to itself of length $k \geq 1$ is called a *loop*; for instance, for the program of Example 3.2 the path (test, loop, upd, test) is a loop. A path from 'begin' to 'end' in a flowchart program is called a path *through* this program.

A flowchart program is called *well-constructed*, if every label which occurs in the program is on a path through this program. A well-constructed program may not contain a command

$$l: x := t; \; goto \; l$$

but may contain the (semantically equivalent) command

$$l: if \; true \; then \; goto \; l \; else \; goto \; l' \; fi$$

(provided there is a path from l' to 'end'). In limiting the attention to well-constructed programs it will be possible to slightly simplify the treatment of Floyd's verification methods in Chapter 7 without reducing the 'semantical power' of the programming language $\mathscr{L}_1$.

3.2 The While-Programming Language $\mathscr{L}_2$

While-programs are built up of assignments, if-then-else statements, and while-loops. The language constitutes the 'kernel' of any ALGOL-like language.

3.2.1 Syntax

Like the flowchart programming language, the while-programming language is built upon a basis B for predicate logic. In addition to these symbols, while-programs make use of the following set of symbols:

$$\{ :=, \; ;, \; if, \; then, \; else, \; fi, \; while, \; do, \; od \}$$

DEFINITION 3.7 (Syntax of $\mathscr{L}_2$) Let B be a basis for predicate logic. The set L_2^B of *while-programs* (for the basis B) is inductively defined as follows:

(a) *Assignment statement* For every variable x from V and every term t from T_B,

$$x := t$$

is a while-program.
(b) *Composed statement, conditional statement*, and *while-statement* If S_1, S_2 are while-programs and e is a quantifier-free formula from QFF_B then

$$\begin{aligned} &S_1 ; S_2 \\ &if \; e \; then \; S_1 \; else \; S_2 \; fi \\ &while \; e \; do \; S_1 \; od \end{aligned}$$

are while-programs $\qquad\qquad\qquad\qquad\qquad\qquad\qquad\qquad\qquad\qquad\qquad\square$

Notice that this inductive definition of the set of all while-programs is not free, because a while-program

$$S_1; S_2; S_3$$

(where S_1, S_2, and S_3 are again while-programs) may be constructed in two ways. This leads to a difficulty in Chapter 5 where the 'meaning function' of the semantics is defined inductively. A first solution consists in replacing the definition of the syntax of $\mathscr{L}_2$ by a more elaborate but free inductive definition. The solution chosen here consists in explicitly proving that the meaning function introduced in Chapter 5 is well-defined although the underlying inductive definition is not free.

3.2.2 Semantics

The operational semantics of while-programs for a basis B is developed similarly to the semantics of flowchart programs. First, an interpretation $\mathscr{I}$ of the basis B is fixed. Next, configurations for while-programs are defined, and a transition relation '$\Rightarrow$' on configurations is introduced. Finally, a meaning $\mathscr{M}_\mathscr{I}(S): \Sigma \rightsquigarrow \Sigma$ is defined.

A *configuration* (for a basis B and an interpretation $\mathscr{I}$ of B) is a pair (S, σ) of the Cartesian product $(L_2^B \cup \{\varepsilon\}) \times \Sigma_\mathscr{I}$. The first element of the pair is meant to be the rest of the program to be executed; the second element is the contents of the variables. Now the transition relation is defined.

DEFINITION 3.8 (Transition Relation) For every basis B and every interpretation $\mathscr{I}$ of B, the relation $\Rightarrow$ on the set of configurations $(L_2^B \cup \{\varepsilon\}) \times \Sigma_\mathscr{I}$ is defined by:

$(S_1, \sigma_1) \Rightarrow (S_2, \sigma_2)$ iff one of the following six conditions holds:

(1) There is a variable $x \in V$ and a term $t \in T_B$ such that

$$S_1 \text{ is } x := t; S_2$$

and

$$\sigma_2 = \sigma_1[x/\mathscr{I}(t)(\sigma_1)];$$

(2) There are while-programs S_1', S_2', S_3' and there is a quantifier-free formula e such that

$$S_1 \text{ is } \textit{if } e \textit{ then } S_1' \textit{ else } S_2' \textit{ fi}; S_3'$$

$$\sigma_2 = \sigma_1$$

and

$$S_2 \text{ is } \begin{cases} S_1'; S_3' & \text{if } \mathscr{I}(e)(\sigma_1) = \text{true} \\ S_2'; S_3' & \text{if } \mathscr{I}(e)(\sigma_1) = \text{false}; \end{cases}$$

(3) There are while-programs S_1', S_2' and there is a quantifier-free formula e such that

$$S_1 \text{ is } while \ e \ do \ S_1' \ od; \ S_2'$$

$$\sigma_2 = \sigma_1$$

and

$$S_2 \text{ is } \begin{cases} S_1'; S_1 & \text{if } \mathscr{I}(e)(\sigma_1) = \text{true} \\ S_2' & \text{if } \mathscr{I}(e)(\sigma_1) = \text{false}; \end{cases}$$

(4) There is a variable $x \in V$ and a term $t \in T_B$ such that

$$S_1 \text{ is } x := t$$

$$S_2 \text{ is } \varepsilon$$

and

$$\sigma_2 = \sigma_1[x/\mathscr{I}(t)(\sigma_1)];$$

(5) and (6): similar to (4) for (2) and (3). □

Notice that in this definition the conditions (4) to (6) are necessary because a while-program does not end with the symbol ';'. Notice also that contrasting with Definition 3.4 the relation '⇒' does not depend on a particular program.

The relation '⇒' is easily seen to be a (partial) function whose value for a configuration (S, σ) is defined iff $S \neq \varepsilon$.

A *computation sequence* (of a while-program S) for a state σ (called *input state*) is a—possibly infinite—sequence of configurations

$$(S_1, \sigma_1), (S_2, \sigma_2), \ldots$$

such that $S_1 = S$, $\sigma_1 = \sigma$ and for every pair of consecutive configurations in the sequence

$$(S_i, \sigma_i) \Rightarrow (S_{i+1}, \sigma_{i+1}) \qquad (i \geq 1).$$

A computation sequence which is

either infinite
or ends with a configuration (S_k, σ_k) such that $S_k = \varepsilon$

is called a *computation*. A while-program S is said to *terminate* for an input state σ, if there is a finite computation

$$(S_1, \sigma_1), \ldots, (S_k, \sigma_k)$$

for this input state. The state σ_k is then called the *output state*.

DEFINITION 3.9 (Operational Semantics of $\mathscr{L}_2$) Let S be a while-program from L_2^B over the basis B and $\mathscr{I}$ be an interpretation of this basis. The *meaning* of S (in the interpretation $\mathscr{I}$) is the function $\mathscr{M}_{\mathscr{I}}(S): \Sigma \to \Sigma$—or $\mathscr{M}(S)$ for short—defined by:

$$\mathscr{M}_{\mathscr{I}}(S)(\sigma) = \begin{cases} \sigma' & \text{if S terminates for the input} \\ & \text{state } \sigma \text{ with output state } \sigma'; \\ \text{undefined} & \text{if S does not terminate for} \\ & \text{the input state } \sigma. \end{cases}$$

□

$\mathcal{M}_{\mathcal{J}}(S)$ is indeed a function because of the definition of the relation '$\Rightarrow$', just as in the case of flowchart programs.

EXAMPLE 3.10   Let $B = (F, P)$ be a basis for predicate logic with $F = \{0, 1, \ldots, +\}$ and $P = \{\leq\}$. The following is an example of a while-program from L_2^B:

$$y_1 := 0; \; y_2 := 1; \; y_3 := 1;$$

$$while \; y_3 \leq x \; do \; y_1 := y_1 + 1;$$
$$y_2 := y_2 + 2;$$
$$y_3 := y_3 + y_2$$
$$od$$

For the usual interpretation of B, this program computes the integer square root of x, as in Example 3.3. A computation sequence of this while-program for an input state with $\sigma(x) = 15$ looks like (keeping track of only a state vector instead of the whole state):

$$(y_1 := 0; \ldots od, (15, \sigma(y_1), \sigma(y_2), \sigma(y_3)))$$
$\Rightarrow \quad (y_2 := 1; \ldots od, (15, 0, \sigma(y_2), \sigma(y_3)))$
$\vdots$

$\Rightarrow \quad (while \ldots od, (15, 0, 1, 1))$
$\Rightarrow \quad (y_1 := y_1 + 1; \; y_2 := y_2 + 2; \; y_3 := y_3 + y_2; \; while \ldots od,$
$$(15, 0, 1, 1))$$
$\vdots$

$\Rightarrow \quad (while \ldots od, (15, 1, 3, 4))$
$\vdots$

$\Rightarrow \quad (while \ldots od, (15, 3, 7, 16))$
$\Rightarrow \quad (\varepsilon, (15, 3, 7, 16))$ $\qquad\qquad \square$

It is possible to translate every while-program to a flowchart program with the same meaning. The basic idea is that a while-statement

$$while \; e \; do \; S \; od$$

is translated into the program segment:

$$l_1: if \; e \; then \; goto \; l_2 \; else \; goto \; l_3;$$
$$l_2: \ldots; \; goto \; l_1;$$
$$l_3:$$

where '$\ldots$' stands for the translation of S. (For a more precise statement and proof see Exercise 3.2–1.) The result of such a translation is a flowchart program that may have 'nested' and 'separate' loops but never any 'interleaved' ones, as illustrated by the following figure:

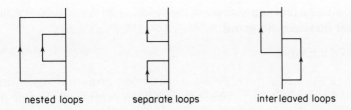

nested loops   separate loops   interleaved loops

3.3 The Language $\mathscr{L}_3$ of Recursive Programs

While $\mathscr{L}_1$ and $\mathscr{L}_2$ are imperative languages, $\mathscr{L}_3$ is a functional language. A program in this language consists of a single term, which can contain recursive calls of the program as well as calls to 'sub-programs'. Recursive programs are, hence, similar to programs in the language LISP and to recursive function schemes encountered in the theory of computation.

Unlike $\mathscr{L}_1$ and $\mathscr{L}_2$, $\mathscr{L}_3$ cannot build upon predicate logic. The reason, as will become clear in the treatment of the semantics of $\mathscr{L}_3$, is the necessity to model partial functions. This leads to the introduction of an 'undefined value'. For this reason, the definition of the syntax of recursive programs starts from scratch.

3.3.1 Syntax

As contrasted with predicate logic and the two previous programming languages, no difference is made between terms and formulas. Instead, formulas will be considered terms and the connectives will be considered additional function symbols. In order to distinguish the different kinds of terms, it is necessary to given every function symbol a 'type' which keeps track of what 'domain' (either D or *Bool*) the arguments and the function's value are.

Three sets of symbols are needed:

(1) The set of auxiliary symbols $\{(,),,,=\}$;
(2) A recursively enumerable set V of *variables*

$$V = \{x, y, z, x_1, \ldots, x', \ldots\};$$

(3) A recursively enumerable set W of *function variables*

$$W = \{F, G, \ldots, F_1, \ldots, F', \ldots\};$$

each of these function variables is associated with a number called its *arity*.

As usually these symbols are common to all languages $\mathscr{L}_3$ of recursive programs. The only one of these sets which is of a kind not encountered before is the set of function variables. Informally, these variables serve as names for the (main) program and for the sub-programs; formally they are mere variables which are intended to range over functions (with the corresponding arity); they should not be confused with the function symbols which will be added to the language in a moment.

Let b and d be two symbols which should remind one of the sets *Bool* and D respectively. The set of *types* is inductively defined as follows:

(a) b and d are types;
(b) if $\beta_1, \ldots, \beta_s, \beta_{s+1} \in \{b, d\}$ for $s \geq 1$, then $(\beta_1, \ldots, \beta_s \to \beta_{s+1})$ is a type.

A *basis* for a language of recursive programs is simply a set F of *function symbols* each of which is assigned a type. A function symbol of type b or d is called a *constant*. It will be assumed that every basis F has at least the following symbols:

true, false	of type b
$\neg$	of type $(b \to b)$
$\wedge, \vee, \supset, \equiv$	of type $(b, b \to b)$
if-then-else	of type $(b, d, d \to d)$
$=$	of type $(d, d \to b)$

Terms will be defined as in predicate logic but with type information taken under consideration. Moreover, function variables can also appear. The end result will be that each term has itself a type b or d.

DEFINITION 3.11 (Syntax of Terms)   The sets of *terms* of type b and of type d over the basis F are defined by simultaneous induction as follows:

(a) Every constant from F of type b or d is a term of type b or d, respectively. Every variable $x \in V$ is a term of type d.
(b) If $f \in F$ is a function symbol of type $(\beta_1, \ldots, \beta_s \to \beta_{s+1})$ and if $t_1, \ldots, t_s$ are terms of type $\beta_1, \ldots, \beta_s$ respectively, then $f(t_1, \ldots, t_s)$ is a term of type β_{s+1}. If $F \in W$ is a function variable of arity s and $t_1, \ldots, t_s$ are terms of type d, then $F(t_1, \ldots, t_s)$ is a term of type d. $\square$

Since the strict observance of this syntax leads to programs that are difficult to read, the customary manner of writing terms will be adopted. For example,

$$\textbf{if } x = 0 \textit{ then } 1 \textit{ else } x * F(x - 1) \, fi$$

will be written instead of

$$\textit{if-then-else } (= (x, 0), 1, *(x, F(-(x, 1)))).$$

DEFINITION 3.12 (Syntax of $\mathcal{L}_3$)   A *recursive program* over the basis F is defined to be a set of **n** *recursive equations*, $n \geq 1$,

$$F_1(x_{11}, \ldots, x_{1s_1}) \Leftarrow t_1$$
$$\vdots$$
$$F_n(x_{n1}, \ldots, x_{ns_n}) \Leftarrow t_n$$

together with a function variable F_k, $1 \leq k \leq n$, called the *main function variable*; it is understood that $F_1, \ldots, F_n$ are n different function variables and that for $i = 1, \ldots, n$ the following conditions hold:

$F_i \in W$ is an s_i-ary function variable;
$x_{i1}, \ldots, x_{is_i}$ are s_i different variables;
t_i is a term of type d which can only contain $F_1, \ldots, F_n$ as function variables and
$x_{i1}, \ldots, x_{is_i}$ as variables.   □

EXAMPLE 3.13   (1) For $n = 1$ the following recursive program is intended to compute the factorial of x:

$$F(x) \Leftarrow \textit{if } x = 0 \textit{ then } 1 \textit{ else } x * F(x - 1) \textit{ fi}.$$

(See also Example 3.28.)
(2) Now a recursive program with two recursive equations:

$$F_1(x) \Leftarrow \textit{if } x = 0 \textit{ then } 0 \textit{ else } F_2(x - 1) \textit{ fi}$$
$$F_2(x) \Leftarrow \textit{if } x = 0 \textit{ then } 1 \textit{ else } F_1(x - 1) \textit{ fi}.$$

and F_1 as the main function variable; this program is intended to compute the remainder modulo 2. (See also Example 5.14.)

3.3.2 Semantics

Informally each recursive equation of a recursive program represents a declaration of a function procedure. A computation of a recursive program is started by a call to the function procedure identified by the main function variable. This call may lead to recursive calls as well as to calls to the other function procedures.

The semantics will be again defined operationally with the help of 'computation sequences'. The elements of such a sequence will be produced by 'substitution' and 'simplification'. Substitution corresponds to a procedure call, or, more precisely, to an application of the 'copy rule'. Simplification corresponds to the evaluation of the value of the procedure body.

These various concepts will now be more precisely defined. First, the 'interpretation' of a term will be seen to lead to the notion of undefined values. Next, simplification and substitution will be treated. Finally, computation sequences will be defined, and then it will be possible to give a precise semantics of the language of recursive programs.

3.3.3 Undefined Values

In the programming languages $\mathcal{L}_1$ and $\mathcal{L}_2$ the value of a term or a (quantifier-free) formula is always defined and may be obtained in finite time. In fact, in these programming languages non-terminating computations only result from programming constructs such as jumps and while-statements. Hence it was possible to take over the definition of the semantics of terms and (quantifier-free) formulas from predicate logic.

The situation is different with regard to the programming language $\mathcal{L}_3$ which contains no programming constructs other than terms. In contrast to $\mathcal{L}_1$ or $\mathcal{L}_2$

the computation of a term of $\mathscr{L}_3$ may be non-terminating. The reason is that a function variable (together with its arguments) stands for the result of a call which may fail to terminate. In that case the term constituted by this function variable (together with its arguments) has an 'undefined' value. Since such a term can appear as the argument of a function or of another function variable, it is necessary to explicitly define the value of a function for undefined arguments. The problem is approached by extending the function domains to include 'undefined values'.

Let D—as in an interpretation of a basis in predicate logic—be a non-empty set called *domain*. Put

$$D_\omega = D \cup \{\omega_d\}$$

where ω_d is an element that does not belong to D. It stands for the undefined value of type d, where d is the type associated with the domain D. Similarly put

$$Bool_\omega = Bool \cup \{\omega_b\}.$$

So long as it does not lead to confusion, ω will be written instead of ω_d or ω_b.

Now let $f : S_1 \times \cdots \times S_n \to S_{n+1}$ be a total function where $S_i = D$ or $S_i = Bool$ for every i, $1 \le i \le n + 1$. Any extension $g : S_{1\omega} \times \cdots \times S_{n\omega} \to S_{(n+1)\omega}$ of f is called ω-*extension* of f. An ω-extension is called *strict* if whenever an argument is ω, it takes the value ω.

Mostly strict ω-extensions will be considered. There is, however, one important exception, the so-called *sequential* (ω-extension of the) if-then-else function, which is also denoted by if-then-else:

$$\text{if-then-else} : Bool_\omega \times D_\omega \times D_\omega \to D_\omega \text{ defined by}$$

$$\text{if-then-else } (b, d_1, d_2) = \begin{cases} d_1 & \text{if } b = \text{true}, \\ d_2 & \text{if } b = \text{false}, \\ \omega & \text{if } b = \omega. \end{cases}$$

This function is not strict, since at the argument (true, d_1, d_2), this function has the value d_1, even when $d_2 = \omega$. (See Exercise 3.3–8 for another possible ω-extension of the if-then-else function.)

Arbitrary ω-extensions can lead to problems in calculating their values. Suppose one wanted to have an ω-extension of the subtraction function on integers such that $\omega - \omega = 0$. This means that the difference of two terms whose calculation did not terminate would be equal to zero. Whereas the difference of two terms whose calculation did terminate could be different from zero. Since it is not decidable whether a calculation terminates or not, it should in general be impossible to determine the difference of two terms (in finite time). To avoid this problem only 'monotonic' functions are considered. The concept of monotonicity refers to particular partial orders which will now be defined.

3.3.4 Flat Partial Orders and Monotonicity

Let D be a domain, and let $S = D$ or $S = Bool$. Define a relation '$\sqsubseteq$' on S_ω by

$$a \sqsubseteq b \qquad \text{iff } (a = \omega \text{ or } a = b)$$

(read 'a is less or equally defined than b'). Then $(S_\omega, \sqsubseteq)$ is a partial order and is called the *flat partial order* pertaining to S.

According to Section 1.1 these flat partial orders induce a partial order on any Cartesian product $S_{1\omega} \times S_{2\omega} \times \cdots \times S_{n\omega}, n \geq 1$, with $S_i = D$ or $S_i = Bool$ for any i, $1 \leq i \leq n$.

EXAMPLE 3.14 The flat partial order pertaining to *Bool* can be graphically represented like:

true$\diagdown$ false

ω

This flat partial order induces in turn a partial order $(Bool_\omega^2, \sqsubseteq)$ on the Cartesian product that has the following form:

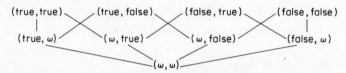

For instance,

$$(\omega, true) \sqsubseteq (true, true)$$

and

$$(\omega, \omega) \sqsubseteq (\omega, true)$$

but

$$(true, \omega) \quad \text{and} \quad (\omega, true)$$

are incomparable. $\qquad\qquad\qquad\qquad\qquad\qquad\qquad\qquad\qquad\qquad\qquad\Box$

Here the interest lies in monotonic functions with respect to these partial orders. So, next, some functions are examined for monotonicity.

Every strict function

$$g: S_{1\omega} \times \cdots \times S_{n\omega} \to S_{(n+1)\omega}$$

with $S_i = D$ or $S_i = Bool$ for any i, $1 \leq i \leq n+1$, is monotonic. For suppose $s_i, s_i' \in S_{i\omega}$ for any i, $1 \leq i \leq n$, such that $(s_1, \ldots, s_n) \sqsubseteq (s_1', \ldots, s_n')$. If $(s_1, \ldots, s_n) = (s_1', \ldots, s_n')$, then the function values must agree and

$$g(s_1, \ldots, s_n) \sqsubseteq g(s_1', \ldots, s_n')$$

If $(s_1, \ldots, s_n) \neq (s_1', \ldots, s_n')$, then for at least one i, $1 \leq i \leq n$, $s_i \neq s_i'$, so that $s_i = \omega$; since g is strict,

$$g(s_1, \ldots, s_n) = \omega \sqsubseteq g(s_1', \ldots, s_n')$$

The sequential if-then-else function is monotonic, as the following argument shows. Suppose $b, b' \in Bool_\omega$ and $d_1, d_2, d_1', d_2' \in D_\omega$ such that $(b, d_1, d_2) \sqsubseteq (b', d_1', d_2')$. There are three cases depending on the value of b. If $b = \omega$, then

$$\text{if-then-else}(b, d_1, d_2) = \omega \sqsubseteq \text{if-then-else}(b', d_1', d_2').$$

If $b = \text{true}$, then $b' = \text{true}$ by $b \sqsubseteq b'$; hence

$$\text{if-then-else}(b, d_1, d_2) = d_1 \sqsubseteq \text{if-then-else}(b', d_1', d_2') = d_1'$$

because $d_1 \sqsubseteq d_1'$ by hypothesis. The case where $b = \text{false}$ is similar.

There is no monotonic ω-extension $(Int_\omega)^2 \to Int_\omega$ of the subtraction function on integers such that

$$\omega - \omega = 0.$$

For consider that

$$(\omega, \omega) \sqsubseteq (a, b) \qquad \text{for all } a, b \in Int_\omega.$$

If the (ω-extension of the) subtraction were monotonic, then

$$\omega - \omega = 0 \sqsubseteq a - b \qquad \text{for all } a, b \in Int_\omega$$

hence

$$a - b = 0 \qquad \text{for all } a, b \in Int_\omega$$

To make it more plausible that indeed the calculation of the value of a monotonic function can be effectively carried out, a characterization of monotonic functions is given:

A function

$$g: S_{1\omega} \times \cdots \times S_{n\omega} \to S_{(n+1)\omega}$$

(with $S_{1\omega}, \ldots, S_{(n+1)\omega}$ as above) is monotonic iff for any i, $1 \le i \le n$, and any $(n-1)$-tuple

$$(s_1, \ldots, s_{i-1}, s_{i+1}, \ldots, s_n) \in S_{1\omega} \times \cdots \times S_{(i-1)\omega} \times S_{(i+1)\omega} \times \cdots \times S_{n\omega}$$

one of the following two conditions holds:

(1) $g(s_1, \ldots, s_{i-1}, \omega, s_{i+1}, \ldots, s_n) = \omega$
(2) for every $s_i \in S_{i\omega}$:

$$g(s_1, \ldots, s_{i-1}, \omega, s_{i+1}, \ldots, s_n) = g(s_1, \ldots, s_{i-1}, s_i, s_{i+1}, \ldots, s_n)$$

(The proof that this characterization is correct is left to Exercise 3.3–3.) From this characterization one sees intuitively that the calculation of the value of a function, which is a monotonic ω-extension of a (computable total) function, can be carried out effectively. For suppose condition (1) holds; the calculation of the value of g does not terminate (hence 'delivers' the value 'undefined') because the calculation of its ith argument does not terminate. On the other hand, suppose condition (2) holds. In this case the computation of the ith argument may be skipped. (What is exactly meant by an effective calculation of the value of a function will be made more precise when simplification is taken up.)

According to Section 1.1 the flat partial orders induce a partial order on any set

$$(S_{1\omega} \times \cdots \times S_{n\omega} \xrightarrow{\vec{m}} S_{(n+1)\omega})$$

of monotonic functions, where $S_{1\omega}, \ldots, S_{(n+1)\omega}$ are as above. For two functions g_1, g_2 of this set,

$$g_1 \sqsubseteq g_2 \quad \text{iff } g_1(s_1, \ldots, s_n) \sqsubseteq g_2(s_1, \ldots, s_n) \text{ for all } (s_1, \ldots, s_n) \in S_{1\omega} \times \cdots \times S_{n\omega}$$

or, equivalently,

$$g_1 \sqsubseteq g_2 \quad \text{iff } g_1(s_1, \ldots, s_n) = \omega \text{ or } g_1(s_1, \ldots, s_n) = g_2(s_1, \ldots, s_n)$$

$$\text{for all } (s_1, \ldots, s_n) \in S_{1\omega} \times \cdots \times S_{n\omega}$$

Thus $g_1 \sqsubseteq g_2$ means that g_2 is defined at least for all arguments for which g_1 is defined, and that both functions agree for these arguments. This partial order on functions will play an important role in the next sections.

3.3.5 Interpretations and Assignments

The groundwork has been laid to allow the definition of an interpretation for the programming language $\mathcal{L}_3$.

DEFINITION 3.15 (Interpretations)   Let F be a basis for $\mathcal{L}_3$. An *interpretation* of the basis F is a pair $\mathscr{I} = (D, \mathscr{I}_0)$ such that D is a non-empty set called the domain, and $\mathscr{I}_0$ is a function that makes the following mapping:

(1) An element of *Bool* or an element of D is made to correspond to every constant from F of type b or of type d, respectively.
(2) A monotonic ω-extension of a total function is made to correspond to every function symbol $f \in F$ of type $(\beta_1, \ldots, \beta_n \to \beta_{n+1})$ where $n \geq 1$ and $\beta_i \in \{b, d\}$ for $i = 1, \ldots, n + 1$. This function must have domain $S_{1\omega} \times \cdots \times S_{n\omega}$ and range in $S_{(n+1)\omega}$, where

$$S_i = \begin{cases} Bool & \text{if } \beta_i = b \\ D & \text{if } \beta_i = d \end{cases}$$

for $i = 1, \ldots, n + 1$.   □

It should be stressed that the constants are assigned values from *Bool* and D, *not* from $Bool_\omega$ and D_ω. The reason is that ω represents the result of a non-terminating computation, and not some particular element of the universe under consideration.

For technical reasons—namely, to simplify the definition of operational semantics—it is assumed that $\mathscr{I}_0$ is a one-to-one function from the constants onto $D \cup Bool$. This means that the basis must contain exactly one constant for every member of the domain.

An interpretation $\mathscr{I} = (D, \mathscr{I}_0)$ is called *standard* if $\mathscr{I}_0(true) = \text{true}$, $\mathscr{I}_0(false) = \text{false}$, and the function symbols $\neg$, $\wedge$, $\vee$, $\supset$, $\equiv$, $=$, and *if-then-else* are given respectively the strict ω-extension of their usual interpretations and the sequential ω-extension of the if-then-else function. If not differently specified only standard interpretations will be considered in the examples; these interpretations will also have recursively enumerable domains and the function symbols (other than *if-then-else*) will all be given strict ω-extensions of computable functions. But outside the examples arbitrary interpretations will be permitted.

As in predicate logic an 'assignment' is introduced which assigns a value to the variables from V and the function variables from W.

DEFINITION 3.16   An *assignment* for a basis F and an interpretation $\mathcal{I} = (D, \mathcal{I}_0)$ of F is a function which maps every variable $x \in V$ to an element from D_ω, and every s-ary function variable $F \in W$ to a monotonic function from $(D_\omega^s \xrightarrow{m} D_\omega)$, $s \geq 1$. □

The set of all assignments is denoted $\Gamma_{\mathcal{I}}$ or Γ-for short. As a difference with the set Σ introduced in the predicate logic (Section 2.2) and used in the description of the semantics of $\mathcal{L}_1$ and $\mathcal{L}_2$, an element of Γ maps also function variables and, more importantly, has ω (and ω-extensions) among its values.

The partial orders on the domain D_ω and on monotonic functions induce a partial order on the set Γ of all assignments in the familiar way. Hence, for all $\gamma, \gamma' \in \Gamma$:

$$\gamma \sqsubseteq \gamma' \quad \text{iff} \quad \begin{cases} \gamma(x) \sqsubseteq \gamma'(x) & \text{for all } x \in V, \text{ and} \\ \gamma(F) \sqsubseteq \gamma'(F) & \text{for all } F \in W. \end{cases}$$

Again, as in the case of predicate logic, there is a semantic functional associated to every interpretation.

DEFINITION 3.17 (Semantics of Terms)   Let $\mathcal{I} = (D, \mathcal{I}_0)$ be an interpretation of the basis F. The semantic functional of this interpretation—also denoted $\mathcal{I}$—assigns to every term t of type b or type d a function

$$\mathcal{I}(t): \Gamma \to Bool_\omega$$

or

$$\mathcal{I}(t): \Gamma \to D_\omega$$

respectively. These functions are inductively defined by

(a) $\mathcal{I}(c)(\gamma) = \mathcal{I}_0(c)$ if $c \in F$ is a constant;
     $\mathcal{I}(x)(\gamma) = \gamma(x)$ if $x \in V$ is a variable;
(b) $\mathcal{I}(f(t_1, \ldots, t_s))(\gamma) = \mathcal{I}_0(f)(\mathcal{I}(t_1)(\gamma), \ldots, \mathcal{I}(t_s)(\gamma))$ if $f \in F$ is an s-ary function symbol, $s \geq 1$;
     $\mathcal{I}(F(t_1, \ldots, t_s))(\gamma) = \gamma(F)(\mathcal{I}(t_1)(\gamma), \ldots, \mathcal{I}(t_s)(\gamma))$ if $F \in W$ is an s-ary function variable. □

Two terms t, t' are said to be *equivalent* in the interpretation $\mathcal{I}$, if $\mathcal{I}(t)(\gamma) = \mathcal{I}(t')(\gamma)$ for all assignments $\gamma \in \Gamma$.

The following theorem ensures that terms represent monotonic functions. This result is essential since it has already been seen that monotonic functions avoid a problem of computability.

THEOREM 3.18   Let t be a term over a basis F and $\mathscr{I}$ an interpretation of F. Then $\mathscr{I}(t)$ is a monotonic function.

Proof. Let $\gamma, \gamma' \in \Gamma$ be two assignments with $\gamma \sqsubseteq \gamma'$. It must be proved that $\mathscr{I}(t)(\gamma) \sqsubseteq \mathscr{I}(t)(\gamma')$ for every term t. The proof is by structural induction on term t.

(a) If $t = c$, with c a constant, then the function $\mathscr{I}(t)$ has a constant value, so
$$\mathscr{I}(t)(\gamma) = \mathscr{I}(t)(\gamma').$$
If $t = x$ with $x \in V$, then
$$\mathscr{I}(x)(\gamma) = \gamma(x) \sqsubseteq \gamma'(x) = \mathscr{I}(x)(\gamma').$$

(b) If $t = f(t_1, \ldots, t_s)$ with $f \in F$, then
$$\begin{aligned}
\mathscr{I}(t)(\gamma) &= \mathscr{I}_0(f)(\mathscr{I}(t_1)(\gamma), \ldots, \mathscr{I}(t_s)(\gamma)) \\
&\sqsubseteq \mathscr{I}_0(f)(\mathscr{I}(t_1)(\gamma'), \ldots, \mathscr{I}(t_s)(\gamma'))
\end{aligned}$$
(since $\mathscr{I}_0(f)$ is monotonic and by induction hypothesis $\mathscr{I}(t_i)(\gamma) \sqsubseteq \mathscr{I}(t_i)(\gamma')$ for $i = 1, \ldots, s$).
$$= \mathscr{I}(t)(\gamma').$$

If $t = F(t_1, \ldots, t_s)$ with $F \in W$, then
$$\begin{aligned}
\mathscr{I}(t)(\gamma) &= \gamma(F)(\mathscr{I}(t_1)(\gamma), \ldots, \mathscr{I}(t_s)(\gamma)) \\
&\sqsubseteq \gamma(F)(\mathscr{I}(t_1)(\gamma'), \ldots, \mathscr{I}(t_s)(\gamma'))
\end{aligned}$$
(because $\gamma(F)$ is monotonic and by induction hypothesis $\mathscr{I}(t_i)(\gamma) \sqsubseteq \mathscr{I}(t_i)(\gamma')$ for $i = 1, \ldots, s$).
$$\begin{aligned}
&\sqsubseteq \gamma'(F)(\mathscr{I}(t_1)(\gamma'), \ldots, \mathscr{I}(t_s)(\gamma')) \qquad \text{(since } \gamma \sqsubseteq \gamma') \\
&= \mathscr{I}(t)(\gamma'). \qquad\qquad\qquad\qquad\qquad\qquad \square
\end{aligned}$$

In order to be able to define the semantics of recursive programs it is still necessary to introduce the notions of simplification and substitution. While an intuitive understanding of these notions is easy, their formal treatment is not trivial. If preferred, the reader may in a first reading skip the details of the formal definitions and the proofs of Theorems 3.21 to 3.26.

*3.3.6 Simplification

Simplification consists—informally expressed—of replacing a term by another more simple, equivalent term. For example, in the usual interpretation $3 + 2$ can be replaced by 5, and

$$\textit{if true then } F(x) \textit{ else } F(y) \textit{ fi}$$

can be replaced by $F(x)$. Simplifications are carried out with the aid of so-called 'simplification schemes'. Examples of simplification schemes (to be precisely defined shortly) are

$$(1 * x, x)$$

and

$$(z \vee z, z);$$

they (are intended to) express that $1 * x$ may be replaced by x and $z \vee z$ by z respectively. The elements of these ordered pairs look like terms of $\mathscr{L}_3$ except for one difference. In the examples above x has been used to stand for a term of type d and, clearly, z is to stand for a term of type b. Hence x may be viewed as a variable (of type d) and z as a variable of type b. But the syntax of $\mathscr{L}_3$ does not provide variables of type b. Hence, in order to be able to define simplification schemes one is led to introduce the notion of *generalized terms*; these are defined like the terms in Definition 3.11 but with a set of variables of type b added.

DEFINITION 3.19 (Simplification Rules)   A *simplification scheme* (for a basis F and an interpretation $\mathscr{I}$ of F) is an ordered pair (t, t') of generalized terms such that

(1) the length of t' is less than that of t;
(2) t and t' are equivalent in $\mathscr{I}$.

A *simplification rule* is a set of simplification schemes.   □

For the usual interpretation the following pairs constitute a simplification rule—with $x, x_1, \ldots$ (usual) variables and z a variable of type b:

$$(0 + 0, 0)$$
$$(0 = 0, true)$$
$$(x + x + x, 3 * x)$$
$$(if\ true\ then\ x_1\ else\ x_2\ fi, x_1)$$
$$(if\ \neg z\ then\ x_1\ else\ x_2\ fi, if\ z\ then\ x_2\ else\ x_1\ fi)$$
$$(z \vee z, z).$$

On the other hand, $(x = x, true)$ is not a simplification scheme because $\mathscr{I}_0(=)(\omega, \omega) = \omega \neq true$. Neither is $(0*x, 0)$ because $\mathscr{I}_0(*)(0, \omega) = \omega \neq 0$. By the way, $(0 * x, 0)$ is a simplification scheme for an interpretation where $\mathscr{I}_0(*)$ is a (non-strict but monotonic) ω-extension of the multiplication with $\mathscr{I}_0(*)(0, \omega) = 0 = \mathscr{I}_0(*)(\omega, 0)$. But $(x = x, true)$ cannot be a simplification scheme in any (monotonic) ω-extension of the equality.

Note that, if a simplification rule for an interpretation $(D, \mathscr{I}_0)$ contains a simplification scheme

$$(f(x, c_1), c_2)$$

where f is a function symbol, x a (usual) variable and c_1, c_2 constants, then

$$\mathscr{I}_0(f)(d, \mathscr{I}_0(c_1)) = \mathscr{I}_0(c_2)$$

for all $d \in D_\omega$. Thus, the value of $\mathscr{I}_0(f)$ is independent of the value of its first argument when its second argument is $\mathscr{I}_0(c_1)$.

The *application of a simplification scheme* (t, u) on a (non-generalized) term v consists in the replacement of a subterm $t_{x_1,\ldots,x_n}^{t_1,\ldots,t_n}$ of v by $u_{x_1,\ldots,x_n}^{t_1,\ldots,t_n}$, where $x_1, \ldots, x_n$ are the variables occurring in t and $t_1, \ldots, t_n$ are some (non-generalized) terms (of the corresponding type).

The *application of a simplification rule* consists in the application of one of its schemes. For a simplification rule r the relation

$$t \xrightarrow{r} u$$

expresses that the term u is obtained from the term t by an application of r. As customary '$\xrightarrow{*}$' denotes the reflexive, transitive closure of the relation '$\rightarrow$'. With the simplification rule of the example above one has for instance

$$F(0 + 0) \xrightarrow{r} F(0)$$

$$\textit{if } 0 = 0 \textit{ then } F(4 + 4 + 4) \textit{ else} \ldots fi \xrightarrow{*}_{r} F(3 * 4)$$

A term t is said to be *maximally simplified* (with respect to a simplification rule r) if there is no term u such that

$$t \xrightarrow{r} u.$$

In the following a special simplification rule, called 'standard', will play an important rule.

DEFINITION 3.20 (Standard Simplification Rule)   The *standard simplification rule* (for a basis F and an interpretation $\mathscr{I}$ of F) is the set of *all* simplification schemes (for F and $\mathscr{I}$) of the form $(f(t_1, \ldots, t_n), c)$ where:

f is a function symbol of arity $n \geq 1$;
each t_i is either a variable or a constant (of the appropriate type);
no variable occurs more than once in $f(t_1, \ldots, t_n)$;
c is a constant.

The standard simplification rule is denoted $s_{\mathscr{I}}$ or, shortly, s.   □

The standard simplification rule contains in particular the simplification scheme

$$(\textit{if true then } 1 \textit{ else } x \textit{ fi}, 1)$$

but not

$$(\textit{if true then } x_1 \textit{ else } x_2 \textit{ fi}, x_1)$$

(because the second element of the simplification scheme is not a constant symbol). Hence

$$\textit{if true then } 1 \textit{ else } F(1) \textit{ fi} \xrightarrow{s} 1$$

but not

$$\textit{if true then } F(0) \textit{ else } F(1) \textit{ fi} \xrightarrow{s} F(0).$$

62

It will now be shown that, despite the elementary character of the standard simplification rule, it is powerful enough to express the semantics of the programming language $\mathscr{L}_3$. The basis for this observation is Theorem 3.22. But first a definition and lemma will be introduced.

The *everywhere-ω assignment* (for given basis and interpretation) is the element $\gamma_0 \in \Gamma$ defined by

$$\gamma_0(x) = \omega \qquad \text{for all variables } x \in V$$

and

$$\gamma_0(F) = \text{the } s\text{-ary constant function with value } \omega,$$
$$\text{for all } s\text{-ary function variables } F \in W, s \geq 1.$$

LEMMA 3.21 Let t be a term over a basis F and γ_0 the everywhere-ω assignment for an interpretation $\mathscr{I}$ of F. If t is not equivalent to a constant, then $\mathscr{I}(t)(\gamma_0) = \omega$.

Proof. Suppose to the contrary that $\mathscr{I}(t)(\gamma_0) = d \neq \omega$. Clearly,

$$\gamma_0 \sqsubseteq \gamma$$

for every assignment γ. By Theorem 3.18, $\mathscr{I}(t)$ is monotonic, hence

$$\mathscr{I}(t)(\gamma_0) \sqsubseteq \mathscr{I}(t)(\gamma)$$

So $\mathscr{I}(t)(\gamma) = d$ for every assignment γ. But this is not possible since t would be equivalent to that constant c for which $\mathscr{I}_0(c) = d$. (Remember that $\mathscr{I}_0$ is one-to-one.)

THEOREM 3.22 Let F be a basis, $\mathscr{I}$ an interpretation of F, t a term over F, and s the standard simplification rule. If t is equivalent to a constant c (in $\mathscr{I}$), then $t \xrightarrow[s]{*} c$.

Proof. Assume that t and c are equivalent in $\mathscr{I}$; then $\mathscr{I}(t)(\gamma) = \mathscr{I}_0(c)$ for every assignment γ. The proof that $t \xrightarrow[s]{*} c$ is by structural induction on the term t.

(a) If $t = c'$, then $c = c'$ because $\mathscr{I}_0(c') = \mathscr{I}_0(c)$ and $\mathscr{I}_0$ is one-to-one.

If $t = x$, then t cannot be equivalent to a constant c, because there are assignments γ such that $\gamma(x) \neq \mathscr{I}_0(c)$.

(b) If $t = f(t_1, \ldots, t_s)$, let $t_{i_1}, \ldots, t_{i_h}$ be those terms from $t_1, \ldots, t_s$ which are equivalent to constants, say $c_{i_1}, \ldots, c_{i_h}$. By induction hypothesis

$$t_{i_j} \xrightarrow[s]{*} c_{i_j} \qquad \text{for } j = 1, \ldots, h.$$

By setting $t_i' = c_i$ for $i = i_1, \ldots, i_h$ and $t_i' = t_i$ otherwise, one obtains

$$t \xrightarrow[s]{*} t' = f(t_1', \ldots, t_s').$$

Now since t and c are equivalent (by assumption) and t and t' are equivalent (by definition of simplification), the following holds for all assignments γ:

$$\mathscr{I}(t')(\gamma) = \mathscr{I}_0(c)$$

or

$$\mathscr{I}_0(f)(\mathscr{I}(t_1')(\gamma), \ldots, \mathscr{I}(t_s')(\gamma)) = \mathscr{I}_0(c). \tag{1}$$

In particular it holds for the everywhere-ω assignment γ_0. By the previous lemma

$$\mathscr{I}(t_i')(\gamma_0) = \omega \qquad \text{for } i \neq i_1, \ldots, i_h.$$

Moreover

$$\mathscr{I}(t_i')(\gamma_0) = \mathscr{I}_0(c_i) \qquad \text{for } i = i_1, \ldots, i_h.$$

Setting $d_i = \mathscr{I}_0(c_i)$ for $i = i_1, \ldots, i_h$ and $d_i = \omega$ otherwise, the following is obtained from equation (1) above:

$$\mathscr{I}_0(f)(d_1, \ldots, d_s) = \mathscr{I}_0(c). \tag{2}$$

Since $\mathscr{I}_0(c) \neq \omega$ and $\mathscr{I}_0(f)$ is monotonic, the equation (2) is also true for arbitrary values of d_i for $i \neq i_1, \ldots, i_h$ (and not only for $d_i = \omega$). Hence the standard simplification rule s necessarily contains the simplification scheme

$$(f(t_1'', \ldots, t_s''), c)$$

with $t_i'' = c_i$ for $i = i_1, \ldots, i_h$ and $t_i'' = $ a variable, say x_i, for $i \neq i_1, \ldots, i_h$. Hence

$$f(t_1', \ldots, t_s') \underset{s}{\rightarrow} c.$$

Consequently,

$$t \underset{s}{\overset{*}{\rightarrow}} t' \underset{s}{\rightarrow} c.$$

If $t = F(t_1, \ldots, t_s)$, then t cannot be equivalent to the constant c, because

$$\mathscr{I}(t)(\gamma_0) = \gamma_0(F)(\ldots) = \omega \neq \mathscr{I}(c)(\gamma_0).$$

(where γ_0 is the everywhere-ω assignment). $\qquad\qquad\qquad\qquad\qquad\qquad\square$

*3.3.7 Substitution

Informally, substitution (or unfolding) consists in replacing a function by its definition. Formally, let

$$F_j(x_{j_1}, \ldots, x_{js_j}) \Leftarrow t_j \qquad \text{for } 1 \leq j \leq n$$

be the equations of a recursive program S over a basis F. The *substitution function* for S is a function $\mathscr{S}$ with domain equal to the set of all terms over F and defined inductively as follows:

(a) $\mathscr{S}(c) = c$, for all constants $c \in F$;
$\mathscr{S}(x) = x$, for all variables $x \in V$;
(b) $\mathscr{S}(f(u_1, \ldots, u_s)) = f(\mathscr{S}(u_1), \ldots, \mathscr{S}(u_s))$, for all s-ary function symbols $f \in F$ and terms $u_1, \ldots, u_s$;
$\mathscr{S}(F(u_1, \ldots, u_s)) = F(\mathscr{S}(u_1), \ldots, \mathscr{S}(u_s))$, for all s-ary function variables $F \in W$ with $F \neq F_1, \ldots, F_n$ and terms $u_1, \ldots, u_s$;
$\mathscr{S}(F_j(u_1, \ldots, u_{s_j})) = (t_j)_{x_{j1}, \ldots, x_{js_j}}^{\mathscr{S}(u_1), \ldots, \mathscr{S}(u_{s_j})}$, for all j, $1 \leq j \leq n$ and terms $u_1, \ldots, u_{s_j}$.

When $t' = \mathscr{S}(t)$, one says that the term t' is obtained from the term t by (*simultaneous*) *substitution* (with respect to program S). In contrast to simplification, substitution is a purely syntactic process: the substitution function does not depend in any way on an interpretation.

EXAMPLE 3.23   (1) Let S be the recursive program

$$F(x) \Leftarrow if \ x = 0 \ then \ 1 \ else \ x * F(x - 1) \ fi.$$

Then

$$\mathscr{S}(F(2)) = (if \dots fi)_x^{\mathscr{S}(2)}$$
$$= (if \dots fi)_x^2$$
$$= if \ 2 = 0 \ then \ 1 \ else \ 2 * F(2 - 1) \ fi$$

(2) Let S be the recursive program

$$F(x) \Leftarrow if \ x > 100 \ then \ x - 10 \ else \ F(F(x + 11)) \ fi.$$

Then

$$\mathscr{S}(F(F(111))) = (if \dots fi)_x^{\mathscr{S}(F(111))}$$

But

$$\mathscr{S}(F(111)) = (if \dots fi)_x^{\mathscr{S}(111)}$$
$$= if \ 111 > 100 \ then \ 111 - 10 \ else \ F(F(111 + 11)) \ fi.$$

So

$$\mathscr{S}(F(F(111))) = if \ (if \ 111 > 100 \ then \ 111 - 10 \ else \ F(F(111 + 11)) \ fi) > 100$$
$$then \ (if \ 111 > 100 \ then \ 111 - 10 \ else \ F(F(111 + 11)) \ fi) - 10$$
$$else \ F(F((if \ 111 > 100 \ then \ 111 - 10 \ else \ F(F(111 + 11)) \ fi) + 11)) \ fi.$$

$\square$

Since substitution is defined similarly in the predicate logic, it is not astonishing that one obtains a similar result:

THEOREM 3.24 (Substitution Theorem): Let

$$F_j(x_{j1}, \dots, x_{js_j}) \Leftarrow t_j \qquad for \ j = 1, \dots, n$$

be the equations of a recursive program S over the basis F, and let $\mathscr{S}$ be the substitution function for S. In addition, let $\mathscr{I} = (D, \mathscr{I}_0)$ be an interpretation of F, $\gamma \in \Gamma$ an assignment, and t a term over F. Then

$$\mathscr{I}(\mathscr{S}(t))(\gamma) = \mathscr{I}(t)(\gamma[F_1/g_1] \dots [F_n/g_n])$$

where for $j = 1, \dots, n$ the function $g_j: D_\omega^{s_j} \to D_\omega$ is defined by

$$g_j(d_1, \dots, d_{s_j}) = \mathscr{I}(t_j)(\gamma[x_{j1}/d_1] \dots [x_{js_j}/d_{s_j}])$$

Proof. The proof is by structural induction on the term t.

(a) If $t = c$ or $t = x$, then the claim is trivial, since then

$$\mathscr{S}(t) = t.$$

(b) If $t = f(u_1, \dots, u_n)$, then by definition of $\mathscr{S}$

$$\mathscr{S}(t) = f(\mathscr{S}(u_1), \dots, \mathscr{S}(u_n)).$$

The property to be proved follows immediately from the induction hypothesis.

Similarly for the case $t = F(u_1, \ldots, u_n)$ where $F \neq F_1, \ldots, F_n$.

The only interesting case is for $t = F_j(u_1, \ldots, u_n)$ where F_j is among $F_1, \ldots, F_n$. Then

$$\mathscr{I}(\mathscr{S}(t))(\gamma) = \mathscr{I}((t_j)_{x_{j1}, \ldots, x_{js_j}}^{\mathscr{S}(u_1), \ldots, \mathscr{S}(u_{sj})})(\gamma) \qquad \text{(by definition of } \mathscr{S})$$

$$= \mathscr{I}(t_j)(\gamma[x_{j1}/\mathscr{I}(\mathscr{S}(u_1))(\gamma)] \ldots)$$

$$\text{(by the Substitution Theorem of predicate logic)}$$

$$= g_j(\mathscr{I}(\mathscr{S}(u_1))(\gamma), \ldots, \mathscr{I}(\mathscr{S}(u_{s_j}))(\gamma)) \qquad \text{(by definition of } g_j)$$

and

$$\mathscr{I}(t)(\gamma[F_1/g_1] \ldots [F_n/g_n]) = \mathscr{I}(F_j(u_1, \ldots, u_{s_j}))(\gamma[F_1/g_1] \ldots [F_n/g_n])$$

$$= (\gamma[F_1/g_1] \ldots [F_n/g_n])(F_j)$$

$$(\mathscr{I}(u_1)(\gamma[F_1/g_1] \ldots [F_n/g_n]), \ldots)$$

$$\text{(by definition of } \mathscr{I})$$

$$= g_j(\mathscr{I}(u_1)(\gamma[F_1/g_1] \ldots [F_n/g_n]), \ldots)$$

$$= g_j(\mathscr{I}(\mathscr{S}(u_1))(\gamma), \ldots, \mathscr{I}(\mathscr{S}(u_{s_j}))(\gamma))$$

$$\text{(by induction hypothesis)}. \qquad \square$$

COROLLARY 3.25 Let F be a basis, t and t' two terms over F, and $\mathscr{S}$ the substitution function for a recursive program over F. For every interpretation $\mathscr{I}$ (of the basis F), whenever t and t' are equivalent in $\mathscr{I}$, then so are $\mathscr{S}(t)$ and $\mathscr{S}(t')$.

$\square$

3.3.8 The Meaning Function

Let F be a basis and $\mathscr{I} = (D, \mathscr{I}_0)$ an interpretation of F. Consider a simplification rule r for F and $\mathscr{I}$, which is 'at least as powerful' as the standard simplification rule s or, in other words, for which $s \subseteq r$ holds. Furthermore, let S be the recursive program over F, defined by the equations

$$F_j(x_{j1}, \ldots, x_{js_j}) \Leftarrow t_j \qquad \text{for } j = 1, \ldots, n$$

and F_k as the main function variable. Finally, let $\mathscr{S}$ be the substitution function for S.

Now a relation '$\underset{r}{\Rightarrow}$' depending on S, $\mathscr{I}$, and r is defined on the set of terms over F. For two terms, $t \underset{r}{\Rightarrow} t'$ is defined to hold if the following three conditions are met:

(1) t contains at least one function variable;
(2) $\mathscr{S}(t) \underset{r}{\overset{*}{\rightarrow}} t'$;
(3) t' is maximally simplified.

Informally, this relation expresses that t' is gained from t by simultaneous substitution and subsequent simplification.

A *computation sequence* (for the recursive program S with respect to the interpretation $\mathscr{I}$ and the simplification rule r) for the *input vector* $(d_1, \ldots, d_{s_k}) \in D^{s_k}$ (not $D^{s_k}_\omega$!) is a—possibly infinite—sequence of terms

$$t_1, t_2, t_3, \ldots$$

such that $t_1 = F_k(c_1, \ldots, c_{s_k})$ where $\mathscr{I}_0(c_j) = d_j$ for $j = 1, \ldots, s_k$, and such that for consecutive terms in the sequence

$$t_i \underset{r}{\Rightarrow} t_{i+1}.$$

(Computation sequences consist, therefore, always of terms without variables from V.)

A computation sequence which is

either infinite
or ends with a term without function variables (that is, a constant)

is called a *computation*.

As usual the function computed by a program will be defined with the help of computations. However, since the relation '$\underset{r}{\Rightarrow}$' is not necessarily a function (see Exercise 3.3–7), a preliminary theorem is needed.

THEOREM 3.26 Consider a recursive program, an interpretation and a simplification rule r which is at least as powerful as the standard simplification rule s or, in other words, for which $s \subseteq r$ holds. For a given input vector either all computations (with respect to r) are infinite or they have the same (finite) length and end with the same constant.

Proof. It is sufficient to prove that, if there is a finite computation (for the given input vector)

$$t_0, t_1, \ldots, t_m = c$$

and if

$$t'_0, t'_1, \ldots, t'_{m'}$$

is any computation sequence (for that input vector) with $m \le m'$, then $m = m'$, and $t'_m = c$ holds.

First notice that $t_0 = t'_0$. After simplifying one always obtains a term equivalent to the original one (by the definition of the simplification). Substitution applied on equivalent terms leads to terms which are equivalent again (by Corollary 3.25). So it follows by induction (on the index i) that the term t_i is equivalent to the term t'_i (in the given interpretation) for $i = 0, \ldots, m$. Hence, in particular t'_m is equivalent to c. So, by Theorem 3.22, $t'_m \underset{s}{\overset{*}{\rightarrow}} c$ and hence $t'_m \underset{r}{\overset{*}{\rightarrow}} c$. Since every member of a computation sequence is maximally simplified, it must be the case that $t'_m = c$. Finally $m' = m$. $\qquad\square$

This theorem establishes that the last term of a finite computation is uniquely determined and that this term in no way depends on the particular simplification rule r, as long as it is powerful enough. Furthermore, if there is a finite computation, then there are no infinite computations.

In light of the previous theorem, a recursive program is said to *terminate* for an input vector (with respect to an interpretation $\mathcal{I} = (D, \mathcal{I}_0)$), if there is a finite computation

$$t_0, t_1, t_2, \ldots, t_m = c$$

for this input vector with respect to a simplification rule which is at least as powerful as the standard simplification rule. $\mathcal{I}_0(c)$ is called the *output value* of the program for the given input vector. Because of the previous theorem this value is uniquely defined.

The climax of this section is the following definition.

DEFINITION 3.27 (Operational Semantics of $\mathcal{L}_3$) Let S be a recursive program over a basis F with an m-ary main function variable. Let $\mathcal{I} = (D, \mathcal{I}_0)$ be an interpretation of F. The·*meaning* of S (in $\mathcal{I}$) is the function $\mathcal{M}_{\mathcal{I}}(S): D^m \rightsquigarrow D$—or $\mathcal{M}(S)$ for short—defined by

$$\mathcal{M}_{\mathcal{I}}(S)(d_1, \ldots, d_m) = \begin{cases} d, \text{ if S terminates for the input vector } (d_1, \ldots, d_m) \\ \quad \text{with the output value } d; \\ \text{undefined, if S does not terminate for the input} \\ \quad \text{vector } (d_1, \ldots, d_m) \end{cases}$$
$\square$

Note that the meaning of a recursive program is defined as a function mapping (a subset of) D^m into D, *not* as a function mapping D^m into D_ω or D_ω^m into D_ω; in other words, the meaning of a recursive program is a 'normal' function, not an ω-extension. Note also the difference with the meaning of a program from $\mathcal{L}_1$ or $\mathcal{L}_2$ which maps states (from Σ) into states rather than data (from D) into data. This section ends with three examples.

EXAMPLE 3.28 Let S be the recursive program

$$F(x) \Leftarrow \textit{if } x = 0 \textit{ then } 1 \textit{ else } x * F(x-1) \textit{ fi}$$

and let $\mathcal{I}$ be the usual interpretation. Using the standard simplification rule (denoted by s), the computation of $\mathcal{M}_{\mathcal{I}}(S)(2)$ leads to:

$F(2) \underset{s}{\Rightarrow} \textit{if false then } 1 \textit{ else } 2 * F(1) \textit{ fi}$
  (because $\mathcal{S}(F(2)) = \textit{if } 2 = 0 \textit{ then } 1 \textit{ else } 2 * F(2-1) \textit{ fi}$ and because
  $2 = 0 \underset{s}{\rightsquigarrow} \textit{false}$ and $2 - 1 \underset{s}{\rightsquigarrow} 1$)

  $\underset{s}{\Rightarrow} \textit{if false then } 1 \textit{ else } 2 * (\textit{if false then } 1 \textit{ else } 1 * F(0) \textit{ fi})$
    (because $\mathcal{S}(\textit{if false then } 1 \textit{ else } 2 * F(1) \textit{ fi})$
      $= \textit{if false then } 1 \textit{ else } 2 * (\textit{if } 1 = 0 \textit{ then } 1 \textit{ else } 1 * F(1-1) \textit{ fi}) \textit{ fi}$
      and because $1 = 0 \underset{s}{\rightsquigarrow} \textit{false}$ and $1 - 1 \underset{s}{\rightsquigarrow} 0$)

68

$\underset{s}{\Rightarrow} 2$

(because $\mathscr{S}(if \ldots else\ 2 * (if \ldots fi)\ fi) = \cdots$ and because $0 = 0 \underset{s}{\to} true, if$
$true\ then\ 1\ else \ldots fi \underset{s}{\to} 1, 1 * 1 \underset{s}{\to} 1$, and so on)

So $\mathscr{M}_{\mathscr{S}}(S)(2) = 2$. $\qquad\qquad\qquad\qquad\qquad\qquad\qquad\qquad\qquad\qquad\square$

EXAMPLE 3.29 Consider the same program S as in the last example with the usual interpretation. This time consider the simplification rule r consisting of the simplification schemes of the standard simplification rule together with

$$(if\ true\ then\ x_1\ else\ x_2\ fi, x_1)$$

and

$$(if\ false\ then\ x_1\ else\ x_2\ fi, x_2).$$

The computation of $\mathscr{M}_{\mathscr{S}}(S)(2)$ leads to:

$F(2) \underset{r}{\Rightarrow} 2 * F(1)$

(as in the previous example, but now $if\ false\ then\ 1\ else\ 2 * F(1)\ fi$
$\underset{r}{\to} 2 * F(1)$)

$\underset{r}{\Rightarrow} 2 * F(0)$

$\underset{r}{\Rightarrow} 2$

One sees that this 'stronger' simplification rule leads to significantly shorter terms (but not to fewer terms!) in the computation. $\qquad\qquad\qquad\qquad\qquad\square$

EXAMPLE 3.30 Let S be the recursive program

$$F(x) \Leftarrow if\ x > 100\ then\ x - 10\ else\ F(F(x + 11))\ fi$$

and consider the simplification rule of the previous example. The computation of $\mathscr{M}_{\mathscr{S}}(S)(100)$ leads to

$F(100) \underset{r}{\Rightarrow} F(F(111))$

(because $\mathscr{S}(F(100)) = if\ 100 > 100\ then\ 100 - 10\ else\ F(F(100 + 11))\ fi$
and because $100 > 100 \underset{r}{\to} false, if\ false\ then \ldots else\ F(F(100 + 11))\ fi$
$\underset{r}{\to} F(F(100 + 11)), 100 + 11 \underset{r}{\to} 111)$

$\underset{r}{\Rightarrow} 91$

(because $\mathscr{S}(F(F(111))) = \cdots$ (see Example 3.23) and $111 > 100 \underset{r}{\to} true$,
and so on). $\qquad\qquad\qquad\qquad\qquad\qquad\qquad\qquad\qquad\qquad\square$

EXERCISES

3.1-1 Justify why the meaning $\mathscr{M}_{\mathscr{S}}(S)$ of a flowchart program S is in fact a function and not just a relation.

3.1-2 Let S be a flowchart program and $x_1, \ldots, x_n$ the variables the occur in S. Prove for a computation sequence $(l_0, \sigma_0), (l_1, \sigma_1), \ldots$ of S that:

(a) Two states of the sequence differ in at most $x_1, \ldots, x_n$.

(b) Every state σ_i in the sequence depends only on the values $\sigma_0(x_1), \ldots, \sigma_0(x_n)$ or, more precisely, if $(l_0, \tau_0), (l_1, \tau_1), \ldots$ is another computation sequence such that

$$\text{then} \quad \begin{aligned} \tau_0(x_k) &= \sigma_0(x_k) &&\text{for } k = 1, \ldots, n, \\ \tau_i(x_k) &= \sigma_i(x_k) &&\text{for } k = 1, \ldots, n. \end{aligned}$$

3.2–1 Let B be a basis for predicate logic. For every while-program S over B define inductively a flowchart program S′ over B such that they are in the following—very strong—sense equivalent:

$$\mathcal{M}_{\mathscr{I}}(\text{S}) = \mathcal{M}_{\mathscr{I}}(\text{S}') \quad \text{for all interpretations } \mathscr{I} \text{ of } B.$$

3.3–1 Find all monotonic ω-extensions of the following functions (given their usual interpretation):

(a) $\neg : Bool \to Bool$
(b) $\wedge, \vee, \supset, \equiv\, : Bool^2 \to Bool$
(c) $=, \leq, <\,: Nat^2 \to Bool$
(d) $+, * : Nat^2 \to Nat$.

3.3–2 Let S, T be non-empty sets. Show that a function $f : S_\omega \to T_\omega$ is monotonic iff it is a strict or a constant function. Does this also hold for functions $f : S_\omega^n \to T_\omega$ with $n > 1$?

3.3–3 Let $(D_1, \sqsubseteq), \ldots, (D_n, \sqsubseteq), (E, \sqsubseteq)$ be partial orders, $n \geq 1$. A function $g : D_1 \times \cdots \times D_n \to E$ is called *monotonic in the ith argument* if whenever $d_i, d_i' \in D_i$ such that $d_i \sqsubseteq d_i'$, then for all

$$(d_1, \ldots, d_{i-1}, d_{i+1}, \ldots, d_n) \in D_1 \times \cdots \times D_{i-1} \times D_{i+1} \times \cdots \times D_n$$

one has:

$$g(d_1, \ldots, d_{i-1}, d_i, d_{i+1}, \ldots, d_n) \sqsubseteq g(d_1, \ldots, d_{i-1}, d_i', d_{i+1}, \ldots, d_n)$$

Show that g is monotonic (in the usual sense) iff it is monotonic in every argument. Now prove that the characterization of monotonic ω-extensions given in Section 3.3 is correct.

3.3–4 (a) Present the partial order $(Bool_\omega \rightarrowtail Bool_\omega, \sqsubseteq)$ graphically. How many elements does it have? How many elements are maximal?
(b) How many elements does the partial order $(Bool_\omega^2 \rightarrowtail Bool_\omega, \sqsubseteq)$ have?

3.3–5 Suppose $\mathscr{I}$ is the 'usual' interpretation. In particular the symbols $\wedge$, $\vee$, and $\neg$ represent the strict ω-extensions of their usual meaning. Which of the following pairs are simplification schemes for $\mathscr{I}$? Which are schemes of the standard simplification rule for $\mathscr{I}$?

(a) $(\neg\neg x, x)$ (b) $(x \vee true, true)$
(c) $(x \wedge \neg x, false)$ (d) $(x \wedge x, x)$

What happens when the symbols $\wedge$ and $\vee$ represent non-strict ω-extensions of their usual meaning?

3.3–6 In the definition of the standard simplification rule it was required that no variable occurs more than once in $f(t_1, \ldots, t_n)$. Would the standard simplification rule be more powerful without this restriction? (Look first at Exercise 3.3–5.)

*3.3–7 Let r be a simplification rule (for given basis and interpretation). One says that r has the *Church–Rosser property* if whenever $t \to_r t_1$ and $t \to_r t_2$ for terms $t, t_1,$ and t_2, then there is a term t' such that $t_1 \twoheadrightarrow_r t'$ and $t_2 \twoheadrightarrow_r t'$.

Let now r be a simplification rule with the Church–Rosser property. Show that a term can be simplified to a maximally simplified term in only one way; that is, if $t \twoheadrightarrow_r t_1, t \twoheadrightarrow_r t_2,$ and t_1, t_2 are maximally simplified, then $t_1 = t_2$. It follows that the associated relation '$\Rightarrow_r$', which is used to define computation sequences, is a function in this case.

3.3–8 For just this once let $\mathscr{I}_0(if\text{-}then\text{-}else)$ be the so-called parallel if-then-else function which differs from the sequential if-then-else in that if-then-else $(\omega, d, d) = d$ for all $d \in D_\omega$.

(a) Show that this function is monotonic.

70

(b) Show that for this interpretation the pair

$$(if \ x \ then \ y \ else \ y \ fi, \ y)$$

is a simplification scheme.

(c) Write a recursive program that computes a different function depending on whether $\mathscr{I}_0(if\text{-}then\text{-}else)$ is the sequential or the parallel if-then-else function.

3.3–9 Let $\mathscr{I}$ be an interpretation in which every function symbol is mapped to a strict function. Show that the meaning of a recursive program in this interpretation is either total or nowhere defined. (So in order to be able to program all computable partial functions one needs at least one non-strict function such as if-then-else.)

HISTORICAL AND BIBLIOGRAPHICAL REMARKS

The formal description of semantics goes back to the early sixties. Pioneering papers are McCarthy (1963) and some of those contained in Steel (1966). Most of these early semantics descriptions are operational or have a strong operational flavour.

The three programming languages introduced are essentially those of Manna (1974) or Greibach (1975). The latter also contains a formal description of operational semantics. The papers by Cadiou (1972) and Vuillemin (1976) contain detailed discussions on the operational semantics of recursive programs. The book Bauer and Wössner (1982) contains an operational semantics of recursive programs which is based on a stack machine.

4
Fixpoints in Complete Partial Orders

In the previous chapter operational semantics for various programming languages were introduced. All these operational semantics had something in common: the meaning $\mathcal{M}_{\mathcal{I}}(S)$ of a program S (in an interpretation $\mathcal{I}$) was defined algorithmically, namely with help of computation sequences. In other words, to each program an algorithm was associated which computes the function $\mathcal{M}_{\mathcal{I}}(S)$ or, more precisely, which computes the value of $\mathcal{M}_{\mathcal{I}}(S)$ (called output value) for any argument (called input value).

Denotational semantics has a 'mathematical' rather than an algorithmic flavour. The meaning $\mathcal{M}_{\mathcal{I}}(S)$ of a program S is now defined 'directly' as a function without making use of an algorithm. (Hence, the name 'denotational', since every program 'denotes' its meaning.) More precisely, the function $\mathcal{M}_{\mathcal{I}}(S)$ is defined inductively—in a way similar to the semantic functional $\mathcal{I}$ in the predicate logic. This inductive definition is based on the inductive definition of the (syntactic) set of all programs. Constructs, the execution of which can lead to a loop, cause problems in defining this function. Such constructs are, for instance: jumps, while-statements, and recursive calls. These problems will be made clear using an example of a recursive program.

A recursive program, say

$$F(x) \Leftarrow \textit{if } x = 0 \textit{ then } 1 \textit{ else } x * F(x - 1) \textit{ fi},$$

is considered an equation for F in denotational semantics by interpreting '⇐' as an equality sign. The meaning of this program is then defined as a solution for F to this equation. The definition of objects as the solution to equalities is found frequently in mathematics. Quadratic equations like

$$x^2 = x + 1$$

or differential equations like

$$F(x) = F'(x)$$

come immediately to mind. For such equations one first defines what is meant by a solution, for example a real number r such that

71

$$r^2 = r + 1$$

in the case of the quadratic equation above, and a differentiable function f such that

$$f(s) = f'(s)$$

for all real numbers s in the case of the differential equations. Then one asks about the existence and uniqueness of the solutions.

What should be understood by a solution to the recursive program

$$F(x) \Leftarrow \textit{if } x = 0 \textit{ then } 1 \textit{ else } x * F(x - 1)\, fi?$$

In Chapter 3 the domain of the function variable F was limited to monotonic functions; this will prove to be useful here too. A solution to the equation above is then a monotonic function $f: Nat_\omega \rightarrow Nat_\omega$ such that

$$f(n) = \text{if-then-else}(n = 0, 1, n * f(n - 1))$$

for all $n \in Nat_\omega$. Notice that these functions are exactly the (monotonic) fixpoints of the functional $\Phi: (Nat_\omega \xrightarrow{m} Nat_\omega) \rightarrow (Nat_\omega \rightarrow Nat_\omega)$ defined by

$$\Phi(f)(n) = \text{if-then-else}(n = 0, 1, n * f(n - 1))$$

As a consequence the questions of the existence and uniqueness of the solutions to a recursive program are questions about the existence and uniqueness of fixpoints. The question of uniqueness can be answered negatively here. Just look at the recursive program

$$F(x) \Leftarrow F(x);$$

clearly, every 1-ary function is a solution. Or examine the recursive program

$$F(x) \Leftarrow \textit{if } x = 0 \textit{ then } F(x) \textit{ else } 0\, fi$$

for which every function $f_i: Nat_\omega \rightarrow Nat_\omega$ defined by

$$f_i(n) = \begin{cases} \omega & \text{if } n = \omega, \\ i & \text{if } n = 0, \\ 0 & \text{otherwise,} \end{cases}$$

where $i \in Nat_\omega$, is a solution. However, a property will be introduced which characterizes exactly one solution.

The theory of complete partial orders concerns itself with these questions—the existence of fixpoints and the characterization of particular fixpoints. This theory will be treated in the current chapter. Although it is totally independent of programming languages, the connection to programs will be brought out in the examples. The definition of denotational semantics and the proof of the equivalence of the operational and denotational semantics follow in the next chapter.

4.1 Complete Partial Orders

The theory of complete partial orders rests on the concept of the least upper bound of a set.

DEFINITION 4.1 (Least Upper Bounds) Let $(D, \sqsubseteq)$ be a partial order and S a (possibly empty) subset of D. An element $u \in D$ is said to be an *upper bound* of S (in D), if $d \sqsubseteq u$ for all $d \in S$; u is said to be the *least upper bound* (*lub*) of S (in D), if u is the least element of the set of all upper bounds of S in D. $\qquad\qquad\square$

Notice that a subset S of a partial order $(D, \sqsubseteq)$ does not necessarily have an upper bound in D. Alternatively S can have many upper bounds in D. However, since a set can have at most one smallest element, the set S can have at most one lub in D; it is denoted $\sqcup_D S$ or, shortly, $\sqcup S$, provided it exists. Furthermore, an upper bound u of S in D is an element of D which does not have to lie in S. Should, however, u lie in S, then u is in fact the greatest element of S and, therefore, also the lub of S.

A *lower bound* and the *greatest lower bound* (*glb*), denoted $\sqcap S$, can be analogously defined. Similar arguments hold for these elements.

In Section 1.1 it was indicated how partial orders may be extended to their Cartesian product and to (the set of) total functions which have these partial orders as range. Now it will be investigated how lub's of these extended partial orders behave. The following notation will be needed:

(1) For a Cartesian product $D_1 \times \cdots \times D_n, n \geq 1$, and for $i = 1, \ldots, n$, pr_i denotes the ith projection function $\mathrm{pr}_i : D_1 \times \cdots \times D_n \to D_i$ defined by

$$\mathrm{pr}_i(d_1, \ldots, d_n) = d_i$$

(2) For a set $S \subseteq (D \to E)$ of functions and an element $d \in D, S(d)$ denotes the set

$$S(d) = \{f(d) \mid f \in S\} \subseteq E$$

THEOREM 4.2 (Cartesian Products and lubs) Let $(D_1, \sqsubseteq), \ldots, (D_n, \sqsubseteq)$ be partial orders and let S be a subset of the Cartesian product $D_1 \times \cdots \times D_n, n \geq 1$. Then, $\sqcup S$ exists iff $\sqcup \mathrm{pr}_i(S)$ exists for $i = 1, \ldots, n$. Moreover, if $\sqcup S$ exists, then

$$\sqcup S = (\sqcup \mathrm{pr}_1(S), \ldots, \sqcup \mathrm{pr}_n(S)).$$

Proof. Assume all the $\sqcup \mathrm{pr}_i(S)$ exist. Put $S_i = \mathrm{pr}_i(S)$ for $i = 1, \ldots, n$ and put $l = (\sqcup S_1, \ldots, \sqcup S_n)$. It must be proved that l is the lub of S. For an arbitrary element $(d_1, \ldots, d_n) \in S, d_i \in S_i$ and hence $d_i \sqsubseteq \sqcup S_i$ holds for $i = 1, \ldots, n$. By the definition of $\sqsubseteq$ on $D_1 \times \cdots D_n$ it follows that $(d_1, \ldots, d_n) \sqsubseteq l$, so l is an upper bound of S. Suppose now $u = (u_1, \ldots, u_n)$ is some arbitrary upper bound of S; it must be proved that $l \sqsubseteq u$. Now u_i is an upper bound of S_i, so $\sqcup S_i \sqsubseteq u_i$ for $i = 1, \ldots, n$. Hence $l \sqsubseteq u$, and it now follows that l is the lub of S. In summary, $\sqcup S$ exists and $\sqcup S = l$.

Conversely, assume that $\sqcup S$ exists and put $l = (l_1, \ldots, l_n) = \sqcup S$. In order to prove that l_i is the lub of $\mathrm{pr}_i(S)$ for $i = 1, \ldots, n$ consider an arbitrary element

$d_i \in \mathrm{pr}_i(S)$; then $d_i = \mathrm{pr}_i(d)$ for some $d \in S$. Since l is an upper bound of S, $d \sqsubseteq l$, and so in particular $d_i \sqsubseteq l_i$. Consequently l_i is an upper bound of the set $\mathrm{pr}_i(S)$. Now let u_i be an arbitrary upper bound of $\mathrm{pr}_i(S)$. Then $l' = (l_1, \ldots, l_{i-1}, u_i, l_{i+1}, \ldots, l_n)$ is an upper bound of S. So $l \sqsubseteq l'$, and hence $l_i \sqsubseteq u_i$. Therefore, l_i is the lub of $\mathrm{pr}_i(S)$. $\quad\square$

Theorem 4.2 and its proof can be extended without difficulty to infinite Cartesian products.

THEOREM 4.3 (Functions and lubs)   Let D be a set, $(E, \sqsubseteq)$ be a partial order, and S be a subset of the set $(D \to E)$ of all total functions from D to E. Then, $\sqcup S$ exists iff $\sqcup S(d)$ exists for every $d \in D$. Moreover, if $\sqcup S$ exists, then $(\sqcup S)(d) = \sqcup S(d)$, for every $d \in D$.

Proof. Assume $\sqcup S(d)$ exists for all $d \in D$. Set $l: D \to E$ to be the function defined by

$$l(d) = \sqcup S(d)$$

It must be proved that l is the lub of S. For an arbitrary $f \in S$, $f(d) \in S(d)$ and hence $f(d) \sqsubseteq \sqcup S(d)$ for every $d \in D$. By the definition of $\sqsubseteq$ on $(D \to E)$ it follows that $f \sqsubseteq l$, so l is an upper bound of S. Now suppose $h: D \to E$ is some arbitrary upper bound of S. Then $h(d)$ is an upper bound of $S(d)$, so $\sqcup S(d) \sqsubseteq h(d)$ for every $d \in D$. Hence $l \sqsubseteq h$, and it now follows that l is the lub of S. In summary, $\sqcup S$ exists and $\sqcup S = l$.

Conversely, set $l: D \to E$ equal to $\sqcup S$. It must be proved that $l(d)$ is the lub of $S(d)$ for every $d \in D$. Let $e \in S(d)$, then $e = f(d)$ for some $f \in S$. Since l is an upper bound of S, $f \sqsubseteq l$, and so in particular $e \sqsubseteq l(d)$. Consequently $l(d)$ is an upper bound of the set $S(d)$. Now let u be an arbitrary upper bound of $S(d)$. Then $l' = l[d/u]$ is an upper bound of S. So $l \sqsubseteq l'$, and hence $l(d) \sqsubseteq u$. Therefore, $l(d)$ is the lub of $S(d)$. $\quad\square$

The observant reader will have noticed the strong similarity in the proofs of Theorems 4.2 and 4.3. This results from the fact mentioned in Section 1.1 that an n-tuple $(d_1, \ldots, d_n) \in D_1 \times \cdots \times D_n$ can be considered as a function $d: \{1, \ldots, n\} \to D_1 \cup \cdots \cup D_n$.

After this preparation it is time to introduce the notion of complete partial orders.

Let $(D, \sqsubseteq)$ be a partial order. A non-empty subset S of D is called a *chain* (in D) if $d \sqsubseteq d'$ or $d' \sqsubseteq d$ (or both) holds for every two elements $d, d' \in S$. Said another way, S is a chain if the order relation '$\sqsubseteq$' restricted to S is total.

DEFINITION 4.4 (Complete Partial Orders)   A partial order $(D, \sqsubseteq)$ is a *complete partial order* (*cpo*) if the following two conditions hold:

(1) The set D has a least element. This element is denoted by $\perp_D$ or simply $\perp$ (read 'bottom').

(2) For every chain S in D the lowest upper bound $\sqcup S$ exists. $\quad\square$

The flat partial orders introduced in Section 3.3 are simple examples of cpo's (with $\perp = \omega$). More generally the following theorem holds:

THEOREM 4.5 Every partial order which has a least element and contains only finite chains, is a cpo.

(The proof is left to Exercise 4.1–5.) □

Since chains in flat partial orders have at most two elements, an immediate consequence of the previous theorem is the fact that flat partial orders are complete. From the following two theorems it will result that all partial orders introduced in Section 3.3 are complete.

THEOREM 4.6 (Cartesian Products and cpo's)   If $(D_1, \sqsubseteq), \ldots, (D_n, \sqsubseteq)$ are cpo's, then $(D_1 \times \cdots \times D_n, \sqsubseteq)$ is a cpo.

Proof. First observe that $(\perp_{D_1}, \ldots, \perp_{D_n})$ is the least element of $D_1 \times \cdots \times D_n$. Now let $S \subseteq D_1 \times \cdots \times D_n$ be any chain. It is sufficient to show that the sets $S_i = \mathrm{pr}_i(S)$ for $i = 1, \ldots, n$ are chains, since by Theorem 4.2 the lub of S would then exist. So let $d_i, d_i' \in S_i$ such that $d_i = \mathrm{pr}_i(d)$ and $d_i' = \mathrm{pr}_i(d')$ where $d, d' \in S$. Then $d \sqsubseteq d'$ or $d' \sqsubseteq d$, hence $d_i \sqsubseteq d_i'$ or $d_i' \sqsubseteq d_i$. Therefore, S_i is a chain. □

This theorem and proof can also be extended to infinite Cartesian products.

A particular consequence of Theorem 4.6 is that the Cartesian products of flat partial orders, as for example $(Nat_\omega^2, \sqsubseteq)$ are cpo's. One can also obtain this result using Theorem 4.5, since the product of flat partial orders have only finite chains (see Exercise 4.1–5).

More interesting cpo's can be obtained by using functions.

THEOREM 4.7 (Functions and cpo's)   If D is a set and $(E, \sqsubseteq)$ a cpo, then $((D \to E), \sqsubseteq)$ is a cpo.

Proof. The first step is to prove that $(D \to E)$ has a least element. Consider the function $\perp_{(D \to E)}: D \to E$ defined by

$$\perp_{(D \to E)}(d) = \perp_E$$

($\perp_{(D \to E)}$ is the 'everywhere-$\perp_E$' function.)

For every function $g: D \to E$ it is the case that

$$\perp_{(D \to E)}(d) = \perp_E \sqsubseteq g(d) \qquad \text{for all } d \in D.$$

So by definition $\perp_{(D \to E)} \sqsubseteq g$, and $\perp_{(D \to E)}$ is the least element of $(D \to E)$.

Secondly, let $S \subseteq (D \to E)$ be a chain. To conclude that the lub of S exists, it is sufficient to show that for every $d \in D$ the set $S(d)$ is a chain (Theorem 4.3). So let $e, e' \in S(d)$; then there are $f, g \in S$ such that $e = f(d)$ and $e' = g(d)$. Then $f \sqsubseteq g$ or $g \sqsubseteq f$, hence $e \sqsubseteq e'$ or $e' \sqsubseteq e$. Therefore, $S(d)$ is a chain. □

EXAMPLE 4.8   By Theorem 4.7 $((Nat_\omega \to Nat_\omega), \sqsubseteq)$ is a cpo. An example of a chain in this cpo is the set $S = \{f_i \mid i \in Nat\}$ where $f_i\colon Nat_\omega \to Nat_\omega$ is defined by

$$f_i(n) = \begin{cases} \omega & \text{if } n = \omega \text{ or } n \in Nat, n \geq i \\ n! & \text{if } n \in Nat, 0 \leq n \leq i - 1. \end{cases}$$

The lub of S is obtained by using Theorem 4.3:

$$(\sqcup S)(n) = \sqcup S(n) = \begin{cases} \omega & \text{if } n = \omega \\ n! & \text{if } n \in Nat. \end{cases}$$

The function $\sqcup S$ is the strict ω-extension of the factorial function. Chains of this type will play a role in the denotational semantics of recursive programs. $\square$

Thus far the property of 'completeness' has carried over from $(D_1, \sqsubseteq), \ldots, (D_n, \sqsubseteq)$ to the Cartesian product $(D_1 \times \cdots \times D_n, \sqsubseteq)$ and from $(E, \sqsubseteq)$ to the set of functions $((D \to E), \sqsubseteq)$. This is not necessarily the case for a subset of a partial order: if $(D, \sqsubseteq)$ is a cpo and E is a subset of D, then it is not always true that $(E, \sqsubseteq)$ is a cpo. First of all, E does not necessarily have a least element. Secondly, while it is true that every chain $S \subseteq E$ has a lub in D, this does not mean that it must lie in E. An example of this is the set $E \subseteq S$ of all functions of the set S of Example 4.8 which are not 'total':

$$E = \{f \in S \mid f(n) = \omega \text{ for some } n \in Nat\}.$$

The set E contains S but not $\sqcup S$. This suggests the following definition:

DEFINITION 4.9 (Sub-cpo's)   Let $(D, \sqsubseteq)$ be a cpo and E a subset of D. E is called a *sub-cpo* of D, if

(1) the partial order $(E, \sqsubseteq)$ is a cpo, and
(2) $\sqcup_E S = \sqcup_D S$, for every chain S in E. $\square$

It must be stressed that the second condition does not necessarily follow from the first: $(E, \sqsubseteq)$ can be a cpo such that the lub's $\sqcup_E S$ and $\sqcup_D S$ do not agree. (See Exercise 4.1–6.)

A characterization of a sub-cpo which is more useful in practice is given by the following theorem.

THEOREM 4.10   Let $(D, \sqsubseteq)$ be a cpo and let E be a subset of D. Then E is a sub-cpo of D iff the following two conditions hold:

(1) E has a least element,
(2) $\sqcup_D S$ lies in E for every chain S in E.

(The proof is left to Exercise 4.1–7.) $\square$

This theorem will be useful in the investigation of partial orders of monotonic functions. In addition, the following lemma will be necessary.

77

LEMMA 4.11   Let $(D, \sqsubseteq)$ be a cpo. Let S and T be subsets of D whose lub's exist. If for every element $d \in S$ there exists an element $d' \in T$ such that $d \sqsubseteq d'$, then $\sqcup S \sqsubseteq \sqcup T$.

Proof. It is sufficient to show that $\sqcup T$ is an upper bound of the set S. So, let $d \in S$. Then by assumption there exists an element $d' \in T$ such that $d \sqsubseteq d'$, hence $d \sqsubseteq \sqcup T$. Therefore, $\sqcup T$ is indeed an upper bound of S.   □

THEOREM 4.12   Let $(D, \sqsubseteq)$ be a partial order and $(E, \sqsubseteq)$ a cpo. The set of all monotonic functions $(D \xrightarrow{m} E)$ is a sub-cpo of $((D \to E), \sqsubseteq)$.

Proof. By Theorem 4.10 it must be shown that

(1) $(D \xrightarrow{m} E)$ has a least element, and
(2) the lub $\sqcup_{(D \to E)} S$ is monotonic for all chains S in $(D \xrightarrow{m} E)$.

The first condition is clear since the least element $\perp_{(D \to E)}$(defined in Theorem 4.7) is monotonic.

For (2) let S be an arbitrary chain and choose $d, d' \in D$ such that $d \sqsubseteq d'$. It must be proved that $(\sqcup S)(d) \sqsubseteq (\sqcup S)(d')$ or, equivalently (by Theorem 4.3), $\sqcup S(d) \sqsubseteq \sqcup S(d')$. Let $e \in S(d)$, hence $e = f(d)$ for some $f \in S$. Then $e \sqsubseteq f(d')$ because f is monotonic. Because $f(d') \in S(d')$ the conclusion ensues by Lemma 4.11.   □

4.2 Continuous Functions

Intuitively speaking, a function is continuous if it is compatible with the construction of least upper bounds. This is similar to the case in analysis where a function is called continuous if it is compatible with the construction of limits. Both concepts are instances of continuity in a topological sense. The reader with some knowledge of topology can work out the connection in Exercise 4.2–6.

DEFINITION 4.13 (Continuity)   Let $(D, \sqsubseteq)$ and $(E, \sqsubseteq)$ be cpo's. A function $f : D \to E$ is said to be *continuous* if for every chain S in D the lub $\sqcup f(S)$ exists and $f(\sqcup S) = \sqcup f(S)$.   □

The set of all continuous functions from D to E will be denoted $[D \to E]$.

The following theorem establishes the connection between continuity and monotonicity, and moreover gives an equivalent—somewhat more manageable—definition of continuity.

THEOREM 4.14 (Continuity versus Monotonicity)   Let $(D, \sqsubseteq)$ and $(E, \sqsubseteq)$ be cpo's and $f : D \to E$ be a function.

(1) The function f is continuous iff f is monotonic and for every chain S in D, $f(\sqcup S) \sqsubseteq \sqcup f(S)$. (Notice that, by Exercise 4.2–1, the monotonicity of f implies that $f(S)$ is a chain, so $\sqcup f(S)$ exists.)
(2) If D contains only finite chains, then f is continuous iff f is monotonic.

Proof. (1) Assume that f is continuous. The only claim that is not obvious is that f is monotonic. So let $d, d' \in D$ be such that $d \sqsubseteq d'$. Then $S = \{d, d'\}$ is a chain so $\sqcup\{f(d), f(d')\}$ exists and agrees with $f(\sqcup S) = f(d')$. This means that $f(d) \sqsubseteq f(d')$.

Conversely, suppose that f is monotonic and for every chain S in D, $f(\sqcup S) \sqsubseteq \sqcup f(S)$. It remains to show that $\sqcup f(S) \sqsubseteq f(\sqcup S)$, or, put another way, that $f(\sqcup S)$ is an upper bound of $f(S)$. Let $e \in f(S)$. Then there is a $d \in S$ such that $e = f(d)$. Since $d \sqsubseteq \sqcup S$, by the monotonicity of f, $e \sqsubseteq f(\sqcup S)$. Therefore, $f(\sqcup S)$ is an upper bound of $f(S)$.

(2) By (1) it is enough to show that for every chain S in D and every monotonic function $f: D \rightarrow E$, $f(\sqcup S) \sqsubseteq \sqcup f(S)$. So let $S \subseteq D$ be a finite chain, say $S = \{d_1, \ldots, d_n\}$, $n \geq 1$, where $d_1 \sqsubseteq d_2 \sqsubseteq \cdots \sqsubseteq d_n$. Then $\sqcup S = d_n$, so that $f(\sqcup S) \in f(S)$, and hence $f(\sqcup S) \sqsubseteq \sqcup f(S)$. $\qquad\square$

To get the feel for continuous functions some easy-to-prove examples will be given. The sets used in these examples are assumed to constitute cpo's.

(1) Let $D_{1\omega}, \ldots, D_{n\omega}, D_{(n+1)\omega}$ be flat cpo's. Then, by the second part of Theorem 4.14, every monotonic function $f: D_{1\omega} \times \cdots \times D_{n\omega} \rightarrow D_{(n+1)\omega}$ is continuous, since the Cartesian product of flat cpo's contains only finite chains.

(2) Every constant function is continuous. Let $e \in E$ and $f: D \rightarrow E$ defined by

$$f(d) = e.$$

Then for every chain S in D, $f(S) = e$, so $\sqcup f(S) = e = f(\sqcup S)$.

(3) The identity function $\mathrm{id}: D \rightarrow D$ for which $\mathrm{id}(d) = d$ for all $d \in D$, is continuous. For every chain $S \subseteq D$, $\mathrm{id}(S) = S$, so $\sqcup \mathrm{id}(S) = \sqcup S = \mathrm{id}(\sqcup S)$.

(4) For $i = 1, \ldots, n$ the projection function $\mathrm{pr}_i: D_1 \times \cdots \times D_n \rightarrow D_i$ is continuous. This follows from Theorem 4.2, for in particular $\sqcup \mathrm{pr}_i(S)$ exists for every chain S in $D_1 \times \cdots \times D_n$, and agrees with $\mathrm{pr}_i(\sqcup S)$.

A particularly important example of a continuous function, which will be used in denotational semantics, is given next.

EXAMPLE 4.15 Let the functional $\Phi: (Nat_\omega \rightarrow Nat_\omega) \rightarrow (Nat_\omega \rightarrow Nat_\omega)$ be defined by

$$\Phi(f)(n) = \mathscr{I} \ (\textit{if } x = 0 \textit{ then } 1 \textit{ else } x * \mathrm{F}(x-1) \ fi)(\gamma[\mathrm{F}/f][x/n])$$

where $\mathscr{I}$ is the usual interpretation and $\gamma \in \Gamma$ is an arbitrary assignment in the sense of Section 3.3. For any function $g: Nat_\omega \rightarrow Nat_\omega$, the function obtained by applying the functional Φ to g, namely $\Phi(g)$, will be denoted $\tilde{g}$ for increased perspicuity. Thus $\tilde{f}: Nat_\omega \rightarrow Nat_\omega$ is the function defined by:

$$\tilde{f}(n) = \begin{cases} \omega & \text{if } n = \omega, \text{ or } (n \neq 0 \text{ and } f(n-1) = \omega), \\ 1 & \text{if } n = 0, \\ n * f(n-1) & \text{otherwise.} \end{cases}$$

It will now be shown that the functional Φ is continuous. Only elementary means will be used here; later a theorem will be derived which guarantees that all such functionals are continuous.

So, by Theorem 4.14 it needs only be shown that Φ is monotonic and that for every chain S in $(Nat_\omega \to Nat_\omega)$, $\Phi(\sqcup S) \sqsubseteq \sqcup \Phi(S)$.

To show that the functional is monotonic, choose $f, g: Nat_\omega \to Nat_\omega$ such that $f \sqsubseteq g$. If $n = \omega$, then $\tilde{f}(n) = \omega$, and $\tilde{f}(n) \sqsubseteq \tilde{g}(n)$. If $n = 0$, then $\tilde{f}(n) = 1 = \tilde{g}(n)$. Suppose now $n \neq \omega, 0$. If $f(n-1) = \omega$, then $\tilde{f}(n) = \omega \sqsubseteq \tilde{g}(n)$. If $f(n-1) \neq \omega$, $f(n-1) = g(n-1)$ since $f \sqsubseteq g$. Therefore,

$$\tilde{f}(n) = n * f(n-1) = n * g(n-1) = \tilde{g}(n).$$

Put all together, $\tilde{f} \sqsubseteq \tilde{g}$, which is the same as $\Phi(f) \sqsubseteq \Phi(g)$.

To show that $\Phi(\sqcup S) \sqsubseteq \sqcup \Phi(S)$, set $g = \sqcup S$. It remains to show

$$\tilde{g} \sqsubseteq \sqcup \{\tilde{f} \mid f \in S\}$$

or, equivalently (by Theorem 4.3),

$$\tilde{g}(n) \sqsubseteq \sqcup \{\tilde{f}(n) \mid f \in S\} \qquad \text{for every } n \in Nat_\omega. \tag{1}$$

If $n = \omega$, then $\tilde{g}(n) = \omega$, so (1) holds. If $n = 0$, $\tilde{g}(n) = 1$, and $\tilde{f}(n) = 1$ for all $f \in S$, so even equality holds in (1). Suppose now $n \neq 0, \omega$. If $f(n-1) = \omega$ for all $f \in S$, then so is $g(n-1) = \omega$, hence $\tilde{g}(n) = \omega$ and again (1) holds. If $f(n-1) = m \neq \omega$ for at least one function $f \in S$, then $g(n-1) = \sqcup\{f(n-1)|f \in S\}$ can only be m. So $\tilde{g}(n) = n * g(n-1) = n * m$. On the other hand, $\sqcup\{\tilde{f}(n)|f \in S\} = \sqcup\{n * f(n-1)|f \in S\}$ can also only by $n * m$. So (1) holds. $\qquad \square$

After these examples one might be led to believe that all monotonic functions are continuous. This is not the case. The next example is of a function that is monotonic but not continuous.

EXAMPLE 4.16   Let the function $\Phi: (Nat_\omega \to Nat_\omega) \to Nat_\omega$ be defined by

$$\Phi(f) = \begin{cases} 0 & \text{if } f(n) \neq \omega \text{ for all } n \in Nat, \\ \omega & \text{otherwise.} \end{cases}$$

Informally, $\Phi(f)$ is 0 exactly when the function f is 'total'.

To show that the function is monotonic, pick $f, g: Nat_\omega \to Nat_\omega$ such that $f \sqsubseteq g$. If $\Phi(f) = \omega$, then of course $\Phi(f) \sqsubseteq \Phi(g)$. Should $\Phi(f) = 0$, that is, $f(n) \neq \omega$ for all $n \in Nat$, then $g(n) \neq \omega$ for all $n \in Nat$ because $f \sqsubseteq g$. Therefore $\Phi(g) = 0$, and hence $\Phi(f) \sqsubseteq \Phi(g)$.

But Φ is not continuous. As already seen in an example preceding Definition 4.9, a chain S of functions which are not 'total' can indeed have a 'total' function for the lub; hence $\sqcup \Phi(S) = \omega \neq \Phi(\sqcup S) = 0$. $\qquad \square$

Now partial orders of continuous functions will be investigated. The following lemma is the starting point.

80

LEMMA 4.17   Let $(D, \sqsubseteq)$ be a partial order. Let I, J be two arbitrary sets whose elements will be used as indices. Let a_i^j be an element of D for each i in I and j in J.

(1) If the lub $a^j = \sqcup\{a_i^j \mid i \in I\}$ exists for each $j \in J$, and if the lub $l^0 = \sqcup\{a^j \mid j \in J\}$ exists, then the lub $l = \sqcup\{a_i^j \mid i \in I, j \in J\}$ exists and furthermore, $l^0 = l$.

(2) The same holds for $a_i = \sqcup\{a_i^j \mid j \in J\}$ and $l_0 = \sqcup\{a_i \mid i \in I\}$.

(3) If the hypotheses of (1) and (2) are fulfilled, then $l^0 = l_0$.

The lemma is illustrated by the following diagram.

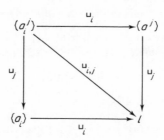

The proof is left to Exercise 4.2–7.   □

THEOREM 4.18 (Continuous Functions and cpo's)   Let $(D, \sqsubseteq)$ and $(E, \sqsubseteq)$ be cpo's. Then the set $[D \to E]$ of all continuous functions from D to E is a sub-cpo of $((D \to E), \sqsubseteq)$.

Proof. By Theorem 4.10 it is enough to show that

(1) $[D \to E]$ has a least element, and
(2) for every chain S in $[D \to E]$ the lub $\sqcup_{(D \to E)}S$ is continuous.

The first condition holds, since the least element $\perp_{(D \to E)}$ is continuous. To prove (2) put $g = \sqcup_{(D \to E)}S$. Since every continuous function is monotonic, it follows from Theorem 4.12 that g is also monotonic. By Theorem 4.14 it remains to show that for every chain T in D, $g(\sqcup T) \sqsubseteq \sqcup g(T)$.

$$
\begin{aligned}
g(\sqcup T) &= (\sqcup S)(\sqcup T) \\
&= \sqcup(S(\sqcup T)) \quad \text{(by Theorem 4.3)} \\
&= \sqcup\{f(\sqcup T) \mid f \in S\} \\
&= \sqcup\{\sqcup f(T) \mid f \in S\} \quad \text{(since every } f \in S \text{ is continuous)} \\
&= \sqcup\{\sqcup\{f(x) \mid x \in T\} \mid f \in S\}.
\end{aligned}
$$

$$
\begin{aligned}
\sqcup g(T) &= \sqcup\{g(x) \mid x \in T\} \\
&= \sqcup\{(\sqcup S)(x) \mid x \in T\} \\
&= \sqcup\{\sqcup S(x) \mid x \in T\} \quad \text{(by Theorem 4.3)} \\
&= \sqcup\{\sqcup\{f(x) \mid f \in S\} \mid x \in T\}.
\end{aligned}
$$

With the help of Lemma 4.17 (whereby $I = T$, $J = S$, and $a_x^f = f(x)$) it follows that $g(\sqcup T) = \sqcup g(T)$.   □

This section concludes with a few theorems about continuity which enable one to prove the continuity of many functions without checking each one individually.

LEMMA 4.19   Let $(D, \sqsubseteq)$, $(E, \sqsubseteq)$, and $(F, \sqsubseteq)$ be cpo's and $g: D \to E$ and $f: E \to F$ continuous functions. Then their composition $f \circ g: D \to F$ is also continuous.

Proof. Let $S \subseteq D$ be a chain. Then

$$\begin{aligned} f(g(\sqcup S)) &= f(\sqcup g(S)) && \text{(because } S \text{ is a chain and } g \text{ is continuous)} \\ &= \sqcup f(g(S)) && \text{(because } g(S) \text{ is a chain and } f \text{ is continuous)} \end{aligned}$$

(That $g(S)$ is a chain follows from the monotonicity of g.) Hence, $f \circ g$ is continuous. $\qquad\square$

THEOREM   4.20   Let $(D, \sqsubseteq), (E_i, \sqsubseteq)$ for $i = 1, \ldots, n$ be cpo's, $n \geq 1$. Let $f: D \to E_1 \times \cdots \times E_n$ be a function. Then f is continuous iff $\mathrm{pr}_i \circ f$ is continuous for $i = 1, \ldots, n$, where pr_i is the ith projection function.

Proof. Since the functions pr_i are continuous, it is clear by the previous lemma that if f is continuous, then so is $\mathrm{pr}_i \circ f$.

Conversely suppose that $\mathrm{pr}_i \circ f$ is continuous and let $S \subseteq D$ be a chain. Then

$$\begin{aligned} f(\sqcup S) &= (\mathrm{pr}_1(f(\sqcup S)), \ldots, \mathrm{pr}_n(f(\sqcup S))) \\ &= (\sqcup \mathrm{pr}_1(f(S)), \ldots, \sqcup \mathrm{pr}_n(f(S))) && \text{(since } \mathrm{pr}_i \circ f \text{ is continuous)} \\ &= \sqcup f(S) && \text{(by Theorem 4.2)} \end{aligned}$$

So f is continuous. $\qquad\square$

THEOREM 4.21 (Composition Preserves Continuity)   Let $(D, \sqsubseteq), (E_i, \sqsubseteq), (F, \sqsubseteq)$ be cpo's; furthermore, let $g_i \in [D \to E_i]$ and $f \in [E_1 \times \cdots \times E_n \to F]$ be continuous functions, $i = 1, \ldots, n$, $n \geq 1$. The composition of f and $g_1, \ldots, g_n$, that is, the function $h: D \to F$ defined by

$$h(d) = f(g_1(d), \ldots, g_n(d))$$

is continuous. (This theorem is a generalization of Lemma 4.19.)

Proof. Set $g: D \to E_1 \times \cdots \times E_n$ to be the function defined by

$$g(d) = (g_1(d), \ldots, g_n(d)).$$

This function is continuous by Theorem 4.20, since $\mathrm{pr}_i \circ g = g_i$ for $i = 1, \ldots, n$. Now $h = f \circ g$. So, by Lemma 4.19, the function h is continuous. $\qquad\square$

Now these theorems will be used to prove some functions continuous.

EXAMPLE   4.22   Let $\Phi: (Nat_\omega \to Nat_\omega) \to (Nat_\omega \to Nat_\omega)$ be the functional defined in Example 4.15. Then, by Theorem 4.21, if f is continuous, then so is $\Phi(f)$, since it is formed by composition from f, and the functions $\mathscr{I}_0$ (*if-then-else*),

$\mathscr{I}_0(=)$, $\mathscr{I}_0(*)$, and $\mathscr{I}_0(-)$; these latter functions are continuous since they are monotonic functions on flat domains. Such functions, as seen earlier, are all continuous.

So the functional Φ can be restricted to a functional from $[Nat_\omega \to Nat_\omega]$ to $[Nat_\omega \to Nat_\omega]$. □

The next theorem will be required in Chapter 10; it makes use of a notion called 'currying' which will now be introduced. Let $D_1, D_2, \ldots, D_n$ $(n \geq 2)$ and E be arbitrary sets, and let $f: D_1 \times D_2 \times \cdots \times D_n \to E$ be a (total) function. Then the *curried function* of f, denoted f^c, is a function from $D_1 \times \cdots \times D_{n-1}$ to the set of functions $(D_n \to E)$ and is defined by

$$f^c(d_1, d_2, \ldots, d_{n-1})(d_n) = f(d_1, d_2, \ldots, d_n)$$

By 'currying' one obtains an 'equivalent' $(n-1)$-ary function from an n-ary function, or, by repeated currying, a one-place function.

THEOREM 4.23 (Currying Preserves Continuity)   Let $(D_1, \sqsubseteq), (D_2, \sqsubseteq), \ldots, (D_n, \sqsubseteq)$ and $(E, \sqsubseteq)$ be cpo's, $n \geq 2$. Let f be a function from $D_1 \times D_2 \times \cdots \times D_n$ to E. Then

$$f \in [D_1 \times \cdots \times D_n \to E] \qquad \text{iff} \quad f^c \in [D_1 \times \cdots \times D_{n-1} \to [D_n \to E]]$$

where f^c is the curried function of f.

Proof. The proof here is for $n = 2$, but the argument holds for any n.

(i) Suppose first $f \in [D_1 \times D_2 \to E]$; that is, f is a continuous function. In order to prove that both f^c and $f^c(d_1)$ with $d_1 \in D_1$ are continuous let S_2 be a chain in D_2. Then for every $d_1 \in D_1$:

$$\begin{aligned} f^c(d_1)(\sqcup S_2) &= f(d_1, \sqcup S_2) \\ &= f(\sqcup\{d_1\} \times S_2) && \text{(by Theorem 4.2)} \\ &= \sqcup f(\{d_1\} \times S_2) && \text{(since } f \text{ is continuous)} \\ &= \sqcup f^c(d_1)(S_2). \end{aligned}$$

Therefore, $f^c(d_1)$ is continuous.

Now let S_1 be a chain in D_1. Then for every $d_2 \in D_2$:

$$\begin{aligned} f^c(\sqcup S_1)(d_2) &= \sqcup f^c(S_1)(d_2) && \text{(analogously to above)} \\ &= (\sqcup f^c(S_1))(d_2) && \text{(by Theorem 4.3)} \end{aligned}$$

So, $f^c(\sqcup S_1) = \sqcup f^c(S_1)$ which means f^c is continuous.

(ii) Conversely, it must be shown that f is continuous if $f^c \in [D_1 \to [D_2 \to E]]$. First it will be shown that f is monotonic.

Let $(d_1, d_2), (d'_1, d'_2) \in D_1 \times D_2$ such that $(d_1, d_2) \sqsubseteq (d'_1, d'_2)$. Then

$$\begin{aligned} f(d_1, d_2) &= f^c(d_1)(d_2) \\ &\sqsubseteq f^c(d_1)(d'_2) && \text{(since } f^c(d_1) \text{ is continuous, hence monotonic)} \\ &\sqsubseteq f^c(d'_1)(d'_2) && \text{(since } f^c \text{ is continuous, hence monotonic)} \\ &= f(d'_1, d'_2) \end{aligned}$$

Therefore, f is monotonic.

Now let S be a chain in $D_1 \times D_2$. By Theorem 4.14(1), it remains to prove that $f(\sqcup S) \sqsubseteq \sqcup f(S)$. However,

$$
\begin{aligned}
f(\sqcup S) &= f(\sqcup \mathrm{pr}_1(S), \sqcup \mathrm{pr}_2(S)) && \text{(by Theorem 4.2)} \\
&= f^c(\sqcup \mathrm{pr}_1(S))(\sqcup \mathrm{pr}_2(S)) \\
&= \sqcup f^c(\sqcup \mathrm{pr}_1(S))(\mathrm{pr}_2(S)) && \text{(since } f^c(\sqcup \mathrm{pr}_1(S)) \text{ is continuous)} \\
&= \sqcup(\sqcup f^c(\mathrm{pr}_1(S)))(\mathrm{pr}_2(S)) && \text{(since } f^c \text{ is continuous)} \\
&= \sqcup\{\sqcup f^c(\mathrm{pr}_1(S))(d_2) \mid d_2 \in \mathrm{pr}_2(S)\} \\
&= \sqcup\{\sqcup\{f^c(d_1)(d_2) \mid d_1 \in \mathrm{pr}_1(S)\} \mid d_2 \in \mathrm{pr}_2(S)\} \\
&= \sqcup\{\sqcup\{f(d_1, d_2) \mid d_1 \in \mathrm{pr}_1(S)\} \mid d_2 \in \mathrm{pr}_2(S)\} \\
&= \sqcup\{f(d_1, d_2) \mid d_1 \in \mathrm{pr}_1(S), d_2 \in \mathrm{pr}_2(S)\} && \text{(by Lemma 4.17)} \\
&= \sqcup f(\mathrm{pr}_1(S) \times \mathrm{pr}_2(S)).
\end{aligned}
$$

It remains to show that

$$\sqcup f(\mathrm{pr}_1(S) \times \mathrm{pr}_2(S)) \sqsubseteq \sqcup f(S). \tag{1}$$

Let $e \in f(\mathrm{pr}_1(S) \times \mathrm{pr}_2(S))$. Then there exist elements $(d_1, d_2), (d_1', d_2') \in S$ so that $e = f(d_1, d_2')$. Since S is a chain either $(d_1, d_2) \sqsubseteq (d_1', d_2')$ or vice versa. Say, $(d_1, d_2) \sqsubseteq (d_1', d_2')$, then, in particular, $d_1 \sqsubseteq d_1'$. Then, by the monotonicity of f, $e = f(d_1, d_2') \sqsubseteq f(d_1', d_2') \in f(S)$. Now (1) follows by Lemma 4.11. $\square$

This theorem can be used to show that the function apply: $[D \to E] \times D \to E$ defined by

$$\mathrm{apply}(f, d) = f(d)$$

is continuous. Just observe that apply^c is the identity function on the set of continuous functions $[D \to E]$.

4.3 Fixpoints

Let $(D, \sqsubseteq)$ be a partial order and $f: D \to D$ a function. The *least fixpoint* of f is defined to be the least element of the set of all fixpoints of f. Concerning its existence and uniqueness, the arguments are similar to those of upper and least upper bounds. If the least fixpoint of a function f exists, it is denoted μf.

THEOREM 4.24 (The Fixpoint Theorem) Let $(D, \sqsubseteq)$ be a cpo and $f: D \to D$ be a continuous function. Then f has a least fixpoint μf, and, in fact,

$$\mu f = \sqcup\{f^i(\perp) \mid i \in Nat\}$$

(where $\perp$ is the least element of the cpo $(D, \sqsubseteq)$ and where f^i is the ith iterate of the function f).

Proof. First, it will be shown by induction that for all $i \in Nat$, $f^i(\perp) \sqsubseteq f^{i+1}(\perp)$.

Induction basis $f^0(\perp) = \perp \sqsubseteq f^1(\perp)$.

84

Induction step   Assume $f^i(\bot) \sqsubseteq f^{i+1}(\bot), i \geq 0$. Then, by the monotonicity of f,

$$f^{i+1}(\bot) = f(f^i(\bot)) \sqsubseteq f(f^{i+1}(\bot)) = f^{i+2}(\bot)$$

Thus, the set $\{f^i(\bot)|i \in Nat\}$ is a chain and its lub, call it $d = \sqcup\{f^i(\bot)|i \in Nat\}$, exists.

Next it will be shown that d is in fact a fixpoint of the function f. By the continuity of f, one obtains

$$
\begin{aligned}
f(d) &= f(\sqcup\{f^i(\bot)\,|\,i \in Nat\}) \\
&= \sqcup f(\{f^i(\bot)\,|\,i \in Nat\}) \\
&= \sqcup\{f^{i+1}(\bot)\,|\,i \in Nat\} \\
&= \sqcup\{f^i(\bot)\,|\,i \in Nat, i \neq 0\} \\
&= \sqcup(\{f^i(\bot)\,|\,i \in Nat, i \neq 0\} \cup \{\bot\}) \\
&= \sqcup\{f^i(\bot)\,|\,i \in Nat\} \\
&= d
\end{aligned}
$$

Thus, d is a fixpoint of f.

Finally, it will be shown that d is the least fixpoint of f. Suppose $d' \in D$ is a fixpoint, i.e. $f(d') = d'$. In order to prove that $d \sqsubseteq d'$ it is sufficient to prove that d' is an upper bound of the set $\{f^i(\bot)\,|\,i \in Nat\}$. This requires that $f^i(\bot) \sqsubseteq d'$ for every $i \in Nat$. This will again be proved by induction.

Induction basis $f^0(\bot) = \bot \sqsubseteq d'$.
Induction step   Assume $f^i(\bot) \sqsubseteq d', i \geq 0$. Then, by the monotonicity of f,

$$f^{i+1}(\bot) = f(f^i(\bot)) \sqsubseteq f(d') = d' \qquad \qquad \square$$

EXAMPLE 4.25   Let $\Phi: (Nat_\omega \to Nat_\omega) \to (Nat_\omega \to Nat_\omega)$ be the continuous functional defined in Example 4.15. As in that example, $\Phi(g)$ will be denoted $\tilde{g}$. Then, by the Fixpoint Theorem, Φ has a least fixpoint $\mu\Phi$ for which

$$\mu\Phi = \sqcup\{\Phi^i(\bot)\,|\,i \in Nat\}.$$

It will now be shown by induction that $\Phi^i(\bot) = f_i$, where $f_i: Nat_\omega \to Nat_\omega$ is the function of Example 4.8:

$$f_i(n) = \begin{cases} \omega & \text{if } n = \omega \text{ or } n \in Nat, n \geq i, \\ n! & \text{if } n \in Nat, 0 \leq n \leq i-1. \end{cases}$$

Induction basis $\Phi^0(\bot) = \bot = f_0$ (because, by Theorem 4.7, $\bot(n) = \omega$ for all $n \in Nat_\omega$).
Induction step   Assume that $\Phi^i(\bot) = f_i$. It must be proved that $\Phi^{i+1}(\bot) = f_{i+1}$. As $\Phi^{i+1}(\bot) = \Phi(f_i) = \tilde{f}_i$, it is sufficient to prove that $\tilde{f}_i = f_{i+1}$. Let $n \in Nat_\omega$. There are three cases. (1) If $n = \omega$, then $\tilde{f}_i(n) = \omega = f_{i+1}(n)$. (2) If $n = 0$, then $\tilde{f}_i(n) = 1 = 0! = f_{i+1}(n)$. (3) For $n \neq \omega, 0$ the proof is further divided into two cases. First, if $n \leq i$, then $f_i(n-1) = (n-1)! \neq \omega$. So $\tilde{f}_i(n) = n * f_i(n-1) = n * (n-1)! = n! = f_{i+1}(n)$. Second, if $n \geq i+1$, then $f_i(n-1) = \omega$, and thus $\tilde{f}_i(n) = n * \omega = \omega = f_{i+1}(n)$.

Therefore $\Phi^i(\bot) = f_i$ and one obtains

$$\mu\Phi = \sqcup\{f_i \mid i \in Nat\}.$$

It is easy to show that $\mu\Phi$ is the strict ω-extension of the factorial function. (See Example 4.8.) □

What the last example demonstrates is that the Fixpoint Theorem can be used to prove properties of the least fixpoint of continuous functions. This method will now be formalized in the so-called Induction Principle of Scott. Unlike the other induction principles introduced so far in this book, this principle cannot be used to (try to) prove any arbitrary properties. Therefore, a suitable class of properties will be defined, the so-called 'admissible predicates'.

DEFINITION 4.26 (Admissible Predicates)   Let $(D, \sqsubseteq)$ be a cpo and $\varphi: D \to Bool$ be a predicate. The predicate φ is called *admissible* if for every chain S in D the following condition holds:

if $\varphi(d) = $ true for all $d \in S$,
then $\varphi(\sqcup S) = $ true. □

Notice that these predicates φ are genuine predicates, namely maps to the set *Bool*, and not—as in the interpretation of predicate symbols in Section 3.3—to the set $Bool_\omega$. This is because the properties now being considered are *about* cpo's or programs, while the interpretation of a predicate symbol is something inside a cpo or program. This will become clearer in the Logic for Computable Functions to be discussed in Chapter 10.

The next theorem guarantees that the predicates to be used later extensively in correctness proofs are admissible.

THEOREM 4.27   Let $(D, \sqsubseteq)$, $(E, \sqsubseteq)$ be cpo's. Let $g_i, h_i \in [D \to E]$ for $i = 1, \ldots, n$ be continuous functions. Then the predicate $\varphi: D \to Bool$ defined by

$$\varphi(d) = \text{true} \qquad \text{iff } g_i(d) \sqsubseteq h_i(d) \text{ for } i = 1, \ldots, n$$

is admissible.

Proof. Let S be a chain in D. Assume that for every $d \in S$, $\varphi(d) = $ true or, equivalently, $g_i(d) \sqsubseteq h_i(d)$ for $i = 1, \ldots, n$. It must be proved that $\varphi(\sqcup S) = $ *true*. For every $e \in g_i(S)$, say $e = g_i(d)$, there exists an $e' \in h_i(S)$, namely $e' = h_i(d)$ such that $e \sqsubseteq e'$. By Lemma 4.11, $\sqcup g_i(S) \sqsubseteq \sqcup h_i(S)$, so $g_i(\sqcup S) \sqsubseteq h_i(\sqcup S)$, by continuity. This is exactly $\varphi(\sqcup S) = $ true. □

COROLLARY 4.28   Let $(D, \sqsubseteq)$, $(E, \sqsubseteq)$ be cpo's and $g, h \in [D \to E]$ be continuous functions. Then the predicate $\varphi: D \to Bool$ defined by

$$\varphi(d) = \text{true} \qquad \text{iff } g(d) = h(d)$$

is admissible.

Proof. This predicate can be rewritten: $g(d) \sqsubseteq h(d)$ and $h(d) \sqsubseteq g(d)$. $\qquad\square$

A word of warning: some meaningful predicates are not admissible. The predicate expressing that a function is 'total' is one example. This predicate, $\varphi: (Nat_\omega \to Nat_\omega) \to Bool$, is defined by:

$$\varphi(f) = \text{true} \qquad \text{iff } f(n) \neq \omega \text{ for all } n \in Nat.$$

Since a chain of functions which are not 'total' can have a 'total' function as lub, φ is not admissible (see Example 4.16).

THEOREM 4.29 (*Induction Principle of Scott*, also called *Fixpoint Induction Principle*) Let $(D, \sqsubseteq)$ be a cpo, $f \in [D \to D]$ a continuous function and $\varphi: D \to Bool$ an admissible predicate. If

(a) *Induction basis* $\varphi(\bot) = \text{true}$, and
(b) *Induction step* $\varphi(d) = \text{true}$ implies $\varphi(f(d)) = \text{true}$ for every $d \in D$,
then $\varphi(\mu f) = \text{true}$.

Remark. In place of (b) a weaker condition would suffice, namely: $\varphi(f^i(\bot)) = \text{true}$ implies $\varphi(f^{i+1}(\bot)) = \text{true}$ for every $i \in Nat$.

Proof. From (a) and (b) one can derive by induction over i that $\varphi(f^i(\bot)) = \text{true}$ for all $i \in Nat$. Since φ is an admissible predicate

$$\varphi(\sqcup \{ f^i(\bot) \mid i \in Nat \}) = \text{true}.$$

So, by the Fixpoint Theorem, $\varphi(\mu f) = \text{true}$. $\qquad\square$

The proof of Theorem 4.29 shows that fixpoint induction is really nothing more than usual induction on i to show the desired property for $f^i(\bot)$, followed by a 'jump' from the chain $\{ f^i(\bot) \mid i \in Nat \}$ to its lub μf. The definition of admissible predicates was made so that this jump is possible.

EXAMPLE 4.30 Again let $\Phi: (Nat_\omega \to Nat_\omega) \to (Nat_\omega \to Nat_\omega)$ be the continuous functional defined in Example 4.15. Let fac_ω be the strict ω-extension of the factorial function. It will be shown using fixpoint induction that $\mu\Phi \sqsubseteq fac_\omega$. The predicate $\varphi: (Nat_\omega \to Nat_\omega) \to Bool$ defined by

$$\varphi(f) = \text{true} \qquad \text{iff } f \sqsubseteq fac_\omega$$

is admissible, since it can be rewritten in the form $g(f) \sqsubseteq h(f)$ where g is the identity function and h is the constant function defined by $h(f) = fac_\omega$.
Now fixpoint induction can be applied.

Induction basis $\varphi(\bot) = \text{true}$, since $\bot \sqsubseteq fac_\omega$.
Induction step Let $f \in (Nat_\omega \to Nat_\omega)$ be any function for which $\varphi(f) = \text{true}$; hence $f \sqsubseteq fac_\omega$ or, by the monotonicity of Φ

$$\Phi(f) \sqsubseteq \Phi(fac_\omega).$$

In order to show that $\varphi(\Phi(f)) = $ true, which means

$$\Phi(f) \sqsubseteq fac_\omega$$

it is sufficient to prove that

$$\Phi(fac_\omega) \sqsubseteq fac_\omega.$$

So let $n \in Nat_\omega$. If $n = \omega$, then

$$\Phi(fac_\omega)(n) = \omega = fac_\omega(n)$$

If $n = 0$, then

$$\Phi(fac_\omega)(n) = 1 = 0! = fac_\omega(n)$$

If $n \neq 0, \omega$, then $fac_\omega(n-1) = (n-1)! \neq \omega$, so

$$\Phi(fac_\omega)(n) = n * fac_\omega(n-1) = n * (n-1)! = n! = fac_\omega(n).$$

Hence, one obtains even $\Phi(fac_\omega) = fac_\omega$.

Unfortunately, this method does not work to prove that $\mu\Phi = fac_\omega$: while $f = fac_\omega$ is still an admissible predicate, the induction basis would require $\perp = fac_\omega$. $\qquad\square$

To avoid the tedium of making some routine steps—like checking the induction basis and the argument that it is sufficient to show $\Phi(fac_\omega) \sqsubseteq fac_\omega$ in the last example—the fixpoint induction principle can be given a somewhat shorter formulation for a common special case.

COROLLARY 4.31 (Park's Theorem)   Let $(D, \sqsubseteq)$ be a cpo, $f : D \to D$ continuous, and e an element of D such that $f(e) \sqsubseteq e$. Then $\mu f \sqsubseteq e$.

Proof. The predicate $\varphi: D \to Bool$ defined $\varphi(d) = $ true iff $d \sqsubseteq e$ is, by Theorem 4.27, an admissible predicate. Moreover,

Induction basis $\perp \sqsubseteq e$, and
Induction step $d \sqsubseteq e$ implies $f(d) \sqsubseteq f(e) \sqsubseteq e$, by the monotonicity of f.

Hence, by fixpoint induction $\mu f \sqsubseteq e$. $\qquad\square$

Using this theorem the proof of $\mu\Phi \sqsubseteq fac_\omega$ in the last example can be reduced to verifying that $\Phi(fac_\omega) \sqsubseteq fac_\omega$. A generalized form of Park's Theorem is in Exercise 4.3–5.

Now a result will be derived that will not find application until Chapter 10.

THEOREM 4.32 (Continuity of the Fixpoint Operator)   Let $(D, \sqsubseteq)$ be a cpo. Then the functional $\mu: [D \to D] \to D$ mapping any function $f \in [D \to D]$ into its least fixpoint μf is continuous; in other words $\mu \in [[D \to D] \to D]$. (The functional μ is called the *fixpoint operator*.)

88

Proof. For all $i \in Nat$ define $\mu_i \colon [D \to D] \to D$ by

$$\mu_i(f) = f^i(\bot).$$

By induction on i it will be shown that all the functions μ_i are continuous. For $i = 0$, $\mu_0(f) = \bot$ for all f. The function μ_0 is therefore constant and hence continuous. For the induction step assume that μ_i is continuous, $i \geq 0$. The value of the function μ_{i+1} for an arbitrary argument $f \in [D \to D]$ is rewritten using the function 'apply' defined earlier in the chapter (after Theorem 4.23):

$$\mu_{i+1}(f) = f^{i+1}(\bot) = f(f^i(\bot)) = \text{apply}(f, \mu_i(f))$$

As 'apply' is continuous, and μ_i is continuous (by induction hypothesis), μ_{i+1} is also continuous by Theorem 4.21. Now

$$
\begin{aligned}
\mu(f) &= \bigsqcup\{f^i(\bot)\,|\,i \in Nat\} && \text{(by the Fixpoint Theorem)} \\
&= \bigsqcup\{\mu_i(f)\,|\,i \in Nat\} && \text{(by the definition of } \mu_i) \\
&= (\bigsqcup\{\mu_i\,|\,i \in Nat\})(f) && \text{(by Theorem 4.3)}
\end{aligned}
$$

so μ is the lub of the set $\{\mu_i\,|\,i \in Nat\}$. Since the lub of a chain of continuous functions is continuous (Theorem 4.18), μ is continuous. $\qquad\square$

This ends the presentation of the theory of complete partial orders. It should be pointed out that the definition of completeness (of partial orders) as well as that of continuity (of functions between cpo's) is not uniform in the literature. The various definitions found differ in being based on a concept different from that of a chain. Sometimes this concept is that of an ω-*chain*, the elements of which must have the form $d_1 \sqsubseteq d_2 \sqsubseteq \cdots$. In other approaches the notion of a *directed set* is used—a directed set being one for which every two elements have a lub in the set. Both these definitions lead to definitions of completeness and continuity which are equivalent to the definitions presented here. If arbitrary sets are permitted, one obtains the (stronger) concept of complete lattices (see Exercise 4.1–9) and also a stronger notion of continuity.

EXERCISES

4.1–1 Let $(D, \sqsubseteq)$ be a partial order.

(i) Which elements of D are upper bounds of the empty set?
(ii) When does the empty set have a lub in D?

4.1–2 Give an example of a partial order $(D, \sqsubseteq)$ and a subset $S \subseteq D$ such that:

(i) S has no upper bounds.
(ii) S has upper bounds but no lub.

Is (ii) possible if S is finite?

4.1–3 Which of the following partial orders $(D, \sqsubseteq)$ are complete?

(i) $D = \{a, b\}^*$ where $v \sqsubseteq w$ iff v is a prefix of w.
(ii) $D = \{a, b\}^* \backslash \{\varepsilon\}$ with $v \sqsubseteq u$ iff v is a prefix of u or there exist strings $x, y, z \in \{a, b\}^*$ such that $v = xay$ and $u = xbz$.

(iii) $D = P(H)$ for an arbitrary set H with the subset relation.

(iv) $D = Nat \cup \{\infty\}$, where $d \sqsubseteq d'$ iff $d' = \infty$ or ($d, d' \neq \infty$ and $d \leq d'$).

(v) $D = Q_+ \cup \{\infty\}$ (where Q_+ is the set of non-negative rational numbers) with $\sqsubseteq$ as defined in (iv).

(vi) $D = R_+ \cup \{\infty\}$ (where R_+ is the set of non-negative real numbers) with $\sqsubseteq$ as defined in (iv).

4.1–4 Let $(D, \sqsubseteq)$ be as defined in Exercise 4.1–3, part (iv). Determine the lub of:

(i) $S = \{(0, n) \mid n \in Nat\} \cup \{(n, 0) \mid n \in Nat\}$ in $(D^2, \sqsubseteq)$.

(ii) $S = \{f_i \mid i \in D\}$ in $((D \to D), \sqsubseteq)$, where $f_i : D \to D$ is defined for each $i \in D$ by $f_i(i) = i$, and $f_i(d) = 0$ for $d \neq i$.

4.1–5 (i) Prove Theorem 4.5.

(ii) Show that if $(D_1, \sqsubseteq), \ldots, (D_n, \sqsubseteq)$ are partial orders which have only finite chains, then $(D_1 \times \cdots \times D_n, \sqsubseteq)$ has only finite chains.

4.1–6 Let $D = P(Nat)$ and $\sqsubseteq$ be the subset relation. Then $(D, \sqsubseteq)$ is a cpo (see Exercise 4.1–3). Furthermore, let $E \subseteq D$ be defined by $E = \{S \subset Nat \mid S \text{ finite}\} \cup \{\emptyset, Nat\}$. Show that $(E, \sqsubseteq)$ is a cpo but not a sub-cpo of $(D, \sqsubseteq)$.

4.1–7 Prove Theorem 4.10.

4.1–8 Let $S_{1\omega}, \ldots, S_{n\omega}, S_{(n+1)\omega}$ be flat partial orders. Prove that the set of all strict functions from $S_{1\omega} \times \cdots \times S_{n\omega}$ to $S_{(n+1)\omega}$ is a sub-cpo of $((S_{1\omega} \times \cdots \times S_{n\omega} \to S_{(n+1)\omega}), \sqsubseteq)$.

4.1–9 Let $(D, \sqsubseteq)$ be a partial order. D is called a *lattice* if every two elements $a, b \in D$—and hence every finite number of elements—has a lub (denoted $a \sqcup b$) and a glb (denoted $a \sqcap b$). A lattice is *complete* if every subset of D has a lub and glb. Prove:

(i) Every complete lattice has a least and a greatest element (hence it is a cpo).

(ii) A (complete) partial order for which every set has a lub is a complete lattice.

4.2–1 Let $(D, \sqsubseteq)$ and $(E, \sqsubseteq)$ be partial orders and let $f : D \to E$ be a monotonic function.

(i) Prove that for every chain S in D the image $f(S)$ of S is a chain in E.

(ii) Is it true that for every chain T in E the pre-image $f^{-1}(T)$ of T is a chain in D?

4.2–2 Let $(Nat_\omega \to Nat_\omega)$ be furnished with the usual ordering and the power set $P(Nat)$ with the subset relation. Which of the following functionals are continuous?

(i) $\Phi : (Nat_\omega \to Nat_\omega) \to P(Nat)$ defined by

$$\Phi(f) = \{n \in Nat \mid f(n) \neq \omega\}.$$

(Φ maps every function f to its domain of definition.)

(ii) $\Phi_1, \Phi_2, \Phi_3 : P(Nat)^2 \to P(Nat)$ defined by

$$\Phi_1(S, T) = S \cup T$$

$$\Phi_2(S, T) = S \cap T$$

$$\Phi_3(S, T) = S \backslash T$$

4.2–3 For all the *complete* partial orders $(D, \sqsubseteq)$ in Exercise 4.1–3 determine the set of continuous functions $f : D \to D$. In each case is there a monotonic function which is not continuous?

4.2–4 Prove that a continuous function restricted to a sub-cpo is still continuous.

4.2–5 (i) Let $(D_1, \sqsubseteq)$, $(D_2, \sqsubseteq)$, and $(E, \sqsubseteq)$ be cpo's and $f : D_1 \times D_2 \to E$ a function. The function f is said to be continuous in the first argument if for every $d_2 \in D_2$ the function $f_{d_2} : D_1 \to E$ defined by

$$f_{d_2}(d_1) = f(d_1, d_2)$$

is continuous. Continuity in the second argument is defined analogously. Show that f is continuous iff it is continuous in both arguments. (*Hint:* Use Theorem 4.20.) Notice that the corresponding theorem in analysis does not hold.

(ii) Let D be a set and $(E, \sqsubseteq)$ a cpo. Show that for every $d \in D$ the function $\mathrm{subst}_d : (D \rightarrow E) \times E \rightarrow (D \rightarrow E)$

$$\mathrm{subst}_d(f, e) = f[d/e]$$

is continuous. Furthermore, show that for every n-tuple $(d_1, \ldots, d_n) \in D^n$ the function

$$\mathrm{subst}_{d_1, \ldots, d_n} : (D \rightarrow E) \times E^n \rightarrow (D \rightarrow E)$$

defined by

$$\mathrm{subst}_{d_1, \ldots, d_n}(f, e_1, \ldots, e_n) = f[d_1/e_1] \ldots [d_n/e_n]$$

is also continuous.

*4.2–6 (Continuity in topology). For every cpo $(D, \sqsubseteq)$ a subset A of D is said to be closed if A is a sub-cpo of D, and $y \in A$ and $x \sqsubseteq y$ imply $x \in A$. Show that this induces a topology on every cpo and that a function between cpo's is continuous iff it is continuous in the way it is defined in topology.

4.2–7 Prove Lemma 4.17.

4.3–1 Which of the following functions $\varphi : [Nat_\omega \rightarrow Nat_\omega] \rightarrow Bool$ are admissible predicates?

(i) $\varphi(f) = $ true   iff $f(0) = \omega$.
(ii) $\varphi(f) = $ true   iff $f(0) = 0$.
(iii) $\varphi(f) = $ true   iff $\{n \in Nat \mid f(n) = \omega\}$ is finite.
(iv) $\varphi(f) = $ true   iff $\{n \in Nat \mid f(n) \neq \omega\}$ is finite.
(v) $\varphi(f) = $ true   iff $f(n) = \omega$ for all $n \in Nat$.

4.3–2 Let $(D, \sqsubseteq)$ and $(E, \sqsubseteq)$ be cpo's. For predicates $\varphi, \psi : D \rightarrow Bool$ and $r : D \times E \rightarrow Bool$ let $\neg \varphi$, $\varphi \wedge \psi$, $\varphi \vee \psi$, $\exists x \in D . r$, and $\forall x \in D . r$ be defined in the obvious way.

(i) Show that if φ, ψ are admissible then $\varphi \wedge \psi$ and $\varphi \vee \psi$ are admissible.
(ii) For which predicates in Exercise 4.3–1 is $\neg \varphi$ admissible?
(iii) If r is admissible, are $\exists x \in D . r$ and $\forall x \in D . r$ admissible?

4.3–3 Consider P(*Nat*) ordered by the subset relation. Prove that each of the following functionals $\Phi : $ P(*Nat*) $\rightarrow$ P(*Nat*) is continuous and determine the least fixpoint.

(i) $\Phi(S) = S \cup T$ for a fixed set $T \subseteq Nat$.
(ii) $\Phi(S) = S \cup \{0\} \cup \{n + 2 \mid n \in S\}$.

4.3–4 Let U be a set and $A \subseteq U$ be defined by induction as in Section 1.2. Show that A can be considered the least fixpoint of a continuous mapping $\Phi : U \rightarrow U$.

*4.3–5 *Knaster–Tarski Fixpoint Theorem*   Let $(D, \sqsubseteq)$ be a cpo.

(i) Show that every *monotonic* function $f : D \rightarrow D$ has a least fixpoint μf. (Sketch of the proof: let $\mathscr{E}_f$ be the set of all sub-cpo's of D which are closed under f and have the same least element as D. $\mathscr{E}_f$ has a least element E, and with help of Zorn's Lemma one can show that E has at least one maximal element m. By using the fact that the set $\{d \in D \mid d \sqsubseteq f(d)\}$ and, for every fixpoint e of f, the set $\{d \in D \mid d \sqsubseteq e\}$ belong to $\mathscr{E}_f$, one can conclude that $m = \mu f$.)

(ii) Show also that for every monotonic function $f : D \rightarrow D$ the fixpoint induction principle holds and hence also the Theorem of Park. (*Hint:* For an admissible predicate Φ which fulfils the hypothesis of the fixpoint induction principle, consider the set $\{d \in D \mid \Phi(d) = \text{true}\}$.)

4.3–6 Show that for a cpo $(D, \sqsubseteq)$ and a monotonic function $f : D \rightarrow D$ the least fixpoint of f (which exists by Exercise 4.3–5) does not necessarily agree with $\bigsqcup \{f^i(\bot) \mid i \in Nat\}$.

4.3–7 Let $(D, \sqsubseteq)$ be a cpo. Then by the fixpoint induction principle every continuous (and by Exercise 4.3–5 even every monotonic) function $f : D \rightarrow D$ has a least fixpoint μf, which is the least element of the set $\{d \in D \mid f(d) \sqsubseteq d\}$. Now conversely, let $(D, \sqsubseteq)$ be a (not necessarily complete) partial order and $f : D \rightarrow D$ a monotonic function for which the glb $y = \sqcap\{x \in D \mid f(x) \sqsubseteq x\}$ exists. Show that $\mu f = y$ and that Park's Theorem is valid.

HISTORICAL AND BIBLIOGRAPHICAL REMARKS

Several of the basic results presented above were already obtained in the framework of recursive function theory. The Fixpoint Theorem, for instance, is essentially the Recursion Theorem of Kleene (1952, p. 348). The study of the theory in the framework of cpo's is more recent and goes back to the development of denotational semantics for programming languages. Pioneering papers in this respect, presenting in particular the Fixpoint Induction Principle, are de Bakker and Scott (1969) and Scott (1970). Park's Theorem is in Park (1969).

There are a large number of publications on cpo's but most of them are not self-contained or are difficult to read. A good book treating the theory of cpo's in a somewhat more general framework is Stoy (1977); it also develops subjects such as self-application of functions which may be needed for the denotational semantics of programming languages more elaborate than those considered here. Another book on the same subject, although more difficult to read, is Milne and Strachey (1976).

5
Denotational Semantics

Now it is time to give denotational semantics to two of the programming languages introduced in Chapter 3. These descriptions will be facilitated by the use of the so-called λ-notation which is the subject of the first section. The denotational semantics of the language $\mathscr{L}_3$ of recursive programs, being very straightforward, is given first. The question of the equivalence to the operational semantics is answered affirmatively. The last section introduces the denotational semantics of the language $\mathscr{L}_2$ of while-programs. The denotational semantics for the language $\mathscr{L}_1$ of flowchart programs is omitted; one of the problems related to making denotational semantics for flowchart programs will be briefly mentioned in Section 11.1.

5.1 The λ-notation

The λ-notation is used in the literature with varying degrees of formality. In its most informal use it is merely a manner of denoting functions whose value is defined by a term. So a 'λ-term', say

$$[\lambda x . x + 1]$$

stands for the one-place function defined by the term $x + 1$ or, more precisely, for the function f defined by $f(x) = x + 1$. Notice among other things that in defining a function in the λ-notation one is spared the trouble of introducing a name for the function.

In this section a formal definition of a λ-notation is given in which syntax and semantics are kept strictly separate, as in the introduction to predicate logic in Chapter 2. In addition, the semantics will be defined specifically with cpo's and continuous functions. This is done because the λ-notation will be used only for the description of denotational semantics. The strict separation of syntax and semantics will, moreover, ease the description of the Logic for Computable Functions in Chapter 10. Finally, the λ-notation to be introduced is a 'typed' one in that a 'type' is associated with each λ-term. The reason for this is that untyped λ-notation is too general for the purposes of this book and leads to some difficult problems connected with self-application.

As usual, the first step in describing the syntax of the λ-notation is to fix the symbols. The auxiliary symbols are those of the set $\{\lambda, (,), [,], .., ,\}$. The only other symbols needed are collected in the basis.

A *basis* for the λ-notation is a triple $B = (BT, F, V)$ of disjoint sets of symbols where:

BT is a set of *basis types*;
F is a set of *function symbols*;
V is a set of *variables*.

Every function symbol and every variable is associated with a type. The set of all *types* over BT is inductively defined by:

(a) Every basis type is a type.
(b) If $\tau_1, \ldots, \tau_n, \tau$ are types $(n \geq 1)$, then $(\tau_1, \ldots, \tau_n \to \tau)$ is a type.

It is assumed that the set V contains an infinite number of variables of each type.

Note that since the variables are divided up by types, and since the types in a λ-notation depend on the basis, the variables have been made part of this basis. This differs from predicate logic where the variables are introduced as logical (that is, auxiliary) symbols.

DEFINITION 5.1 (Syntax of the λ-Notation) For a given basis the sets of λ-*terms* of each type are defined by simultaneous induction:

(a) Every function symbol of type τ and every variable of type τ is a λ-term of type τ.
(b) *Application* If $t_1, \ldots, t_n$ are λ-terms of types $\tau_1, \ldots, \tau_n$ respectively, $n \geq 1$, and u is a λ-term of type $(\tau_1, \ldots, \tau_n \to \tau)$, then $u(t_1, \ldots, t_n)$ is a λ-term of type τ.
λ-abstraction If $x_1, \ldots, x_n$ are *distinct* variables of type $\tau_1, \ldots, \tau_n$ respectively, $n \geq 1$, and t is a λ-term of type σ, then $[\lambda x_1, \ldots, x_n . t]$ is a λ-term of type $(\tau_1, \ldots, \tau_n \to \sigma)$. $\square$

The terms of predicate logic and of the programming language $\mathcal{L}_3$ can be considered special kinds of λ-terms. In the case of predicate logic there is only one basis type and in the case of recursive programs there are two basis types, b and d. In both cases the type of every term is a basis type while in λ-notation terms of a 'function type' such as $(\tau_1, \ldots, \tau_n \to \tau)$ appear.

With the syntax established it is time to define the semantics of the λ-notation. For that an interpretation of the basis is needed.

DEFINITION 5.2 (Interpretations) Let $B = (BT, F, V)$ be a basis for the λ-notation. An *interpretation* $\mathscr{I}$ of B consists of:

a cpo $(D_\tau, \sqsubseteq)$ for every basis type $\tau \in BT$;
a function $\mathscr{I}_0$ that gives every function symbol $f \in F$ of type τ an element $\mathscr{I}_0(f) \in D_\tau$; when τ is not a basis type but of the form $\tau = (\tau_1, \ldots, \tau_n \to \sigma)$, D_τ is taken to be

$$D_\tau = [D_{\tau_1} \times \cdots \times D_{\tau_n} \to D_\sigma] \qquad \square$$

Notice that $(D_\tau, \sqsubseteq)$ is a cpo for every type τ, as follows from the theory developed in Chapter 4, specifically Theorems 4.6 and 4.18. Hence $\mathscr{I}_0(f)$ is a continuous function whenever the type of f is not a basis type.

An *assignment* γ (for the basis B and the interpretation $\mathscr{I}$) is a function which maps every variable x of type τ to an element $\gamma(x) \in D_\tau$. The set of all assignments will be denoted $\Gamma_\mathscr{I}$—or Γ for short.

The set of assignments Γ is made into a partial order (in the now familiar way) by the definition:

$$\gamma \sqsubseteq \gamma' \qquad \text{iff } \gamma(x) \sqsubseteq \gamma'(x) \text{ for all variables } x \text{ from } V.$$

Notice that, strictly speaking, this definition involves different relations '$\sqsubseteq_\tau$' depending on the type τ of the variable x. This partial order $(\Gamma, \sqsubseteq)$ is complete with $(\sqcup S)(x) = \sqcup S(x)$ for every chain $S \subseteq \Gamma$ and every variable $x \in V$ as can be seen by a proof similar to that of Theorem 4.7. (Another—more direct—proof is obtained by considering an assignment γ as a family of functions $\gamma_\tau \colon V_\tau \to D_\tau$, one for each type τ. Here V_τ denotes the set of all variables of type τ. Then the partial order '$\sqsubseteq$' is just the order induced on the infinite Cartesian product of the cpo's $((V_\tau \to D_\tau), \sqsubseteq_\tau).)$

DEFINITION 5.3 (Semantics of the λ-Notation)   For every interpretation $\mathscr{I}$ of a basis for the λ-notation there is a semantic functional, also denoted $\mathscr{I}$, that maps every λ-term t of type τ to a function

$$\mathscr{I}(t) \colon \Gamma \to D_\tau$$

according to the following inductive definition:

(a) $\mathscr{I}(f)(\gamma) = \mathscr{I}_0(f)$ if f is a function symbol
   $\mathscr{I}(x)(\gamma) = \gamma(x)$ if x is a variable
(b) *Application*   With the notation of Definition 5.1 one has:

$$\mathscr{I}(u(t_1, \ldots, t_n))(\gamma) = \mathscr{I}(u)(\gamma)(\mathscr{I}(t_1)(\gamma), \ldots, \mathscr{I}(t_n)(\gamma))$$

λ-abstraction   With the notation of Definition 5.1:

$$\mathscr{I}([\lambda x_1, \ldots, x_n . u])(\gamma) = f_\gamma$$

where the function $f_\gamma \colon D_{\tau_1} \times \cdots \times D_{\tau_n} \to D_\sigma$ is defined by

$$f_\gamma(d_1, \ldots, d_n) = \mathscr{I}(u)(\gamma[x_1/d_1] \ldots [x_n/d_n]) \qquad \square$$

It is not obvious that in fact the semantic functional $\mathscr{I}$ so defined actually maps every λ-term t of type τ to a function $\mathscr{I}(t) \colon \Gamma \to D_\tau$. Take for example the case of a term t of type $\tau = (\tau_1, \ldots, \tau_n \to \sigma)$, where $\tau_1, \ldots, \tau_n$ and σ are all basis types. From the definition it is clear that $\mathscr{I}(t)(\gamma)$ is a function from $(D_{\tau_1} \times \cdots \times D_{\tau_n} \to D_\sigma)$ but not necessarily that $\mathscr{I}(t)(\gamma) \in D_\tau$ or, equivalently, that $\mathscr{I}(t)(\gamma)$ is a continuous function from $[D_{\tau_1} \times \cdots \times D_{\tau_n} \to D_\sigma]$. The non-trivial proof that $\mathscr{I}(t)(\gamma) \in D_\tau$ for all terms t of type τ and all assignments γ is given in Theorem 5.5. But first some simple examples illustrating the semantics of λ-terms are given; more examples follow after the theorem.

EXAMPLE 5.4   Let $B = (BT, F, V)$ be a basis with

$BT = \{nat, bool\}$
$F = \{0, 1, 2, \ldots, +, *, \ldots, <, \leq, \ldots\}$
$V = \{x, y, \ldots, p, q, \ldots, F, G, \ldots\}$,

where

$0, 1, 2, \ldots, x, y, \ldots$ are of type nat,
$p, q, \ldots$ are of type $bool$,
$+, *, \ldots, F, G, \ldots$ are of type $(nat, nat \to nat)$,
$<, \leq, \ldots$ are of type $(nat, nat \to bool)$.

Now let $\mathscr{I}$ be the usual interpretation with $D_{nat} = Nat_\omega$ and $D_{bool} = Bool_\omega$. Finally, let γ be an assignment with, say, $\gamma(x) = 4$. Infix notation is used where customary and $3, 4, \ldots, <, \ldots$ will be written instead of $\mathscr{I}_0(3), \mathscr{I}_0(4), \ldots, \mathscr{I}_0(<), \ldots$.

(1) $\mathscr{I}(3 < x)(\gamma) = \mathscr{I}(<)(\gamma)(\mathscr{I}(3)(\gamma), \mathscr{I}(x)(\gamma))$
$\qquad\qquad = \mathscr{I}_0(<)(\mathscr{I}_0(3), \gamma(x))$
$\qquad\qquad = \text{true}$

(2) $\mathscr{I}([\lambda x . 3 + x])(\gamma) = f_\gamma$,
$\qquad$ where $f_\gamma \colon Nat_\omega \to Nat_\omega$ is defined by

$\qquad\qquad f_\gamma(n) = \mathscr{I}(3 + x)(\gamma[x/n])$
$\qquad\qquad\qquad = \mathscr{I}(+)(\gamma[x/n])(\mathscr{I}(3)(\gamma[x/n]), \mathscr{I}(x)(\gamma[x/n]))$
$\qquad\qquad\qquad = \mathscr{I}_0(+)(\mathscr{I}_0(3), \gamma[x/n](x))$
$\qquad\qquad\qquad = 3 + n$

(3) $\mathscr{I}([\lambda x . 3 + x](5))(\gamma) = f_\gamma(5) \qquad$ (with f_γ defined as above)
$\qquad\qquad\qquad\qquad = 3 + 5$
$\qquad\qquad\qquad\qquad = 8$

(4) $\mathscr{I}([\lambda F . F(3, x)])(\gamma) = g_\gamma$,
$\qquad$ where $g_\gamma \colon (Nat_\omega^2 \to Nat_\omega) \to Nat_\omega$ is defined by

$\qquad\qquad g_\gamma(\text{op}) = \mathscr{I}(F(3, x))(\gamma[F/\text{op}])$
$\qquad\qquad\qquad = \mathscr{I}(F)(\gamma[F/\text{op}])(\mathscr{I}(3)(\gamma[F/\text{op}]), \mathscr{I}(x)(\gamma[F/\text{op}]))$
$\qquad\qquad\qquad = \text{op}(\mathscr{I}_0(3), \gamma[F/\text{op}](x))$
$\qquad\qquad\qquad = \text{op}(3, 4)$

(5) $\mathscr{I}([\lambda F . F(3, x)](*))(\gamma) = g_\gamma(*) \qquad$ (with g_γ defined as above)
$\qquad\qquad\qquad\qquad = 3 * 4$
$\qquad\qquad\qquad\qquad = 12$ $\qquad\qquad\qquad\qquad\qquad\qquad\qquad\qquad$ $\square$

Now the claim made in the definition of the semantics of the λ-notation that for any term t of type τ and any assignment γ, $\mathscr{I}(t)(\gamma) \in D_\tau$, is shown. The proof is simplified by proving simultaneously, that the function $\mathscr{I}(t)$ is continuous.

THEOREM 5.5 (Consistency of Definition 5.3)   Let $\mathscr{I}$ be an interpretation of a basis for the λ-notation. For every λ-term t of type τ

(1) $\mathscr{I}(t)(\gamma) \in D_\tau$ for every assignment $\gamma \in \Gamma$, and

(2) $\mathscr{I}(t): \Gamma \to D_\tau$ is continuous.

Proof. The proof is by simultaneous structural induction on the term t.

(a) If f is a function symbol of type τ, then, by definition, $\mathscr{I}(f)(\gamma) = \mathscr{I}_0(f)$ for all assignments γ. Then (1) holds since $\mathscr{I}_0(f) \in D_\tau$. Assertion (2) holds, because $\mathscr{I}(f)$ is a constant function and hence, continuous.

If x is a variable of type τ, then, by definition, $\mathscr{I}(x)(\gamma) = \gamma(x)$ for all assignments γ. Then (1) holds since $\gamma(x) \in D_\tau$. To prove (2), let S be a chain in Γ. Then

$$\begin{aligned} \mathscr{I}(x)(\sqcup S) &= (\sqcup S)(x) \\ &= \sqcup S(x) \qquad \text{(by the remark about the cpo } (\Gamma, \sqsubseteq)) \\ &= \sqcup \mathscr{I}(x)(S). \end{aligned}$$

(b) *Application*   With the notation of Definition 5.1 and $t = u(t_1, \ldots, t_n)$,

$$\mathscr{I}(t)(\gamma) = \mathscr{I}(u)(\gamma)(\mathscr{I}(t_1)(\gamma), \ldots, \mathscr{I}(t_n)(\gamma))$$

for every assignment γ. By induction hypothesis

$$\mathscr{I}(u)(\gamma) \in [D_{\tau_1} \times \cdots \times D_{\tau_n} \to D_\tau]$$

and $\mathscr{I}(t_i)(\gamma) \in D_{\tau_i}$ for $i = 1, \ldots, n$.

Clearly, $\mathscr{I}(t)(\gamma) \in D_\tau$, so (1) holds. Next, define the function

$$g: \Gamma \to D_{\tau_1} \times \cdots \times D_{\tau_n}$$

by

$$g(\gamma) = (\mathscr{I}(t_1)(\gamma), \ldots, \mathscr{I}(t_n)(\gamma)).$$

This function is continuous by Theorem 4.20 since each of the $\mathscr{I}(t_i)$ is continuous, by induction hypothesis. Using the continuous function 'apply' defined after Theorem 4.23, $\mathscr{I}(t)(\gamma)$ can be rewritten:

$$\mathscr{I}(t)(\gamma) = \text{apply}(\mathscr{I}(u)(\gamma), g(\gamma)).$$

Since by induction hypothesis $\mathscr{I}(u)$ is continuous and since it has just been shown that g is continuous, $\mathscr{I}(t)$ is continuous, so (2) holds.

λ-abstraction   With the notation of Definition 5.1 and $t = [\lambda x_1, \ldots, x_n . u]$, for every assignment γ it is the case that $\mathscr{I}(t)(\gamma)$ is the function from $D_{\tau_1} \times \cdots \times D_{\tau_n}$ to D_σ defined by

$$\mathscr{I}(t)(\gamma)(d_1, \ldots, d_n) = \mathscr{I}(u)(\gamma[x_1/d_1] \ldots [x_n/d_n]).$$

(Notice that $\mathscr{I}(t)(\gamma)(d_1, \ldots, d_n) \in D_\sigma$ since, for every assignment γ', $\mathscr{I}(u)(\gamma') \in D_\sigma$ by induction hypothesis.) Now introduce the function

$$h: \Gamma \times (D_{\tau_1} \times \cdots \times D_{\tau_n}) \to D_\sigma$$

defined by

$$h(\gamma, (d_1, \ldots, d_n)) = \mathscr{I}(t)(\gamma)(d_1, \ldots, d_n).$$

Then for every assignment γ and every $(d_1, \ldots, d_n)$ from

$$D_{\tau_1} \times \cdots \times D_{\tau_n}: h(\gamma, (d_1, \ldots, d_n)) = \mathscr{I}(u)(\gamma[x_1/d_1] \ldots [x_n/d_n])$$
$$= \mathscr{I}(u)(\text{subst}(\gamma, (d_1, \ldots, d_n))),$$

where subst: $\Gamma \times (D_{\tau_1} \times \cdots \times D_{\tau_n}) \to \Gamma$ is defined by

$$\text{subst}(\gamma, (d_1, \ldots, d_n)) = \gamma[x_1/d_1] \ldots [x_n/d_n].$$

The function subst is continuous (Exercise 4.2–5). Since $\mathscr{I}(u)$ is also continuous by induction hypothesis, the function h is continuous (another application of Theorem 4.21). Now $\mathscr{I}(t)$ is nothing other than the curried version of the function h, hence, by Theorem 4.23,

$$\mathscr{I}(t) \in [\Gamma \to [D_{\tau_1} \times \cdots \times D_{\tau_n} \to D_\sigma]].$$

Assertions (1) and (2) follow immediately. $\qquad\qquad\qquad\qquad\qquad\square$

EXAMPLE 5.6 (1) Let $x_1, \ldots, x_n$ be variables and let u be some λ-term of the appropriate type. Then for all assignments γ

$$\mathscr{I}([\lambda x_1, \ldots, x_n . u(x_1, \ldots, x_n)])(\gamma) = \mathscr{I}(u)(\gamma).$$

A specific instance of this is:

$$\mathscr{I}([\lambda x, y . x + y])(\gamma) = \mathscr{I}_0(+).$$

(2) With appropriate variables F and x, and interpretation $\mathscr{I}$, the apply function can be expressed in λ-notation by

$$\text{apply} = \mathscr{I}([\lambda F, x . F(x)])(\gamma)$$

for any assignment γ.

(3) Let $(D_1, \sqsubseteq)$, $(D_2, \sqsubseteq)$, and $(E, \sqsubseteq)$ be cpo's. Let the function curry: $[D_1 \times D_2 \to E] \to [D_1 \to [D_2 \to E]]$ be the function defined in Section 4.2 which takes a function $f \in [D_1 \times D_2 \to E]$ of two arguments and returns a function $f^c \in [D_1 \to [D_2 \to E]]$ of one argument whose value is yet another function. With appropriate variables F, x, y, and interpretation $\mathscr{I}$, the (two-place) function curry can be expressed in the λ-notation by

$$\text{curry} = \mathscr{I}([\lambda F . [\lambda x . [\lambda y . F(x, y)]]])(\gamma)$$

for any assignment γ. By Theorem 4.23, the curry function is continuous:

$$\text{curry} \in [[D_1 \times D_2 \to E] \to [D_1 \to [D_2 \to E]]].$$

The inverse function is also continuous since it can also be expressed as a λ-term:

$$[\lambda F . [\lambda x, y . F(x)(y)]].$$

(From this it is seen that the cpo's $[D_1 \times D_2 \to E]$ and $[D_1 \to [D_2 \to E]]$ are connected by an isomorphism. This makes precise and stronger the statement already made that every two-place function—and, in general, every n-ary function—can be replaced by a one-place function.) □

In the previous examples it was made clear that the interpretation of a λ-term like

$$[\lambda F . [\lambda x . F(x)]]$$

has a value which is independent of the assignment. This is the result of the Coincidence Theorem, so-called because of its resemblance to the theorem of the same name in the predicate logic. The Renaming Theorem and Substitution Theorem of the predicate logic also have an analogue in the λ-notation. Before these theorems can be given, the syntactic notions of bound and free occurrences of a variable must be given their meaning in the λ-notation.

Let (for a given basis) t be a λ-term and x a variable. An occurrence of x in t is said to be *bound* if it appears in a subterm of t of the form $[\lambda x . \ldots]$. An occurrence which is not bound is called *free*.

THEOREM 5.7 (Coincidence Theorem) Let $\mathscr{I}$ be an interpretation of a basis for the λ-notation and let t be a λ-term. If two assignments γ and γ' agree on all variables that occur free in t, then $\mathscr{I}(t)(\gamma) = \mathscr{I}(t)(\gamma')$.

Proof. The proof proceeds by structural induction; the reader is entrusted with the details. □

In particular, for λ-terms with no free variables (called *closed λ-terms*) the value of $\mathscr{I}(t)(\gamma)$ is independent of the assignment γ.

THEOREM 5.8 (Renaming Theorem) Let $\mathscr{I}$ be an interpretation of a basis for the λ-notation. Let t be a λ-term, x a variable which occurs bound in t, and x' a variable of the same type which does not occur in t at all. Set t' to be the λ-term which is obtained by replacing every bound occurrence of x in t by x'. Then for all assignments γ

$$\mathscr{I}(t)(\gamma) = \mathscr{I}(t')(\gamma).$$

(The proof is left to Exercise 5.1–3.) □

Let s, t be λ-terms and x a variable of the same type as t. The λ-term created by *substituting* t for x in s, denoted s^t_x, may now be defined as in Definition 2.9.

THEOREM 5.9 (Substitution Theorem) Let $\mathscr{I}$ be an interpretation of a basis for the λ-notation. Let s, t be λ-terms and x a variable of the same type as t. Then for all assignments γ

$$\mathcal{I}(s_x^t)(\gamma) = \mathcal{I}(s)(\gamma[x/\mathcal{I}(t)(\gamma)]) \qquad (= \mathcal{I}([\lambda x.s](t))(\gamma))$$

(The proof is left to Exercise 5.1–3.) □

5.2 Denotational Semantics of Recursive Programs

In many of the examples given in the last chapter (for instance, Example 4.15) a functional $\Phi: (Nat_\omega \to Nat_\omega) \to (Nat_\omega \to Nat_\omega)$ resembling a recursive program appeared as if out of thin air. This functional proved to be continuous and the least fixpoint of Φ had exactly the semantics of the program. This will be exploited to provide another definition of the semantics of the programming language $\mathscr{L}_3$—the denotational semantics. For that purpose it must be shown that every recursive program can be given such a functional and that this functional is continuous. The λ-notation allows both these objectives to be met with elegance. The functional given a recursive program can be simply and exactly described. The continuity of the functional (and hence the existence of the least fixpoint) follows immediately from Theorem 5.5.

Now consider the programming language $\mathscr{L}_3$ as defined in Section 3.3, with variable sets V and W and basis F (a set of functions). Next define a basis $B = (BT, F', V')$ for the λ-notation by setting

(1) $BT = \{b, d\}$;
(2) $F' = F$, where the type of every function symbol is carried over;
(3) $V' = V \cup W$, where any variable $x \in V$ gets the type d and any s-ary function symbol $F \in W$ gets the type $(d, \ldots, d \to d)$, where $d, \ldots, d$ stands for a sequence of s symbols d.

Furthermore, let $\mathcal{I} = (D, \mathcal{I}_0)$ be an interpretation of the basis F for the-programming language $\mathscr{L}_3$. Then an interpretation of the basis B for the λ-notation is easily created as follows. The cpo's corresponding to the basis types b and d are the flat cpo's $Bool_\omega$ and D_ω respectively. The interpretation of the function symbols of $F' = F$ is nothing more than that given by $\mathcal{I}_0$. To see that this is in fact an interpretation for a λ-notation it needs only be recalled that $\mathcal{I}_0$ maps the function symbols to monotonic functions: since in flat cpo's there are only finite chains these functions are continuous. The interpretation for the λ-notation thus defined will also be denoted by $\mathcal{I}$.

EXAMPLE 5.10 Consider a basis of $\mathscr{L}_3$ containing the function symbols *if-then-else*, $=, +, -, 1, 2$. If x, y are variables from V and if G is a function variable from W then

$$if \ x = y \ then \ x + 1 \ else \ G(y - 2) \ fi$$

is a term of type d in the programming language. This term is a λ-term of type d in the λ-notation described above (with infix notation). From this term, one can build another λ-term

$$[\lambda x, y . if \ x = y \ then \ x + 1 \ else \ G(y - 2) \ fi]$$

which given an interpretation for $\mathscr{L}_3$ can be interpreted in the λ-notation as a function $f \in [D_\omega^2 \to D_\omega]$ which depends on the value of the assignment for the (function) variable G. Likewise

$$[\lambda G \cdot [\lambda x, y \cdot if \ x = y \ then \ x + 1 \ else \ G(y - 2) \ fi]]$$

can be interpreted as a functional from $[[D_\omega \to D_\omega] \to [D_\omega^2 \to D_\omega]]$. $\qquad \square$

Now it is simple to associate a functional to any recursive program.

DEFINITION 5.11 (The Semantic Functional $\Phi(S)$) Let $\mathscr{I} = (D, \mathscr{I}_0)$ be an interpretation of a basis for the programming language $\mathscr{L}_3$ and let S be the recursive program defined by the set of recursive equations

$$F_i(x_{i1}, \ldots, x_{is_i}) \Leftarrow t_i$$

for $i = 1, \ldots, n$, $n \geq 1$ (and by a main function symbol). Put

$$D^* = [D_\omega^{s_1} \to D_\omega] \times \cdots \times [D_\omega^{s_n} \to D_\omega].$$

The semantic functional $\Phi_\mathscr{I}(S) \colon D^* \to D^*$—$\Phi(S)$ for short—associated with the recursive program S (and the interpretation $\mathscr{I}$) is defined in each component by using projection functions as follows:

$$pr_1 \circ \Phi_\mathscr{I}(S) = \mathscr{I}([\lambda F_1, \ldots, F_n \cdot [\lambda x_{11}, \ldots, x_{1s_1} \cdot t_1]])(\gamma)$$
$$\vdots$$
$$pr_n \circ \Phi_\mathscr{I}(S) = \mathscr{I}([\lambda F_1, \ldots, F_n \cdot [\lambda x_{n1}, \ldots, x_{ns_n} \cdot t_n]])(\gamma),$$

where $\gamma \in \Gamma_\mathscr{I}$ is an arbitrary assignment. $\qquad \square$

Note that in the case of a recursive program S consisting of a single recursive equation

$$F(x_1, \ldots, x_s) \Leftarrow t$$

the definition of the semantical functional

$$\Phi_\mathscr{I}(S) \colon [D_\omega^s \to D_\omega] \to [D_\omega^s \to D_\omega]$$

of S reduces to:

$$\Phi_\mathscr{I}(S) = \mathscr{I}([\lambda F \cdot [\lambda x_1, \ldots, x_s \cdot t]])(\gamma)$$

where $\gamma \in \Gamma_\mathscr{I}$ is an arbitrary assignment.

Now all the work that has been done with cpo's and the λ-notation can finally be applied to see that this semantic functional is the sort of thing that is wanted. First of all, each of the $pr_i \circ \Phi_\mathscr{I}(S)$ is independent of the assignment γ chosen in the definition. This is by the Coincidence Theorem because the λ-terms are all closed. Second, the domain of $\Phi_\mathscr{I}(S)$ is indeed D^*, and D^* constitutes a cpo. By examining the type of the λ-terms above one obtains, by Theorem 5.5, that each $pr_i \circ \Phi_\mathscr{I}(S)$ belongs to $[D^* \to [D_\omega^{s_i} \to D_\omega]]$. In particular this means each $pr_i \circ \Phi_\mathscr{I}(S)$ is continuous. Third, since each of the $pr_i \circ \Phi_\mathscr{I}(S)$ is continuous, by Theorem 4.20, $\Phi_\mathscr{I}(S)$ is continuous and so the least fixpoint $\mu\Phi_\mathscr{I}(S)$ exists. By the Fixpoint Theorem,

$$\mu\Phi_\mathscr{I}(S) = \sqcup\{(\Phi_\mathscr{I}(S))^i(\bot, \ldots, \bot) \mid i \geq 0\}.$$

Moreover $pr_i(\mu\Phi_\mathscr{I}(S)) \in [D_\omega^{s_i} \to D_\omega]$.

DEFINITION 5.12 (Denotational Semantics of $\mathscr{L}_3$)   Let S be the recursive program over a basis F defined by the set of recursive equations

$$F_i(x_{i1}, \ldots, x_{is_i}) \Leftarrow t_i$$

for $i = 1, \ldots, n$ and the main function variable F_k, $1 \le k \le n$. Let $\mathscr{I} = (D, \mathscr{I}_0)$ be an interpretation of F and $\Phi_{\mathscr{I}}(S)$ the semantic functional associated with S and $\mathscr{I}$. The *meaning* of S (in $\mathscr{I}$) is the function $\mathscr{M}_{\mathscr{I}}(S): D^{s_k} \rightarrow D$—or $\mathscr{M}(S)$ for short— defined by:

$$\mathscr{M}_{\mathscr{I}}(S)(d_1, \ldots, d_{s_k}) = \begin{cases} \mathrm{pr}_k(\mu\Phi_{\mathscr{I}}(S))(d_1, \ldots, d_{s_k}) \text{ if this value is different from } \omega; \\ \text{undefined otherwise.} \end{cases} \qquad \square$$

Note that in the case of a recursive program S consisting of a single recursive equation

$$F(x_1, \ldots, x_s) \Leftarrow t$$

the definition of the meaning $\mathscr{M}_{\mathscr{I}}(S): D^s \rightarrow D$ reduces to

$$\mathscr{M}_{\mathscr{I}}(S)(d_1, \ldots, d_s) = \begin{cases} \mu\Phi_{\mathscr{I}}(S)(d_1, \ldots, d_s) \text{ if this value is different from } \omega; \\ \text{undefined otherwise.} \end{cases}$$

EXAMPLE 5.13   Let S be the recursive program

$$F(x) \Leftarrow \text{if } x = 0 \text{ then } 1 \text{ else } x * F(x - 1) \text{ fi.}$$

Then for the usual interpretation, $\mathscr{M}(S)$ is the restriction to Nat of the function

$$\mu\mathscr{I}([\lambda F . [\lambda x . \text{if } x = 0 \text{ then } 1 \text{ else } x * F(x - 1) \text{ fi}]])(\gamma)$$

for an arbitrary assignment γ. Hence, by Example 4.25 $\mathscr{M}(S)$ is the factorial function. $\qquad \square$

EXAMPLE 5.14   Let S be the recursive program defined by

$$F_1(x) \Leftarrow \text{if } x = 0 \text{ then } 0 \text{ else } F_2(x - 1) \text{ fi}$$

$$F_2(x) \Leftarrow \text{if } x = 0 \text{ then } 1 \text{ else } F_1(x - 1) \text{ fi}$$

with F_1 as the main function variable (see Example 3.13(2)). Let $\mathscr{I}$ be the usual interpretation. Then

$$\mathscr{M}(S) = f_1 \,|\, Nat$$

with $(f_1, f_2) = \mu\Phi(S)$ and the functional $\Phi(S): [[Nat_\omega \rightarrow Nat_\omega]^2 \rightarrow [Nat_\omega \rightarrow Nat_\omega]^2]$ defined by

$$\mathrm{pr}_1 \circ \Phi(S) = \mathscr{I}([\lambda F_1, F_2 . [\lambda x . \text{if } x = 0 \text{ then } 0 \\ \text{else } F_2(x - 1) \text{ fi}]])(\gamma)$$

$$\mathrm{pr}_2 \circ \Phi(S) = \mathscr{I}([\lambda F_1, F_2 . [\lambda x . \text{if } x = 0 \text{ then } 1 \\ \text{else } F_1(x - 1) \text{ fi}]])(\gamma)$$

for an arbitrary assignment γ.

In addition it is easy to prove (by induction on i) that, for all $i \in Nat$, $\Phi(S)^i(\bot, \bot) = (f_1^{(i)}, f_2^{(i)})$ where

$$f_1^{(i)}(n) = \begin{cases} 0 & \text{if } n \in Nat, n < i, \text{ and } n \text{ even} \\ 1 & \text{if } n \in Nat, n < i, \text{ and } n \text{ odd} \\ \omega & \text{otherwise} \end{cases}$$

$$f_2^{(i)}(n) = \begin{cases} 1 & \text{if } n \in Nat, n < i, \text{ and } n \text{ even} \\ 0 & \text{if } n \in Nat, n < i, \text{ and } n \text{ odd} \\ \omega & \text{otherwise.} \end{cases}$$

Therefore it is easy to see that for all $n \in Nat_\omega$:

$$\mathrm{pr}_1(\mu\Phi(S))(n) = f_1(n) = \begin{cases} 0 & \text{if } n \in Nat \text{ and } n \text{ even} \\ 1 & \text{if } n \in Nat \text{ and } n \text{ odd} \\ \omega & \text{if } n = \omega \end{cases}$$

and $\mathrm{pr}_2(\mu\Phi(S))(n)$ is similar. $\qquad\square$

*5.3 Equivalence of the Operational and Denotational Semantics of Recursive Programs

In Section 3.3 a definition was given for the meaning of a recursive program with the help of operational semantics. It remains to see if the definition just given with the help of the denotational semantics is the same. Before the proof of equivalence is given, the connection between the terms of a computation sequence (from Section 3.3) and the semantic functional $\Phi(S)$ (of Definition 5.11) is worked out.

LEMMA 5.15   Let S be the recursive program defined by the system of recursive equations

$$F_i(x_{i1}, \ldots, x_{is_i}) \Leftarrow t_i$$

for $i = 1, \ldots, n$ and the main function symbol F_k. Let $\mathscr{I} = (D, \mathscr{I}_0)$ be an appropriate interpretation and

$$u_0, u_1, u_2, \ldots$$

be a computation for the input vector $(d_1, \ldots, d_{s_k}) \in D^{s_k}$. Finally let $\Phi_{\mathscr{I}}(S): D^* \to D^*$ be the semantic functional of Definition 5.11. Then for every $i \in Nat$ for which the term u_i exists and for every assignment γ:

$$\mathscr{I}(u_i)(\gamma) = \mathrm{pr}_k(\Phi_{\mathscr{I}}(S)^i(\gamma(F_1), \ldots, \gamma(F_n)))(d_1, \ldots, d_{s_k}).$$

(Recall that u_i exists for every $i \in Nat$ only when the computation is infinite.)

Remark. This lemma can be intuitively understood to say that u_i is that term which one obtains after i substitutions and subsequent simplifications. $\Phi_{\mathscr{I}}(S)$ corresponds to the use of one substitution, so $\Phi_{\mathscr{I}}(S)^i$ corresponds to the use of i

successive substitutions. The lemma expresses that u_i and the value of $\Phi_{\mathscr{I}}(S)^i$ are the same.

Proof. The proof is carried out by induction over the number i.

Induction basis By definition $u_0 = F_k(c_1, \ldots, c_{s_k})$, where $\mathscr{I}_0(c_j) = d_j$ for $j = 1, \ldots, s_k$. Hence

$$\mathscr{I}(u_0)(\gamma) = \gamma(F_k)(d_1, \ldots, d_{s_k}).$$

On the other hand

$$\mathrm{pr}_k(\Phi(S)^0(\gamma(F_1), \ldots, \gamma(F_n)))(d_1, \ldots, d_{s_k}) = \mathrm{pr}_k(\gamma(F_1), \ldots, \gamma(F_n))(d_1, \ldots, d_{s_k})$$
$$= \gamma(F_k)(d_1, \ldots, d_{s_k}).$$

Induction step Assume the property holds for i. From the definition of a computation in Section 3.3, $u_i \Rightarrow u_{i+1}$, where $\mathscr{S}(u_i) \overset{*}{\twoheadrightarrow} u_{i+1}$ and u_{i+1} is maximally simplified. So, by the definitions of the relation '$\overset{*}{\twoheadrightarrow}$' and of a simplification rule, for every assignment γ:

$$\mathscr{I}(u_{i+1})(\gamma) = \mathscr{I}(\mathscr{S}(u_i))(\gamma). \tag{1}$$

By the Substitution Theorem 3.24,

$$\mathscr{I}(\mathscr{S}(u_i))(\gamma) = \mathscr{I}(u_i)(\gamma[F_1/g_1] \ldots [F_n/g_n]) \tag{2}$$

where for $j = 1, \ldots, n$, $g_j \colon D_\omega^{s_j} \to D_\omega$ is defined by

$$g_j(e_1, \ldots, e_{s_j}) = \mathscr{I}(t_j)(\gamma[x_{j1}/e_1] \ldots [x_{js_j}/e_{s_j}]).$$

That is, by the definition of the semantics of the λ-notation

$$g_j = \mathscr{I}([\lambda x_{j1}, \ldots, x_{js_j} . t_j])(\gamma). \tag{3}$$

(1), (2), and the induction hypothesis lead to

$$\mathscr{I}(u_{i+1})(\gamma) = \mathrm{pr}_k(\Phi(S)^i(g_1, \ldots, g_n))(d_1, \ldots, d_{s_k}). \tag{4}$$

Now for $j = 1, \ldots, n$ and every assignment γ':

$$\mathrm{pr}_j(\Phi(S)(\gamma(F_1), \ldots, \gamma(F_n)))$$
$$= \mathscr{I}([\lambda F_1, \ldots, F_n . [\lambda x_{j1}, \ldots, x_{js_j} . t_j]])(\gamma')(\gamma(F_1), \ldots, \gamma(F_n))$$
$$\text{(by the definition of } \Phi(S))$$

$$= \mathscr{I}([\lambda x_{j1}, \ldots, x_{js_j} . t_j])(\gamma'[F_1/\gamma(F_1)] \ldots [F_n/\gamma(F_n)])$$
$$\text{(by the semantics of } \lambda\text{-notation)}$$

$$= \mathscr{I}([\lambda x_{j1}, \ldots, x_{js_j} . t_j])(\gamma)$$
(by the Coincidence Theorem, because the only variables occurring free in $[\lambda x_{j1}, \ldots, x_{js_j} . t_j]$ are $F_1, \ldots, F_n$)

$$= g_j. \quad \text{(by (3))}$$

104

Equation (4) can now be rewritten:

$$\mathscr{I}(u_{i+1})(\gamma) = \mathrm{pr}_k(\Phi(\mathrm{S})^i(\mathrm{pr}_1(\Phi(\mathrm{S})(\gamma(\mathrm{F}_1), \ldots, \gamma(\mathrm{F}_n))),$$
$$\vdots$$
$$\mathrm{pr}_n(\Phi(\mathrm{S})(\gamma(\mathrm{F}_1), \ldots, \gamma(\mathrm{F}_n))))(d_1, \ldots, d_{s_k})$$
$$= \mathrm{pr}_k(\Phi(\mathrm{S})^{i+1}(\gamma(\mathrm{F}_1), \ldots, \gamma(\mathrm{F}_n)))(d_1, \ldots, d_{s_k}). \qquad \square$$

THEOREM 5.16 (Equivalence of Operational and Denotational Semantics)   The definition of the meaning of a recursive program with help of the operational semantics (Definition 3.27) and its definition with help of the denotational semantics (Definition 5.12) are equivalent.

Proof. Let S, F_k, $\mathscr{I} = (D, \mathscr{I}_0)$, $\Phi(\mathrm{S})$, and the computation $u_0, u_1, \ldots$ be as in the previous lemma. Put $f_k = \mathrm{pr}_k(\mu\Phi(\mathrm{S}))$. Then

$$f_k = \mathrm{pr}_k(\sqcup\{\Phi(\mathrm{S})^i(\bot, \ldots, \bot) \mid i \in Nat\}) \qquad \text{(by the Fixpoint Theorem)}$$
$$= \sqcup\{\mathrm{pr}_k(\Phi(\mathrm{S})^i(\bot, \ldots, \bot)) \mid i \in Nat\} \qquad \text{(since } \mathrm{pr}_k \text{ is continuous)}$$

so for every d from D^{s_k}:

$$f_k(d) = (\sqcup\{\mathrm{pr}_k(\Phi(\mathrm{S})^i(\bot, \ldots, \bot)) \mid i \in Nat\})(d)$$
$$= \sqcup\{\mathrm{pr}_k(\Phi(\mathrm{S})^i(\bot, \ldots, \bot))(d) \mid i \in Nat\} \qquad \text{(by Theorem 4.3)} \qquad (1)$$

From the definitions of the meaning $\mathscr{M}(\mathrm{S})$ it remains to show:

(i) If the computation $u_0, u_1, \ldots$ is finite ending in the term u_m, then $\mathscr{I}_0(u_m) = f_k(d) \neq \omega$.
(ii) If the computation is infinite, then $f_k(d) = \omega$.

(Proof of (i).)   By the definition of $\mathscr{I}$, $\mathscr{I}(u_m)(\gamma) = \mathscr{I}_0(u_m)$ for all assignments γ. In particular, $\mathscr{I}_0(u_m) = \mathscr{I}(u_m)(\bot_\Gamma)$ where $\bot_\Gamma$ is the least element of the cpo Γ or, equivalently, the everywhere-ω assignment of Section 3.3 (see Lemma 3.21). Since for $i = 1, \ldots, n$, $\bot_\Gamma(\mathrm{F}_i) = \bot$, applying Lemma 5.15 yields:

$$\mathscr{I}(u_m)(\bot_\Gamma) = \mathrm{pr}_k(\Phi(\mathrm{S})^m(\bot, \ldots, \bot))(d).$$

So the chain in D_ω

$$\{\mathrm{pr}_k(\Phi(\mathrm{S})^i(\bot, \ldots, \bot))(d) \mid i \in Nat\}$$

contains the element $\mathscr{I}_0(u_m) \neq \omega$. Thus the lub of this chain is $\mathscr{I}_0(u_m)$. By equation (1) above, this lub is $f_k(d)$. Therefore $\mathscr{I}_0(u_m) = f_k(d) \neq \omega$.

(Proof of (ii).)   By Lemma 3.21 $\mathscr{I}(u_i)(\bot_\Gamma) = \omega$ for all $i \in Nat$.
On the other hand, from Lemma 5.15

$$\mathscr{I}(u_i)(\bot_\Gamma) = \mathrm{pr}_k(\Phi(\mathrm{S})^i(\bot, \ldots, \bot))(d)$$

for all $i \in Nat$. So

$$\{\mathrm{pr}_k(\Phi(\mathrm{S})^i(\bot, \ldots, \bot))(d) \mid i \in Nat\} = \{\omega\}$$

and by (1)

$$f_k(d) = \sqcup\{\omega\} = \omega.$$ □

5.4 Denotational Semantics of while-Programs

The semantics of while-programs will be inductively defined using the inductive definition of their syntax. This definition will make use of the Fixpoint Theorem. Again, the applicability of this theorem requires the underlying functions to be continuous and this in turn requires the underlying domain to be a cpo.

As in Section 2.2 let V be the set of variables and B a basis for the predicate logic. Furthermore, let $\mathcal{I} = (D, \mathcal{I}_0)$ be an interpretation of this basis and let Σ be the set of all states. In order to turn the set Σ into a cpo it is extended by an element ω yielding the flat cpo Σ_ω. This element ω stands for the 'undefined state'. Note that, while ω is an element of Σ_ω, it is *not* a function from $(V \to D)$.

An alternative way to turn Σ into a cpo is to extend the domain D by an 'undefined value' ω leading to the flat cpo D_ω, and to consider (instead of Σ_ω) the (non-flat) cpo $(V \to D_\omega)$ of functions. This solution was not adopted here for two reasons. First, the cpo $(V \to D_\omega)$ contains a lot of superfluous 'states', namely those which are 'defined' for some variables and 'undefined' for others. Second, extending the domain D by an undefined value only makes sense in a programming language such as $\mathcal{L}_3$ in which the computation of terms may not terminate, but it does not in a language such as $\mathcal{L}_2$ in which only statements possess this property.

The meaning $\mathcal{M}_\mathcal{I}(S): \Sigma \to \Sigma$ of a while-program S is deduced from a total function $\mathcal{M}_\mathcal{I}^\omega(S): \Sigma_\omega \to \Sigma_\omega$, called '$\omega$-extended meaning', in a way similar to the deduction of $\mathcal{M}_\mathcal{I}(S)$ from $\mathrm{pr}_k(\mu\Phi_\mathcal{I}(S))$ in Definition 5.12. Hence, the real effort is done by the function $\mathcal{M}_\mathcal{I}^\omega(S)$ which is defined next.

DEFINITION 5.17 (ω-Extended Meaning) Let S be a while-program over a given basis and $\mathcal{I}$ an interpretation of this basis. The ω-*extended meaning* of S in $\mathcal{I}$ is the function $\mathcal{M}_\mathcal{I}^\omega(S): \Sigma_\omega \to \Sigma_\omega$, or $\mathcal{M}^\omega(S)$ for short, defined by structural induction on S as follows (using the notation of Definition 3.7):

(a) *Assignment statement*

$$\mathcal{M}_\mathcal{I}^\omega(x := t)(\sigma) = \begin{cases} \sigma[x/\mathcal{I}(t)(\sigma)] & \text{if } \sigma \neq \omega \\ \omega & \text{if } \sigma = \omega \end{cases}$$

  for all $\sigma \in \Sigma_\omega$.

(b) *Composed statement*

$$\mathcal{M}_\mathcal{I}^\omega(S_1 ; S_2) = \mathcal{M}_\mathcal{I}^\omega(S_2) \circ \mathcal{M}_\mathcal{I}^\omega(S_1)$$

  where '$\circ$' denotes composition.

Conditional statement

$\mathscr{M}_\mathscr{I}^\omega(if\ e\ then\ S_1\ else\ S_2\ fi)(\sigma)$

$$= \begin{cases} \text{if-then-else}(\mathscr{I}(e)(\sigma),\ \mathscr{M}_\mathscr{I}^\omega(S_1)(\sigma),\ \mathscr{M}_\mathscr{I}^\omega(S_2)(\sigma)) & \text{if } \sigma \neq \omega \\ \omega & \text{if } \sigma = \omega, \end{cases}$$

for all $\sigma \in \Sigma_\omega$.

While-statement

$\mathscr{M}_\mathscr{I}^\omega(while\ e\ do\ S_1\ od) = \mu\Phi$ where the functional Φ:

$$[\Sigma_\omega \to \Sigma_\omega] \to [\Sigma_\omega \to \Sigma_\omega]$$

is defined by

$$\Phi(f)(\sigma) = \begin{cases} \text{if-then-else}(\mathscr{I}(e)(\sigma),\ f(\mathscr{M}_\mathscr{I}^\omega(S_1)(\sigma)),\ \sigma) & \text{if } \sigma \neq \omega \\ \omega & \text{if } \sigma = \omega \end{cases}$$

for all $f \in [\Sigma_\omega \to \Sigma_\omega]$ and $\sigma \in \Sigma_\omega$. $\qquad\qquad\square$

Several things must be stressed about this definition. First, the functions $\mathscr{I}(t)$ and $\mathscr{I}(e)$ are the functions of predicate logic (with domain Σ, not Σ_ω). Next, though the inductive definition of the syntax of while-programs is not free (see Section 3.2), the function $\mathscr{M}_\mathscr{I}^\omega(S)$ is well-defined; this is a direct result from the associativity of the composition used in the definition of $\mathscr{M}_\mathscr{I}^\omega(S_1 ; S_2)$ (see Exercise 5.4–2). Third, in order for the definition of $\mathscr{M}_\mathscr{I}^\omega(while\ e\ do\ S'\ od)$ to be meaningful it must be shown that the functional Φ actually has a least fixpoint. This latter property is proved in the following theorem; the proof is simplified by proving simultaneously that the function $\mathscr{M}_\mathscr{I}^\omega(S)$ is continuous.

THEOREM 5.18 (Consistency of Definition 5.17)   For every while-program S

(1) $\mathscr{M}^\omega(S)$ is well defined.
(2) $\mathscr{M}^\omega(S)$ is continuous.

Proof. The proof is by structural induction on S.

Assignment statement   Assume S has the form $x := t$. Assertion (1) holds trivially. For proving (2) notice that $\mathscr{M}^\omega(x := t)$ is strict and hence continuous.

Composed statement   Assume S has the form $S_1 ; S_2$. Assertion (1) holds as, by induction hypothesis $\mathscr{M}^\omega(S_1)$ and $\mathscr{M}^\omega(S_2)$ are well defined. Assertion (2) holds because $\mathscr{M}^\omega(S_1)$ and $\mathscr{M}^\omega(S_2)$ are continuous by induction hypothesis and because composition preserves continuity (Theorem 4.21).

Conditional statement   When S is a conditional statement, assertion (1) is proved as in the case of a composed statement and assertion (2) as in the case of an assignment statement.

While-statement   Assume S has the form *while e do* S_1 *od* and let Φ be as in Definition 5.17.

First note that $\mathcal{M}^\omega(S_1)$ is well defined. In order to prove that Φ indeed maps the set $[\Sigma_\omega \to \Sigma_\omega]$ of continuous functions into itself and, moreover, that Φ is itself continuous, it is now simply expressed as a λ-term:

$$\Phi = [\lambda F . [\lambda\sigma . \textit{if } \sigma = \sigma$$
$$\textit{then if } \mathcal{I}(e)(\sigma) \textit{ then } F(\mathcal{M}^\omega(S_1)(\sigma)) \textit{ else } \sigma \textit{ fi}$$
$$\textit{else} \ldots \textit{fi}]]$$

where ... stands for any (correctly typed) λ-term. Several things must be noted about this λ-term. First, the purpose of the test '$\sigma = \sigma$' (where '$=$' stands for the strict ω-extension of the equality in Σ) is to make sure that $\Phi(f)(\omega) = \omega$ for every $f \in [\Sigma_\omega \to \Sigma_\omega]$. Next, one should have written

$$\Phi = \mathcal{I}([\lambda F . [\lambda\sigma . \ldots]])(\gamma) \qquad \text{for any assignment } \gamma$$

rather than

$$\Phi = [\lambda F . [\lambda\sigma . \ldots]]$$

Third, $\mathcal{I}(e)$ and $\mathcal{M}^\omega(S_1)$ should be regarded as function symbols rather than as functions. Finally (the interpretation of the function symbol) $\mathcal{I}(e)$ is a—not further defined—monotonic ω-extension of the function $\mathcal{I}(e)$ from predicate logic. The desired properties of Φ now result from the induction hypothesis stating that $\mathcal{M}^\omega(S_1)$ is continuous. This finally implies the validity of the assertions (1) and (2) for the case of the while-statement. $\square$

DEFINITION 5.19 (Denotational Semantics of $\mathcal{L}_2$)   Let S be a while-program over a given basis, $\mathcal{I}$ an interpretation of this basis. The *meaning* of S (in $\mathcal{I}$) is the function $\mathcal{M}_{\mathcal{I}}(S): \Sigma \rightsquigarrow \Sigma$ defined by

$$\mathcal{M}_{\mathcal{I}}(S)(\sigma) = \begin{cases} \mathcal{M}^\omega_{\mathcal{I}}(S)(\sigma) & \text{if } \mathcal{M}^\omega_{\mathcal{I}}(S)(\sigma) \neq \omega \\ \text{undefined} & \text{if } \mathcal{M}^\omega_{\mathcal{I}}(S)(\sigma) = \omega \end{cases} \qquad \square$$

The logical next step is to prove the equivalence of operational and denotational semantics of $\mathcal{L}_2$. Instead of a formal proof, a few informal remarks are given.

The only big problem in this equivalence proof is the while-statement; the other cases are more or less evident. Now, for every state $\sigma \in \Sigma$:

$$\mathcal{M}^\omega(\textit{while e do } S_1 \textit{ od})(\sigma)$$

$$= \textit{if-then-else } (\mathcal{I}(e)(\sigma),$$
$$\mathcal{M}^\omega(\textit{while e do } S_1 \textit{ od})(\mathcal{M}^\omega(S_1)(\sigma)),$$
$$\sigma)$$
$$(\text{since } \mathcal{M}^\omega(\textit{while e do } S_1 \textit{ od}) \text{ is a fixpoint of } \Phi)$$

$$= \text{if-then-else}(\mathscr{I}(e)(\sigma),$$
$$\mathscr{M}^{\omega}(S_1\,;\, while\ e\ do\ S_1\ od)(\sigma),$$
$$\sigma) \tag{1}$$
(by the definition of $\mathscr{M}^{\omega}$ for the composed statement)

The right-hand side of equation (1) reflects the operational semantics of *while e do* S_1 *od*. For essentially the same reason as in $\mathscr{L}_3$, the solution of this equation or, more precisely, the least fixpoint of the appropriate functional is the one computed by the operational semantics.

It is also worth pointing out that equation (1) cannot be used in the part 'while-statement' of Definition 5.17. This is because the definition is an inductive one: if the function to be defined also occurs in the right-hand side of the equation, its argument has to be syntactically shorter. This is not the case in (1): 'S_1; *while* ... *od*' is even longer than '*while* ... *od*'.

EXERCISES

5.1–1 Let $\mathscr{I}$ be the 'usual' interpretation and let $\gamma \in \Gamma$ be an assignment with $\gamma(x) = 3$ and $\gamma(y) = 4$. For each of the following λ-terms t calculate $\mathscr{I}(t)(\gamma)$:

(i) $[\lambda x, y . (x + y)]$ (ii) $[\lambda x . [\lambda y . (x + y)]]$

(iii) $[\lambda x . [\lambda x . (x + y)]]$ (iv) $[\lambda x . [\lambda y . (x + y)]](y)$

(v) $[\lambda x . [\lambda y . (x + y)](y)]$

5.1–2 In Definition 5.2 the domain D_τ for a type τ of the form $(\tau_1, \ldots, \tau_n \to \sigma)$ was defined to be the set of all continuous functions

$$[D_{\tau_1} \times \cdots \times D_{\tau_n} \to D_\sigma] \tag{I}$$

Alternatively D_τ could have been defined to be the set of all monotonic functions

$$(D_{\tau_1} \times \cdots \times D_{\tau_n} \xrightarrow{m} D_\sigma) \tag{II}$$

or even the set of all functions

$$(D_{\tau_1} \times \cdots \times D_{\tau_n} \to D_\sigma). \tag{III}$$

(i) Consider the definition with the domain (II). Prove that $\mathscr{I}(t)(\gamma)$ is monotonic for every λ-term t and every assignment γ.
(ii) Consider the (classical) definition with the domain (I). Prove that for every cpo $(D, \sqsubseteq)$ the composition operator

$$\text{comp}: [D \to D]^2 \to [D \to D]$$

defined by

$$\text{comp}(f, g) = f \circ g$$

is continuous. (*Hint*: Express it as a λ-term.)
(iii) Consider again the definition with the domain (II). Prove that the extension of the function comp (defined sub (ii)) to the set of all monotonic functions—which is monotonic by part (i)—need not be continuous.
(iv) Consider the definition with the domain (III). Prove that the extension of the function comp to the set of all functions need not be monotonic.

5.1–3 (i) Prove the Renaming Theorem 5.8.
(ii) Prove the Substitution Theorem 5.9.

5.1–4 (i) Assume that the definition of the λ-notation is extended by allowing applications of the μ-operator (fixpoint operator). Prove that still $\mathscr{I}(t)(\gamma)$ is continuous for every λ-term t and every assignment γ.

*(ii) Let $(D_1, \sqsubseteq)$, $(D_2, \sqsubseteq)$ be complete partial orders and $f: D_1 \times D_2 \to D_1 \times D_2$ a continuous function. Let

$$g = \text{curry}(\text{pr}_2 \circ f): D_1 \to [D_2 \to D_2]$$

and let

$$h: D_1 \to D_1$$

be defined by

$$h(d_1) = \text{pr}_1(f(d_1, \mu(g(d_1))))$$

Prove that h is continuous and that

$$\mu f = (\mu h, \mu(g(\mu h))).$$

(*Hint:* Prove first that $(\mu h, \mu(g(\mu h)))$ is a fixpoint of f and then that $h(e_1) \sqsubseteq e_1$ and $g(\mu h)(e_2) \sqsubseteq e_2$ for every fixpoint (e_1, e_2) of f.)

Part (ii) of this exercise proves that 'simultaneous recursion' and 'nested recursion' lead to the same result. This property is useful in the study of more complex programming languages such as ALGOL-60 where both kinds of procedure declarations—simultaneous procedure declaration as well as nested ones—are possible.

5.2–1 (i) *Simultaneous fixpoint induction*   Let $(D, \sqsubseteq)$, $(E, \sqsubseteq)$ be cpo's, $f: D \to D$, $g: E \to E$ continuous functions and $\varphi: D \times E \to Bool$ an admissible predicate. Prove that if

(a) $\varphi(\perp_D, \perp_E) = true$ and
(b) $\varphi(d, e) = true$ implies $\varphi(f(d), g(e))$ for all $d \in D$ and $e \in E$

then $\varphi(\mu f, \mu g) = true$.

(ii) Consider the following two recursive programs

$$S: F(x) \Leftarrow if\ x = 0\ then\ 1\ else\ x * F(x - 1)\ fi$$

$$S': F(x) \Leftarrow if\ x = 0\ then\ 1$$
$$else\ x * (if\ x = 1\ then\ 1\ else\ (x - 1) * F(x - 2)\ fi)\ fi$$

Prove—with the aid of part (i)—that $\mathscr{M}(S) \sqsubseteq \mathscr{M}(S')$. Does the equality also hold? Can this equality be proved with the method of part (i)? Does the equality hold for other interpretations than the classical one?

(iii) Generalize the result of part (ii) to arbitrary recursive programs.

5.4–1 In Definition 5.17 the ω-extended meaning $\mathscr{M}^\omega(while\ e\ do\ S\ od)$ of a while-statement was defined as the least fixpoint of a functional Φ. ˙

(i) Determine this functional Φ for the statement $while\ x \neq 0\ do\ x := x - 1\ od$ (in the usual interpretation).

(ii) Give an example of a while-statement for which Φ is the identity function.

5.4–2 The inductive definition for while-programs given in Definition 3.7 is not free. Prove that nevertheless the ω-extended meaning of a while-program—which is based on this inductive definition—is well-defined (see Definition 5.17).

5.4–3 Prove that for every while-statement the ω-extended meaning $\mathscr{M}^\omega(while\ e\ do\ S\ od)$ is also a fixpoint of the functional

$$\Psi: [\Sigma_\omega \to \Sigma_\omega] \to [\Sigma_\omega \to \Sigma_\omega]$$

defined by

$$\Psi(f) = f \circ \mathscr{M}^\omega(if\ e\ then\ S\ else\ x := x\ fi)$$

Is the ω-extended meaning necessarily the least fixpoint of this functional?

5.4–4 Prove that for every while-program S the ω-extended meaning $\mathscr{M}^\omega(S)$ is a strict function on Σ_ω. (*Hint:* Prove simultaneously that the functional Φ, used to define the

110

meaning of a while-statement, can be restricted to the sub-cpo of all strict functions and that $\mathcal{M}^{\omega}$(*while e do* S *od*) is also the least fixpoint of this restricted functional.)
*5.4–5 Prove the equivalence of operational and denotational semantics for while-programs. (*Hint:* The proof requires some—more or less trivial—properties of the operational semantics such as

$$(S, \sigma) \stackrel{*}{\Rightarrow} (\varepsilon, \sigma') \qquad \text{iff } (S; S', \sigma) \stackrel{*}{\Rightarrow} (S', \sigma') \text{ for all S, S}' \in L_2^B \text{ and } \sigma, \sigma' \in \Sigma).$$

HISTORICAL AND BIBLIOGRAPHICAL REMARKS

The theory of cpo's having been developed in view of denotational semantics, the historical references are the same as for Chapter 4.

Denotational semantics are treated extensively in Stoy (1977). An informal introduction is given in Gordon (1979) and a short tutorial in Tennent (1976). The proof of the equivalence of operational and denotational semantics may also be found in Vuillemin (1976) or de Bakker (1980). An extensive treatment of the λ-notation is given in Barendregt (1981).

PART C
Program Verification Methods

6
Correctness of Programs

The semantics of programs was a prelude necessary to make explicit exactly what programs do. The direction of this book now turns to the central issue: how to establish that a program does the right things. It is assumed to begin with that programs are syntactically correct. The detection of syntax errors—missing parentheses and the like—belongs to the study of formal languages. Here the issue is detecting semantic errors—incorrect loop initialization and the like.

A common approach to the problem of program correctness consists in program testing: the program is made to run on a sample of 'critical' input data. This method may increase confidence in the correctness of a program but it is far from guaranteeing that the program is free from semantic errors. The reason is that the notion of critical input data is much too vague. Another approach is program verification and is the subject of the rest of this book. This approach avoids the deficiencies of program testing by proving mathematically that the meaning of the program (as described in Chapter 3) satisfies its specifications. These specifications must, of course, be defined with mathematical precision. In the case where a formal definition of these specifications is available, for instance as a formula of predicate logic, the program verification may be performed formally, even with the aid of a computer.

The different principles of program verification that are introduced will be illustrated with some small programs. Their application to 'real-life' programs is still disputed by some—de Millo, Lipton, and Perlis (1979) is a provocative paper on the issue. The main difficulty in applying the techniques of program verification to 'real-life' programs is the combinatorial complexity of large proofs. Several verification systems have been proposed in hopes of finding a way to overcome this difficulty; a few of them are mentioned in Chapter 11.

The present chapter introduces the basic concepts necessary in program verification, sets the limits to what is possible (from the point of view of the theory of computation) and gives the first examples of proving programs correct.

6.1 Specifying Program Correctness

As indicated above the verification of a program consists in proving that it

113

satisfies a given specification. An informal version of such a specification is, for example,

> for all input values $a, b \in Nat$ with $a, b > 0$
> the program computes $gcd(a, b)$. (1)

(What the program does if $a = 0$ or $b = 0$ may also be interesting but is left open by this specification.) Actually, specification (1) implicitly assumes that the program terminates. Hence a more precise formulation of the specification is:

> for all input values $a, b \in Nat$ with $a, b > 0$
> the program terminates with output value $gcd(a, b)$. (2)

For a recursive program S the specification (2) may be written:

> for all $a, b \in Nat$
> if $a, b > 0$
> then $\mathcal{M}(S)(a, b)$ is defined and $\mathcal{M}(S)(a, b) = gcd(a, b)$. (2′)

A specification such as (2) or (2′) is called a specification of 'total correctness'.

Now the specification of total correctness (2) is clearly equivalent to the following two specifications:

> for all input values $a, b \in Nat$ with $a, b > 0$
> if the program terminates, then it terminates with the
> output value $gcd(a, b)$, (3)

and

> for all input values $a, b \in Nat$ with $a, b > 0$
> the program terminates. (4)

For a recursive program S one obtains

> for all $a, b \in Nat$
> if $a, b > 0$ and $\mathcal{M}(S)(a, b)$ is defined
> then $\mathcal{M}(S)(a, b) = gcd(a, b)$, (3′)

and

> for all $a, b \in Nat$
> if $a, b > 0$
> then $\mathcal{M}(S)(a, b)$ is defined. (4′)

A specification such as (3) or (3′) is called a specification of 'partial correctness'; (4) and (4′) are called specifications of 'termination'. One reason these notions are introduced separately is that a proof of partial correctness—or, more precisely, a proof that a specification of partial correctness is satisfied—and a proof of termination are often simpler than a proof of total correctness. Another reason for this is that the notions of 'partial correctness' and of 'termination' are of a fundamentally different nature and lead to different proof techniques. (This difference is discussed in Section 8.4.)

These informal notions of total correctness, partial correctness, and termination will suffice for the study of verification of recursive programs. For flowchart programs and while-programs it is useful to introduce a more formal definition. This will be especially useful in the treatment of the Hoare calculus in Chapter 8. Two definitions of correctness are given. The first one is based on the use of predicates, the second one on the use of formulas.

DEFINITION 6.1 (Correctness with respect to Predicates)   Let B be a basis for predicate logic, $\mathscr{I}$ an interpretation of this basis and Σ the corresponding set of states. Let S be a flowchart program from L_1^B or a while-program from L_2^B, and let $\mathscr{M}_{\mathscr{I}}(S)$ be the program's meaning. Furthermore, let $\varphi: \Sigma \to Bool$ and $\psi: \Sigma \to Bool$ be two predicates called the *precondition* and *postcondition* respectively. The program S is said

(i) to be *partially correct with respect to* the predicates φ and ψ (in the interpretation $\mathscr{I}$) if for all states $\sigma \in \Sigma$:

  if $\varphi(\sigma) = true$ and $\mathscr{M}_{\mathscr{I}}(S)(\sigma)$ is defined
  then $\psi(\mathscr{M}_{\mathscr{I}}(S)(\sigma)) = true$;

(ii) to *terminate with respect to* the predicate φ (in the interpretation $\mathscr{I}$) if for all states $\sigma \in \Sigma$:

  if $\varphi(\sigma) = true$
  then $\mathscr{M}_{\mathscr{I}}(S)(\sigma)$ is defined;

(iii) to be *totally correct with respect to* the predicates φ and ψ (in the interpretation $\mathscr{I}$) if for all states $\sigma \in \Sigma$:

  if $\varphi(\sigma) = true$
  then $\mathscr{M}_{\mathscr{I}}(S)(\sigma)$ is defined and $\psi(\mathscr{M}_{\mathscr{I}}(S)(\sigma)) = true$.   □

DEFINITION 6.2 (Correctness with respect to Formulas)   Let B, $\mathscr{I}$, and S be as in Definition 6.1 and p and q two formulas from WFF_B. The program S is said to be *partially correct with respect to* the formulas p and q (in the interpretation $\mathscr{I}$) if it is partially correct with respect to the predicates $\mathscr{I}(p)$ and $\mathscr{I}(q)$. Termination and total correctness with respect to formulas are defined similarly.   □

Note that Definition 6.1 is more general than Definition 6.2 because it allows the use of predicates that cannot be expressed as formulas of (first-order) predicate logic—as will be illustrated in Section 8.2. In examples—such as those now following—Definition 6.2 is used; in theoretical considerations—such as in Theorem 6.5—Definition 6.1 is used.

EXAMPLE 6.3   (a) The specification of total correctness of the program of Example 3.2 or 3.10 may now be stated: the program is totally correct with respect to the precondition

$$true$$

and the postcondition

$$y_1^2 \leq x \wedge x < (y_1 + 1)^2.$$

(b) Let S be a flowchart program or a while-program that is to compute the greatest common divisor. More precisely, for any input state σ the program is intended to terminate with an output state σ' such that

$$\sigma'(x) = gcd(\sigma(x), \sigma(y)),$$

where x and y are variables occurring in the program. Specification (2) at the beginning of the chapter may then be restated as: the program is totally correct with respect to

$$x = a \wedge y = b \wedge a > 0 \wedge b > 0$$

and

$$x = gcd(a, b).$$

In this statement a and b are variables not occurring in the program. The introduction of these extra variables is a technical trick allowing the input values $\sigma(x)$ and $\sigma(y)$ to be accessible in the postcondition.

(c) A flowchart program or while-program is partially correct with respect to the precondition *true* and the postcondition *false* iff its meaning is the everywhere undefined function.

(d) A flowchart program or while-program terminates with respect to the precondition *true* iff its meaning is a total function. $\qquad\square$

The examples make it clear that specifications—either formal ones according to Definition 6.1 or informal ones—may express more than just the 'correctness' of a program. Some specifications, like 'a (given) program is partially correct with respect to *true* and *true*', express nothing significant at all, for, of course, every program which terminates, terminates in a state which satisfies the formula *true*. (See Exercise 6.1–1.)

In view of some theoretical considerations in Section 8.2 three further notions will be introduced.

DEFINITION 6.4 (Weakest Preconditions and Strongest Postconditions) Let B, $\mathscr{I}$, Σ, S, and φ be as in Definition 6.1.

The *weakest liberal precondition* of the program S and the predicate φ is defined to be that predicate $\psi : \Sigma \to Bool$ such that $\psi(\sigma) =$ true iff $\mathscr{M}_\mathscr{I}(S)(\sigma)$ is undefined or $\mathscr{M}_\mathscr{I}(S)(\sigma)$ is defined and $\varphi(\mathscr{M}_\mathscr{I}(S)(\sigma)) =$ true.

The *weakest precondition* of the program S and the predicate φ is the predicate $\psi : \Sigma \to Bool$ such that $\psi(\sigma) =$ true iff $\mathscr{M}_\mathscr{I}(S)(\sigma)$ is defined and $\varphi(\mathscr{M}_\mathscr{I}(S)(\sigma)) =$ true.

The *strongest postcondition* of the predicate φ and the program S is the predicate $\psi : \Sigma \to Bool$ such that $\psi(\sigma) =$ true iff there is a state $\sigma' \in \Sigma$ for which $\varphi(\sigma') =$ true and $\mathscr{M}_\mathscr{I}(S)(\sigma') = \sigma$. $\qquad\square$

As in Definition 6.2 it is possible to replace the predicates φ and ψ of Definition 6.4 by formulas of first-order predicate logic. For instance, the *weakest liberal precondition of a program S and a formula p* is a formula q such that $\mathscr{I}(q)$ is the weakest liberal precondition of the program S and the predicate $\mathscr{I}(p)$. Note that the formula g is defined up to equivalence only. As in the case of Definition 6.2 this definition is less general than Definition 6.4.

The following theorem shows how these notions relate to partial and total correctness and justifies the use of the adjectives 'weakest' and 'strongest'.

THEOREM 6.5   Let B, $\mathscr{I}$, Σ, S, and φ be as in Definition 6.1 or 6.4.

(i) Let ψ be the weakest liberal precondition of S and φ. Then (a) S is partially correct with respect to ψ and φ, and (b) for any predicate ξ such that S is partially correct with respect to ξ and φ it is the case that

$$\xi(\sigma) \supset \psi(\sigma)$$

for all states $\sigma \in \Sigma$.

(ii) Similarly but for 'weakest precondition' and 'totally correct' instead of 'weakest liberal precondition' and 'partially correct' respectively.

(iii) Let ψ be the strongest postcondition of φ and S. Then (a) S is partially correct with respect to φ and ψ, and (b) for any predicate ξ such that S is partially correct with respect to φ and ξ it is the case that

$$\psi(\sigma) \supset \xi(\sigma)$$

for all states $\sigma \in \Sigma$.

(The proof is left to the reader. See Exercise 6.1–3.)   □

Notice that in part (iii)(a) of the previous theorem the program is *partially* correct with respect to φ and ξ. It need not be totally correct as one might at first suspect. The reason is that the precondition φ itself determines whether the program terminates. More properties of the weakest precondition and the strongest postcondition may be found in the Exercises 6.1–4 to 6.1–7.

*6.2 Decision Problems

The goal of the chapters to come will be to develop methods of proving the correctness of programs. The following observations from the theory of computation show that there are some fundamental limits to the applicability of such methods.

The remarks in this section will be made about the flowchart programming language. They apply equally well to the language of while-programs and—in the appropriately modified formalism—to the language of recursive programs.

To begin with the following lemma is needed. No proof will be given, but the result should be intuitively apparent to the reader acquainted with the theory of computation.

LEMMA 6.6   Let $B = (F, P)$ be a basis for predicate logic and let $\mathscr{I} = (Nat, \mathscr{I}_0)$ be an interpretation of this basis such that F contains at least the symbols 0, 1, and $+$, and $\mathscr{I}_0$ gives these symbols their usual meaning. Let $f : Nat^n \rightsquigarrow Nat, n \geq 1$, be an arbitrary computable function defined by, say, a Turing machine. Let

118

$x_1, \ldots, x_n, y$ be variables. Then one can construct a flowchart program S from L_1^B such that for all states $\sigma \in \Sigma$ either $f(\sigma(x_1), \ldots, \sigma(x_n))$ and $\mathscr{M}_\mathscr{I}(S)(\sigma)(y)$ are both undefined, or they are both defined and equal. $\square$

Informally this lemma states that, as soon as the domain D of the interpretation $\mathscr{I} = (D, \mathscr{I}_0)$ contains the natural numbers, flowchart programs have the same computing power as, say, Turing machines. This means there is a flowchart program for any computable function.

With the help of Lemma 6.6 it is possible to connect assertions about the correctness of programs with the halting problem for Turing machines. The following theorem uses the lemma to prove that the problems of partial correctness, termination, and total correctness are hopelessly undecidable, as soon as the natural numbers are available.

THEOREM 6.7 Let B and $\mathscr{I}$ be defined as in Lemma 6.6. Then none of the following sets is recursively enumerable:

(i) $PC = \{(p, S, q) | p, q$ are formulas from WFF_B, S is a flowchart program from L_1^B, and S is partially correct with respect to p and q in $\mathscr{I}\}$;
(ii) $TE = \{(p, S) | p$ is a formula from WFF_B, S is a flowchart program from L_1^B, and S terminates with respect to p in $\mathscr{I}\}$;
(iii) TC is defined like PC but with total instead of partial correctness.

Proof. (i) Assume for purposes of finding a contradiction that the set PC is recursively enumerable. Then so would be the set

$$\{S \in L_1^B | (true, S, false) \in PC\},$$

since during an enumeration of PC the elements of the form $(true, S, false)$ could be picked out. This is exactly the set of all flowchart programs the meaning of which is the everywhere undefined function. So by Lemma 6.6 the set of all Turing machines that halt on no input is recursively enumerable. From the theory of computation, this cannot be true, so the assumption that PC is recursively enumerable is false.

(ii) Assume the set TE is recursively enumerable. Then so would be the set $\{S \in L_1^B | (true, S) \in TE\}$. But this is exactly the set of all flowchart programs the meaning of which is a total function. So by Lemma 6.6, the set of all Turing machines that halt on every input is recursively enumerable. This also contradicts a result from the theory of computation.

(iii) Assume the set TC is recursively enumerable. Then the set TE would also be recursively enumerable, since $TE = \{(p, S) | (p, S, true) \in TC\}$. This assumption led in (ii) to a contradiction. $\square$

6.3 Ingenuous Correctness Proofs

In this section a few proofs of correctness will be given that illustrate the use of the notions introduced in Section 6.1. These correctness proofs are 'ingenuous' in that they are based on common mathematical argumentation rather than on one of the methods for program verification to be discussed later. Such 'free-style' proofs start from the semantics of the programming language and use induction as the main tool. Typically, the induction is on (the length of) computation sequences in the case of operational semantics and on chains in the case of denotational semantics.

Proofs of this type are often tedious and, above everything else, repetitive in that the same argumentation appears over and over again. This justifies the development of methods for program verification which use more appropriate notation and which filter out the arguments that would otherwise have to be repeated in each proof. Such methods, however, will not be presented until the following chapters.

In what follows there are a few proofs based on operational semantics followed by a proof based on denotational semantics. Notice that the choice of the semantics can influence the complexity of the proof. If the program is built around an 'iterative idea' a proof using operational semantics is appropriate, while if it is built around a 'recursive idea' a proof using denotational semantics is likely to be simpler (see Exercise 6.3–1).

In the first example the partial correctness of a flowchart program is proved with the help of operational semantics. Typically such a proof has the following pattern: one first proves a lemma about computation sequences using induction; then the partial correctness is derived from this lemma.

EXAMPLE 6.8 (Partial Correctness in Operational Semantics)   Consider the flowchart program from Examples 3.2 or 3.3 with the usual interpretation $\mathscr{I}$ over the natural numbers. This program is partially correct with respect to the formulas $x = c$ and $y_1 = \sqrt{c}$ (where c is some variable different from x, y_1, y_2, and y_3).

First a lemma is proved which expresses a relation between the values of the variables each time the label $test$ is reached. Specifically the lemma is: let

$$(l_1, \sigma_1) \Rightarrow \cdots \Rightarrow (l_n, \sigma_n)$$

be a computation sequence with $n \geq 1$ and $l_n = test$. Then

$$\sigma_n(x) = \sigma_1(x)$$
$$(\sigma_n(y_1))^2 \leq \sigma_n(x)$$
$$\sigma_n(y_2) = 2\sigma_n(y_1) + 1$$
$$\sigma_n(y_3) = (\sigma_n(y_1) + 1)^2.$$

(The symbol '+' is used here to mean addition, just as the juxtaposition of symbols is used to mean multiplication. In this example the symbol '+' will also be used for one of the function symbols in the basis which, of course, is interpreted in the usual interpretation to mean addition.) The proof of the lemma is by induction on the length of the computation sequence.

Induction basis   Since $n = 1, l_n = l_1 = begin$. So $l_1 = test$ is not possible and the proposition holds vacuously.

Induction step   Assume the proposition holds for $j = 1, \ldots, n$. The proposition is now proved for $n + 1$.

Assume that $l_{n+1} = test$. The proof proceeds by breaking into two cases according to the value of l_n. If $l_n = begin$, so that $n = 1$, then

$$\sigma_{n+1}(x) = \sigma_n(x) = \sigma_1(x)$$
$$\sigma_{n+1}(y_1) = 0$$
$$\sigma_{n+1}(y_2) = 1$$
$$\sigma_{n+1}(y_3) = 1.$$

It is now obvious that the proposition holds for this case. Suppose that $l_n = upd$, then

$$\sigma_{n+1} = \sigma_n[\,y_3/\mathscr{I}(y_2 + y_3)(\sigma_n)].$$

Moreover $l_{n-1} = loop$ and

$$\sigma_n = \sigma_{n-1}[\,y_1/\mathscr{I}(y_1 + 1)(\sigma_{n-1})][\,y_2/\mathscr{I}(y_2 + 2)(\sigma_{n-1})].$$

Finally $l_{n-2} = test$, $\sigma_{n-1} = \sigma_{n-2}$ and

$$\mathscr{I}(y_3 \le x)(\sigma_{n-2}) = \text{true}. \tag{1}$$

Hence,

$$\sigma_{n+1}(x) = \sigma_n(x) = \sigma_{n-1}(x) = \sigma_{n-2}(x) \tag{2}$$
$$\sigma_{n+1}(y_1) = \sigma_n(y_1) = \sigma_{n-1}(y_1) + 1 = \sigma_{n-2}(y_1) + 1 \tag{3}$$
$$\sigma_{n+1}(y_2) = \sigma_n(y_2) = \sigma_{n-1}(y_2) + 2 = \sigma_{n-2}(y_2) + 2 \tag{4}$$
$$\sigma_{n+1}(y_3) = \sigma_n(y_2) + \sigma_n(y_3)$$
$$= \sigma_{n-1}(y_2) + 2 + \sigma_{n-1}(y_3)$$
$$= \sigma_{n-2}(y_2) + 2 + \sigma_{n-2}(y_3). \tag{5}$$

The induction hypothesis with $j = n - 2$ can now be used to get the desired result:

$$\sigma_{n+1}(x) = \sigma_{n-2}(x) \quad \text{(by (2))}$$
$$= \sigma_1(x) \quad \text{(by induction hypothesis)}$$
$$(\sigma_{n+1}(y_1))^2 = (\sigma_{n-2}(y_1) + 1)^2 \quad \text{(by (3))}$$
$$= \sigma_{n-2}(y_3) \quad \text{(by induction hypothesis)}$$
$$\le \sigma_{n-2}(x) \quad \text{(by (1))}$$
$$= \sigma_{n+1}(x) \quad \text{(by (2))}$$

$$\sigma_{n+1}(y_2) = \sigma_{n-2}(y_2) + 2 \quad \text{(by (4))}$$
$$= 2\sigma_{n-2}(y_1) + 3 \quad \text{(by induction hypothesis)}$$
$$= 2\sigma_{n+1}(y_1) + 1 \quad \text{(by (3))}$$

$$\sigma_{n+1}(y_3) = \sigma_{n-2}(y_2) + \sigma_{n-2}(y_3) + 2 \quad \text{(by (5))}$$
$$= 2\sigma_{n-2}(y_1) + 1 + (\sigma_{n-2}(y_1) + 1)^2 + 2 \quad \text{(by induction hypothesis)}$$
$$= (\sigma_{n-2}(y_1) + 2)^2$$
$$= (\sigma_{n+1}(y_1) + 1)^2. \quad \text{(by (3))}$$

This completes the second case and the proof of the lemma.

To prove partial correctness, consider a finite computation

$$(l_1, \sigma_1) \Rightarrow \cdots \Rightarrow (l_k, \sigma_k),$$

where $k \geq 2$, $l_1 = begin$, $l_k = end$, and $\sigma_1(x) = \sigma_1(c)$. To prove is that $\sigma_k(y_1) = \sqrt{\sigma_1(c)}$ or, equivalently, that $(\sigma_k(y_1))^2 \leq \sigma_1(c)$ and $\sigma_1(c) < (\sigma_k(y_1) + 1)^2$. Now $l_{k-1} = test$, $\sigma_{k-1} = \sigma_k$, and $\mathscr{I}(y_3 \leq x)(\sigma_{k-1}) = \text{false}$. So,

$$\sigma_{k-1}(y_3) > \sigma_{k-1}(x). \qquad (6)$$

This together with the lemma yields

$$
\begin{aligned}
\sigma_k(y_1))^2 &= (\sigma_{k-1}(y_1))^2 \\
&\leq \sigma_{k-1}(x) && \text{(by the lemma)} \\
&= \sigma_1(x) && \text{(by the lemma)} \\
&= \sigma_1(c)
\end{aligned}
$$

and

$$
\begin{aligned}
(\sigma_k(y_1) + 1)^2 &= (\sigma_{k-1}(y_1) + 1)^2 \\
&= \sigma_{k-1}(y_3) && \text{(by the lemma)} \\
&> \sigma_{k-1}(x) && \text{(by (6))} \\
&= \sigma_1(x) && \text{(by the lemma)} \\
&= \sigma_1(c). && \qquad\qquad \square
\end{aligned}
$$

The following example contains a proof of termination with the help of operational semantics. A typical pattern for such a proof is the following: one assumes that there is an infinite computation sequence and then derives a contradiction with the help of a lemma which expresses some property of the computation sequences. This lemma is proved—as in the last example—by induction over the length of the sequence.

EXAMPLE 6.9 (Termination in Operational Semantics) The same flowchart program as in the last example is considered and proved to terminate with respect to *true* (that is, it always terminates).

The following lemma is needed, the proof of which is left to the reader: for any computation sequence

$$(l_1, \sigma_1) \Rightarrow \cdots \Rightarrow (l_n, \sigma_n)$$

$(n \geq 1)$ of the flowchart program one has for all $j \in Nat$ with $0 \leq j \leq (n - 2)/3$,

$$
\begin{aligned}
l_{3j+2} &= test \\
\sigma_{3j+2}(y_3) &> j \\
\sigma_{3j+2}(x) &= \sigma_1(x).
\end{aligned}
$$

Assume there is an infinite computation sequence. Choose $j \geq \sigma_1(x)$. Then $l_{3j+2} = test$, $\sigma_{3j+2}(y_3) > j$, and so $\sigma_{3j+2}(y_3) > \sigma_1(x) = \sigma_{3j+2}(x)$. But then $l_{3j+3} = end$ which is a contradiction to the assumption that the computation sequence is infinite. $\qquad \square$

From the proof of partial correctness in Example 6.8 and the proof of termination in Example 6.9 one may combine the results and conclude that the flowchart program considered in these examples is totally correct with respect to $x = c$ and $y_1 = \sqrt{c}$. The same total correctness property will now be proved directly without explicit reference to partial correctness or termination. The main idea is to first prove a preliminary lemma describing the configurations in a computation sequence.

EXAMPLE 6.10 (Total Correctness in Operational Semantics) The same flowchart program as in the last two examples is considered and proved to be totally correct with respect to $x = c$ and $y_1 = \sqrt{c}$.

First the following lemma is proved: for every state $\sigma_1 \in \Sigma$ and every number $k \in Nat$ such that

$$0 \le k \le \sqrt{\sigma_1(x)}$$

there is a computation sequence

$$(l_1, \sigma_1) \Rightarrow \cdots \Rightarrow (l_{3k+2}, \sigma_{3k+2})$$

for this state σ_1 such that

$$l_{3k+2} = test$$
$$\sigma_{3k+2}(x) = \sigma_1(x)$$
$$\sigma_{3k+2}(y_1) = k$$
$$\sigma_{3k+2}(y_2) = 2k + 1$$
$$\sigma_{3k+2}(y_3) = (k + 1)^2.$$

The proof of this lemma is by induction on k.

Induction basis   In view of the operational semantics of the flowchart program it is obvious that the property holds for $k = 0$; in particular, $l_2 = test$, $\sigma_2(x) = \sigma_1(x)$, and so on.

Induction step   Assume that $k + 1 \le \sqrt{\sigma_1(x)}$. As

$$\sigma_{3k+2}(y_3) = (k = 1)^2 \quad \text{and} \quad \sigma_{3k+2}(x) = \sigma_1(x)$$

one obtains

$$\sigma_{3k+2}(y_3) \le \sigma_{3k+2}(x).$$

So $l_{3k+3} = loop$, $l_{3k+4} = upd$, and $l_{3(k+1)+2} = test$. Moreover, it follows easily that

$$\sigma_{3(k+1)+2}(x) = \sigma_{3k+2}(x) = \sigma_1(x)$$
$$\sigma_{3(k+1)+2}(y_1) = \sigma_{3k+2}(y_1) + 1 = k + 1$$
$$\sigma_{3(k+1)+2}(y_2) = \sigma_{3k+2}(y_2) + 2 = 2(k + 1) + 1$$
$$\sigma_{3(k+1)+2}(y_3) = \sigma_{3k+2}(y_3) + \sigma_{3k+2}(y_2) + 2$$
$$= (k + 1)^2 + 2k + 1 + 2 = (k + 2)^2.$$

This completes the proof of the lemma.

Consider now the computation sequence for the state $\sigma_1 \in \Sigma$

$$(l_1, \sigma_1) \Rightarrow \cdots \Rightarrow (l_{3k+2}, \sigma_{3k+2})$$

with $k = \sqrt{\sigma_1(x)}$. By the lemma

$$
\begin{aligned}
\sigma_{3k+2}(y_3) &= (k+1)^2 \\
&= (\sqrt{\sigma_1(x)} + 1)^2 \\
&> \sigma_1(x) \\
&= \sigma_{3k+2}(x)
\end{aligned}
$$

and $l_{3k+2} = test$. So $l_{3k+3} = end$ and the computation sequence

$$(l_1, \sigma_1) \Rightarrow \cdots \Rightarrow (l_{3k+3}, \sigma_{3k+3})$$

is a computation (that is, it terminates). Moreover

$$
\begin{aligned}
\sigma_{3k+3}(y_1) &= \sigma_{3k+2}(y_1) \\
&= k \qquad \text{(by the lemma)} \\
&= \sqrt{\sigma_1(x)}. \qquad \qquad \qquad \Box
\end{aligned}
$$

In Section 6.1 it was mentioned that a direct proof of total correctness is in general more difficult than two proofs, one of partial correctness and another of termination. This is illustrated by the three previous examples in the following way: the lemma used in the proof of total correctness is much stronger—and, hence, more difficult to find—than the lemmas used in the proofs of partial correctness and termination. In particular, the lemma in Example 6.10 provides the number of passes through the loop (namely $\sqrt{\sigma_1(x)}$). This number is not needed in the proof in Example 6.8 and the proof in Example 6.9 needs only an upper bound on this number. Finding a direct proof of total correctness is difficult particularly for programs with several loops, especially interleaved loops.

Notice also how Example 6.8 differs from the last two examples. The lemmas in the last two examples established a connection between the values of the variables and the length of the computation sequence. (Such an induction is called *external induction* by some authors.) The lemma proved in Example 6.8 needed no reference to the length of the computation sequence. This difference is related to the fact that partial correctness and termination are properties with essentially different natures.

Correctness proofs for while-programs or recursive programs may be conducted along the same lines. Such proofs are again relatively involved and so the technique will be illustrated on just a simple recursive program.

EXAMPLE 6.11 (Termination of a Recursive Program using Operational Semantics)   Consider the recursive program

$$
\begin{aligned}
F_1(x) &\Leftarrow F_2(0, 1, 0, x) \\
F_2(y_1, y_2, y_3, x) &\Leftarrow \text{if } y_2 + y_3 \leq x \text{ then } F_2(y_1 + 1, y_2 + 2, y_2 + y_3, x) \\
&\qquad\qquad else \ y_1 \ fi
\end{aligned}
$$

with the main function symbol F_1. (Notice the similarity to the flowchart program considered in the examples above.) Let $\mathscr{I} = (Nat, \mathscr{I}_0)$ be the usual interpretation over the natural numbers. It is proved that this program terminates for any input.

As usual, first a lemma is proved which expresses some property of the computation sequences. Let $t_1, \ldots, t_n$ with $n \geq 2$ be a finite computation sequence for an input $m \in Nat$. If the term t_n is not a constant (or, equivalently, if the computation sequence is not a computation), then (1) the term t_n contains exactly one function variable, namely F_2 and (2) for the subterm $F_2(c_1, c_2, c_3, c_4)$ of the term t_n: c_1, c_2, c_3, and c_4 are constants, $\mathscr{I}_0(c_2) > 0$, $\mathscr{I}_0(c_3) + 3 > n$, and $\mathscr{I}_0(c_4) = m$. The proof is by induction on n.

Induction basis Since $t_1 = F_1(m)$, $t_2 = F_2(0, 1, 0, m)$ and the lemma is obvious for $n = 2$. (Technically one should have written c instead of m, where c is the constant defined by $\mathscr{I}_0(c) = m$ whose existence follows from the assumption in Section 3.3 that $\mathscr{I}_0$ is one-to-one.)

Induction step Now assume that $n > 2$ and that the lemma holds for $n - 1$. Hence, the term t_{n-1} contains exactly one function variable, namely F_2. As the term t_n is assumed not to be constant, it must contain at least one function variable (by the very definition of a computation sequence). This function variable must be F_2 by the form of the recursive equations. This proves the first part of the lemma.

Now let $F_2(c_1, c_2, c_3, c_4)$ be the subterm of t_{n-1} provided by the induction hypothesis. Substitution leads to

$$F_2(c_1 + 1, c_2 + 2, c_2 + c_3, c_4).$$

Simplification then leads to

$$F_2(c_1', c_2', c_3', c_4)$$

where c_1', c_2', c_3' are the constants defined by

$$\mathscr{I}_0(c_1') = \mathscr{I}_0(c_1) + 1$$
$$\mathscr{I}_0(c_2') = \mathscr{I}_0(c_2) + 2$$
$$\mathscr{I}_0(c_3') = \mathscr{I}_0(c_2) + \mathscr{I}_0(c_3).$$

(Formally, one should have written $\mathscr{I}_0(+)(\mathscr{I}_0(c_1), \mathscr{I}_0(1))$ for $\mathscr{I}_0(c_1) + 1$ and so on.) Hence $\mathscr{I}_0(c_2') > 0$ and $\mathscr{I}_0(c_3') + 3 > n$, because $\mathscr{I}_0(c_2) > 0$ and $\mathscr{I}_0(c_3) + 3 > n - 1$. This completes the proof of the lemma.

Suppose now that the recursive program does not terminate for an input $m \in Nat$. Then there exist arbitrarily long computation sequences for m. Let $t_1, \ldots, t_n$ be such a computation sequence with $n > m + 3$. Let $F_2(c_1, c_2, c_3, c_4)$ be the subterm occurring in t_n given by the lemma just proved. By this lemma

$$\mathscr{I}_0(c_2) + \mathscr{I}_0(c_3) + 3 > n$$

and $\mathscr{I}_0(c_4) = m$. Hence, $\mathscr{I}_0(c_2) + \mathscr{I}_0(c_3) > \mathscr{I}_0(c_4)$ and substitution applied to t_n delivers a term without function variables. As a consequence there exists a finite computation for m (consisting of $n + 1$ terms). This contradicts the assumption that the recursive program does not terminate for m. □

The last example in this chapter proves the total correctness of a recursive program with the help of denotational semantics. In Example 5.13 it was shown that the meaning of the recursive program S defined by

$$F(x) \Leftarrow if\ x = 0\ then\ 1\ else\ x * F(x - 1)\ fi$$

is the factorial function. Essentially the strategy used in that example (and in the related Examples 4.25 and 4.8) was to

(1) Find an expression for $\Phi(S)^i(\bot)$;
(2) From this expression find one for $\sqcup\{\Phi(S)^i(\bot) | i \in Nat\}$;
(3) From this expression derive the desired property of the program S.

The following example uses the same strategy.

EXAMPLE 6.12 (Total Correctness of a Recursive Program with Denotational Semantics) Let S be the recursive program

$$F(x, y) \Leftarrow if\ x = y\ then\ 1\ else\ (y + 1) * F(x, y + 1)\ fi.$$

Assuming the usual interpretation it is shown that for all $m \in Nat$: $\mathscr{M}(S)(m, 0)$ is defined and $\mathscr{M}(S)(m, 0) = m!$.

The first step is to show that for all $i \in Nat$

$$\Phi(S)^i(\bot) = f_i, \tag{1}$$

where $f_i: Nat_\omega^2 \to Nat_\omega$ is defined by

$$f_i(m, n) = \begin{cases} m!/n! & \text{if } m, n \neq \omega, n \leq m, \text{ and } m < n + i \\ \omega & \text{otherwise.} \end{cases}$$

The proof is by induction on i.

Induction basis For all $m, n \in Nat_\omega$

$$\Phi(S)^0(\bot)(m, n) = \omega.$$

But also

$$f_0(m, n) = \omega,$$

because $n \leq m$ and $m < n$ is impossible.

Induction step For all $m, n \in Nat_\omega$

$$\Phi(S)^{i+1}(\bot)(m, n) = \Phi(S)(f_i)(m, n) \quad \text{(by induction hypothesis)}$$
$$= if\ m = n\ then\ 1\ else\ (n + 1) * f_i(m, n + 1)\ fi \tag{2}$$

by the definition of $\Phi(S)$. The proof of (1) proceeds by cases. If $m = \omega$ or $n = \omega$ (or both), then (2) becomes

$$\Phi(S)^{i+1}(\bot)(m, n) = \omega$$
$$= f_{i+1}(m, n).$$

If $m, n \neq \omega$ and $n > m$, then

$$\Phi(S)^{i+1}(\bot)(m, n) = (n + 1) * f_i(m, n + 1)$$
$$= (n + 1) * \omega \qquad \text{(because } n > m \text{ implies}$$
$$= \omega = f_{i+1}(m, n). \qquad\qquad n + 1 > m)$$

If $m, n \neq \omega$ and $m \geq n + i + 1$, then

$$\Phi(S)^{i+1}(\bot)(m, n) = (n + 1) * f_i(m, n + 1)$$
$$= (n + 1) * \omega \qquad \text{(because } m \geq (n + 1) + i)$$
$$= \omega$$
$$= f_{i+1}(m, n). \qquad \text{(because } m \geq n + (i + 1))$$

If $m, n \neq \omega$ and $m = n$, then

$$\Phi(S)^{i+1}(\bot)(m, n) = 1$$
$$= f_{i+1}(m, n). \qquad \text{(because } n \leq m \text{ and}$$
$$m < n + (i + 1))$$

Finally, if $m, n \neq \omega$, $n < m$, and $m < n + i + 1$, then

$$\Phi(S)^{i+1}(\bot)(m, n) = (n + 1) * f_i(m, n + 1)$$
$$= (n + 1) * (m!/(n + 1)!) \qquad \text{(because } (n + 1) \leq m \text{ and}$$
$$= m!/n! \qquad\qquad m < (n + 1) + i)$$
$$= f_{i+1}(m, n). \qquad \text{(because } n \leq m \text{ and}$$
$$m < n + (i + 1))$$

This completes the proof of (1).

Next it is shown that

$$\sqcup\{\Phi(S)^i(\bot) \mid i \in Nat\} = f, \tag{3}$$

where $f: Nat_\omega^2 \to Nat_\omega$ is defined by

$$f(m, n) = \begin{cases} m!/n! & \text{if } m, n \neq \omega \text{ and } n \leq m \\ \omega & \text{otherwise} \end{cases}$$

In order to show that (3) holds one shows

$$f_i \sqsubseteq f \qquad \text{for any } i \in Nat \tag{4}$$
$$f \sqsubseteq g \qquad \text{for any upper bound } g \text{ of } \{f_i \mid i \in Nat\}. \tag{5}$$

For all $i \in Nat$ and $m, n \in Nat_\omega$

$$f_i(m, n) \sqsubseteq f(m, n)$$

because whenever $f_i(m, n) \neq \omega$ one has

$$f_i(m, n) = m!/n! = f(m, n).$$

This proves (4).

Let g be an upper bound of $\{f_i \mid i \in Nat\}$ such that $f \sqsubseteq g$ does *not* hold. Then there must be $m, n \in Nat_\omega$ such that

$$f(m, n) \neq \omega \quad \text{and} \quad f(m, n) \neq g(m, n).$$

Hence $m, n \neq \omega$ and $n \leq m$. Consider now the function f_i with $i = m - n + 1$; by definition of f_i one has

$$f_i(m, n) = m!/n! \neq \omega.$$

As f and g are both upper bounds of $\{f_i \mid i \in Nat\}$, one obtains $f(m, n) = m!/n! = g(m, n)$ which contradicts the assumption. This completes the proof of (5) and thus of (3).

By definition of the meaning of a recursive program one has for all $m, n \in Nat$

$$\mathscr{M}(S)(m, n) = \begin{cases} f(m,n) & \text{if } f(m,n) \neq \omega \\ \text{undefined} & \text{otherwise} \end{cases}$$

and, in particular, for all $m \in Nat$

$$\mathscr{M}(S)(m, 0) = f(m, 0) = m!.$$ $\square$

As for the proof of total correctness in Example 6.10 the lemma needed in the previous example was a 'strong' one. It gave an expression for each element $\Phi(S)^i(\bot)$ of the chain $\{\Phi(S)^i(\bot) \mid i \in Nat\}$ (as well as an expression for $\mathscr{M}(S)$).

EXERCISES

6.1–1 What does it mean for a program to be partially or totally correct with respect to the following pairs of formulas:

(i) *true* and *true*;   (ii) *true* and *false*;
(iii) *false* and *true*;   (iv) *false* and *false*.

What does it mean for a program to terminate with respect to the formula:

(v) *true*;   (vi) *false*.

6.1–2 Let S be a program, which is totally correct with respect to the formulas $x = y$ and $x = y!$ (in the usual interpretation). Under which conditions does S calculate the factorial function? (Note that the variable y may occur in S.)

6.1–3 Prove Theorem 6.5.

6.1–4 Let B be a basis for predicate logic and $\mathscr{I}$ an interpretation of B. Let $wp(S, \varphi)$ denote the weakest precondition of a while-program S from L_2^B and a predicate $\varphi: \Sigma \to Bool$. Similarly, let $wlp(S, \varphi)$ and $sp(\varphi, S)$ stand for the weakest liberal precondition and the strongest postcondition respectively. Finally, introduce for a fixed program S the function

$$wp_S: (\Sigma \to Bool) \to (\Sigma \to Bool)$$

defined by

$$wp_S(\varphi) = wp(S, \varphi)$$

and define similarly the functions wlp_S and sp_S. These functions which map predicates into predicates are often called *predicate transformers*.

(i) Let S be the while-program

$$while \; x \neq y \; do \; x := x + 1 \; od$$

and $\mathscr{I}$ the usual interpretation. Determine the following predicates:

$$wp(S, \mathscr{I}(x = y))$$
$$wp(S, \mathscr{I}(x \neq y))$$
$$wlp(S, \mathscr{I}(x = y))$$
$$wlp(S, \mathscr{I}(x \neq y))$$
$$sp(\mathscr{I}(true), S)$$
$$sp(\mathscr{I}(x > y), S)$$

(ii) Determine the predicates $wp_S(\varphi)$, $wlp_S(\varphi)$, and $sp_S(\varphi)$ for an arbitrary predicate φ if predicate φ if

S is a while-program which does not terminate for any input, say

$$\text{while } true \text{ do } x := x \text{ od};$$

S is a 'dummy statement', say $x := x$;
S is the while-program

$$\text{while } e \text{ do } x := x \text{ od}.$$

6.1–5 For an arbitrary basis B for predicate logic and an interpretation $\mathscr{I}$ of B consider the set $P = (\Sigma \to Bool)$ of all predicates from Σ. This set P can be made into a complete lattice by introducing the relation '$\sqsubseteq$' on P defined by:

$$\varphi \sqsubseteq \psi \qquad \text{iff } \{\sigma \mid \phi(\sigma) = true\} \subseteq \{\sigma \mid \psi(\sigma) = true\}$$

(in words: $\varphi \sqsubseteq \psi$ means that φ is stronger than ψ). The (well-known) operations 'and' and 'or' on P—denoted $\wedge$ and $\vee$—play the role of glb and lub on this lattice. (See Exercise 4.1–9.) Let now S be a fixed while-program. The predicate transformers wp_S, wlp_S, and sp_S of Exercise 6.1–4 are functions on this lattice.

(i) Prove that the functions wp_S, wlp_S, and sp_S are monotonic. Examine if they also respect the operations $\neg$, $\wedge$, and $\vee$, for instance whether

$$wp_S(\varphi \wedge \psi) = wp_S(\varphi) \wedge wp_S(\psi)$$

holds for all predicates φ and ψ from P.

(ii) Prove that for every predicate φ from P:

$$\varphi \sqsubseteq wlp_S(sp_S(\varphi));$$
$$sp_S(wlp_S(\varphi)) \sqsubseteq \varphi.$$

Prove that in both cases the equality does not necessarily hold. Can wlp_S be replaced by wp_S?

(iii) Conclude from (i) and (ii) that for every predicate φ from P:

$$sp_S(\varphi) = sp_S(wlp_S(sp_S(\varphi)));$$
$$wlp_S(\varphi) = wlp_S(sp_S(wlp_S(\varphi))).$$

(iv) Examine which of the results of (i), (ii), and (iii) also hold for arbitrary programs S (rather than while-programs S). Consider also the case of non-deterministic programs.

6.1–6

(i) Prove the following properties (the notation is from Exercise 6.1–4): for all while-programs S_1 and S_2, and all predicates $\varphi : \Sigma \to Bool$:

$$wp(S_1; S_2, \varphi) = wp(S_1, wp(S_2, \phi))$$
$$wlp(S_1; S_2, \varphi) = wlp(S_1, wlp(S_2, \varphi))$$
$$sp(\varphi, S_1; S_2) = sp(sp(\varphi, S_1), S_2)$$

(ii) The equations of (i) are related to the compound statement. Find similar equations for the conditional statement and prove them.

*6.1–7 Consider again the complete lattice of predicates introduced in Exercise 6.1–5. Let S be a fixed while-program and wp_S, wlp_S, and sp_S as in Exercise 6.1–4. Let finally $T \subseteq (\Sigma \to Bool)$ be a set of predicates.

(i) Prove that

$$wp_S(\sqcup T) = \sqcup wp_S(T)$$
$$wlp_S(\sqcup T) = \sqcup wlp_S(T)$$
$$sp_S(\sqcup T) = \sqcup sp_S(T)$$

As a result the functions wp_S, wlp_S, and sp_S are continuous and hence possess least fixpoints.

(ii) Prove that moreover

$$wp_S(\sqcap T) = \sqcap wp_S(T)$$
$$wlp_S(\sqcap T) = \sqcap wlp_S(T)$$

but that

$$sp_S(\sqcap T) = \sqcap sp_S(T)$$

only holds if the set $T \subseteq (\Sigma \to Bool)$ is a chain. As a result the functions wp_S, wlp_S, and sp_S are also continuous on the lattice with the reversed order '$\sqsupseteq$' and hence possess greatest fixpoints.

(iii) Let $\varphi : \Sigma \to Bool$ be a fixed predicate and S' a while-statement of the form:

$$while\ e\ do\ S\ od.$$

Define the functions

$$\Delta_1, \Delta_2, \Delta_3 : (\Sigma \to Bool) \to (\Sigma \to Bool)$$

by:

$$\Delta_1(\psi) = (\mathscr{I}(\neg e) \supset \varphi) \wedge (\mathscr{I}(e) \supset wlp_S(\psi))$$
$$\Delta_2(\psi) = (\mathscr{I}(\neg e) \wedge \varphi) \vee (\mathscr{I}(e) \wedge wp_S(\psi))$$
$$\Delta_3(\psi) = \varphi \vee sp_S(\mathscr{I}(e) \wedge \psi)$$

Prove that:

$wlp(S', \varphi)$ is the greatest fixpoint of Δ_1;
$wp(S', \varphi)$ is the least fixpoint of Δ_2;
$sp(\varphi, S')$ is the conjunction of $\mathscr{I}(\neg e)$ and the least fixpoint of Δ_3.

(iv) Examine which of the results of (i) and (ii) hold for arbitrary programs (rather than while-programs).

6.2–1 Let B and $\mathscr{I}$ be defined as in Lemma 6.6. Establish whether the following sets are recursively enumerable:

(i) $WLP = \{(p, S, q) \mid p, q \in WFF_B, S \in L_1^B$ and $\mathscr{I}(p)$ is the weakest liveral precondition of S and $\mathscr{I}(q)\}$;

(ii) WP defined as WLP but with the weakest precondition instead of the weakest liberal precondition;

(iii) $SP = \{(p, S, q) \mid p, q \in WFF_B, S \in L_1^B$ and $\mathscr{I}(q)$ is the strongest postcondition of $\mathscr{I}(p)$ and $S\}$.

6.2–2 Let B be a basis for predicate logic and let $\mathscr{I} = (D, \mathscr{I}_0)$ be an interpretation of B, for which the domain D is finite. Prove that then the sets PC, TE, and TC of Theorem 6.7 are decidable. Why does this not contradict the results of computation theory?

*6.2–3 Let B, $\mathscr{I}$, and the sets PC, TE, TC be defined as in Theorem 6.7. For given formulas $p, q \in WFF_B$ prove the following properties:

(i) The set $\{S \mid (p, S, q) \in PC\}$ is decidable iff at least one of the two formulas $\neg p$ and q is valid in $\mathscr{I}$.

(ii) The set $\{S \mid (p, S) \in TE\}$ is decidable iff $\neg p$ is valid in $\mathscr{I}$.

(iii) The set $\{S \mid (p, S, q) \in TC\}$ is decidable iff at least one of the two formulas $\neg p$ and $\neg q$ is valid in $\mathcal{I}$.

(*Hint:* For (i) consider programs S which are independent of the precondition $\mathcal{I}(p)$ and which guarantee that the postcondition $\mathcal{I}(q)$ is satisfied. (ii) and (iii) can be solved similarly. Disregard the undecidability of the $\mathcal{I}$-validity of first-order predicate formulas as this undecidability does not affect the (un-)decidability of the above sets for *given* formulas p and q.)

Hence, as soon as the domain D of the interpretation $(D, \mathcal{I}_0)$ contains the natural numbers, partial or total correctness of a program as well as its termination are decidable (or recursively enumerable) problems in trivial cases only.

6.3–1 In Example 6.8 the partial correctness of a program calculating the square root of a natural number was proved. The proof made use of a lemma stating that a certain property holds whenever the label *test* is reached during a computation of the program. In order to find such a property it is necessary to understand the idea behind the program. In the case of Example 6.8 this idea may be illustrated as follows: if n is the (initial) value of x, the sequences of the values assigned to y_1, y_2, and y_3 are:

$$y_1 : 0, 1, 2, \ldots, k, \ldots$$
$$y_2 : 1, 3, 5, \ldots, 2k + 1, \ldots$$
$$y_3 : 1, 4, 9, \ldots, (k + 1)^2, \ldots$$

as long as $k \leq \sqrt{n}$. (For a more precise formulation see Example 6.10.) Hence the following property holds:

'There exists a number $k \leq \sqrt{n}$, such that
$$\sigma(y_1) = k, \, \sigma(y_2) = 2k + 1, \, \sigma(y_3) = (k + 1)^2.'$$

The elimination of k yields the property used in Example 6.8.

Consider now the following while-program S intended to calculate the gcd of two natural numbers:

> *while* $x \neq y$ *do*
>   *if* $x > y$ *then* $x := x - y$
>   *else* $y := y - x$ *fi od*

For this program it is difficult to express the values assigned to the variables x and y. The reason is that the 'idea behind the program' is a recursive rather than an iterative one. This recursive idea is expressed by the equations

$$\gcd(a, b) = \gcd(a - b, b)$$

or

$$\gcd(a, b) = \gcd(a, b - a).$$

These equations make it easy to establish a property, which is satisfied whenever the test '$x \neq y$' is reached, namely:

$$\gcd(\sigma(x), \sigma(y)) = \gcd(m, n)$$

where m, n are the initial values of x and y.

(i) Prove—with the aid of this property—the partial correctness of the program S with respect to the formulas $x = a \wedge y = b$ and $x = \gcd(a, b)$ using the operational semantics of while-programs.

(ii) Prove the same result using denotational semantics. Note that denotational semantics is more adequate due to the recursive nature of the idea behind the program.

6.3–2 Consider again the while-program S of Exercise 6.3–1. Prove that S terminates with respect to the formula $x > 0 \wedge y > 0$ by using the same method as in Example 6.9. This proof together with the result of Exercise 6.3–1 implies the total correctness of S with respect to the formulas $x = a \wedge y = b \wedge x > 0 \wedge y > 0$ and $x = \gcd(a, b)$. What do you think of proving this total correctness result 'directly' by the method of 'external induction' illustrated in Example 6.10?

HISTORICAL REMARKS

The notions of partial and total correctness came up with the first papers on program verification by Floyd (1967) and Hoare (1969). The notion of weakest precondition was introduced in Dijkstra (1976). The proof method implicitly used in the proofs using operational semantics (Example 6.8 through 6.11) is essentially that of Burstall (1974).

7
The Classical Methods of Floyd

Two proof methods for the verification of flowchart programs will now be introduced: the inductive assertions method and the well-founded sets method. The former method applies to proofs of partial correctness, the latter to proofs of termination. These proof methods capture the essence of the reasoning used in Example 6.8 (in the case of the inductive assertions method) and Example 6.9 (in the case of the well-founded sets method). Their improvement over the *ad hoc* reasoning lies in the use of predicate logic which leads to more elegant notation and in that some routine proof steps are filtered out.

As mentioned above the methods to be described in this chapter are only for flowchart programs. But they are strongly related to the axiomatic method of Hoare for while-programs, which will be presented in Chapter 8.

7.1 The Inductive Assertions Method

The inductive assertions method presented here performs proofs in the framework of first-order predicate logic. More precisely, let B be a basis for predicate logic and $\mathscr{I}$ an interpretation of this basis. Let further $p, q \in WFF_B$ be formulas and $S \in L_1^B$ a flowchart program. The inductive assertions method is a way to prove the partial correctness of the program S with respect to the formulas p and q. This method may be generalized to partial correctness with respect to arbitrary (not necessarily first-order) predicates (see, for instance, de Bakker and Meertens (1975)).

The basic idea of the inductive assertions method is to reason about the paths in a program rather than about the program itself. To this end, the following definitions are introduced.

Let $\alpha = (l_0, \ldots, l_k)$, $k \geq 0$, be a path in a flowchart program S (remember the definitions at the end of Section 3.1). In analogy to Definition 3.5 of the meaning of a flowchart program, the *meaning* of the path α (in the flowchart program S and in the interpretation $\mathscr{I}$) is the function $\mathscr{M}_{\mathscr{I}}(\alpha): \Sigma \to \Sigma$ defined by:

$$\mathcal{M}_{\mathcal{I}}(\alpha)(\sigma) = \begin{cases} \sigma' & \text{if there are } (k+1) \text{ states } \sigma_0, \sigma_1, \ldots, \sigma_k \text{ such that} \\ & \sigma = \sigma_0, \sigma' = \sigma_k, \text{ and } (l_i, \sigma_i) \overset{S}{\Rightarrow} (l_{i+1}, \sigma_{i+1}) \\ & \text{for } i = 0, \ldots, k-1 \\ \text{undefined} & \text{otherwise} \end{cases}$$

Note that the sequence $(l_0, \sigma_0), \ldots, (l_k, \sigma_k)$ is not necessarily a computation sequence of the program as l_0 may be a label different from *begin*. Note also the following important difference: the meaning of a program is undefined if the (input) state σ leads into an infinite loop; the meaning of a path is undefined if the path is 'impossible' for σ because of its incompatibility with the conditional jumps. The notions of *partial correctness*, *termination*, *total correctness*, *weakest* (*liberal*) *precondition*, and *strongest postcondition* may now be generalized for paths (see Definitions 6.1, 6.2, 6.4). Again, it is important to notice the difference between the notions of, for instance, termination of a program and termination of a path.

It is obvious that for all states $\sigma, \sigma' \in \Sigma$,

$$\mathcal{M}_{\mathcal{I}}(S)(\sigma) = \sigma' \qquad \text{iff there is a path } \alpha \text{ through S such that } \mathcal{M}_{\mathcal{I}}(\alpha)(\sigma) = \sigma'$$

As an immediate consequence, one gets the following lemma.

LEMMA 7.1 A flowchart program S is partially correct with respect to the formulas p and q iff every path through S is partially correct with respect to p and q. $\qquad\qquad\square$

Informally speaking, the preceding lemma allows one to replace the study of a flowchart program by that of the (infinitely many) paths through it. Paths are essentially simpler than programs because the loops are unwound and hence explicit. In particular, if $\mathcal{M}_{\mathcal{I}}(\alpha)(\sigma)$ is defined, each label of the path α is passed exactly once. On the other hand, the infinitely many paths may be considered as being built up from a finite number of 'elementary' paths. It will emerge that the reasoning about the infinitely many paths through a program may be replaced by reasoning about these (finitely many) elementary paths.

First it will be shown how the partial correctness of an arbitrary path α with respect to formulas p and q may be proved. To that purpose two formulas are going to be defined:

a formula $wlp(\alpha, q)$; the name stems from the fact—which will be proved in Theorem 7.4—that $wlp(\alpha, q)$ expresses the weakest liberal precondition of α and $\mathcal{I}(q)$;

a formula $vc(p, \alpha, q)$ called the 'verification condition'.

DEFINITION 7.2 Let B be a basis for predicate logic, $p, q \in WFF_B$ two formulas, $S \in L_1^B$ a flowchart program and $\alpha = (l_0, \ldots, l_k)$ a path in S.

(i) The formula $wlp(\alpha, q)$ is defined by induction on the length k of the path:

Induction basis For $k = 0$ the formula $wlp(\alpha, q)$ is defined to be q.

Induction step   For $k > 0$ let β be the path $(l_1, \ldots, l_k)$ and r the (already defined) formula $wlp(\beta, q)$. Depending on the form of the command at the label l_0, two cases are distinguished. If the command is a parallel assignment of the form

$$l_0 : (x_1, \ldots, x_n) := (t_1, \ldots, t_n);\ goto\ l_1,$$

then the formula $wlp(\alpha, q)$ is defined to be $r_{x_1, \ldots, x_n}^{t_1, \ldots, t_n}$. If the command is a conditional jump of the form

$$l_0 : if\ e\ then\ goto\ l\ else\ goto\ l'\ fi,$$

then the formula $wlp(\alpha, q)$ is defined to be:

$$
\begin{array}{ll}
e \supset r & \text{if } l = l_1 \text{ and } l' \neq l_1; \\
(\neg e) \supset r & \text{if } l' = l_1 \text{ and } l \neq l_1
\end{array}
$$

(remember that $l \neq l'$ by the syntax of flowchart programs).

(ii) The *verification condition* for the path α and the formulas p and q is denoted $vc(p, \alpha, q)$ and is defined to be the formula

$$p \supset wlp(\alpha, q). \qquad \square$$

Note that the definitions of $wlp(\alpha, q)$ and $vc(p, \alpha, q)$ are purely syntactical, that is, they do not depend on the interpretation of the basis B.

EXAMPLE 7.3 (Determining wlp and vc)   Consider the flowchart program of Examples 3.2 and 3.3. Three examples of determining the wlp's and verification conditions will be given. The choice of the paths and the formulas in these examples are made to simplify the treatment of Example 7.8 illustrating the inductive assertions method. One of these formulas is denoted q_{test} and stands for:

$$x = a \wedge y_1^2 \leq x \wedge y_3 = (y_1 + 1)^2 \wedge y_2 = 2 * y_1 + 1$$

where a is a variable not occurring in the program.

(1) The wlp of the path $(begin, test)$ and the formula q_{test} is

$$
\begin{aligned}
wlp((begin, test), q_{test}) &= (wlp((test), q_{test}))_{y_1, y_2, y_3}^{0,1,1} \\
&= (q_{test})_{y_1, y_2, y_3}^{0,1,1} \\
&= (x = a \wedge 0^2 \leq x \wedge 1 = (0 + 1)^2 \wedge 1 = 2 * 0 + 1)
\end{aligned}
$$

Note that in the usual interpretation this formula may be replaced by the (equivalent) formula $x = a$. Such replacements will not be made here in order to stress the fact that the definitions of $wlp(\alpha, q)$ and of the verification condition do not depend on any particular interpretation.

(2) To determine

$$wlp((test, loop, upd, test), q_{test})$$

one works backward using the definition of $wlp(\alpha, q)$:

$$wlp((test), q_{test}) = q_{test}$$
$$wlp((upd, test), q_{test}) = (q_{test})_{y_3}^{y_3 + y_2}$$
$$wlp((loop, upd, test), q_{test}) = ((q_{test})_{y_3}^{y_3 + y_2})_{y_1, y_2}^{y_1 + 1, y_2 + 2}$$
$$wlp((test, loop, upd, test), q_{test}) = (y_3 \leq x \supset ((q_{test})_{y_3}^{y_3 + y_2})_{y_1, y_2}^{y_1 + 1, y_2 + 2})$$
$$= (y_3 \leq x \supset (x = a \wedge (y_1 + 1)^2 \leq x \wedge$$
$$y_3 + y_2 + 2 = (y_1 + 1 + 1)^2 \wedge$$
$$y_2 + 2 = 2 * (y_1 + 1) + 1))$$

(3) The wlp of the path (*test, end*) and the formula $y_1 = \sqrt{a}$ is

$$\neg(y_3 \leq x) \supset y_1 = \sqrt{a}.$$

(4) The verification condition $vc(x = a, (begin, test), q_{test})$ is

$$(x = a) \supset (x = a \wedge 0^2 \leq x \wedge 1 = (0 + 1)^2 \wedge 1 = 2 * 0 + 1).$$

(5) The verification condition $vc(q_{test}, (test, loop, upd, test), q_{test})$ is

$$(x = a \wedge y_1^2 \leq x \wedge y_3 = (y_1 + 1)^2 \wedge y_2 = 2 * y_1 + 1 \wedge y_3 \leq x)$$
$$\supset (x = a \wedge (y_1 + 1)^2 \leq x \wedge y_3 + y_2 + 2 = (y_1 + 1 + 1)^2 \wedge y_2 + 2$$
$$= 2 * (y_1 + 1) + 1)$$

(Remember that $p \supset (q \supset r)$ and $p \wedge q \supset r$ are logically equivalent for all formulas p, q, r.)

(6) The verification condition $vc(q_{test}, (test, end), y_1 = \sqrt{a})$ is

$$(x = a \wedge y_1^2 \leq x \wedge y_3 = (y_1 + 1)^2 \wedge y_2 = 2 * y_1 + 1 \wedge \neg(y_3 \leq x) \supset$$
$$(y_1 = \sqrt{a}) \quad \square$$

The following theorem says that the formula $wlp(\alpha, q)$ expresses the weakest liberal precondition. The subsequent corollary states that the formula $vc(p, \alpha, q)$ expresses partial correctness.

THEOREM 7.4 ($wlp(\alpha, q)$ is the Weakest Liberal Precondition)   Let B be a basis for predicate logic, $S \in L_1^B$ a flowchart program, α a path in S, and $q \in WFF_B$ a formula. For every interpretation $\mathscr{I}$ of B the predicate $\mathscr{I}(wlp(\alpha, q))$ is the weakest liberal precondition of the path α and the predicate $\mathscr{I}(q)$.

Proof. Suppose $\alpha = (l_0, \ldots, l_k)$. The proof is by induction on the length k of α.

Induction basis   For $k = 0$ the meaning $\mathscr{M}_{\mathscr{I}}(\alpha)$ is the identity function. Hence $\mathscr{I}(q)$ is the weakest liberal precondition of α and $\mathscr{I}(q)$.

Induction step   For $k > 0$ set $\beta = (l_1, \ldots, l_k)$. By induction hypothesis $\mathscr{I}(wlp(\beta, q))$ is the weakest liberal precondition of β and $\mathscr{I}(q)$. It is to prove that for every state $\sigma \in \Sigma$:

$$\mathscr{I}(wlp(\alpha, q))(\sigma) = \text{true} \quad \text{iff}$$
$$\text{either } \mathscr{M}_\mathscr{I}(\alpha)(\sigma) \text{ is undefined} \tag{1}$$
$$\text{or } \mathscr{M}_\mathscr{I}(\alpha)(\sigma) \text{ is defined and } \mathscr{I}(q)(\mathscr{M}_\mathscr{I}(\alpha)(\sigma)) = \text{true}$$

Two cases are distinguished:

(i) *Parallel assignment* There is a command

$$l_0 : (x_1, \dots, x_n) := (t_1, \dots, t_n); \; goto \; l_1$$

in the program S. Let $\sigma \in \Sigma$ be an arbitrary state. Then:

$$\mathscr{I}(wlp(\alpha, q))(\sigma) = \mathscr{I}((wlp(\beta, q))_{x_1, \dots, x_n}^{t_1, \dots, t_n})(\sigma)$$
$$\text{(by definition of } wlp(\alpha, q))$$
$$= \mathscr{I}(wlp(\beta, q))(\sigma')$$

where $\sigma' = \sigma[x_1/\mathscr{I}(t_1)(\sigma)] \dots [x_n/\mathscr{I}(t_n)(\sigma)]$ (by the Substitution Theorem). Now, by induction hypothesis:

$$\mathscr{I}(wlp(\beta, q))(\sigma') = \text{true} \quad \text{iff}$$
$$\text{either } \mathscr{M}_\mathscr{I}(\beta)(\sigma') \text{ is undefined}$$
$$\text{or } \mathscr{M}_\mathscr{I}(\beta)(\sigma') \text{ is defined and } \mathscr{I}(q)(\mathscr{M}_\mathscr{I}(\beta)(\sigma')) = \text{true.}$$

Because $(l_0, \sigma) \Rightarrow (l_1, \sigma')$ one has:

$\mathscr{M}_\mathscr{I}(\alpha)(\sigma)$ is undefined, iff $\mathscr{M}_\mathscr{I}(\beta)(\sigma')$ is;
if $\mathscr{M}_\mathscr{I}(\alpha)(\sigma)$ is defined, then $\mathscr{M}_\mathscr{I}(\alpha)(\sigma) = \mathscr{M}_\mathscr{I}(\beta)(\sigma')$ and $\mathscr{I}(q)(\mathscr{M}_\mathscr{I}(\alpha)(\sigma)) = \mathscr{I}(q)(\mathscr{M}_\mathscr{I}(\beta)(\sigma'))$

This concludes the proof of (1).

(ii) *Conditional jump* There is a command

$$l_0 : if \; e \; then \; goto \; l \; else \; goto \; l' \; fi$$

Consider first the case $l = l_1$. Let $\sigma \in \Sigma$ be an arbitrary state. Then:

$$\mathscr{I}(wlp(\alpha, q))(\sigma) = \mathscr{I}(e \supset wlp(\beta, q))(\sigma)$$

If $\mathscr{I}(e)(\sigma) = \text{true}$ then

$$\mathscr{I}(e \supset wlp(\beta, q))(\sigma) = \text{true} \quad \text{iff}$$
$$\text{either } \mathscr{M}_\mathscr{I}(\beta)(\sigma) \text{ is undefined}$$
$$\text{or } \mathscr{M}_\mathscr{I}(\beta)(\sigma) \text{ is defined and } \mathscr{I}(q)(\mathscr{M}_\mathscr{I}(\beta)(\sigma)) = \text{true}$$

Because $(l_0, \sigma) \Rightarrow (l_1, \sigma)$:

$\mathscr{M}_\mathscr{I}(\alpha)(\sigma)$ is undefined, iff $\mathscr{M}_\mathscr{I}(\beta)(\sigma)$ is;
if $\mathscr{M}_\mathscr{I}(\alpha)(\sigma)$ is defined, then $\mathscr{M}_\mathscr{I}(\alpha)(\sigma) = \mathscr{M}_\mathscr{I}(\beta)(\sigma)$.

This proves (1).

If, on the contrary, $\mathscr{I}(e)(\sigma) = \text{false}$, then $\mathscr{I}(e \supset wlp(\beta, q))(\sigma) = \text{true}$. Because $(l_0, \sigma) \Rightarrow (l', \sigma)$, $\mathscr{M}_\mathscr{I}(\alpha)(\sigma)$ is undefined. This again proves (1).

The case $l \neq l_1$ may be treated similarly. $\qquad\square$

Corollary 7.5   Let B be a basis for predicate logic, $p, q \in WFF_B$ two formulas and α a path in a flowchart program from L_1^B. For every interpretation $\mathscr{I}$ of B, the path α is partially correct with respect to the formulas p and q, iff the verification condition $vc(p, \alpha, q)$ is valid in $\mathscr{I}$.

Proof. The corollary follows directly from Theorems 7.4 and 6.5.   □

As an immediate consequence of Lemma 7.1 and Corollary 7.5 one obtains the following result:

Theorem 7.6 (Partial Correctness is a First-order Property)   Let B be a basis for predicate logic, $p, q \in WFF_B$ two formulas, and $S \in L_1^B$ a flowchart program. For every interpretation $\mathscr{I}$ of B the program S is partially correct with respect to the formulas p and q (in the interpretation $\mathscr{I}$) iff for every path α through S the verification condition $vc(p, \alpha, q)$ is valid in $\mathscr{I}$.   □

This theorem says that partial correctness is a first-order property in the following sense: partial correctness in an interpretation $\mathscr{I}$ depends only on the (first-order) theory $Th(\mathscr{I})$, not on $\mathscr{I}$ itself. In fact, according to Theorem 7.6 a program is partially correct (in $\mathscr{I}$) iff the verification conditions are formulas from $Th(\mathscr{I})$. As a consequence, partial correctness results are also valid in non-standard models; in other words, if $\mathscr{I}$ and $\mathscr{J}$ are interpretations such that $Th(\mathscr{I}) = Th(\mathscr{J})$, then a program is partially correct in $\mathscr{I}$ exactly when it is partially correct in $\mathscr{J}$—even if the interpretations $\mathscr{I}$ and $\mathscr{J}$ are not isomorphic. It will be shown in Theorem 7.11 that termination—and hence, total correctness—do not possess this property. This is the deeper reason why partial correctness and termination are often proved separately.

Corollary 7.5 and Theorem 7.6 now allow the introduction of the inductive assertions method (Definition 7.7) and the proof of its soundness (Theorem 7.9).

Definition 7.7 (Inductive Assertions Method)   Let B be a basis for predicate logic, $p, q \in WFF_B$ two formulas, $S \in L_1^B$ a flowchart program, and $\mathscr{I}$ an interpretation of B. The inductive assertions method proving the partial correctness of S with respect to the formulas p and q in the interpretation $\mathscr{I}$ consists of the following three steps:

(i) Choose a subset C of the set of all labels occurring in S such that the labels *begin* and *end* are in C, and every loop in S contains at least one element of C. The elements of C are called *cutpoints*.

(ii) Associate a formula $q_l \in WFF_B$ with each cutpoint $l \in C$, namely: the formula p with the cutpoint *begin*, the formula q with the cutpoint *end*, and an 'appropriate' formula with every other cutpoint. This formula can be arbitrary as long as step (iii) can be carried out. If a cutpoint l is contained in a loop, the associated formula q_l is called an *invariant*.

(iii) For each path $\alpha = (l_0, \ldots, l_k)$ in S, $k \geq 1$, such that $l_0, l_k \in C$ and

$l_1, \ldots, l_{k-1} \notin C$, prove that the verification condition $vc(q_{l_0}, \alpha, q_{l_k})$ is valid in $\mathscr{I}$. $\qquad \square$

Note that due to the definition of the set C of cutpoints, only finitely many paths must be examined in step (iii). Indeed the length of such a path α cannot exceed the number of labels occurring in the program S, because otherwise it would contain a loop and, hence, at least one further cutpoint.

Before proving the soundness of the inductive assertions method, an example is given.

EXAMPLE 7.8 (Inductive Assertions Method)   Consider again the flowchart program of Examples 3.2 and 3.3. The inductive assertions method is used to show that this program is partially correct with respect to the formulas $x = a$ and $y_1 = \sqrt{a}$ in the usual interpretation (a is a variable not occurring in the program).

(i) C is chosen to be the set $\{begin, test, end\}$.

(ii) One takes ($x = a$) for q_{begin}, ($y_1 = \sqrt{a}$) for q_{end} and chooses the formula

$$x = a \wedge y_1^2 \leq x \wedge y_3 = (y_1 + 1)^2 \wedge y_2 = 2 * y_1 + 1$$

of Example 7.3 for q_{test}.

(iii) It is sufficient to examine the paths ($begin, test$), ($test, loop, upd, test$), and ($test, end$). Hence the verification conditions which have to be proved valid (in the usual interpretation) are those of (4) to (6) in Example 7.3. These proofs are left to the reader who may note their similarity to the arguments used in Example 6.8. $\qquad \square$

THEOREM 7.9 (Soundness of the Inductive Assertions Method)   If steps (i), (ii), and (iii) of the inductive assertions method as described in Definition 7.7 can be carried out successfully, then the program S is partially correct with respect to the formulas p and q in the interpretation $\mathscr{I}$.

Proof. The idea of the proof is to show that a path through S consists of paths that were examined in step (iii). The partial correctness of the path then results from the partial correctness of these 'elementary' paths.

Specifically, consider a computation sequence

$$(l_0, \sigma_0), (l_1, \sigma_1), \ldots, (l_k, \sigma_k)$$

with $k \geq 0$ such that $\mathscr{I}(p)(\sigma_0) = $ true and l_k is a cutpoint. Then $\mathscr{I}(q_{l_k})(\sigma_k) = $ true. The proof of this claim is by induction on the number m of (occurrences of) cutpoints in the path $(l_0, \ldots, l_k)$.

Induction basis   If $m = 1$ then $k = 0$, because $l_0 = begin$ is a cutpoint. Then $\mathscr{I}(q_{l_k})(\sigma_k) = \mathscr{I}(p)(\sigma_0) = $ true.

Induction step   Assume $m > 1$. Let l_j be the last cutpoint before l_k or, more precisely, $j < k$ is such that $l_j \in C$ and $l_{j+1}, \ldots, l_{k-1} \notin C$. Then

$$\mathscr{I}(q_{l_j})(\sigma_j) = \text{true}$$

by induction hypothesis. Moreover the path $(l_j, \ldots, l_k)$ is among those examined in step (iii). By Corollary 7.5 this path is partially correct with respect to q_{l_j} and q_{l_k} which leads to $\mathscr{I}(q_{l_k})(\sigma_k) = \text{true}$. This concludes the proof of the claim.

Now for a computation or, in other words, for a computation sequence

$$(l_0, \sigma_0) \Rightarrow \cdots \Rightarrow (l_k, \sigma_k)$$

with $l_k = end$, every path $(l_0, \ldots, l_k)$ through the program S is partially correct with respect to p and q. The soundness of the inductive assertions method then follows from Theorem 7.6.   □

EXAMPLE 7.10 (Inductive Assertions Method)   Consider the following flowchart program.

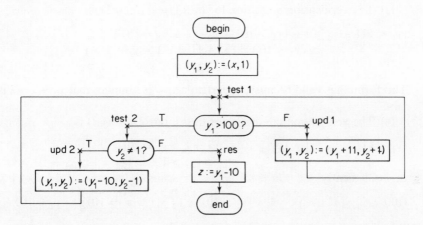

The inductive assertions method is used to prove that the program is partially correct with respect to the formulas $x \leq 100$ and $z = 91$ (in the usual interpretation). This means, whenever the input value of x does not exceed 100, the output value of z is 91. (A recursive version of this '91-program' may be found in Example 9.7.)

(i) C is chosen to be the set $\{begin, test\,1, end\}$.

(ii) One takes $(x \leq 100)$ for q_{begin}, $(z = 91)$ for q_{end} and chooses

$$y_1 \leq 111 \wedge y_2 \geq 1 \wedge (y_1 \geq 101 \wedge y_2 = 1 \supset y_1 = 101)$$

for q_{test1}. It is clear that only insight into the way the program works allows one to find an appropriate formula for q_{test1}.

(iii) There are four paths to be considered: $(begin, test\,1)$, $(test\,1, test\,2, upd\,2, test\,1)$, $(test\,1, upd\,1, test\,1)$, and $(test\,1, test\,2, res, end)$.

(1) It is easy to see that for the path ($begin, test$ 1) the verification condition is:

$$x \leq 100 \supset (x \leq 111 \wedge 1 \geq 1 \wedge (x \geq 101 \wedge 1 = 1 \supset x = 101))$$

The validity of this formula is evident (note in particular that $x \geq 101$ is false).

(2) The verification condition for ($test$ 1, $test$ 2, upd 2, $test$ 1) is:

$$(y_1 \leq 111 \wedge y_2 \geq 1 \wedge (y_1 \geq 101 \wedge y_2 = 1 \supset y_1 = 101))$$
$$\supset (y_1 > 100 \supset (y_2 \neq 1 \supset (y_1 - 10 \leq 111 \wedge y_2 - 1 \geq 1$$
$$\wedge (y_1 - 10 \geq 101 \wedge y_2 - 1 = 1 \supset y_1 - 10 = 101))))$$

or, equivalently (remembering that $p \supset (q \supset r)$ and $p \wedge q \supset r$ are equivalent and that $y_2 \geq 1$ and $y_2 \neq 1$ imply $y_2 \geq 2$):

$$(101 \leq y_1 \leq 111 \wedge y_2 \geq 2 \wedge (y_1 \geq 101 \wedge y_2 = 1 \supset y_1 = 101))$$
$$\supset (y_1 \leq 121 \wedge y_2 \geq 2 \wedge (y_1 \geq 111 \wedge y_2 = 2 \supset y_1 = 111)).$$

The validity of this formula is a result from the fact that $y_1 \leq 111$ and $y_1 \geq 111$ imply $y_1 = 111$.

(3) The verification condition for ($test$ 1, upd 1, $test$ 2) is:

$$(y_1 \leq 111 \wedge y_2 \geq 1 \wedge (y_1 \geq 101 \wedge y_2 = 1 \supset y_1 = 101))$$
$$\supset (y_1 \leq 100 \supset (y_1 + 11 \leq 111 \wedge y_2 + 1 \geq 1$$
$$\wedge (y_1 + 11 \geq 101 \wedge y_2 + 1 = 1 \supset y_1 + 11 = 101)))$$

This formula is valid because, in particular, $y_2 \geq 1$ implies that $y_2 + 1 = 1$ is false.

(4) The verification condition for ($test$ 1, $test$ 2, res, end) is:

$$(y_1 \leq 111 \wedge y_2 \geq 1 \wedge (y_1 \geq 101 \wedge y_2 = 1 \supset y_1 = 101))$$
$$\supset (y_1 > 100 \supset (y_2 = 1 \supset y_1 - 10 = 91))$$

or, equivalently:

$$(100 < y_1 \leq 111 \wedge y_2 = 1 \wedge (y_1 \geq 101 \wedge y_2 = 1 \supset y_1 = 101)) \supset y_1 = 101 \quad \Box$$

The section concludes with a few remarks. The most difficult part in the proofs of Examples 7.8 and 7.10 is to find an invariant. This requires a thorough understanding of the program. Hence it seems reasonable to establish the invariants (and to perform the verification) during, rather than after, the design of the program. As a matter of fact, the proof of Theorem 8.16 indicates a method which allows one to construct such an invariant in the case where the interpretation is that of Peano arithmetic. Unfortunately, the invariant thus obtained is much too complicated to be of any practical use.

Theorem 7.9 states the soundness of the inductive assertions method. Another interesting question is whether the inductive assertions method is complete or, more precisely, whether the method is effectual enough to prove the program partially correct whenever the program is indeed partially correct by Definition 6.1. The answer is not simple for the general case but is affirmative for the case of Peano arithmetic (and for any other interpretation that is at least as 'powerful' as Peano arithmetic); this problem will be discussed in Section 8.2.

7.2 The Well-Founded Sets Method

In the previous section it was proved that partial correctness is a first-order property (Theorem 7.6). Termination is not, as will be shown in the next theorem. The proof of this theorem moveover justifies why termination proofs need well-founded sets.

THEOREM 7.11 (Termination is not a First-order Property) The flowchart program

$$begin: x := 0; \; goto \; test;$$
$$test: \; if \; x = y \; then \; goto \; end \; else \; goto \; loop \; fi;$$
$$loop: \; x := x + 1; \; goto \; test$$

terminates with respect to the formula *true* in the standard model of Peano arithmetic but it does not in a non-standard model.

Proof. The program terminates in the standard model of Peano arithmetic because, informally speaking, the value of x eventually reaches the input value of y. This does not happen in the non-standard model when the input value of y is an infinite number (see Section 2.4 or Exercise 2.4–5). $\qquad \square$

Informally, Theorem 7.11 states that the termination of a program in an interpretation $\mathscr{I}$ depends on more than its first-order theory $Th(\mathscr{I})$. As the standard model of Peano arithmetic differs from a non-standard model by the validity of the principle of induction over the natural numbers (as explained in Section 2.4) it is not astonishing that this induction principle is required in termination proofs. Actually the induction principle to be used in this section is Noetherian induction which has been introduced in Section 1.2 as a generalization of the induction over natural numbers and which makes use of well-founded sets.

DEFINITION 7.12 (Well-founded Sets Method) Let B be a basis for predicate logic, $p \in WFF_B$ a formula, $S \in L_1^B$ a flowchart program, and $\mathscr{I}$ an interpretation of B. The well-founded sets method proving the termination of S with respect to the formula p in the interpretation $\mathscr{I}$ consists of the following seven steps:

 (i) Choose a subset C of the set of all labels occurring in S such that the label *begin* is in C, and every loop of S contains at least one element of C.
 (ii) Associate a formula $q_l \in WFF_B$ with each label $l \in C$, namely: the formula p with the cutpoint *begin*, and an 'appropriate' formula with every other cutpoint.
(iii) For each path $\alpha = (l_0, \ldots, l_k)$ in S, $k \geq 1$, such that $l_0, l_k \in C$ and $l_1, \ldots, l_{k-1} \notin C$, prove that the verification condition $vc(q_{l_0}, \alpha, q_{l_k})$ is valid in $\mathscr{I}$.
(iv) Choose a (not necessarily proper) subset C' of the set C such that each loop of S contains at least one element of C'.

(v) Choose an 'appropriate' well-founded set $(W, \sqsubseteq)$.

(vi) Associate to each label $l \in C'$ a function $g_l: \Sigma \to W$ mapping the set of all states into the well-founded set.

(vii) For each path $\alpha = (l_0, \ldots, l_k)$ in S, $k \geq 1$, such that $l_0, l_k \in C'$ and $l_1, \ldots, l_{k-1} \notin C'$ prove that for all states $\sigma \in \Sigma$:

$$\text{if } \mathcal{I}(q_{l_0})(\sigma) = \text{true}$$
$$\text{and if } \mathcal{M}_{\mathcal{I}}(\alpha)(\sigma) \text{ is defined}$$
$$\text{then } g_{l_k}(\mathcal{M}_{\mathcal{I}}(\alpha)(\sigma)) \sqsubseteq g_{l_0}(\sigma). \qquad \square$$

Note that the first three steps of the well-founded sets method are identical with those of the inductive assertions method except that the label *end* must not occur in C. The goal of these steps is to establish the validity of the formulas q_l. This validity plays a role in (the soundness of) step (vii). If no such properties are required, steps (i) to (iii) may be skipped or, more precisely, in step (ii) the formula *true* is chosen for each q_l.

Before the well-founded sets method is proved to be sound, it is illustrated by an example.

EXAMPLE 7.13 (Well-founded Sets Method) Consider again the flowchart program of Examples 3.2 and 3.3. The well-founded sets method is used to prove that this program terminates with respect to the formula *true* in the usual interpretation; that is, it is proved that the program always terminates. The steps (i) to (iii) are skipped.

(iv) Choose C' to be the set $\{test\}$.

(v) Choose $(W, \sqsubseteq)$ to be $(Nat, \leq)$.

(vi) Let $g_{test}: \Sigma \to Nat$ be defined by $g_{test}(\sigma) = \sigma(x) + 1 - \sigma(y_3)$.

(vii) The only path that must be examined is $\alpha = (test, loop, upd, test)$. Let $\sigma \in \Sigma$ be a state such that $\mathcal{M}_{\mathcal{I}}(\alpha)(\sigma)$ is defined or, equivalently, such that

$$\sigma(y_3) \leq \sigma(x) \qquad (1)$$

As q_{test} was implicitly chosen to be the formula *true*, one has to prove that

$$(\mathcal{M}_{\mathcal{I}}(\alpha)(\sigma))(x) + 1 - (\mathcal{M}_{\mathcal{I}}(\alpha)(\sigma))(y_3) < \sigma(x) + 1 - \sigma(y_3) \qquad (2)$$

Clearly,

$$(\mathcal{M}_{\mathcal{I}}(\alpha)(\sigma))(x) = \sigma(x)$$
$$(\mathcal{M}_{\mathcal{I}}(\alpha)(\sigma))(y_3) = \sigma(y_3) + \sigma(y_2) + 2.$$

Hence (2) becomes

$$\sigma(x) + 1 - (\sigma(y_3) + \sigma(y_2) + 2) < \sigma(x) + 1 - \sigma(y_3). \qquad (3)$$

By (1) it is the case that

$$\sigma(x) + 1 - \sigma(y_3) > 0.$$

Hence (3) holds because $\sigma(y_2) + 2 > 0$. (Remember the somewhat peculiar properties of the subtraction in *Nat* recalled in Section 1.1.) This concludes the termination proof.

Note that it is possible to choose a simpler function g_{test} at the price of a more elaborate well-founded set. For instance, in step (v) choose $(W, \sqsubseteq)$ to be $(Nat^2, \sqsubseteq)$ with '$\sqsubseteq$' defined by:

$$(m_1, n_1) \sqsubseteq (m_2, n_2) \qquad \text{iff } m_1 + 1 - n_1 \leq m_2 + 1 - n_2.$$

(That this is a well-founded set is easy to prove.) In step (vi) let

$$g_{test} \colon \Sigma \to Nat^2$$

be defined by

$$g_{test}(\sigma) = (\sigma(x), \sigma(y_3))$$

The proof in step (vii) is then essentially the same as above. $\qquad\square$

THEOREM 7.14 (Soundness of the Well-founded Sets Method)   If steps (i) through (vii) of the well-founded sets method as described in Definition 7.12 can be carried out successfully, then the program S terminates with respect to the formula p in the interpretation $\mathscr{I}$.

Proof. The proof is by contradiction. Assume that there is a state $\sigma_0 \in \Sigma$ such that $\mathscr{I}(p)(\sigma_0) = $ true and that the computation

$$(l_0, \sigma_0), (l_1, \sigma_1), \ldots$$

for σ_0 is infinite. From steps (i) to (iii) one may deduce—in a way similar to that used in the proof of Theorem 7.9—that

$$\mathscr{I}(q_{l_j})(\sigma_j) = \text{true} \qquad (1)$$

for every label $l_j \in C$. As C' is a subset of C, (1) also holds for every label $l_j \in C'$.

As the computation is infinite and the program contains only a finite number of labels, there exists at least one label which occurs infinitely often in the computation. As each loop contains at least one label from C' the computation contains an infinite number of occurrences of labels from C'. Let $l_{i_1}, l_{i_2}, \ldots,$ be these (infinite number of) occurrences of labels, $i_1 < i_2 < \cdots$. Consider two successive occurrences of these, say l_{i_k} and $l_{i_{k+1}}$. Then the path $\alpha = (l_{i_k}, l_{i_k+1}, \ldots, l_{i_{k+1}-1}, l_{i_{k+1}})$ is among those examined in step (vii) because $l_{i_k}, l_{i_{k+1}} \in C'$ and $l_{i_k+1}, \ldots, l_{i_{k+1}-1} \notin C'$. By (1) and because $\mathscr{M}_{\mathscr{I}}(\alpha)(\sigma_{i_k}) = \sigma_{i_{k+1}}$ is defined, one may conclude

$$g_{l_{i_{k+1}}}(\sigma_{i_{k+1}}) \sqsubset g_{l_{i_k}}(\sigma_{i_k})$$

Hence there exists an infinite descending sequence

$$\cdots \sqsubset g_{l_{i_2}}(\sigma_{i_2}) \sqsubset g_{l_{i_1}}(\sigma_{i_1})$$

of elements from W. This contradicts the assumption that $(W, \sqsubseteq)$ is a well-founded set. $\qquad\square$

It is often the case that the domain D of the interpretation $\mathscr{I} = (D, \mathscr{I}_0)$—or at least a definable subset of D—is a well-founded set. If moreover each of the functions g_l of step (vi) of the well-founded sets method can be expressed by a term, then step (vii) is reduced to a validity proof of first-order predicate formulas.

DEFINITION 7.15 (Well-founded Sets Method with Terms) The well-founded sets method, using terms is identical with the well-founded sets method as described in Definition 7.12, except for steps (v) to (vii) which are replaced by the following five steps:

(v) Choose a formula $w \in WFF_B$ in which (at most) one variable, say x, occurs free and a predicate symbol of B, say $\sqsubseteq$.

(vi) Prove that

$$(\{\sigma(x) \mid \sigma \in \Sigma, \mathscr{I}(w)(\sigma) = \text{true}\}, \mathscr{I}_0(\sqsubseteq))$$

is a well-founded set.

(vii) Associate to each label $l \in C'$ an appropriate term $t_l \in T_B$.

(viii) Prove that the formula

$$q_l \supset w_x^{t_l}$$

is valid in the interpretation $\mathscr{I}$ for each $l \in C'$.

(ix) For each path $\alpha = (l_0, \ldots, l_k)$ in S, $k \geq 1$, such that $l_0, l_k \in C'$ and $l_1, \ldots, l_{k-1} \notin C'$ prove the validity in $\mathscr{I}$ of the verification condition

$$vc(q_{l_0} \wedge t_{l_0} = a, \alpha, t_{l_k} \sqsubseteq a)$$

where a is a variable not occurring in q_{l_0}, t_{l_0}, and t_{l_k}. □

Note that the formulas q_l associated in step (ii) with each label $l \in C$ have now an additional role: according to step (vii) they guarantee that the values of the terms t_l are in the well-founded set.

The proof of the soundness of the method is left to the reader.

EXAMPLE 7.16 (Well-founded Sets Method with Terms) Reconsider Example 7.13. Steps (i) to (iv) are identical.

(v) The formula w is chosen to be *true* and the predicate symbol '$\sqsubseteq$' to be '$\leq$'.

(vi) $(Nat, \leq)$ is a well-founded set.

(vii) The term t_{test} is chosen to be $x + 1 - y_3$.

(viii) As w is the formula *true* nothing has to be proved.

(ix) The only path to be considered is again $\alpha = (test, loop, upd, test)$. The verification condition to be examined is

$$vc(true \wedge t_{test} = a, \alpha, t_{test} < a)$$

or, equivalently

$$t_{test} = a \supset wlp(\alpha, t_{test} < a). \tag{1}$$

It is easy to check that

$$wlp(\alpha, t_{test} < a) = (y_3 \leq x \supset x + 1 - (y_3 + y_2 + 2) < a).$$

Hence (1) is valid if

$$x + 1 - y_3 = a \wedge y_3 \leq x \supset x + 1 - (y_3 + y_2 + 2) < a.$$

The validity of this formula is established by the same arguments as in step (vii) of Example 7.13.

This concludes the termination proof.

Note that unlike Example 7.13 it is not possible to choose $(W, \sqsubseteq)$ to be $(Nat^2, \sqsubseteq)$ with '$\sqsubseteq$' defined appropriately because Nat^2 is not a subset of the domain Nat of the interpretation. $\qquad\square$

EXAMPLE 7.17 (Well-founded Sets Method with Terms) Consider again the flowchart program of Examples 7.13 and 7.16 but this time with a different interpretation $\mathcal{I} = (Int, \mathcal{I}_0)$, where $\mathcal{I}_0$ maps the symbols used into their usual meanings for the integers. It is shown that this program terminates with respect to the formula $x \geq 0$.

(i) Choose $C = \{begin, test\}$.

(ii) Take $x \geq 0$ for q_{begin} and choose $y_2 > 0 \wedge x + y_2 - y_3 \geq 0$ for q_{test}.

(iii) The verification condition for $(begin, test)$ is

$$x \geq 0 \supset x + 1 - 1 \geq 0.$$

The verification condition for $(test, loop, upd, test)$ is

$$y_2 > 0 \wedge x + y_2 - y_3 \geq 0 \wedge y_3 \leq x \supset y_2 + 2 > 0 \wedge x + y_2 + 2 - (y_3 + y_2 + 2) \geq 0.$$

The validity of these conditions is evident. For the latter formula, $y_2 + 2 > 0$ results from $y_2 > 0$ and $x - y_3 \geq 0$ results from $y_3 \leq x$.

(iv) Choose $C' = \{test\}$.

(v) Choose the formula $x \geq 0$ for w and the symbol '$\leq$' for '$\sqsubseteq$'.

(vi) As the set $\{\sigma(x) \mid \sigma \in \Sigma, \sigma(x) \geq 0\}$ is the set of natural numbers,

$$(\{\sigma(x) \mid \sigma \in \Sigma, \sigma(x) \geq 0\}, \mathcal{I}_0(\leq))$$

is a well-founded set.

(vii) Choose the term $x + y_2 - y_3$ for t_{test}.

(viii) The formula

$$y_2 > 0 \wedge x + y_2 - y_3 \geq 0 \supset x + y_2 - y_3 \geq 0$$

is clearly valid.

(ix) The verification condition to be examined is

$$vc(y_2 > 0 \wedge x + y_2 - y_3 \geq 0 \wedge x + y_2 - y_3 = a, (test, loop, upd, test), \\ x + y_2 - y_3 < a)$$

or, equivalently

$$y_2 > 0 \wedge x + y_2 - y_3 \geq 0 \wedge x + y_2 - y_3 = a \wedge y_3 \leq x \supset \\ x + y_2 + 2 - y_3 - y_2 - 2 < a$$

or

$$y_2 > 0 \land x + y_2 - y_3 \geq 0 \land y_3 \leq x \supset x - y_3 < x + y_2 - y_3.$$

The right-hand side of this implication is a direct consequence of the fact that $y_2 > 0$.

This concludes the proof of termination. □

Note that this proof bears strong similarities with that of Example 7.16. The main difference lies in the well-founded set *Nat* (implicitly defined by the choice in step (v)) which is a *proper* subset of the domain *Int* of the interpretation. Note also that the function symbol '−', for instance, occurring in the term t_{test}, is interpreted as subtraction on *Int*. As a consequence of this difference the formula q_{test} chosen in step (ii) has to be more elaborate than in Example 7.16. See also Exercise 8.4–3(i).

EXAMPLE 7.18 (Well-founded Sets Method with Terms) It is proved in this example that the flowchart program of Example 7.10 terminates with respect to the formula $x \leq 100$.

(i) Choose C to be the set $\{begin, test\,1\}$.
(ii) Take $x \leq 100$ for q_{begin} and choose $y_1 \leq 111 \land y_2 \geq 1$ for q_{test1}.
(iii) The paths to be examined are $(begin, test\,1)$, $(test\,1, test\,2, upd\,2, test\,1)$, and $(test\,1, upd\,1, test\,1)$. The proofs that the verification conditions are valid are left to the reader.
(iv) Choose C' to be the set $\{test\,1\}$.
(v) Choose *true* for w and '≤' for '⊑'.
(vi) The proof that $(Nat, \leq)$ is well-founded is trivial.
(vii) Choose $201 + 21y_2 - 2y_1$ for t_{test1}.
(viii) This step is trivial since $w = true$.
(ix) For the path $(test\,1, test\,2, upd\,2, test\,1)$ the verification condition is (equivalent to)

$$y_1 \leq 111 \land y_2 \geq 1 \land y_1 > 100 \land y_2 \neq 1$$
$$\supset 201 + 21(y_2 - 1) - 2(y_1 - 10) < 201 + 21y_2 - 2y_1.$$

For the path $(test\,1, upd\,1, test\,1)$ it is

$$y_1 \leq 111 \land y_2 \geq 1 \land y_1 \leq 100$$
$$\supset 201 + 21(y_2 + 1) - 2(y_1 + 11) < 201 + 21y_2 - 2y_1.$$

The proofs that these formulas are valid are left to the reader. In these proofs it is essential to remember the somewhat peculiar property of subtraction on *Nat*. For the case at hand this means that

$$201 + 21(y_2 - 1) - 2(y_1 - 10)$$

simplifies to

$$201 + 21y_2 - 21 - (2y_1 - 20)$$

and, because $y_1 > 100$, to

$$200 + 21y_2 - 2y_1.$$ $\qquad\qquad\qquad\qquad\qquad\qquad$ □

EXERCISES

7.1–1 In Definition 7.2 formulas $wlp(\alpha, q)$ were introduced to express weakest liberal preconditions of paths and were used to construct so-called verification conditions for paths. Try to give a similar definition with strongest postconditions instead of weakest liberal preconditions.

7.1–2 Prove with the aid of the inductive assertions method the partial correctness of the (translation into a flowchart program of the) gcd-program of Exercise 6.3–1. Note that in Exercise 6.3–1 some hints have already been given how to find invariants for partial correctness proofs.

7.1–3 A natural number n is called *perfect*, if it is the sum of all $m \in Nat, 1 \leq m < n$, which divide n. The number 6, for instance, is perfect because $6 = 3 + 2 + 1$. Write a flowchart program which determines whether a number is perfect and prove its partial correctness.

7.2–1 (i) Let α be a path in a flowchart program and q a formula from WFF_B. Give an inductive definition of a formula $wp(\alpha, q)$ from WFF_B expressing the weakest precondition of α and $\mathscr{I}(q)$ in every interpretation $\mathscr{I}$.

(ii) In the case of partial correctness the formulas $wlp(\alpha, q)$ were used to reduce the proof of partial correctness of a program to the proof of—possibly infinitely many—formulas from WFF_B, called verification conditions. Convince yourself that a similar reduction for total correctness with the aid of the formulas $wp(\alpha, q)$ introduced above does not work. (That it cannot work results from Theorem 7.11.)

7.2–2 Prove the termination of the (translation into a flowchart program of the) gcd-program of Exercise 6.3–1:

(i) With the aid of the general well-founded sets method (Definition 7.12);
(ii) With the aid of the well-founded sets method with terms (Definition 7.15).

7.2–3 Consider the following flowchart program S

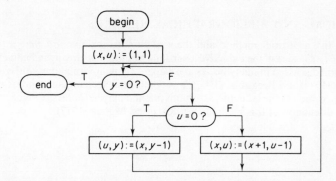

(i) Prove that S is totally correct with respect to the formulas $y = a$ and $x = 2^a$.
(ii) Assume that only the predicate and function symbols of Peano arithmetic (with their usual interpretation) are available. Prove that the well-founded sets method with terms does not allow a proof of the termination of S with respect to the formula *true*. (*Hint*: Note that for a term t associated with a cutpoint the value $\mathscr{I}(t)(\sigma)$ must decrease each time this cutpoint is reached.)

148

*7.2-4 *Well-founded sets method with formulas* Consider the method obtained by replacing steps (vii) to (ix) of the well-founded sets method with terms (Definition 7.15) by:

(vii') Associate with each label $l \in C'$ an appropriate formula $p_l \in WFF_B$ containing a free variable a, which occurs neither in the program nor in the invariants q_l of step (ii). If the label l is contained in a loop, then p_l is called a *convergent* of this loop.

(viii') Prove that the formula

$$q_l \supset \exists a . (w_x^a \wedge p_l)$$

is valid in the interpretation $\mathscr{I}$ for each label $l \in C'$.

(ix') For each path $\alpha = (l_0, \ldots, l_k)$ in S, $k \geq 1$, such that $l_0, l_k \in C'$ and $l_1, \ldots, l_{k-1} \notin C'$, prove the validity in $\mathscr{I}$ of the verification condition

$$vc(q_{l_0} \wedge w_x^a \wedge p_{l_0}, \alpha, \exists b . (w_x^b \wedge b \sqsubset a \wedge (p_{l_k})_a^b))$$

where b is a variable not occurring in p_{l_k}.

The exercise is:

(i) Prove the soundness of this new method.
(ii) Prove that the well-founded sets method with terms can be obtained as a special case of this new method.
(iii) Prove the termination (with respect to *true*) of the program of Exercise 7.2–3 with this new method (*without* the restriction that the formulas p_l are over the basis of Peano arithmetic).
(iv) As (iii) but *with* the restriction that the formulas p_l are over the basis of Peano arithmetic. (*Hint:* Consult the remark preceding Theorem 8.16 which indicates how to construct a formula over the basis of Peano arithmetic which is equivalent to the formula $a = 2^x$).

Note that (iv) illustrates a completeness property of the well-founded sets method with formulas contrasting with the incompleteness property of the well-founded sets method with terms proved in Exercise 7.2–3. The point is that there is a formula in the Peano arithmetic which is equivalent to the formula $a = 2^x$ but there is no term t in the Peano arithmetic such that $t = 2^x$ is valid. A more precise treatment of this problem may be found in Section 8.3.

HISTORICAL AND BIBLIOGRAPHICAL REMARKS

The inductive assertions method and the well-founded sets method were introduced in Floyd (1967); the idea of the inductive assertions method was already in Naur (1966). Both methods are discussed in many books and papers. Good informal descriptions are found in Manna (1974) and Berg *et al.* (1982); a very informal account is in Anderson (1979). A formal description of the inductive assertions method may be found in Greibach (1975). An extensive discussion of this method is in Katz and Manna (1977).

8
The Axiomatic Method
of Hoare

This chapter discusses the verification method of Hoare, well known for proving the partial correctness of while-programs. This method is usually presented in the form of a calculus, the so-called Hoare calculus. Essentially this approach is identical with the inductive assertions method introduced in the last chapter, as may become plausible from the following considerations. The inductive assertions method can be used on while-programs, since every while-program can be easily transformed to an equivalent flowchart program. Because this translation produces flowchart programs of a special form—namely flowchart programs without interleaved loops—the inductive assertions method can be simplified. This simplified form leads naturally to a calculus, namely the Hoare calculus. In the last section it will be seen how (a slight variant of) the well-founded sets method can be likewise incorporated in the Hoare calculus to achieve a method for proving the total correctness of while-programs.

8.1 Hoare Logic and Hoare Calculus

The Hoare calculus is a calculus for a logic, called Hoare logic, in which one can formulate propositions about the partial correctness of while-programs. This logic will now be introduced. Just as in the definition of the while-programming language, the definition of the Hoare logic builds on the predicate logic.

DEFINITION 8.1 (Syntax of Hoare Logic)   Let B be a basis for predicate logic. A *Hoare formula* over the basis B is an expression of the form

$$\{p\}\, S\, \{q\}$$

where $p, q \in WFF_B$ are formulas of the predicate logic and $S \in L_2^B$ is a while-program. $\square$

The set of all Hoare formulas over the basis B will be denoted by HF_B.

Unlike the predicate logic where there were two sorts of syntactic objects—terms and formulas—here there is only one (new) object, the Hoare formulas.

149

Thus the semantics of the Hoare logic need only describe the meaning of Hoare formulas.

DEFINITION 8.2 (Semantics of Hoare Logic)   Let an interpretation $\mathscr{I}$ of a basis B for predicate logic be given, and let Σ be the corresponding set of states. Every Hoare formula $\{p\}\,S\,\{q\} \in HF_B$ is mapped by a semantic functional—also denoted $\mathscr{I}$—to a function

$$\mathscr{I}(\{p\}\,S\,\{q\}): \Sigma \to Bool$$

defined as follows:

$$\mathscr{I}(\{p\}\,S\,\{q\})(\sigma) = \text{true}$$
$$\text{iff} \begin{cases} \text{if } \mathscr{I}(p)(\sigma) = \text{true} \\ \text{and if } \mathscr{M}_{\mathscr{I}}(S)(\sigma) \text{ is defined,} \\ \text{then } \mathscr{I}(q)(\mathscr{M}_{\mathscr{I}}(S)(\sigma)) = \text{true.} \end{cases} \qquad \square$$

It is naturally a matter of indifference whether the meaning $\mathscr{M}_{\mathscr{I}}(S)$ of the program S is defined by operational or denotational semantics.

Analogously to the predicate logic, the Hoare formula $\{p\}\,S\,\{q\}$ is said to be *valid* in an interpretation $\mathscr{I}$—denoted

$$\models_{\mathscr{I}} \{p\}\,S\,\{q\}$$

—if $\mathscr{I}(\{p\}\,S\,\{q\})(\sigma) = \text{true}$ for all states $\sigma \in \Sigma$. If $\models_{\mathscr{I}} \{p\}\,S\,\{q\}$ for all interpretations $\mathscr{I}$, then the Hoare formula is called *logically valid*; this fact is denoted

$$\models \{p\}\,S\,\{q\}.$$

A Hoare formula is called a *logical consequence* of a set $W \subseteq WFF_B$ of formulas of the predicate logic—denoted

$$W \models \{p\}\,S\,\{q\}$$

—if $\models_{\mathscr{I}} \{p\}\,S\,\{q\}$ holds for all models $\mathscr{I}$ of W.

Notice that $\mathscr{I}(\{p\}\,S\,\{q\})(\sigma)$ is true whenever $\mathscr{I}(p)(\sigma)$ is false—like $\mathscr{I}(p \supset q)(\sigma)$ in the predicate logic—or whenever $\mathscr{M}_{\mathscr{I}}(S)(\sigma)$ is undefined. This is why $\models_{\mathscr{I}} \{p\}\,S\,\{q\}$ means exactly that $\mathscr{M}_{\mathscr{I}}(S)$ is partially correct with respect to the formulas p and q in the interpretation $\mathscr{I}$. Thus Hoare logic essentially expresses partial correctness.

EXAMPLE 8.3   (1) Let $\{p\}\,S\,\{q\}$ be the Hoare formula

$$\{x > 5\}\; x := 2 * x\; \{x > 20\}.$$

Then in the usual interpretation $\mathscr{I}$:

$$\mathscr{I}(\{p\}\,S\,\{q\})(\sigma) = \text{true}$$
$$\text{iff } \mathscr{I}(p)(\sigma) = \text{false, or } \mathscr{I}(q)(\mathscr{M}_{\mathscr{I}}(S)(\sigma)) = \text{true}$$
$$\text{iff } \sigma(x) \le 5, \text{ or } \mathscr{M}_{\mathscr{I}}(S)(\sigma)(x) > 20$$
$$\text{iff } \sigma(x) \le 5, \text{ or } \sigma(x) > 10.$$

(2) Let $\{p\}\,S\,\{q\}$ be the Hoare formula

$$\{true\}\ while\ x \neq 10\ do\ x := x + 1\ od\ \{x = 10\}.$$

Then $\models_{\mathscr{I}}\{p\}\,S\,\{q\}$ in the usual interpretation $\mathscr{I}$, because for every state $\sigma \in \Sigma$:

either $\sigma(x) \leq 10$ and hence $\mathscr{M}_{\mathscr{I}}(S)(\sigma)(x) = 10$,
or $\sigma(x) > 10$ and hence $\mathscr{M}_{\mathscr{I}}(S)(\sigma)$ is undefined.

(3) The Hoare formula

$$\{true\}\ x := y + 1\ \{x > y\}$$

is valid in the usual interpretation $\mathscr{I}$. It is also a logical consequence of the set $W = \{y + 1 > y\}$, because for *all* interpretations $\mathscr{I}$,

$\mathscr{I}(x > y)(\mathscr{M}_{\mathscr{I}}(x := y + 1)(\sigma)) = $ true, for all $\sigma \in \Sigma$
    iff $\mathscr{I}(x > y)(\sigma[x/\mathscr{I}(y + 1)(\sigma)]) = $ true, for all $\sigma \in \Sigma$
    iff $\mathscr{I}(y + 1 > y)(\sigma) = $ true, for all $\sigma \in \Sigma$ (by the Substitution Theorem)
    iff $\mathscr{I}$ is a model of W. $\qquad\qquad\qquad\qquad\qquad\qquad\qquad\qquad$ □

8.1.1 The Hoare Calculus

The Hoare calculus is intended to derive the 'true' Hoare formulas. Like the predicate calculus, the Hoare calculus is not tailored to a specific interpretation, but includes only those axioms and rules which are valid in all interpretations. In practice one is of course interested in the Hoare formulas valid in some particular interpretation $\mathscr{I}$, say the interpretation of Peano arithmetic. Hence, to obtain significant results one must call upon the formulas of predicate logic which are valid in this interpretation $\mathscr{I}$; in other words, the interesting Hoare formulas are those which are derivable from the theory $Th(\mathscr{I})$. As a consequence the Hoare calculus 'works' not only with Hoare formulas but also with predicate logic formulas.

More formally, the *Hoare calculus* (over a basis B for predicate logic) is a calculus over the union of the set HF_B of Hoare formulas and the set WFF_B of formulas of the predicate logic and consists of an axiom (scheme) and five inference rules (the notations are the same as in Definition 3.7):

(i) *Assignment axiom*

$$\{p^t_x\}\ x := t\ \{p\} \qquad \text{for all } p \in WFF_B, x \in V, t \in T_B.$$

(ii) *Composition rule*

$$\frac{\{p\}\,S_1\,\{r\}, \{r\}\,S_2\,\{q\}}{\{p\}\,S_1;S_2\,\{q\}} \qquad \text{for all } p, q, r \in WFF_B, S_1, S_2 \in L_2^B.$$

(iii) *Conditional rule*

$$\frac{\{p \wedge e\}\,S_1\,\{q\}, \{p \wedge \neg e\}\,S_2\,\{q\}}{\{p\}\ if\ e\ then\ S_1\ else\ S_2\ fi\ \{q\}}$$

$$\text{for all } p, q \in WFF_B, e \in QFF_B, S_1, S_2 \in L_2^B.$$

152

(iv) *While-rule*

$$\frac{\{p \wedge e\}\, S_1\, \{p\}}{\{p\}\ while\ e\ do\ S_1\ od\ \{p \wedge \neg e\}} \qquad \text{for all } p \in WFF_B,\, e \in QFF_B,\, S_1 \in L_2^B.$$

(v) *Consequence rule*

$$\frac{p \supset q,\, \{q\}\, S\, \{r\},\, r \supset s}{\{p\}\, S\, \{s\}} \qquad \text{for all } p, q, r, s \in WFF_B,\, S \in L_2^B.$$

Before proceeding a few words should be said about the 'meaning' of these axioms and rules. The assignment axiom states that every property p that holds of a term t before the execution of the assignment, holds afterwards for the variable x. The composition rule needs no explanation. The conditional rule is clear when one recalls that in a conditional statement S_1 is carried out exactly when e holds and S_2 when $\neg e$ holds. The while-rule is the core of the calculus, since this is where the inductive assertions method is captured. If one translates the while-statement into a flowchart program, then the premises mean exactly that p is an invariant (in the sense of the inductive assertions method) at the point before the test of condition e. Hence, if p holds when entering the loop, then p holds when the loop is left. In addition $\neg e$ holds, since this is the only way the loop can end. The consequence rule makes it possible to relate the Hoare formulas to the predicate logic formulas of the theory under consideration.

Before a deduction from a given theory is attempted in this calculus, it is useful to extend the somewhat awkward axioms and rules by so-called derived rules. The application of a derived rule replaces several applications of the original rules (and hence reduces the length of a deduction). More precisely,

$$\frac{s_1, s_2, \ldots, s_n}{s}$$

is a *derived rule*, if there exists a deduction of s from $\{s_1, s_2, \ldots, s_n\}$ and the set of all logically valid formulas of predicate logic. Note that the use of logically valid formulas is allowed because they are contained in any theory. Three derived rules, labelled (i'), (ii'), and (iv'), will now be introduced.

(i') $$\frac{p \supset q_x^t}{\{p\}\ x := t\ \{q\}} \qquad \text{for all } p, q \in WFF_B,\, x \in V,\, t \in T_B.$$

This derived rule results from (or: is a shorthand for) the following deduction (from $p \supset q_x^t$ and an arbitrary theory):

(1) $p \supset q_x^t$ by assumption
(2) $\{q_x^t\}\ x := t\ \{q\}$ from the assignment axiom (i)
(3) $q \supset q$ from predicate logic
(4) $\{p\}\ x := t\ \{q\}$ consequence rule (v) applied to (1), (2), (3)

(ii')
$$\frac{\{p_0\}\, S_1\, \{p_1\},\, \{p_1\}\, S_2\, \{p_2\},\, \ldots,\, \{p_{n-1}\}\, S_n\, \{p_n\}}{\{p_0\}\, S_1;\, S_2;\, \ldots;\, S_n\, \{p_n\}}$$

for all $p_0, \ldots, p_n \in WFF_B$, $S_1, \ldots, S_n \in L_2^B$, $n \geq 2$.

This derived rule results from $(n-1)$ applications of the composition rule.

(iv')
$$\frac{p \supset r,\, \{r \wedge e\}\, S_1\, \{r\},\, (r \wedge \neg e) \supset q}{\{p\}\, while\ e\ do\ S_1\ od\ \{q\}}$$

for all $p, q, r \in WFF_B$, $e \in QFF_B$, and $S_1 \in L_2^B$.

This derived rule results from the following deduction:

(1) $p \supset r$ by assumption
(2) $\{r \wedge e\}\, S_1\, \{r\}$ by assumption
(3) $r \wedge \neg e \supset q$ by assumption
(4) $\{r\}\, while\ e\ do\ S_1\ od\ \{r \wedge \neg e\}$ while-rule (iv) applied to (2)
(5) $\{p\}\, while\ e\ do\ S_1\ od\ \{q\}$ consequence rule (v) applied to (1), (4) and (3).

EXAMPLE 8.4   Let T be the (theory of) Peano arithmetic. Suppose one wants to prove:

$$T \vdash \{x = a\}\ y_1 := 0;\ y_2 := 1;\ y_3 := 1;$$
$$while\ y_3 \leq x\ do\ y_1 := y_1 + 1;\ y_2 := y_2 + 2;\ y_3 := y_3 + y_2\ od\ \{y_1 = \sqrt{a}\}$$

Less formally, one wants to prove that the program of Example 3.9 is partially correct with respect to $x = a$ and $y = \sqrt{a}$ in the usual interpretation.

The proof consists in a deduction of the Hoare formula to the right of '$\vdash$' from T. Actually such a 'forward' proof, in which one starts with some axioms and formulas from T and then applies inference rules until the result appears is often not transparent. In the present example the inference rules will instead be applied 'backwards' until eventually axioms and formulas of T are obtained. More precisely, the 'backward' application of an inference rule (r)

$$\frac{s_1, s_2, \ldots, s_n}{s}$$

on the formula s replaces the 'goal' s by the 'subgoals' $s_1, s_2, \ldots, s_n$ and is written

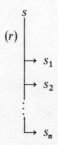

154

A subgoal is 'reached' if it is a formula of T or an (assignment) axiom; otherwise it has to be replaced in its turn by subgoals. The goal to be started with is, of course, the Hoare formula to be proved.

In the following proof the only inference rules applied are the derived rules (i'), (ii'), and (iv').

(1) $\{x = a\}\ y_1 := 0;\ y_2 := 1;\ y_3 := 1;$
   $while\ y_3 \leq x\ do\ y_1 := y_1 + 1;\ y_2 := y_2 + 2;$
   $y_3 := y_3 + y_2\ od\ \{y_1 = \sqrt{a}\}$

(ii')

$\rightarrow$ (2) $\{x = a\}\ y_1 := 0\ \{x = a \wedge y_1 = 0\}$

$\rightarrow$ (3) $\{x = a \wedge y_1 = 0\}\ y_2 := 1\ \{x = a \wedge y_1 = 0 \wedge y_2 = 1\}$

$\rightarrow$ (4) $\{x = a \wedge y_1 = 0 \wedge y_2 = 1\}$
   $y_3 := 1\ \{x = a \wedge y_1 = 0 \wedge y_2 = 1 \wedge y_3 = 1\}$

$\rightarrow$ (5) $\{x = a \wedge y_1 = 0 \wedge y_2 = 1 \wedge y_3 = 1\}$
   $while\ y_3 \leq x\ do\ y_1 := y_1 + 1;\ y_2 := y_2 + 2;$
   $y_3 := y_3 + y_2\ od\ \{y_1 = \sqrt{a}\}$

(2)

(i')

$\rightarrow$ (6) $x = a \supset x = a \wedge 0 = 0$ \qquad Formula of T

(3)

(i')

$\rightarrow$ (7) $x = a \wedge y_1 = 0 \supset x = a \wedge y_1 = 0 \wedge 1 = 1$ \qquad Formula of T

(4)

(i')

$\rightarrow$ (8) $x = a \wedge y_1 = 0 \wedge y_2 = 1 \supset x = a \wedge y_1 = 0 \wedge y_2 = 1 \wedge 1 = 1$
   Formula of T

(5)

(iv')

$\rightarrow$ (9) $x = a \wedge y_1 = 0 \wedge y_2 = 1 \wedge y_3 = 1$
   $\supset x = a \wedge y_1^2 \leq x \wedge y_3 = (y_1 + 1)^2 \wedge y_2 = 2 * y_1 + 1$
   Formula of T

$\rightarrow$ (10) $\{x = a \wedge y_1^2 \leq x \wedge y_3 = (y_1 + 1)^2 \wedge y_2 = 2 * y_1 + 1 \wedge y_3 \leq x\}$
   $y_1 := y_1 + 1;\ y_2 := y_2 + 2;\ y_3 := y_3 + y_2$
   $\{x = a \wedge y_1^2 \leq x \wedge y_3 = (y_1 + 1)^2 \wedge y_2 = 2 * y_1 + 1\}$

$\rightarrow$ (11) $x = a \wedge y_1^2 \leq x \wedge y_3 = (y_1 + 1)^2 \wedge y_2 = 2 * y_1 + 1 \wedge \neg y_3 \leq x$
   $\supset y_1 = \sqrt{a}$ \qquad Formula of T

(10)

(ii′) $\mapsto$ (12) $\{x = a \wedge y_1^2 \le x \wedge y_3 = (y_1 + 1)^2 \wedge y_2 = 2 * y_1 + 1 \wedge y_3 \le x\}$
$y_1 := y_1 + 1 \ \{x = a \wedge y_3 = y_1^2 \wedge$
$\qquad\qquad y_2 = 2 * y_1 - 1 \wedge y_3 \le x \wedge y_1 > 0\}$

$\mapsto$ (13) $\{x = a \wedge y_3 = y_1^2 \wedge y_2 = 2 * y_1 - 1 \wedge y_3 \le x \wedge y_1 > 0\}$
$y_2 := y_2 + 2 \ \{x = a \wedge y_1^2 \le x \wedge y_3 = y_1^2 \wedge y_2 = 2 * y_1 + 1\}$

$\mapsto$ (14) $\{x = a \wedge y_1^2 \le x \wedge y_3 = y_1^2 \wedge y_2 = 2 * y_1 + 1\}$
$y_3 := y_3 + y_2 \ \{x = a \wedge y_1^2 \le x \wedge$
$\qquad\qquad y_3 = (y_1 + 1)^2 \wedge y_2 = 2 * y_1 + 1\}$

(12)

(i′) $\mapsto$ (15) $x = a \wedge y_1^2 \le x \wedge y_3 = (y_1 + 1)^2 \wedge y_2 = 2 * y_1 + 1 \wedge y_3 \le x$
$\supset x = a \wedge y_3 = (y_1 + 1)^2 \wedge y_2 = 2 * (y_1 + 1) - 1 \wedge y_3 \le x$
$\wedge y_1 + 1 > 0$ \qquad Formula of T

(13)

(i′) $\mapsto$ (16) $x = a \wedge y_3 = y_1^2 \wedge y_2 = 2 * y_1 - 1 \wedge y_3 \le x \wedge y_1 > 0$
$\supset x = a \wedge y_1^2 \le x \wedge y_3 = y_1^2 \wedge y_2 + 2 = 2 * y_1 + 1$
Formula of T (note that $2 * y_1 - 1 + 2 = 2 * y_1 + 1$ because
$y_1 > 0$)

(14)

(i′) $\mapsto$ (17) $x = a \wedge y_1^2 \le x \wedge y_3 = y_1^2 \wedge y_2 = 2 * y_1 + 1$
$\supset x = a \wedge y_1^2 \le x \wedge y_3 + y_2 = (y_1 + 1)^2 \wedge y_2 = 2 * y_1 + 1$
Formula of T

Note that a 'forward' proof leads to the same formulas but in a different order, for instance:

(6), (2), (7), (3), (8), (4), (9), (15), (12), (16), (13), (17), (14), (10), (11), (5), (1).

The two proof methods ('backward' and 'forward') may be illustrated by the following 'goal tree'.

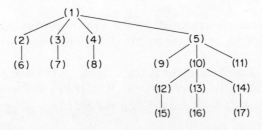

The 'backward' proof corresponds to a 'top-down', the 'forward' proof to a 'bottom-up' traversal of this tree. $\qquad\square$

One of the lessons of the previous example is that for every construct of the programming language—assignment, composition, conditional, and while-statement—there exists an inference rule—namely (i'), (ii), (iii), and (iv') respectively——which by 'backward application' leads to 'simpler' Hoare formulas or, more precisely, to Hoare formulas involving syntactically shorter program segments. Whereas these simpler Hoare formulas are univocally defined in the case of the rules (i') and (iii), for the rules (ii) and (iv') one must bring in some 'understanding' of the program to find the formula r constituting the intermediate assertion for a composition of statements or the invariant for a while-loop. It will be seen in the next section that this fact plays an important role in the completeness of the calculus.

In what preceded, the application of the Hoare calculus to a given theory consisted in considering the derivations in the Hoare calculus from this theory. It is interesting to note that there exists an alternative way to apply the Hoare calculus to a theory when this theory is axiomatizable. To this end the Hoare calculus is augmented with the axioms and inference rules of the predicate calculus and with the axioms of this theory. The derivations of interest are then the derivations in this extended calculus from the empty set. This alternative view was not taken here because it is only applicable to axiomatizable theories; hence it is for instance not applicable to Peano arithmetic. Moreover, the use of predicate calculus is too clumsy to be practical.

8.2 Soundness and Relative Completeness

Now the two questions asked about every calculus will be investigated:

(1) Is the Hoare calculus sound (that is, is every derivable formula 'true')?
(2) Is the Hoare calculus complete (that is, is every 'true' formula derivable)?

To formulate both questions precisely, recall the purpose of the Hoare calculus is to derive Hoare formulas from a given theory. This leads one to investigate the (slightly more general) question whether for every set W of formulas (where W need not be a theory) and every Hoare formula h the following hold:

(1) If $W \vdash h$, then $W \models h$,
(2) If $W \models h$, then $W \vdash h$.

First, soundness (as expressed by (1)) will be proved. On the other hand completeness in this form turns out to be false; it will be restated in a weaker form.

THEOREM 8.5 (Soundness of the Hoare Calculus) Let B be a basis for predicate logic. Then for every set of formulas $W \subseteq WFF_B$ and every Hoare formula $\{p\} S \{q\}$ from HF_B (with $p, q \in WFF_B$ and $S \in L_2^B$):

if $W \vdash \{p\} S \{q\}$, then $W \models \{p\} S \{q\}$.

Proof. The proof follows the pattern given in Section 2.3 for the proof of soundness of the predicate calculus. Hence, it is sufficient to show that every axiom is logically valid, and for every interpretation $\mathscr{I}$ of the basis B, if the premises of an inference rule are valid in $\mathscr{I}$, then so is the conclusion. This will now be carried out for the Hoare calculus using the denotational semantics of while-programs. (See also Exercise 8.2–5.)

(i) *Assignment axiom*   It must be proved that for any interpretation $\mathscr{I}$

$$\models_I \{p_x^t\}\ x := t\ \{p\}.$$

Let $\sigma \in \Sigma$ be a state such that $\mathscr{I}(p_x^t)(\sigma) = \text{true}$. Notice that $\mathscr{M}_{\mathscr{I}}(x := t)(\sigma)$ is defined by definition of the semantics (see Definitions 5.17 and 5.19). Set $\sigma' = \mathscr{M}_{\mathscr{I}}(x := t)(\sigma)$. It needs to be shown that $\mathscr{I}(p)(\sigma') = \text{true}$. By the Substitution Theorem

$$\mathscr{I}(p_x^t)(\sigma) = \mathscr{I}(p)(\sigma[x/\mathscr{I}(t)(\sigma)])$$

and by the definition of the semantics

$$\mathscr{M}_{\mathscr{I}}(x := t)(\sigma) = \sigma[x/\mathscr{I}(t)(\sigma)];$$

hence it follows immediately that

$$\mathscr{I}(p)(\sigma') = \text{true}.$$

(ii) *Composition rule*   Assume $\models_{\mathscr{I}} \{p\}\ S_1\ \{r\}$ and $\models_{\mathscr{I}} \{r\}\ S_2\ \{q\}$. In order to show that $\models_{\mathscr{I}} \{p\}\ S_1 ; S_2\ \{q\}$, let $\sigma \in \Sigma$ be such that $\mathscr{I}(p)(\sigma) = \text{true}$. If $\mathscr{M}_{\mathscr{I}}(S_1 ; S_2)(\sigma)$ is undefined, nothing has to be proved. Otherwise set $\sigma' = \mathscr{M}_{\mathscr{I}}(S_1 ; S_2)(\sigma)$. It must be shown that $\mathscr{I}(q)(\sigma') = \text{true}$. As $\sigma' = \mathscr{M}_{\mathscr{I}}^{\omega}(S_2)(\mathscr{M}_{\mathscr{I}}^{\omega}(S_1)(\sigma))$ and $\mathscr{M}_{\mathscr{I}}^{\omega}(S_2)$ is strict by Exercise 5.4–4, $\mathscr{M}_{\mathscr{I}}^{\omega}(S_1)(\sigma)$ must be different from ω. Set $\sigma'' = \mathscr{M}_{\mathscr{I}}(S_1)(\sigma)$; then $\sigma' = \mathscr{M}_{\mathscr{I}}(S_2)(\sigma'')$. From $\models_{\mathscr{I}} \{p\}\ S_1\ \{r\}$ it follows that $\mathscr{I}(r)(\sigma'') = \text{true}$. Consequently $\models_{\mathscr{I}} \{r\}\ S_2\ \{q\}$ leads to $\mathscr{I}(q)(\sigma') = \text{true}$.

(iii) *Conditional rule*   The proof is left to the reader as Exercise 8.2–2.

(iv) *While-rule*   Assume

$$\models_{\mathscr{I}} \{p \wedge e\}\ S_1\ \{p\}. \tag{1}$$

It must be shown that

$$\models_{\mathscr{I}} \{p\}\ \text{while } e \text{ do } S_1 \text{ od } \{p \wedge \neg e\}$$

or equivalently: for all states $\sigma \in \Sigma$,

$$\left. \begin{array}{l} \text{if } \mathscr{I}(p)(\sigma) = \text{true} \\ \text{and if } \mathscr{M}_{\mathscr{I}}(\text{while } e \text{ do } S_1 \text{ od})(\sigma) \text{ is defined} \\ \text{or, equivalently, if } \mathscr{M}_{\mathscr{I}}^{\omega}(\text{while } e \text{ do } S_1 \text{ od})(\sigma) \neq \omega \\ \text{then } \mathscr{I}(p \wedge \neg e)(\mathscr{M}_{\mathscr{I}}(\text{while } e \text{ do } S_1 \text{ od})(\sigma)) = \text{true}. \end{array} \right\} \tag{2}$$

By Definition 5.17 $\mathscr{M}_{\mathscr{I}}^{\omega}(\text{while } e \text{ do } S_1 \text{ od})$ is the minimal fixpoint of the functional

$$\Phi: [\Sigma_{\omega} \to \Sigma_{\omega}] \to [\Sigma_{\omega} \to \Sigma_{\omega}]$$

defined by

$$\Phi(f)(\sigma) = \begin{cases} \text{if-then-else}(\mathscr{I}(e)(\sigma), f(\mathscr{M}_{\mathscr{I}}^{\omega}(S_1)(\sigma)), \sigma), & \text{if } \sigma \neq \omega \\ \omega, & \text{if } \sigma = \omega \end{cases}$$

Hence the property (2) may be proved by fixpoint induction provided it is an admissible predicate (in the sense of Definition 4.26). For this reason a detour is made to prove the following lemma:

LEMMA 8.6 (Partial Correctness is an Admissible Predicate)   Let $\varphi, \psi \colon \Sigma \to Bool$ be predicates and Σ_ω the flat cpo of Section 5.4. Then the predicate $\pi \colon [\Sigma_\omega \to \Sigma_\omega] \to Bool$ defined by

$$\pi(f) = \text{true iff for all states } \sigma \in \Sigma \ (not \ \sigma \in \Sigma_\omega!)$$
$$\begin{cases} \text{if } \varphi(\sigma) = \text{true} \\ \text{and if } f(\sigma) \neq \omega \\ \text{then } \psi(f(\sigma)) = \text{true} \end{cases}$$

is an admissible predicate. (Note that with $\varphi = \mathscr{I}(p)$ and $\psi = \mathscr{I}(p \wedge \neg e)$ the property (2) is $\pi(\mu\Phi) = \text{true}$.)

Proof. Let S be a chain in $[\Sigma_\omega \to \Sigma_\omega]$ such that $\pi(f) = \text{true}$ for all functions f from S. In order to show that $\pi(\sqcup S) = \text{true}$, let σ be a state from Σ such that $\varphi(\sigma) = \text{true}$ and $(\sqcup S)(\sigma) = \sigma' \neq \omega$. It must be shown that $\psi(\sigma') = \text{true}$. Since by Theorem 4.3 $(\sqcup S)(\sigma) = \sqcup S(\sigma)$ and since Σ_ω is a flat cpo, it must be the case that $f(\sigma) = \sigma'$ for at least one function f in S. Since $\pi(f) = \text{true}$, $\psi(\sigma') = \text{true}$. So $\pi(\sqcup S) = \text{true}$. $\square$

Now the proof of (iv) can be continued. Let π be defined as in the lemma with $\varphi = \mathscr{I}(p)$ and $\psi = \mathscr{I}(p \wedge \neg e)$. As already indicated the property (2) to be proved is then

$$\pi(\mu\Phi) = \text{true}. \tag{3}$$

According to the lemma, (3) may be proved by fixpoint induction. Hence it is sufficient to prove:

Induction basis $\pi(\bot) = \text{true}$.

Induction step   If $\pi(f) = \text{true}$, then $\pi(\Phi(f)) = \text{true}$ for all $f \in [\Sigma_\omega \to \Sigma_\omega]$. The first is clear, since $\bot(\sigma) = \omega$ for all $\sigma \in \Sigma$. So it remains to show the induction step. Let $f \in [\Sigma_\omega \to \Sigma_\omega]$ be such that $\pi(f) = \text{true}$. In order to show that $\pi(\Phi(f)) = \text{true}$ let $\sigma_0 \in \Sigma$ be such that

$$\mathscr{I}(p)(\sigma_0) = \text{true} \tag{4}$$

and

$$\Phi(f)(\sigma_0) \neq \omega. \tag{5}$$

It must be shown that

$$\mathscr{I}(p \wedge \neg e)(\Phi(f)(\sigma_0)) = \text{true}. \tag{6}$$

The proof of (6) proceeds by case distinction.

If $\mathscr{I}(e)(\sigma_0) = \text{true}$, then $\Phi(f)(\sigma_0) = f(\mathscr{M}_{\mathscr{I}}^\omega(S_1)(\sigma_0))$ and (5) leads to

$$f(\mathscr{M}_{\mathscr{I}}^\omega(S_1)(\sigma_0)) \neq \omega. \tag{7}$$

If in addition $\mathcal{M}_{\mathscr{I}}^{\omega}(S_1)(\sigma_0) \neq \omega$ (hence $\mathcal{M}_{\mathscr{I}}(S_1)(\sigma_0)$ is defined) then (1) together with (4) gives

$$\mathscr{I}(p)(\mathcal{M}_{\mathscr{I}}^{\omega}(S_1)(\sigma_0)) = \text{true.} \tag{8}$$

The induction hypothesis $\pi(f) = \text{true}$ for $\sigma = \mathcal{M}_{\mathscr{I}}^{\omega}(S_1)(\sigma_0)$ together with (8) and (7) leads to (6). If on the contrary $\mathcal{M}_{\mathscr{I}}^{\omega}(S_1)(\sigma_0) = \omega$, (7) leads to

$$f(\omega) \neq \omega. \tag{9}$$

But then—since f is monotonic and Σ_{ω} a flat cpo—f is a function with the constant value $f(\mathcal{M}_{\mathscr{I}}^{\omega}(S_1)(\sigma_0))$, hence in particular

$$f(\sigma_0) = f(\mathcal{M}_{\mathscr{I}}^{\omega}(S_1)(\sigma_0)) \neq \omega. \tag{10}$$

Then the induction hypothesis for $\sigma = \sigma_0$ together with (4) and (10) leads to (6).

If $\mathscr{I}(e)(\sigma_0) = \text{false}$, then $\Phi(f)(\sigma_0) = \sigma_0$. Then (6) directly results from (4). This completes part (iv) of the soundness proof.

(v) *Consequence rule*   The proof is easy and left to the reader. $\square$

It is worthwhile to mention that in step (iv) of the above proof the case $f(\omega) \neq \omega$ (see (9)) had to be considered. This difficulty could have been avoided by defining the meaning of the while-statement as the least fixpoint of a functional on the cpo of strict functions and not on the cpo of continuous functions (see Exercise 5.4–4).

With a little reflection it can be seen that the inverse of the soundness property proved in the previous theorem, namely

$$\text{if } W \models \{p\} S \{q\} \text{ then } W \vdash \{p\} S \{q\},$$

cannot be true for any set W of formulas. For instance, the Hoare formula $\{true\}$ $x := 1 \{x = 1\}$ is clearly logically valid, but it cannot be derived from $W = \varnothing$. Of course $\{1 = 1\} x := 1 \{x = 1\}$ is an axiom, but in order to use the consequence rule one must have the formula $true \supset (1 = 1)$ 'available'. In accordance with the purpose of the Hoare calculus, which is to derive Hoare formulas from a given theory, the following weaker version of completeness seems reasonable:

$$\text{for every theory } T: \quad \text{if } T \models \{p\} S \{q\} \text{ then } T \vdash \{p\} S \{q\} \tag{I}$$

Now it will be seen in Theorem 8.8 that even this weaker version of completeness is not true. First the following lemma is needed:

LEMMA 8.7 (Hoare Logic is a First-order Logic)   Let B be a basis for predicate logic and $\mathscr{I}$ an interpretation of B. Then for every Hoare formula $h \in HF_B$

$$\models_{\mathscr{I}} h \qquad \text{iff} \qquad Th(\mathscr{I}) \models h.$$

Proof. Since every while-program can be translated into a flowchart program, the conclusion follows directly from Theorem 7.6. $\square$

THEOREM 8.8   Let $B = (\{0, 1, +\}, \{<\})$ be the basis for Presburger arithmetic and $\mathscr{I}$ the usual interpretation. Then there is *no* calculus $\mathscr{K}$ such that for every Hoare formula $h \in HF_B$

$$Th(\mathscr{I}) \models h \qquad \text{iff } Th(\mathscr{I}) \vdash_{\mathscr{K}} h.$$

Proof. In Example 2.25 it was seen that $Th(\mathscr{I})$, the theory of Presburger arithmetic, is decidable. Assume that there was a calculus $\mathscr{K}$ with the property given above. Then the set

$$\{h \in HF_B \,|\, Th(\mathscr{I}) \models h\} = \{h \in HF_B \,|\, Th(\mathscr{I}) \vdash_{\mathscr{K}} h\}$$

would be recursively enumerable. Then by Lemma 8.7, so would the set $\{h \in HF_B \,|\, \models_{\mathscr{I}} h\}$. But this is a contradiction to Theorem 6.7(i).   □

From Theorem 8.8 one may deduce that the completeness property of the Hoare calculus as expressed by (I) above does not hold for the theory of Presburger arithmetic, and moreover that this is not a weakness of the particular calculus, but lies in the nature of the problem.

In order to find a valid completeness result for the Hoare calculus, it is useful to examine carefully why the derivation of a true Hoare formula can fail. As already noted above (after Example 8.4) there exist rules for the assignment and the conditional statement which by 'backward' application generate 'subgoals', namely rules (i') and (iii). On the other hand, for the composition and the while-statement it is necessary to ponder a little to arrive at an intermediate assertion for composition and an invariant for the while-statement. The following lemma provides a lead to the discovery of intermediate assertions. By a little trick which will be explained in the proof of Theorem 8.11 the same method can be used to find invariants too.

LEMMA 8.9   Let B be a basis for predicate logic and $\mathscr{I}$ an interpretation of B. Let $p, q, r \in WFF_B$ be formulas of predicate logic and let $S_1, S_2 \in L_2^B$ be while-programs. If

$$\models_{\mathscr{I}} \{p\} \, S_1 ; S_2 \, \{q\}$$

and $\mathscr{I}(r)$ is the weakest liberal precondition of the program S_2 and the predicate $\mathscr{I}(q)$, then

$$\models_{\mathscr{I}} \{p\} \, S_1 \, \{r\}$$

and

$$\models_{\mathscr{I}} \{r\} \, S_2 \, \{q\}.$$

Proof. Since $\mathscr{I}(r)$ is the weakest liberal precondition of S_2 and $\mathscr{I}(q), \models_{\mathscr{I}} \{r\} \, S_2 \, \{q\}$ by Theorem 6.5.

So it remains to show $\models_{\mathscr{I}} \{p\} \, S_1 \, \{r\}$. For that purpose choose $\sigma, \sigma' \in \Sigma$ such that $\mathscr{I}(p)(\sigma) = \text{true}$ and $\mathscr{M}_{\mathscr{I}}(S_1)(\sigma) = \sigma'$ (hence $\mathscr{M}_{\mathscr{I}}(S_1)(\sigma)$ is defined). It must be shown that $\mathscr{I}(r)(\sigma') = \text{true}$. Because

$$\mathcal{M}_\mathcal{I}^\omega(S_1;S_2)(\sigma) = \mathcal{M}_\mathcal{I}^\omega(S_2)(\mathcal{M}_\mathcal{I}^\omega(S_1)(\sigma))$$
$$= \mathcal{M}_\mathcal{I}^\omega(S_2)(\sigma')$$

and because

$$\models_\mathcal{I}\{p\}\,S_1;S_2\,\{q\}$$

one has

if $\mathcal{M}_\mathcal{I}(S_2)(\sigma')$ is defined then $\mathcal{I}(q)(\mathcal{M}_\mathcal{I}(S_2)(\sigma')) = $ true.

As $\mathcal{I}(r)$ is the weakest liberal precondition of S_2 and $\mathcal{I}(q)$, $\mathcal{I}(r)(\sigma') = $ true (by Definition 6.4). $\square$

Lemma 8.9 will now be used to prove a completeness result which concerns certain interpretations of predicate logic. These interpretations are called expressive, an idea which will now be defined.

DEFINITION 8.10 (Expressiveness) Let B be a basis for predicate logic. An interpretation $\mathcal{I}$ of B is said to be *expressive* (for while-programs) if for every while-program $S \in L_2^B$ and every formula $q \in WFF_B$ there is a formula $r \in WFF_B$ such that $\mathcal{I}(r)$ is the weakest liberal precondition of S and $\mathcal{I}(q)$. In this case the predicate $\mathcal{I}(r)$ is said to be *expressible*. $\square$

Incidentally, Cook's original result (Cook, 1978), which was for a language with procedures, used a definition of expressiveness based on strongest post-conditions. The equivalence of both definitions is left to Exercise 8.2–3.

It will now be shown that the Hoare calculus is complete if only expressive interpretations are considered. The question of which interpretations are expressive and whether there are any at all will be postponed until the next section.

THEOREM 8.11 (Cook's Relative Completeness Theorem) Let B be a basis for predicate logic and $\mathcal{I}$ an expressive interpretation of B. Then for every Hoare formula $h \in HF_B$:

if $Th(\mathcal{I}) \models h$ then $Th(:\mathcal{I}) \vdash h$.

By Lemma 8.7, this implication may be written:

if $\models_\mathcal{I} h$ then $Th(\mathcal{I}) \vdash h$.

Proof. Let $h = \{p\}\,S\,\{q\}$ be an arbitrary Hoare formula. The proof of the theorem is by induction over the structure of the while-program S. In the proof the inference rules (i) to (v) as well as the derived rules (i'), (ii'), and (iv') of the Hoare calculus will be used. The notations are the same as in Definition 3.7.

(i) *Assignment statement* Assume $\models_\mathcal{I}\{p\}\,x := t\,\{q\}$. Similarly to step (i) in the soundness proof (Theorem 8.5) one may prove that $\models_\mathcal{I} p \supset q_x^t$ follows from the assumption. Since $p \supset q_x^t$ is a formula of predicate logic, it must then be contained in the set $Th(\mathcal{I})$, hence $Th(\mathcal{I}) \vdash p \supset q_x^t$. By an application of the derived rule (i') one obtains $Th(\mathcal{I}) \vdash \{p\}\,x := t\,\{q\}$.

(ii) *Composed statement*   Assume $\models_\mathscr{I} \{p\} S_1; S_2 \{q\}$. Since $\mathscr{I}$ is expressive, there exists a formula $r \in WFF_B$ such that $\mathscr{I}(r)$ is the weakest liberal precondition of S_2 and $\mathscr{I}(q)$. By Lemma 8.9, $\models_\mathscr{I} \{p\} S_1 \{r\}$ as well as $\models_\mathscr{I} \{r\} S_2 \{q\}$ and, by induction hypothesis, both formulas are derivable from $Th(\mathscr{I})$. By application of the composition rule one obtains $Th(\mathscr{I}) \vdash \{p\} S_1; S_2 \{q\}$.

(iii) *Conditional statement*   Assume

$$\models_\mathscr{I} \{p\} \text{ if } e \text{ then } S_1 \text{ else } S_2 \text{ } fi \text{ } \{q\}.$$

By Exercise 8.2–2, it follows that $\models_\mathscr{I} \{p \wedge e\} S_1 \{q\}$ and $\models_\mathscr{I} \{p \wedge \neg e\} S_2 \{q\}$. By induction hypothesis both formulas are derivable from $Th(\mathscr{I})$ and by application of the conditional rule one obtains

$$Th(\mathscr{I}) \vdash \{p\} \text{ if } e \text{ then } S_1 \text{ else } S_2 \text{ } fi \text{ } \{q\}.$$

(iv) *While-statement*   Assume $\models_\mathscr{I} \{p\} S \{q\}$ where S is the while-statement *while e do* S_1 *od*. Now an invariant must be found. Since $\mathscr{I}$ is expressive, there exists a formula $r \in WFF_B$ such that $\mathscr{I}(r)$ is the weakest liberal precondition of S and $\mathscr{I}(q)$. It will be shown that r is the required invariant.

Recall that $\mathscr{M}^\omega_\mathscr{I}(S)$ is the least fixpoint of the functional $\Phi: [\Sigma_\omega \to \Sigma_\omega] \to [\Sigma_\omega \to \Sigma_\omega]$ defined by

$$\Phi(f)(\sigma) = \text{if-then-else}(\mathscr{I}(e)(\sigma), f(\mathscr{M}^\omega_\mathscr{I}(S_1)(\sigma)), \sigma)$$

Hence, for each state $\sigma \in \Sigma$:

$$\begin{aligned} \mathscr{M}^\omega_\mathscr{I}(S)(\sigma) &= \Phi(\mathscr{M}^\omega_\mathscr{I}(S))(\sigma) \qquad \text{because } \mathscr{M}^\omega_\mathscr{I}(S) \text{ is a fixpoint} \\ &= \text{if-then-else}(\mathscr{I}(e)(\sigma), \mathscr{M}^\omega_\mathscr{I}(S)(\mathscr{M}^\omega_\mathscr{I}(S_1)(\sigma)), \sigma) \\ &= \mathscr{M}^\omega_\mathscr{I}(\text{if } e \text{ then } S_1; S \text{ else } x := x \text{ } fi)(\sigma) \end{aligned}$$

where x is some arbitrary variable and $x := x$ is just one possible 'dummy' statement which has no effect on the state.

As $\mathscr{I}(r)$ is the weakest liberal precondition of S and $\mathscr{I}(q)$, one has

$$\models_\mathscr{I} \{r\} S \{q\}$$

hence

$$\models_\mathscr{I} \{r\} \text{ if } e \text{ then } S_1; S \text{ else } x := x \text{ } fi \text{ } \{q\}$$

Now as in step (iii) one obtains, on the one hand

$$\models_\mathscr{I} \{r \wedge e\} S_1; S \{q\}$$

from which, by Lemma 8.9, follows

$$\models_\mathscr{I} \{r \wedge e\} S_1 \{r\},$$

and, on the other hand,

$$\models_\mathscr{I} \{r \wedge \neg e\} x := x \{q\},$$

which is nothing other than

$$\models_\mathscr{I} (r \wedge \neg e) \supset q.$$

The first formula is derivable from $Th(\mathscr{I})$ by induction hypothesis, and the second is derivable since it is in $Th(\mathscr{I})$. Finally, by $\models_\mathscr{I} \{p\}\, \text{S}\, \{q\}$ and by Theorem 6.5 one has $\models_\mathscr{I} p \supset r$; this formula is also derivable since it is in $Th(\mathscr{I})$. These are just the three premises needed to use rule (iv') and obtain $Th(\mathscr{I}) \vdash \{p\}\, \text{S}\, \{q\}$ $\square$

*8.3 Expressiveness

The completeness result of the last section is only meaningful when some of the 'usual' interpretations of the 'usual' bases for predicate logic turn out to be expressive. Indeed this is the case, as will now be demonstrated in this section. To make the problem clearer, though, an interpretation which is not expressive is presented first.

THEOREM 8.12   Let $B = (\{0, 1, +\}, \{<\})$ be the basis for Presburger arithmetic. The usual interpretation $\mathscr{I} = (Nat, \mathscr{I}_0)$ is not expressive.

Proof. In Theorem 8.8 it was seen that there is no calculus such that for every Hoare formula $h \in HF_B$

$$Th(\mathscr{I}) \models h \qquad \text{iff } Th(\mathscr{I}) \vdash h.$$

Therefore the expressiveness of $\mathscr{I}$ would contradict Theorem 8.11. $\square$

The above proof does not make clear why the interpretation $\mathscr{I}$ fails to be expressive. So another proof will be made of Theorem 8.12. For this proof some definitions and facts from predicate logic are needed.

DEFINITION 8.13   A set S of natural numbers is said to be *periodic* if there exists a natural number $p \in Nat$ such that for all $n \in Nat$, it is the case that $n \in S$ iff $n + p \in S$. The set S is said to be *eventually periodic* if there exist numbers $p, m \in Nat$ such that for all $n > m$, $n \in S$ iff $n + p \in S$. $\square$

LEMMA 8.14   Let B and $\mathscr{I}$ be respectively the basis and interpretation of Presburger arithmetic and Σ the corresponding set of all assignments. Let $q \in WFF_B$ be a formula in which only one variable, say c, occurs free. Then the set $\{\sigma(c)\,|\,\sigma \in \Sigma$ and $\mathscr{I}(q)(\sigma) = \text{true}\}$ (that is, the subset of Nat 'defined' by q) is eventually periodic.

Proof. The reader is referred to Enderton (1972, p. 192). $\square$

The lemma may be illustrated by the following example. Let q be the formula

$$(c = 1) \vee (\neg\exists y.\,(y + y + y + 1 = c)).$$

The set defined by this formula is $\{0, 1, 2, 3, 5, 6, 8, 9, \ldots\}$. This set is not periodic (since 1 gets in the way), but it is eventually periodic as the reader can check (take $p = 3$, $m = 1$).

164

With the help of the lemma one can easily see that the interpretation $\mathscr{I}$ of Presburger arithmetic is not expressive. Consider the following while-program S:

$$x := 0; \ y := 0; \ while \ y < z \ do \ y := y + 1; \ x := x + z \ od.$$

This program squares the contents of z and stores the result in x. Let c be an arbitrary variable. If there existed a formula $r \in WFF_B$ such that $\mathscr{I}(r)$ is the weakest liberal precondition of the program S and the predicate $\mathscr{I}(x = c)$, then it would have to be the case that, for all $\sigma \in \Sigma$, $\mathscr{I}(r)(\sigma) = \text{true}$ iff $\sigma(c) = \sigma(z)^2$. Hence, $\mathscr{I}(\exists z . r)(\sigma) = \text{true}$ iff $\sigma(c)$ is a perfect square. The existence of such a formula stands in contradiction to Lemma 8.14, since the set of perfect squares is not eventually periodic. (Should the formula $\exists z . r$ have free variables other than c, an equivalent formula can be found by quantifying so that only c occurs free.) Therefore, $\mathscr{I}$ cannot be expressive.

Apparently Presburger arithmetic fails to be expressive because on the one hand multiplication can be performed by repeated addition in a while-program, but on the other, multiplication cannot be expressed by a formula of predicate logic. It would appear that the argument would also apply to Peano arithmetic since exponentiation can be performed by a while-program, but there is no symbol in the basis of Peano arithmetic for it. Actually, this argument does not hold as will appear below.

The key to a proof that the usual interpretation of Peano arithmetic is expressive lies in the existance of a coding (sometimes called Gödelization) of a finite sequence of natural numbers by a pair of natural numbers. This coding—and this is the important fact—is expressible in Peano arithmetic. The following lemma describing the coding requires the Gödel β-predicate β: $Nat^4 \to Bool$ defined by

$$\beta(m, n, i, r) = \text{true}$$
iff r is the remainder of m divided by $(1 + (i + 1) * n)$.

LEMMA 8.15   For every finite sequence of numbers $r_0, \ldots, r_k \in Nat$ $(k \geq 0)$ there exist two numbers $m, n \in Nat$ such that $\beta(m, n, i, r_i) = \text{true}$ for $i = 0, \ldots, k$.

Proof. The lemma is a consequence of a well-known theorem in number theory, namely the Chinese Remainder Theorem. Both can be found—with easy proofs—in Enderton (1972, pp. 248–249). □

Before this lemma is used to prove that the usual interpretation of Peano arithmetic is expressive, it will now be used to illustrate how exponentiation can be expressed in Peano arithmetic. More precisely, the aim is to find a formula expressing that $c = a^b$ for $a, b, c \in Nat$. Now $c = a^b$ if and only if there exist numbers $c_0, \ldots, c_b \in Nat$ such that

$$c_0 = 1$$
$$c_{i+1} = c_i * a, \quad \text{for } i = 0, \ldots, b - 1$$
$$c_b = c.$$

By Lemma 8.15, this is equivalent to: there exist $m, n \in Nat$ such that

(i) $\beta(m, n, 0, 1) = true$
(ii) for all $u, v \in Nat$ and $i = 0, \ldots, b - 1,$ $\beta(m, n, i, u) = true$ and
$\beta(m, n, i + 1, v) = true$ imply $v = u * a$
(iii) $\beta(m, n, b, c) = true$

Considering that the Gödel β-predicate can be written as a predicate logic formula, namely

$$r < (1 + (i + 1) * n) \wedge \exists s . m = s * (1 + (i + 1) * n) + r$$

(where the distinction between variables and their values, this once, is not made explicit), it is clear how one can express the statement $c = a^b$ in Peano arithmetic. This technique is used in the following proof.

THEOREM 8.16 (Expressiveness of Peano Arithmetic) Let $B = (\{0, 1, +, *\}, \{<\})$ be the basis for Peano arithmetic and $\mathscr{I}$ the usual interpretation. Then $\mathscr{I}$ is expressive.

Proof. By Exercise 8.2–3, the proof may just as well show that the strongest postcondition is expressible. Let $p \in WFF_B$ be a formula and $S \in L_2^B$ be a while-program. It has to be shown that there exists a formula $q \in WFF_B$ such that $\mathscr{I}(q)$ is the strongest postcondition of $\mathscr{I}(p)$ and S; in other words, it must be the case that for all states $\sigma \in \Sigma$:

$$\mathscr{I}(q)(\sigma) = true \quad \text{iff there is a state } \sigma' \in \Sigma \text{ such that}$$
$$\mathscr{I}(p)(\sigma') = true \text{ and } \sigma = \mathscr{M}_\mathscr{I}(S)(\sigma').$$

The proof proceeds by induction on the structure of the while-program S.

(i) *Assignment statement* For the assignment statement $x := t$, choose for q the formula $\exists c . (p_x^c \wedge x = t_x^c)$, where c is a variable that does not occur in p and t. Then, in fact, for all $\sigma \in \Sigma$:

$\mathscr{I}(q)(\sigma) = true$ iff there is $d \in Nat$ so that $\mathscr{I}(p_x^c)(\sigma[c/d]) = true$
and $\sigma(x) = \mathscr{I}(t_x^c)(\sigma[c/d])$
iff there is $d \in Nat$ so that $\mathscr{I}(p)(\sigma[x/d]) = true$
and $\sigma(x) = \mathscr{I}(t)(\sigma[x/d])$.
iff there is $\sigma' \in \Sigma$ so that $\sigma'(y) = \sigma(y)$ for all $y \neq x$,
$\mathscr{I}(p)(\sigma') = true$ and $\sigma(x) = \mathscr{I}(t)(\sigma')$
iff there is $\sigma' \in \Sigma$ such that $\mathscr{I}(p)(\sigma') = true$
and $\sigma = \mathscr{M}_\mathscr{I}(x := t)(\sigma')$

(ii) *Composed statement* Consider the composed statement $S_1 ; S_2$. By induction hypothesis there exists a formula $r \in WFF_B$ such that $\mathscr{I}(r)$ is the strongest postcondition of $\mathscr{I}(p)$ and S_1, and a formula $q \in WFF_B$ such that $\mathscr{I}(q)$ is the strongest postcondition of $\mathscr{I}(r)$ and S_2. Then $\mathscr{I}(q)$ is the strongest postcondition of $\mathscr{I}(p)$ and $S_1 ; S_2$ because for all $\sigma \in \Sigma$:

$\mathscr{I}(q)(\sigma) = \text{true}$ iff there is $\sigma'' \in \Sigma$ so that $\mathscr{I}(r)(\sigma'') = \text{true}$
and $\sigma = \mathscr{M}_{\mathscr{I}}(S_2)(\sigma'')$
iff there are $\sigma'', \sigma' \in \Sigma$ so that $\mathscr{I}(p)(\sigma') = \text{true}$,
$\sigma'' = \mathscr{M}_{\mathscr{I}}(S_1)(\sigma')$, and $\sigma = \mathscr{M}_{\mathscr{I}}(S_2)(\sigma'')$
iff there is $\sigma' \in \Sigma$ so that $\mathscr{I}(p)(\sigma') = \text{true}$
and $\sigma = \mathscr{M}_{\mathscr{I}}(S_1 ; S_2)(\sigma')$.

(iii) *Conditional statement*   Consider the conditional statement *if e then* S_1 *else* S_2 *fi*. By induction hypothesis there exists a formula q_1 such that $\mathscr{I}(q_1)$ is the strongest postcondition of $\mathscr{I}(p \wedge e)$ and S_1 and a formula q_2 such that $\mathscr{I}(q_2)$ is the strongest postcondition of $\mathscr{I}(p \wedge \neg e)$ and S_2. Then $\mathscr{I}(q_1 \vee q_2)$ is the strongest postcondition of $\mathscr{I}(p)$ and *if e then* S_1 *else* S_2 *fi*. The proof is left to the reader.

(iv) *While-statement*   Suppose S is the while-statement *while e do* S_1 *od*. This case constitutes the core of the proof where Lemma 8.15 is required. In fact, it would be absurd to try to give a formula, as in the other cases, and then prove that it is the strongest postcondition. Such a formula would be too complicated to be found as may be suggested by the example after Lemma 8.15. Instead, this formula will be developed step by step. The objective is to find a formula q which expresses the statement:

For each state $\sigma \in \Sigma$ there is a state $\sigma' \in \Sigma$ such that $\mathscr{I}(p)(\sigma') = \text{true}$ and $\sigma = \mathscr{M}_{\mathscr{I}}(S)(\sigma')$.

The first step is to 'unwind' the loop and obtain:

For each state $\sigma \in \Sigma$ there is a number $n \in Nat$ and there are states $\sigma_0, \ldots, \sigma_n \in \Sigma$ such that

$\mathscr{I}(p)(\sigma_0) = \text{true}$
$\mathscr{M}_{\mathscr{I}}(S_1)(\sigma_i) = \sigma_{i+1}, \quad \text{for } i = 0, \ldots, n-1$
$\mathscr{I}(e)(\sigma_i) = \text{true}, \quad \text{for } i = 0, \ldots, n-1$
$\mathscr{I}(e)(\sigma_n) = \text{false}$
$\sigma = \sigma_n.$

Suppose that x is the only variable that occurs free in p and S. (The indefatigable reader can generalize to the case of more than one variable.) Since this variable is the only one that 'plays a role', an equivalent formulation of the above is:

For each state $\sigma \in \Sigma$ there are numbers $n, d_0, \ldots, d_n \in Nat$ such that

$$\left.\begin{array}{l} \mathscr{I}(p)(\sigma[x/d_0]) = \text{true} \\ \mathscr{M}_{\mathscr{I}}(S_1)(\sigma[x/d_i]) = \sigma[x/d_{i+1}], \quad \text{for } i = 0, \ldots, n-1 \\ \mathscr{I}(e)(\sigma[x/d_i]) = \text{true}, \quad \text{for } i = 0, \ldots, n-1 \\ \mathscr{I}(e)(\sigma[x/d_n]) = \text{false} \\ \sigma(x) = d_n. \end{array}\right\} \quad (1)$$

Let y be a new variable. By induction hypothesis there is a formula r such that $\mathscr{I}(r)$ is the strongest postcondition of $\mathscr{I}(x = y)$ and S_1. The formula captures the relationship of the value of the variable x before the execution of S_1 to its value afterwards. Thus it can be used to replace the second condition in (1), namely

$$\mathscr{M}_{\mathscr{I}}(S_1)(\sigma[x/d_i]) = \sigma[x/d_{i+1}],$$

by

$$\mathscr{I}(r)(\sigma[y/d_i][x/d_{i+1}]) = \text{true}.$$

After this transformation it looks as though the statement (1) could be made into a formula of predicate logic. The only problem is that the number n of values $d_0, \ldots, d_n$ is existentially quantified. Therefore the Gödelization must come into play. The sequence of values $d_0, \ldots, d_n$ for the variable x is encoded by two numbers d and e. The result is an equivalent formulation of (1):

For each state $\sigma \in \Sigma$ there exist numbers $n, d, e \in Nat$ such that

for all $a \in Nat$, $\beta(d, e, 0, a) = \text{true}$ implies $\mathscr{I}(p)(\sigma[x/a]) = \text{true}$
for $i = 0, \ldots, n - 1$ and all $a, b \in Nat$, $\beta(d, e, i, a) = \text{true}$ and
$\beta(d, e, i + 1, b) = \text{true}$ imply $\mathscr{I}(r)(\sigma[y/a][x/b]) = \text{true}$

and so on.

Since Gödel's β-predicate can be expressed by a formula in Peano arithmetic, it should be clear that the above statement can be translated into such a formula. This ends the case of the existence of the strongest postcondition for the while-statement and the proof of Theorem 8.16. □

The section ends with two remarks.

Theorems 8.12 and 8.16 shed more light on Theorem 6.7 which states that the set of all valid Hoare formulas is not recursively enumerable, neither in the interpretation of Presburger arithmetic nor in that of Peano arithmetic. Now consider the following obvious property:

the set of all Hoare formulas valid in an (arbitrary) interpretation $\mathscr{I}$ is recursively enumerable if:

(i) the theory $Th(\mathscr{I})$ is recursively enumerable, and if moreover
(ii) $\models_{\mathscr{I}} h$ iff $Th(\mathscr{I}) \vdash h$ for any Hoare formula h.

This property is not applicable to Presburger arithmetic because (ii) does not hold; it is not applicable to Peano arithmetic because (i) does not hold. Hence the reasons why Theorem 6.7 holds for Presburger and Peano arithmetic are 'different'.

The second remark concerns the method given in the proof of Theorem 8.16 which allows construction of the strongest postcondition q of an arbitrary formula p and an arbitrary while-program S and hence reduces the validity proof of the Hoare formula $\{p\}\, S\, \{r\}$ to a validity proof of the predicate logic formula $q \supset r$. First, note that the existence of this method does not contradict Theorem 6.7 because Peano arithmetic is a theory which is not recursively enumerable. Next, the method does not absolve one from finding a 'good' invariant for each while-statement because the formula q obtained for a while-statement is so complicated that the validity proof of the formula $q \supset r$ becomes unfeasible.

8.4 Integration of the Well-Founded Sets Method

In this section a variant of the Hoare calculus is presented in which one can prove total correctness of while-programs. The Hoare formulas for the total correctness logic will be written $[p]\,S\,[q]$ for formulas $p, q \in WFF_B$ and a while-program $S \in L_2^B$ in order to distinguish them from the formulas $\{p\}\,S\,\{q\}$ of the partial correctness logic.

What it means for $[p]\,S\,[q]$ to be true is as follows. For every interpretation $\mathscr{I}$ of the basis B and every state $\sigma \in \Sigma$:

$$\mathscr{I}([p]\,S\,[q])(\sigma) = \text{true}$$
$$\text{iff} \begin{cases} \text{if } \mathscr{I}(p)(\sigma) = \text{true}, \\ \text{then } \mathscr{M}_{\mathscr{I}}(S)(\sigma) \text{ is defined} \\ \text{and } \mathscr{I}(q)(\mathscr{M}_{\mathscr{I}}(S)(\sigma)) = \text{true}. \end{cases}$$

The concepts of *validity* in $\mathscr{I}$, *logical validity*, and *logical consequence* are all defined for these formulas analogously to Section 8.1. In particular $\models_{\mathscr{I}} [p]\,S\,[q]$ expresses that the while-program S is totally correct with respect to the formulas p and q in the interpretation $\mathscr{I}$.

The calculus is confined here to the case where the domain D of the interpretation $\mathscr{I}$ contains a well-founded set that can be defined by a formula of predicate logic. Specifically, in this section

(1) B is a basis which contains a two-place predicate symbol '$\leq$';
(2) $\mathscr{I} = (D, \mathscr{I}_0)$ is an interpretation of B;
(3) W is a subset of D such that $(W, \mathscr{I}_0(\leq))$ is a well-founded set;
(4) $w \in WFF_B$ is a formula of predicate logic with one free variable, say x, which 'defines' W, namely $W = \{\sigma(x) \mid \sigma \in \Sigma \text{ and } \mathscr{I}(w)(\sigma) = \text{true}\}$.

For example, in the case $D = Nat$ one may choose $W = D$, $\mathscr{I}_0(\leq)$ to be the relation 'smaller than or equal to'. The formula w may then be the formula *true*.

Under these conditions the axioms and rules (i), (ii), (iii), and (v) of the calculus of partial correctness can be carried over with $\{\ldots\}$ replaced by $[\ldots]$. The while-rule (iv) is replaced by

$$\frac{(p \wedge e) \supset w_x^t, \ [p \wedge e \wedge (t = y)]\,S\,[p \wedge (t < y)]}{[p]\text{ while } e \text{ do } S \text{ od } [p \wedge \neg e]}$$

for all formulas $p \in WFF_B$, quantifier-free formulas $e \in QFF_B$, terms $t \in T_B$, variables y such that y does not occur in e, S, p, or t, and while-programs $S \in L_2^B$.

This new while-rule requires some explanation. The first premise, namely $(p \wedge e) \supset w_x^t$, says that the value of the term t lies in the well-founded set so long as one is in the while-loop. At the moment of leaving the loop, that is when e does not hold, the value of t may lie outside of the well-founded set. This is a relaxation of the well-founded sets method as it was described in the last chapter; it does not affect the correctness of the method, and may make proofs easier. The second premise, namely $[p \wedge e \wedge (t = y)] \, \mathrm{S} \, [p \wedge (t < y)]$, says that p is an invariant and that the value of the term t decreases (with respect to '$<$') after every pass through the loop. It is important that the variable y is completely uninvolved. If y occurred in p, e, or t, it could be possible that $\mathscr{I}(p \wedge e \wedge (t = y))(\sigma) =$ false for all $\sigma \in \Sigma$. Then the premise would be valid without saying something about t decreasing. Something similar might happen, if y was assigned a value to in S. As a final remark note that $t < y$ was used as an abbreviation for $(t \le y) \wedge \neg (t = y)$.

EXAMPLE 8.17   The example is the same as Example 8.4 but with total instead of partial correctness. Taking $W = Nat$, $\mathscr{I}_0(\le) =$ 'smaller than or equal to', and $w = true$ it will be proved that:

$$T \vdash [x = a] \; y_1 := 0; \; y_2 := 1; \; y_3 := 1;$$
$$while \; y_3 \le x \; do \; y_1 := y_1 + 1; \; y_2 := y_2 + 2; \; y_3 := y_3 + y_2 \; od \; [y_1 = \sqrt{a}]$$

Assuming that for (the Hoare calculus for) total correctness derived rules $[\mathrm{i}']$, $[\mathrm{ii}']$, and $[\mathrm{iv}']$ have been established which are similar to those labelled (i'), (ii'), and (iv') respectively in Section 8.1, the proof proceeds along the same lines as in Example 8.4. The main difference lies in the 'backward' application of the new (derived rule from the) while-rule $[\mathrm{iv}']$ on the Hoare formula labelled (5); taking $1 + x - y_3$ for the term t one obtains:

(5)

$[\mathrm{iv}']$ $\longmapsto$ (9)   identical with formula (9) in Example 8.4

$\longmapsto$ (10) $x = a \wedge y_1^2 \le x \wedge y_3 = (y_1 + 1)^2 \wedge y_2 = 2 * y_1 + 1$
$$\wedge \; y_3 \le x \supset true \qquad \text{Formula of } T$$

$\longmapsto$ (11) $[x = a \wedge y_1^2 \le x \wedge y_3 = (y_1 + 1)^2 \wedge y_2 = 2 * y_1 + 1$
$$\wedge \; y_3 \le x \wedge 1 + x - y_3 = y]$$
$$y_1 := y_1 + 1; \; y_2 := y_2 + 2; \; y_3 := y_3 + y_2$$
$$[x = a \wedge y_1^2 \le x \wedge y_3 = (y_1 + 1)^2 \wedge$$
$$y_2 = 2 * y_1 + 1 \wedge 1 + x - y_3 < y]$$

$\longmapsto$ (12)   identical with formula (11) in Example 8.4

(11)

$[\mathrm{ii}']$ $\longmapsto$ (13) $[x = a \wedge y_1^2 \le x \wedge y_3 = (y_1 + 1)^2 \wedge$
$$y_2 = 2 * y_1 + 1 \wedge y_3 \le x \wedge 1 + x - y_3 = y] \; y_1 := y_1 + 1$$
$$[x = a \wedge y_3 = y_1^2 \wedge$$
$$y_2 = 2 * y_1 - 1 \wedge y_3 \le x \wedge y_1 > 0 \wedge 1 + x - y_3 = y]$$

$\longmapsto$ (14) $[x = a \wedge y_3 = y_1^2 \wedge$
$$y_2 = 2 * y_1 - 1 \wedge y_3 \le x \wedge y_1 > 0 \wedge 1 + x - y_3 = y]$$
$$y_2 := y_2 + 2 \; [x = a \wedge y_1^2 \le x \wedge$$
$$y_3 = y_1^2 \wedge y_2 = 2 * y_1 + 1 \wedge 1 + x - y_3 = y]$$

$\hookrightarrow$ (15) $\quad [x = a \wedge y_1^2 \leq x \wedge y_3 = y_1^2 \wedge y_2 = 2 * y_1 + 1 \wedge 1 + x - y_3 = y]$
$$y_3 := y_3 + y_2 \, [x = a \wedge y_1^2 \leq x \wedge y_3 = (y_1 + 1)^2 \wedge$$
$$y_2 = 2 * y_1 + 1 \wedge 1 + x - y_3 < y]$$

(13)

$[i'] \quad \hookrightarrow \; x = a \wedge y_1^2 \leq x \wedge y_3 = (y_1 + 1)^2 \wedge$
$$y_2 = 2 * y_1 + 1 \wedge y_3 \leq x \wedge 1 + x - y_3 = y$$
$$\supset x = a \wedge y_3 = (y_1 + 1)^2 \wedge$$
$$y_2 = 2 * (y_1 + 1) - 1 \wedge y_3 \leq x \wedge y_1 + 1 > 0 \wedge 1 + x - y_3 = y$$

Formula of T

(14)

$[i'] \quad \hookrightarrow \; x = a \wedge y_3 = y_1^2 \wedge y_2 = 2 * y_1 - 1 \wedge y_3 \leq x \wedge y_1 > 0 \wedge 1 + x - y_3 = y$
$$\supset x = a \wedge y_1^2 \leq x \wedge y_3 = y_1^2 \wedge y_2 + 2 = 2 * y_1 + 1 \wedge 1 + x - y_3 = y$$

Formula of T

(15)

$[i'] \quad \hookrightarrow \; x = a \wedge y_1^2 \leq x \wedge y_3 = y_1^2 \wedge y_2 = 2 * y_1 + 1 \wedge 1 + x - y_3 = y$
$$\supset x = a \wedge y_1^2 \leq x \wedge y_3 + y_2 = (y_1 + 1)^2 \wedge$$
$$y_2 = 2 * y_1 + 1 \wedge 1 + x - y_3 - y_2 < y$$

Formula of T (note that $x \geq y_3$, hence $y > 0$ and that $y_2 > 0$) $\quad \square$

This section ends with a few words about the questions of soundness and completeness for the Hoare calculus of total correctness. Naturally these questions only make sense for interpretations $\mathscr{I}$ which satisfy the restrictions indicated above. In particular the domain of the interpretation must contain a well-founded set. For these interpretations one can prove the following soundness property:

$$Th(\mathscr{I}) \vdash [p] \, \mathrm{S} \, [q] \quad \text{implies} \quad \vDash_{\mathscr{I}} [p] \, \mathrm{S} \, [q].$$

The idea of a proof can be gleaned from the remarks about the new while-rule, however the details of a full proof are left to the reader as Exercise 8.4–2.

A reasonable completeness result cannot be obtained for the calculus, as presented here. The reason for this lack of completeness has been discussed in Exercises 7.2–3 and 7.2–4. The idea of convergents was suggested in order to overcome this difficulty. A calculus which uses such convergents is presented and proved complete in some sense in Harel (1979).

Finally, it is instructive to compare partial and total correctness with respect to first-order predicate logic. While partial correctness for while-programs is a first-order property, total correctness is not. (This was seen in Theorem 7.11.) The latter of these facts is reflected in the requirement that the domain of the interpretation has to contain a well-founded set, and this condition is not a first-order property. (See Exercise 2.4–6.) Since partial correctness is a first-order property one might suppose that in contrast to the case for total correctness, only first-order properties play a role in the soundness and completeness proofs. This was the case in the soundness proof of Theorem 8.5, as no restrictions were placed on the interpretation. But in the Relative Completeness Theorem 8.11 it was required that the interpretation is expressive. This is not a first-order property (see Exercise 8.3–3). It is, however, possible to introduce a slightly different notion of completeness which refers to first-order properties only (see Sieber, 1982).

EXERCISES

8.1–1 The greatest common divisor g of two numbers $a, b \in Nat$ may always be represented as a linear combination of these numbers:

$$g = i * a + j * b \qquad \text{with } i, j \in Int.$$

The following while-program S is intended to compute the gcd and the coefficients i and j:

$$i := 1; j := 0; k := 0; l := 1;$$
$$while \ x \neq y \ do$$
$$\quad if \ x > y \ then \ x := x - y; i := i - k; j := j - l$$
$$\quad\quad else \ y := y - x; k := k - i; l := l - j \ fi \ od$$

Try to find the underlying 'recursive idea' and prove with the aid of the Hoare calculus that S is partially correct with respect to the formulas

$$x = a \wedge y = b \wedge a > 0 \wedge b > 0$$

and

$$x = \gcd(a, b) \wedge x = i * a + j * b.$$

(Note that the domain of the interpretation has to be the set Int of *all* integers.)

8.1–2 Write a while-program which checks whether a given number is prime and prove its partial correctness with the aid of the Hoare calculus.

8.1–3 Let $S \in L_2^B$ be a while-program and $p, q \in WFF_B$ formulas for a given basis B.

(i) Prove that for every interpretation $\mathscr{I}$ of B the predicate $\mathscr{I}(\{true\} S \{q\}) \colon \Sigma \to Bool$ is the weakest liberal precondition of S and $\mathscr{I}(q)$.

*(ii) Prove that the weakest precondition of S and $\mathscr{I}(q)$ and the strongest postcondition of $\mathscr{I}(p)$ and S can in general not be expressed by a Hoare formula.

(*Hint*: Prove that every Hoare formula is equivalent to an 'infinite conjunction' of first-order predicate formulas and show that this need not be the case for weakest preconditions or strongest postconditions, if $\mathscr{I}$ is a non-standard model of Peano arithmetic.)

8.2–1

(i) Why is a simple 'assignment axiom' of the form

$$\{true\} \ x := t \ \{x = t\} \qquad \text{for all } x \in V, t \in T_B$$

not sound?

(ii) Extend the language of while-programs by the statement '*repeat* S *until* e' which can be considered as an abbreviation for 'S; *while* $\neg e \ do$ S *od*'. Find an inference rule for this statement which leads again to a sound and complete (in the sense of Theorem 8.11) calculus.

8.2–2 Prove the 'soundness and completeness' of the conditional rule: for every interpretation $\mathscr{I}$, $\models_\mathscr{I} \{p\} \ if \ e \ then \ S_1 \ else \ S_2 \ fi \ \{q\}$ is equivalent to $\models_\mathscr{I} \{p \wedge e\} S_1 \{q\}$ and $\models_\mathscr{I} \{p \wedge e\} S_2 \{q\}$.

8.2–3 It has been mentioned that in the definition of expressiveness weakest liberal preconditions can be replaced by strongest postconditions. This will now be stated more precisely.

Let a basis B, a while-program $S \in L_2^B$, and a formula $q \in WFF_B$ be given. Let $x_1, \ldots, x_n$ be the variables occurring in S and/or q and let $y_1, \ldots, y_n$ be 'new' variables. Prove that for every interpretation $\mathscr{I}$ of B:

(i) If $r \in WFF_B$ is the weakest liberal precondition of S and the formula $\neg(x_1 = y_1 \wedge \cdots \wedge x_n = y_n)$, then the formula $(\exists x_1, \ldots, x_n . (q \wedge \neg r)_{y_1, \ldots, y_n}^{x, \ldots, x}$ is the strongest postcondition of the formula q and S.

(ii) If $r \in WFF_B$ is the strongest postcondition of the formula $(x_1 = y_1 \wedge \cdots \wedge x_n = y_n)$ and S, then the formula $(\forall x_1, \ldots, x_n . (r \supset q))_{y_1, \ldots, y_m}^{x, \ldots, x}$ is the weakest liberal precondition of S and the formula q.

8.2–4

(i) In the proof of the Completeness Theorem 8.11 the weakest precondition r of *while e do S od* and the formula q was shown to be an invariant for the proof of $\{p\}$ *while e do S od* $\{q\}$. Show that r is the weakest of all possible invariants for this proof or, more precisely, that the formula $u \supset r$ is valid in $\mathscr{I}$ for every invariant u.

(ii) Let $x_1, \ldots, x_n$ be the variables occurring in p and S and let $y_1, \ldots, y_n$ be 'new' variables. Let the formula s be the strongest postcondition of the formula p and *while $e \wedge \neg(x_1 = y_1 \wedge \cdots \wedge x_n = y_n)$ do S od* (which also exists in the case of expressiveness by Exercise 8.2–3). Show that $\exists y_1, \ldots, y_n . s$ is the strongest of all possible invariants.

(iii) Is every formula v which lies between r and $\exists y_1, \ldots, y_n . s$ or, more precisely, for which $\exists y_1, \ldots, y_n . s \supset v$ and $v \supset r$ are valid in $\mathscr{I}$, also an invariant? Is the conjunction or disjunction of two invariants again an invariant?

8.2–5 Prove Theorem 8.5 using operational instead of denotational semantics.

8.3–1

(i) Let B be a basis for predicate logic and $\mathscr{I}$ a finite interpretation of B, or, in other words, $\mathscr{I} = (D, \mathscr{I}_0)$ with a finite domain D. Prove that $\mathscr{I}$ is expressive. (*Hint:* The weakest liberal precondition of a program and a formula can be obtained as the conjunction of the weakest preconditions of finitely many paths through this program.)

(ii) Deduce from (i) that, whenever a Hoare calculus exists for a programming language which is sound and complete in the sense of Cook (Theorem 8.11), then the halting problem of the programming language for *finite* interpretations is decidable.

8.3–2 Let B be the basis for Presburger arithmetic and $\mathscr{I}$ its usual interpretation. It was proved in Section 8.3 that $\mathscr{I}$ is not expressive and, moreover, that there is *no* calculus, which is 'complete' for this interpretation (Theorem 8.12). Give a concrete Hoare formula $h \in HF_B$ which cannot be derived from the theory $Th(\mathscr{I})$ of Presburger arithmetic with the aid of the Hoare calculus. (*Hint:* Use again Lemma 8.14.)

*8.3–3 Let B be the basis for Peano arithmetic. It was proved that the standard interpretation $\mathscr{I}$ of B is expressive. Let now $\mathscr{I}^*$ be a non-standard model of $Th(\mathscr{I})$ (see Chapter 2, in particular, Exercise 2.4–5) and let S be the while-program

$$x := 0; \ while \ x \neq y \ do \ x := x + 1 \ od.$$

Prove that in $\mathscr{I}^*$ the weakest liberal precondition of S and $\mathscr{I}(false)$ is not expressible, hence that $\mathscr{I}^*$ is not expressive. This exercise shows that expressiveness is not a first-order property and—as a consequence—that it is not a *necessary* condition for Cook's completeness result (because the completeness holds for $\mathscr{I}^*$ as well as for $\mathscr{I}$).

8.4–1 Let S be the while-program

$$z := 1;$$
$$while \ y > 0 \ do$$
$$\quad if \ odd \ (y) \ then \ y := y - 1; \ z := x * z$$
$$\quad\quad else \ x := x * x; \ y := y/2 \ fi \ od$$

Prove with the aid of the extended Hoare calculus of Section 8.4 that

173

$$\vDash_{\mathscr{I}}[x = a \land y = b]\,S\,[z = a^b]$$

in the usual interpretation $\mathscr{I}$. (*Hint*: Deduce the invariant from the 'recursive idea' behind the program.)

8.4-2 Prove the soundness of the extended Hoare calculus for total correctness.

8.4-3 Consider the term $x + 1 - y_3$ chosen for t_{test} in Example 7.16.

(i) Explain why it was necessary to choose a different term for t_{test} in Example 7.17.

(ii) Explain why it was possible to choose the same term for t in Example 8.17.

HISTORICAL AND BIBLIOGRAPHICAL REMARKS

A large number of publications are devoted to Hoare logic, the pioneering paper being that of Hoare (1969). The total correctness version of the Hoare calculus was first presented in Manna and Pnueli (1974). The notions of expressiveness and relative completeness were introduced in Cook (1978). A further example of a non-expressive language was given in Wand (1978). The expressiveness of finite interpretations plays a role in Clarke (1979). In this paper it is proved that certain programming languages cannot possess a sound and relatively complete Hoare calculus, because the halting problem is undecidable for these languages, even if the underlying interpretation is finite (see Exercise 8.3–1). The theoretical work about Hoare logic culminates in two theorems of Lipton. The first of them says—roughly speaking—that the only expressive interpretations are the standard interpretation of Peano arithmetic and the finite interpretation; the second is in some sense the converse of Clarke's result. A good exposition of these two theorems is given in Clarke, German, and Halpern (1982); the original paper is Lipton (1977). For all these topics Apt's (1981) excellent overview article is a good starting point.

Further aspects of Hoare logic, like calculi for less trivial programming languages or 'axiomatic semantics' are discussed—together with the pertinent literature—in Chapter 11.

9
Verification Methods Based on Denotational Semantics

In Chapters 5 and 6 it has been seen how the Fixpoint Theorem can be used to prove program correctness (Examples 5.16 and 6.12). This proof method based directly on the definition of denotational semantics is powerful but too cumbersome for practical purposes. Other properties of denotational semantics, for example the Fixpoint Induction Principle or Park's Theorem, can also be used for verification of programs and often lead to more wieldy proofs. It is the aim of Section 9.1 to illustrate the use of such properties by some examples. In Section 9.2 the method of subgoal induction will be introduced. It is arrived at from denotational semantics in much the same way as the inductive assertions method was derived from the operational semantics in Chapter 7. In the last section another verification method, called the structural induction method, will be presented.

The usual interpretation over the natural numbers will be used in all the various examples. The difference between syntax and semantics will often not be made explicit, particularly in the use of λ-notation. No difference in notation will be made between the functions and their strict ω-extensions. Furthermore, some straightforward properties of the functions used will be applied, like

$$h(\text{if-then-else}(b, s, t)) = \text{if-then-else}(b, h(s), h(t))$$

for all b, s, t, whenever h is a strict function.

9.1 Applying Properties of Cpo's

By means of some examples with recursive programs the use of the following properties will be illustrated:

(1) fixpoint induction (Examples 9.1 to 9.6);
(2) the property that the least fixpoint is the least of all the fixpoints (Examples 9.7 and 9.8);
(3) Park's Theorem (Example 9.9).

Finally the use of these properties on while-programs will be briefly addressed

174

(Example 9.10). Since these properties are not independent of one another (Park's Theorem is a corollary of the Fixpoint Theorem), the methods are naturally related.

9.1.1 Fixpoint Induction

The use of fixpoint induction (Theorem 4.29) is now illustrated by six examples. In Examples 9.3 and 9.5 the generalized form of fixpoint induction—called simultaneous fixpoint induction—from Exercise 5.2-1 is used.

Proving partial correctness using fixpoint induction is often simple. Already in Example 4.30 it was proved by fixpoint induction that

$$\mu\Phi(S) \sqsubseteq fac,$$

where $\Phi(S)$ was the semantic functional of the recursive program

$$F(x) \Leftarrow if \ x = 0 \ then \ 1 \ else \ x * F(x - 1) \ fi$$

and 'fac' the (strict ω-extension of the) factorial function. From this it is easy to prove a partial correctness result: for all $n \in Nat$

if $\mathcal{M}(S)(n)$ is defined,
then $\mathcal{M}(S)(n) = n!$

(where '!' denotes the factorial function, not its ω-extension).

In this same vein another example is treated.

EXAMPLE 9.1 (Partial Correctness) Let S be the recursive program

$$F(x, y) \Leftarrow if \ x = y \ then \ 1 \ else \ (y + 1) * F(x, y + 1) \ fi$$

(see Example 6.12). It is now proved that for all $n \in Nat$, if $\mathcal{M}(S)(n, 0)$ is defined, then $\mathcal{M}(S)(n, 0) = n!$ or, equivalently, that for all $n \in Nat$, $\mathcal{M}^\omega(S)(n, 0) \sqsubseteq n!$ This is done by first proving by fixpoint induction that

$$\mu\Phi(S) \sqsubseteq [\lambda x, y . x!/y!]. \tag{1}$$

By choosing the predicate φ in the Fixpoint Induction Principle (Theorem 4.29) to be

$$\varphi(f) = true \qquad iff \ g(f) \sqsubseteq h(f),$$

where g is the identity function and h is the function with constant value $[\lambda x, y . x!/y!]$, then it must be shown that

(a) *Induction basis* $\perp \sqsubseteq [\lambda x, y . x!/y!]$

(b) *Induction step* For all $f \in [Nat_\omega^2 \to Nat_\omega]$:

$$f \sqsubseteq [\lambda x, y . x!/y!] \quad implies \quad \Phi(S)(f) \sqsubseteq [\lambda x, y . x!/y!].$$

(a) holds trivially.

For the proof of (b), let $n, m \in Nat_\omega$. It must be shown that

$$\text{if } n = m \text{ then } 1 \text{ else } (m + 1) * f(n, m + 1) \; fi \sqsubseteq n!/m! \tag{2}$$

for every function $f \in [Nat_\omega^2 \to Nat_\omega]$ such that

$$f \sqsubseteq [\lambda x, y . x!/y!]. \tag{3}$$

The proof of (2) continues by dividing into three cases.

Case 1. If $n = \omega$ or $m = \omega$, then (2) becomes $\omega \sqsubseteq \omega$ which holds trivially.

Case 2. If $n, m \in Nat$ and $n = m$, then (2) becomes

$$1 \sqsubseteq n!/n! = 1.$$

Case 3. If $n, m \in Nat$ and $n \neq m$, then (2) becomes

$$(m + 1) * f(n, m + 1) \sqsubseteq n!/m!.$$

This holds, since from (3) one obtains

$$f(n, m + 1) \sqsubseteq n!/(m + 1)!.$$

This ends the proof of (1).

From (1) follows in particular that for all $n \in Nat$,

$$\mu\Phi(S)(n, 0) \sqsubseteq [\lambda x, y . x!/y!](n, 0)$$

so that

$$\mu\Phi(S)(n, 0) \sqsubseteq n!/0! = n!$$

This expresses the property to be proved. $\qquad\square$

EXAMPLE 9.2 (Partial Correctness) Let S be the recursive program defined by the following recursive equations and F_1 as the main function variable:

$$F_1(x) \Leftarrow F_2(0, 1, 0, x) \tag{1}$$

$$F_2(y_1, y_2, y_3, x) \Leftarrow \text{if } y_2 + y_3 \leq x \text{ then } F_2(y_1 + 1, y_2 + 2, y_2 + y_3, x)$$
$$\text{else } y_1 \; fi \tag{2}$$

(See Example 6.11.) In order to prove that for all $n \in Nat$, if $\mathcal{M}(S)(n)$ is defined, then $\mathcal{M}(S)(n) = \sqrt{n}$, it is sufficient to show that for all $n \in Nat_\omega$

$$(n \leq (\text{pr}_1(\mu\Phi(S))(n))^2) \sqsubseteq \text{true} \tag{3}$$

and

$$((\text{pr}_1(\mu\Phi(S))(n))^2 < n + 1) \sqsubseteq \text{true}. \tag{4}$$

(3) and (4) can be derived from a more general property of $\mu\Phi(S')$, where S' is the recursive program that consists of only the recursive equation (2). The details are left to Exercise 9.1–1. $\qquad\square$

Proofs of termination using fixpoint induction come up against a fundamental problem, as illustrated by the following attempt to prove that a recursive program terminates. First a function is defined to distinguish when the program terminates (leading to a value in D) and when it does not (leading to the value ω). Such a function is, for instance, the strict ω-extension of the function with constant value zero. This function zero: $D_\omega \to \{0, \omega\}$ is defined by

$$\text{zero}(x) = \begin{cases} 0 & \text{if } x \in D \\ \omega & \text{if } x = \omega. \end{cases}$$

One could have, for instance, $D = Nat$. To prove that, for a recursive program S, $\mathscr{M}(S)(d)$ is defined for all $d \in D$ satisfying a predicate φ, it is sufficient to show that

$$\text{zero}(d) \sqsubseteq \text{zero}(\mu\Phi(S)(d))$$

for all $d \in D$ such that φ holds. Unfortunately this property cannot be proved without further ado, because the induction basis of the Fixpoint Induction Principle simply does not hold. One solution to this problem is given in the next example.

EXAMPLE 9.3 (Termination)   Let S be the recursive program

$$F(x) \Leftarrow \text{if } x = 0 \text{ then } 1 \text{ else } x * F(x-1) \text{ } fi$$

and S' the recursive program

$$F(x) \Leftarrow \text{if } x = 0 \text{ then } 0 \text{ else } F(x-1) \text{ } fi.$$

Suppose it has been shown that $\mu\Phi(S') = \text{zero}$. (This could have been done 'directly' as demonstrated in Example 6.12 or by the method of structural induction which will be treated in Section 9.3.) Then to prove that $\mathscr{M}(S)(n)$ is defined for all $n \in Nat$, it needs only be proved that

$$\mu\Phi(S') \sqsubseteq \text{zero} \circ \mu\Phi(S).$$

This is now proved by simultaneous fixpoint induction (see Exercise 5.2–1).

Induction basis   Clearly $\bot \sqsubseteq \text{zero} \circ \bot$, since $\bot$ is the least element.

Induction step   Let $f, f' \in [Nat_\omega \to Nat_\omega]$ such that

$$f' \sqsubseteq \text{zero} \circ f.$$

Then it must be proved that
$$\Phi(S')(f') \sqsubseteq \text{zero} \circ \Phi(S)(f).$$

Expanded this yields the assertion that

$$\text{if } n = 0 \text{ then } 0 \text{ else } f'(n-1) \text{ } fi \sqsubseteq \text{zero}(\text{if } n = 0 \text{ then } 1 \text{ else } n * f(n-1) \text{ } fi)$$

for all $n \in Nat_\omega$. This is easily seen to be true by case distinction. For $n = \omega$, the assertion reduces to $\omega \sqsubseteq \text{zero}(\omega) = \omega$. For $n = 0$, $0 \sqsubseteq \text{zero}(1) = 0$. Otherwise the assertion reduces to

$$f'(n-1) \sqsubseteq \text{zero}(n * f(n-1)) = \text{zero}(f(n-1))$$

which holds by induction hypothesis. $\square$

This last example generalizes relatively easily to a certain class of programs (see Exercise 9.1–2). Essentially, fixpoint induction permits a proof of termination depending on the termination of a 'known' program. This method will not be considered here any further, since termination can often be proved with more simple methods—for instance, by the method of structural induction described in Section 9.3.

Other useful properties, besides partial and total correctness, can be proved by fixpoint induction. It can be used to prove a relation between different values computed by a program (Example 9.4) or between the values computed by different programs (Example 9.5).

EXAMPLE 9.4 (Connection between Different Values)   Let S be the recursive program

$$F(x, y) \Leftarrow \text{ if } q(x) \text{ then } y \text{ else } l(F(k(x), y)) \text{ } fi,$$

where q is interpreted as a 1-ary predicate from $(D \to Bool)$, and k and l as 1-place functions from $(D \to D)$. (Actually, S is a *program scheme*—in the sense of, say Greibach (1975)—rather than a program.) Suppose it is to be proved that either

$$\mathcal{M}(S)(m, l(n)) \quad \text{and} \quad l(\mathcal{M}(S)(m, n))$$

are both undefined or

$$\mathcal{M}(S)(m, l(n)) = l(\mathcal{M}(S)(m, n))$$

for all $m, n \in D$. It is sufficient to show that

$$\mu\Phi(S)(m, l(n)) = l(\mu\Phi(S)(m, n))$$

for all $m, n \in D_\omega$ (where l now denotes the strict ω-extension). The proof is by fixpoint induction, where the predicate φ of the Fixpoint Induction Principle is chosen to be

$$\varphi(f) = \text{true} \qquad \text{iff } g(f) = h(f),$$

where

$$g = [\lambda f . [\lambda m, n . f(m, l(n))]]$$
$$h = [\lambda f . [\lambda m, n . l(f(m, n))]].$$

Induction basis   Because l is strict

$$\bot(m, l(n)) = l(\bot(m, n))$$

which proves the base case.

Induction step   The induction hypothesis consists in assuming that $f \in [D_\omega^2 \to D_\omega]$ is such that for all $x, y \in D_\omega$

$$f(x, l(y)) = l(f(x, y)).$$

It must be shown that

$$\Phi(S)(f)(m, l(n)) = l(\Phi(S)(f)(m, n))$$

for all $m, n \in D_\omega$. Expanding $\Phi(S)(f)$ one obtains the equivalent formulation:

$$if\ q(m)\ then\ l(n)\ else\ l(f(k(m), l(n)))\ fi$$
$$= l(if\ q(m)\ then\ n\ else\ l(f(k(m), n))\ fi)$$

This holds for $q(m) = \omega$ since l is strict, and for $q(m) =$ true. For $q(m) =$ false it remains to show that

$$l(f(k(m), l(n))) = l(l(f(k(m), n)))$$

for all $m, n \in D_\omega$. But this follows from the induction hypothesis by letting $x = k(m)$ and $y = n$ which yields

$$f(k(m), l(n)) = l(f(k(m), n)) \qquad\qquad \square$$

EXAMPLE 9.5 (Connection between Programs)   Let S_1 and S_2 be the recursive programs

$$F(x, y, z) \Leftarrow if\ x = 0\ then\ y\ else\ F(x - 1, y + z, z)\ fi$$

and

$$F(x, y) \Leftarrow if\ x = 0\ then\ y\ else\ F(x - 1, 2 * x + y - 1)\ fi.$$

Suppose one wants to prove that, for all $m \in Nat$, either $\mathcal{M}(S_1)(m, 0, m)$ and $\mathcal{M}(S_2)(m, 0)$ are undefined, or they are the same. This can be proved by showing the more general property: for all $x, y \in Nat$ with $x \geq y$

$$\mu\Phi(S_1)(y, x * x - y), x) = \mu\Phi(S_2)(y, x^2 - y^2).$$

(To show that this property is an admissible predicate it is sufficient to write it in an equivalent form such as:

$$[\lambda x, y . if\ x \geq y\ then\ \mu\Phi(S_1)(y, x * (x - y), x)\ else\ x\ fi]$$
$$= [\lambda x, y . if\ x \geq y\ then\ \mu\Phi(S_2)(y, x^2 - y^2)\ else\ x\ fi].)$$

The proof proceeds by simultaneous fixpoint induction.

Induction basis   It is clear that for all $x, y \in Nat$ (even for all $x, y \in Nat_\omega$)

$$\bot(y, x * (x - y), x) = \bot(y, x^2 - y^2)$$

since $\bot(y, x * (x - y), x) = \bot(y, x^2 - y^2) = \omega.$

Induction step   It must be proved that, for all $f_1 \in [Nat_\omega^3 \to Nat_\omega]$ and $f_2 \in [Nat_\omega^2 \to Nat_\omega]$, from the induction hypothesis

$$f_1(y, x * (x - y), x) = f_2(y, x^2 - y^2) \qquad for\ all\ x, y \in Nat\ with\ x \geq y$$

follows

$$\Phi(S_1)(f_1)(n, m * (m - n), m) = \Phi(S_2)(f_2)(n, m^2 - n^2)$$
$$for\ all\ m, n \in Nat\ with\ m \geq n$$

Expanding $\Phi(S_1)(f_1)$ and $\Phi(S_2)(f_2)$ yields

$$if\ n = 0\ then\ m * (m - n)\ else\ f_1(n - 1, m * (m - n) + m, m)\ fi$$
$$= if\ n = 0\ then\ m^2 - n^2\ else\ f_2(n - 1, 2 * n + m^2 - n^2 - 1)\ fi.$$

This last equation follows immediately for $n = 0$, since $m * (m - 0) = m^2 - 0^2$ for all $m \in Nat$. For $n \neq 0$ it must be shown that

$$f_1(n - 1, m * (m - n) + m, m) = f_2(n - 1, m^2 - (n - 1)^2).$$

But this follows from the induction hypothesis by letting $x = m$ and $y = n - 1$. Note in particular that, by $m \geq n$, $m \geq n - 1$ (hence the induction hypothesis is applicable) and $m * (m - n) + m = m * (m - (n - 1))$. $\qquad\square$

Fixpoint induction can also be used to prove that a program does *not* terminate.

EXAMPLE 9.6 (Non-termination)   Let S be the recursive program

$$F(x, y) \Leftarrow if\ x = y\ then\ 1\ else\ (y + 2) * (y + 1) * F(x, y + 2)\ fi.$$

For all $m, n \in Nat$ with $m < n$, $\mathscr{M}(S)(m, n)$ is undefined. This can be proved by showing that for all $m, n \in Nat$ with $m < n$

$$\mu\Phi(S)(m, n) \sqsubseteq \omega$$

The proof proceeds by fixpoint induction.

Induction basis   That

$$\bot(m, n) \sqsubseteq \omega$$

is obvious.

Induction step   Assume f to be such that for all $m, n \in Nat$ with $m < n$

$$f(m, n) \sqsubseteq \omega. \tag{1}$$

It must be proved that for all $m, n \in Nat$ with $m < n$:

$$if\ m = n\ then\ 1\ else\ (n + 2) * (n + 1) * f(m, n + 2)\ fi \sqsubseteq \omega$$

or, because $m < n$:

$$(n + 2) * (n + 1) * f(m, n + 2) \sqsubseteq \omega. \tag{2}$$

From the induction hypothesis (1) one obtains

$$f(m, n + 2) \sqsubseteq \omega$$

(since $m < n$ implies $m < n + 2$). This proves (2) (since $*$ is assumed to be strict or, even more generally, since for each (monotonic) ω-extension $*$ of the multiplication one has

$$n * \omega = \omega$$

for all $n \in Nat$ with $n > 0$). $\qquad\square$

As will be seen in Chapter 10 the principle of fixpoint induction is powerful enough to form the basis of a calculus for program verification. But experience shows—and the previous examples have tried to illustrate—that the use of this principle is not always 'natural'. This is because of its abstract nature as well as a somewhat weak step in the induction. For an introduction to and use of stronger induction steps the reader is referred to, for instance, Manna (1974).

9.1.2 Other Methods

Another method for proving properties about recursive programs takes advantage of the fact that the least fixpoint is always less or equally defined than any function which can be shown to be a fixpoint. Suppose some property of a recursive program S is to be proved. If a function f can be shown to be a fixpoint of $\Phi(S)$, then the conclusion $\mu\Phi(S) \sqsubseteq f$ follows. This technique can be used to prove properties of S as is illustrated in the following examples.

EXAMPLE 9.7 (Partial Correctness) Consider the following recursive program S:

$$F(x) \Leftarrow if \ x > 100 \ then \ x - 10 \ else \ F(F(x + 11)) \ fi.$$

(see Example 3.30). Suppose one wants to show that, for all $n \in Nat$ with $n \leq 100$, either $\mathcal{M}(S)(n)$ is undefined or $\mathcal{M}(S)(n) = 91$. For all $n \in Nat$ with $n \leq 100$, $\mathcal{M}^{\omega}(S)(n) \sqsubseteq 91$, as the following argument shows. First define the function f_{91} by

$$f_{91} = [\lambda x . if \ x > 100 \ then \ x - 10 \ else \ 91 \ fi].$$

Now it is shown that this function is a fixpoint of $\Phi(S)$, in other words, $\Phi(S)(f_{91}) = f_{91}$. By expanding, this becomes

$$f_{91}(n) = if \ n > 100 \ then \ n - 10 \ else \ f_{91}(f_{91}(n + 11)) \ fi \qquad (1)$$

for all $n \in Nat_{\omega}$. If $n = \omega$ or $n > 100$, this is obvious. Otherwise $n \neq \omega$ and $n \leq 100$, so that the fixpoint condition (1) becomes

$$f_{91}(n) = f_{91}(f_{91}(n + 11)).$$

To see this, consider three cases.

If $n = 100$, then the left-hand side becomes $f_{91}(100) = 91$. The right-hand side becomes $f_{91}(f_{91}(111)) = f_{91}(101) = 91$.

If $90 \leq n \leq 99$, then $f_{91}(n) = 91$ and $n + 11 > 100$, so $f_{91}(f_{91}(n + 11)) = f_{91}(n + 1) = 91$.

Finally, if $n \leq 89$, then $f_{91}(n) = 91$ and $n + 11 \leq 100$, so $f_{91}(f_{91}(n + 11)) = f_{91}(91) = 91$.

This shows that f_{91} is a fixpoint of $\Phi(S)$. Since $\mu\Phi(S)$ is the least fixpoint

$$\mathcal{M}^{\omega}(S) = \mu\Phi(S) \sqsubseteq f_{91}.$$

Therefore $\mathcal{M}(S)$ is a restriction of f_{91}. The partial correctness follows from the fact that if $n \neq \omega$ and $n \leq 100$ then $f_{91}(n) = 91$. $\qquad\square$

182

EXAMPLE 9.8 (Termination)   Let S, S' be the recursive programs from Example 9.3. Likewise let the function zero be defined as in that example. To prove that $\mathcal{M}(S)(n)$ is defined for all $n \in Nat$, it is sufficient to show that

$$\mu\Phi(S') \sqsubseteq zero \circ \mu\Phi(S).$$

It is sufficient to prove that $zero \circ \mu\Phi(S)$ is a fixpoint of $\Phi(S')$, that is, for all $n \in Nat_\omega$

$$if\ n = 0\ then\ 0\ else\ zero(\mu\Phi(S)(n-1))\ fi = zero(\mu\Phi(S)(n)). \qquad (1)$$

Since $\mu\Phi(S)$ is a fixpoint of $\Phi(S)$

$$\mu\Phi(S)(n) = if\ n = 0\ then\ 1\ else\ n * \mu\Phi(S)(n-1)\ fi.$$

So (1) becomes

$$if\ n = 0\ then\ 0\ else\ zero(\mu\Phi(S)(n-1))\ fi$$
$$= zero(if\ n = 0\ then\ 1\ else\ n * \mu\Phi(S)(n-1)\ fi).$$

This obviously holds if $n = \omega$ or $n = 0$. Otherwise it follows from the fact that

$$zero(\mu\Phi(S)(n-1)) = zero(n * \mu\Phi(S)(n-1)). \qquad \square$$

The method illustrated in the last two examples is a practical one for proving partial correctness (Example 9.7). On the other hand, as a method for proving termination (Example 9.8) it suffers from the same disadvantages as fixpoint induction.

The following example demonstrates the use of Park's Theorem.

EXAMPLE 9.9 (Partial Correctness)   Let S be the recursive program

$$F(x, y) \Leftarrow if\ x = y\ then\ 1\ else\ (y + 2) * (y + 1) * F(x, y + 2)\ fi$$

from Example 9.6. It must be proved that for all $m, n \in Nat$ with $m \geq n$ either $\mathcal{M}(S)(m, n)$ is undefined or $\mathcal{M}(S)(m, n) = m!/n!$. To prove that for all $m, n \in Nat$ with $m \geq n$, $\mathcal{M}^\omega(S)(m, n) \sqsubseteq m!/n!$, one shows $\mu\Phi(S) \sqsubseteq g$, where g is the (strict) function defined by:

$$g(x, y) = \begin{cases} x!/y! & \text{if } x, y \in Nat \text{ and } x \geq y \\ \omega & \text{otherwise.} \end{cases}$$

By Park's Theorem it is sufficient to show that $\Phi(S)(g) \sqsubseteq g$, or, expanding,

$$if\ m = n\ then\ 1\ else\ (n + 2) * (n + 1) * g(m, n + 2)\ fi \sqsubseteq g(m, n).$$

This follows from considering five cases.

If $m = \omega$ or $n = \omega$, then both sides reduce to ω.

If $m, n \neq \omega$ and $m \geq n + 2$, then one obtains

$$(n + 2) * (n + 1) * g(m, n + 2) \sqsubseteq g(m, n)$$

or, equivalently

$$(n + 2) * (n + 1) * m!/(n + 2)! \sqsubseteq m!/n!.$$

If $m, n \neq \omega$ and $m = n + 1$, then

$$(n + 2) * (n + 1) * g(m, n + 2) \sqsubseteq g(m, n)$$

or, equivalently

$$\omega \sqsubseteq m!/n!.$$

If $m, n \neq \omega$ and $m = n$, then

$$1 \sqsubseteq g(m, n) = m!/m! = 1.$$

If $m, n \neq \omega$ and $m < n$, then

$$(n + 2) * (n + 1) * g(m, n + 2) \sqsubseteq g(m, n)$$

or, equivalently

$$\omega \sqsubseteq \omega.$$

And that completes the proof. □

This proof method can be seen as a generalization of the method used in Examples 9.7 and 9.8. To prove for a given program S and a given function g that $\mu\Phi(S) \sqsubseteq g$, requires only that $\Phi(S)(g) \sqsubseteq g$, and not $\Phi(S)(g) = g$. This generalization is only interesting in those special cases where the function g is not a fixpoint of $\Phi(S)$. Such a case occurred in the previous example, where for $m = n + 1$ one has $\Phi(S)(g)(m, n) \neq g(m, n)$.

9.1.3 The Case of while-Programs

All the previous examples demonstrated the proof methods on recursive programs. But they are also applicable on while-programs. The essential difference is that one has to deal with states (functions from V to D) instead of values. The proofs are correspondingly more tedious.

EXAMPLE 9.10 (Partial Correctness of a while-Program) Let S be the while-program

$$y := 1;$$
$$while \ x > 0 \ do \ y := y * x; \ x := x - 1 \ od$$

The program S is partially correct with respect to the formulas $x = a$ and $y = a!$. This means that for all states $\sigma \in \Sigma$, if $\mathcal{M}(S)(\sigma)$ is defined, then $\mathcal{M}(S)(\sigma)(y) = \sigma(x)!$, or equivalently, that for all states $\sigma \in \Sigma$, $\mathcal{M}^\omega(S)(\sigma)(y) \sqsubseteq \sigma(x)!$. The proof follows from the following arguments.

Let σ be an arbitrary state of Σ. (As was just indicated, it is not necessary to consider the case $\sigma = \omega$.) Then

$$\mathcal{M}^\omega(S)(\sigma) = \mathcal{M}^\omega(while \ x > 0 \ do \ldots od)(\mathcal{M}^\omega(y := 1)(\sigma)).$$

184

Setting $\sigma_1 = \sigma[y/1]$ this simplifies to

$$\mathscr{M}^\omega(S)(\sigma) = \mathscr{M}^\omega(while \ldots od)(\sigma_1).$$

Now let (as in Definition 5.17) $\Phi: [\Sigma_\omega \to \Sigma_\omega] \to [\Sigma_\omega \to \Sigma_\omega]$ be the function defined by

$$\Phi(f)(\sigma) = \begin{cases} \text{if-then-else}(\mathscr{I}(x > 0)(\sigma), f(\mathscr{M}^\omega(y := y * x; x := x - 1)(\sigma)), \sigma) & \text{if } \sigma \\ \omega & \text{if } \sigma = \omega. \end{cases}$$

Then

$$\mathscr{M}^\omega(S)(\sigma) = \mu\Phi(\sigma_1). \tag{1}$$

And it remains to show that

$$\mu\Phi(\sigma_1)(y) \sqsubseteq \sigma(x)!.$$

First one proves a slightly more general property, namely,

$$\mu\Phi \sqsubseteq g \tag{2}$$

where $g: \Sigma_\omega \to \Sigma_\omega$ is the function defined by

$$g(\sigma) = \begin{cases} \sigma[x/0][y/\sigma(x)! * \sigma(y)] & \text{if } \sigma \neq \omega \\ \omega & \text{if } \sigma = \omega. \end{cases}$$

This is done by showing that the function g is a fixpoint of Φ. That is, $\Phi(g) = g$ or, equivalently,

$$\Phi(g)(\sigma) = g(\sigma) \qquad \text{for all } \sigma \in \Sigma_\omega. \tag{3}$$

For $\sigma = \omega$, (3) becomes $\omega = \omega$. For $\sigma \neq \omega$, (3) leads to

$$\text{if-then-else}(\sigma(x) > 0, g(\mathscr{M}^\omega(y := y * x; x := x - 1)(\sigma)), \sigma) = g(\sigma). \tag{4}$$

The proof continues by dividing into two cases.

Case 1. If $\sigma(x) = 0$, then (4) becomes

$$\sigma = \sigma[x/0][y/\sigma(x)! * \sigma(y)].$$

This holds since

$$\sigma[x/0][y/\sigma(x)! * \sigma(y)] = \sigma[x/\sigma(x)][y/\sigma(y)] \qquad (\text{since } \sigma(x) = 0)$$
$$= \sigma.$$

Case 2. If $\sigma(x) \neq 0$, then (4) becomes

$$g(\mathscr{M}^\omega(\ldots)(\sigma)) = g(\sigma) \tag{5}$$

Now $\mathscr{M}^\omega(\ldots)(\sigma)$ yields a state, call it σ_2. This state is determined by the following argument:

$$\begin{aligned} \sigma_2 &= \mathscr{M}^\omega(y := y * x; x := x - 1)(\sigma) \\ &= \mathscr{M}^\omega(x := x - 1)(\sigma[y/\sigma(y) * \sigma(x)]) \\ &= (\sigma[y/\sigma(y) * \sigma(x)])[x/\sigma[y/\sigma(y) * \sigma(x)](x) - 1] \\ &= (\sigma[y/\sigma(y) * \sigma(x)])[x/\sigma(x) - 1] \\ &= \sigma[x/\sigma(x) - 1][y/\sigma(y) * \sigma(x)] \end{aligned}$$

As $\sigma_2 \neq \omega$, (5) can now be reduced to

$$\sigma_2[x/0][y/\sigma_2(x)! * \sigma_2(y)] = \sigma[x/0][y/\sigma(x)! * \sigma(y)].$$

These two functions are equal if they are equal for every argument $z \in V$. For $z = x$, both functions have the value 0. For $z = y$, the left-hand side function has the value $\sigma_2(x)! * \sigma_2(y)$, where by definition of σ_2, $\sigma_2(x) = \sigma(x) - 1$ and $\sigma_2(y) = \sigma(x) * \sigma(y)$, so the value is $(\sigma(x) - 1)! * \sigma(y) * \sigma(x)$. This is equal to the value of the right-hand side function, $\sigma(x)! * \sigma(y)$, since $\sigma(x) \neq 0$. Finally, for $z \neq x$ and $z \neq y$ both functions have the same value since σ_2 does not differ from σ on $z \neq x, y$.

This completes the proof of (3).

Together (1) and (2) result in

$$\mathcal{M}^\omega(S)(\sigma) \sqsubseteq \sigma_1[x/0][y/\sigma_1(x)! * \sigma_1(y)].$$

By definition of σ_1, $\sigma_1(x) = \sigma(x)$ and $\sigma_1(y) = 1$, and so

$$\mathcal{M}^\omega(S)(\sigma) \sqsubseteq \sigma_1[x/0][y/\sigma(x)!]$$

and in particular,

$$\mathcal{M}^\omega(S)(\sigma)(y) \sqsubseteq \sigma(x)!. \qquad \square$$

In the previous example one could also have proved assertion (2) using fixpoint induction or Park's Theorem.

Proofs of termination for while-programs can be performed similarly like those for recursive programs (Examples 9.3 and 9.8).

9.2 Subgoal Induction Method

In Chapter 7 the inductive assertions method for flowchart programs was derived out of the 'ingenious' proof methods based on operational semantics described in Chapter 6. Such proof methods can likewise be derived out of the above proof methods based on denotational semantics. For example, it is possible to derive the inductive assertions method for while-programs from the fixpoint induction principle. Here another method will be derived as an example, the subgoal induction method. This method also allows the proof of the partial correctness of while-programs.

THEOREM 9.11 (Subgoal Induction) Let S be a while-program of the form

$$\text{while } e \text{ do } S_1 \text{ od},$$

where e is a quantifier-free formula, S_1 is another while-program, and $\mathscr{I}$ its interpretation. Furthermore, let $\varphi: \Sigma^2 \to Bool$ be a two-place predicate. In order to prove for all states $\sigma \in \Sigma$:

if $\mathcal{M}(S)(\sigma)$ is defined, then $\varphi(\sigma, \mathcal{M}(S)(\sigma)) = \text{true}$, (1) it is sufficient to prove the following two conditions:

(i) *Induction basis* For all states $\sigma \in \Sigma$,

if $\mathscr{I}(e)(\sigma) = $ false,
then $\varphi(\sigma, \sigma) = $ true.

(ii) *Induction step* For all states $\sigma, \sigma' \in \Sigma$,

if $\mathscr{I}(e)(\sigma) = $ true,
if $\mathscr{M}(S_1)(\sigma)$ is defined and
if $\varphi(\mathscr{M}(S_1)(\sigma), \sigma') = $ true,
then $\varphi(\sigma, \sigma') = $ true.

Proof. If φ also denotes its strict ω-extension, then the assertion (1) can be succinctly written

$$\text{for all } \sigma \in \Sigma, \ \varphi(\sigma, \mathscr{M}^\omega(S)(\sigma)) \sqsubseteq \text{true.}$$

This can be rewritten

$$\text{for all } \sigma \in \Sigma, \ \varphi(\sigma, \mu\Phi(\sigma)) \sqsubseteq \text{true,} \qquad (2)$$

since, by the semantics of the while-statement, $\mathscr{M}^\omega(S) = \mu\Phi$, where Φ is defined as in Definition 5.17 by

$$\Phi(f)(\sigma) = \begin{cases} \text{if-then-else}(\mathscr{I}(e)(\sigma), f(\mathscr{M}^\omega(S_1)(\sigma)), \sigma) & \text{if } \sigma \in \Sigma \\ \omega & \text{if } \sigma = \omega. \end{cases}$$

The proof proceeds by deriving (2) by fixpoint induction from the conditions (i) and (ii) listed above.

Fixpoint induction basis For all $\sigma \in \Sigma$, $\varphi(\sigma, \bot(\sigma)) \sqsubseteq$ true, since φ is strict.

Fixpoint induction step Let by induction hypothesis $f \in [\Sigma_\omega \to \Sigma_\omega]$ be a function such that

$$\text{for all } \sigma \in \Sigma, \ \varphi(\sigma, f(\sigma)) \sqsubseteq \text{true.}$$

Consider an arbitrary $\sigma' \in \Sigma$. It must be proved that

$$\varphi(\sigma', \Phi(f)(\sigma')) \sqsubseteq \text{true.}$$

or, by expanding Φ

$$\varphi(\sigma', \text{if-then-else}(\mathscr{I}(e)(\sigma'), f(\mathscr{M}^\omega(S_1)(\sigma')), \sigma')) \sqsubseteq \text{true.} \qquad (3)$$

(Remember that $\sigma' \in \Sigma$, hence $\sigma' \neq \omega$.) The proof breaks into two cases according to the value of the formula e (remember that $\mathscr{I}(e)(\sigma') \neq \omega$).

Case 1. If $\mathscr{I}(e)(\sigma') = $ false, then (3) reduces to $\varphi(\sigma', \sigma') \sqsubseteq$ true. By condition (i), $\varphi(\sigma', \sigma') = $ true, so (3) follows immediately.

Case 2. If $\mathscr{I}(e)(\sigma') = $ true, then (3) reduces to

$$\varphi(\sigma', f(\mathscr{M}^\omega(S_1)(\sigma'))) \sqsubseteq \text{true.} \tag{4}$$

Should $f(\mathscr{M}^\omega(S_1)(\sigma')) = \omega$, then (4) holds since φ is strict, so suppose $f(\mathscr{M}^\omega(S_1)(\sigma')) \neq \omega$. Consider first the case $\mathscr{M}^\omega(S_1)(\sigma') = \omega$. But since f is monotonic and Σ_ω a flat cpo it must be that $f(\sigma'') = f(\omega) \neq \omega$ for all $\sigma'' \in \Sigma_\omega$. So in particular $f(\mathscr{M}^\omega(S_1)(\sigma')) = f(\sigma')$, hence (4) holds by induction hypothesis with $\sigma = \sigma'$. Consider now the case $\mathscr{M}^\omega(S_1)(\sigma') \neq \omega$, so $\mathscr{M}(S_1)(\sigma')$ is defined. By induction hypothesis with $\sigma = \mathscr{M}^\omega(S_1)(\sigma')$ it holds that

$$\varphi(\mathscr{M}^\omega(S_1)(\sigma'), f(\mathscr{M}^\omega(S_1)(\sigma'))) \sqsubseteq \text{true}$$

or, because $\mathscr{M}^\omega(S_1)(\sigma') \neq \omega$ and $f(\mathscr{M}^\omega(S_1)(\sigma')) \neq \omega$,

$$\mathscr{M}^\omega(S_1)(\sigma') = \mathscr{M}(S_1)(\sigma')$$

and

$$\varphi(\mathscr{M}(S_1)(\sigma'), f(\mathscr{M}(S_1)(\sigma'))) = \text{true.}$$

Now condition (ii) can be applied yielding (4). $\qquad\square$

Theorem 9.11 provides a convenient way to prove partial correctness of a while-program, if one can find an appropriate predicate φ, called an *invariant* (of the subgoal induction method) for each of its while-statements. This method will be illustrated with the next two examples.

EXAMPLE 9.12 (Partial Correctness)   Let S be the while-program from Example 9.10. It is proved again that S is partially correct with respect to the formulas $x = a$ and $y = a!$.

First it is proved that the predicate $\varphi: \Sigma^2 \to Bool$ defined by

$$\varphi(\sigma, \sigma') = \text{true} \qquad \text{iff } \sigma'(y) = \sigma(x)! * \sigma(y)$$

is an invariant of the while-program S':

$$while\ x > 0\ do\ y := y * x; x := x - 1\ od.$$

In other words, it is proved that $\varphi(\sigma, \mathscr{M}(S')(\sigma)) = $ true for all states $\sigma \in \Sigma$ for which $\mathscr{M}(S')(\sigma)$ is defined. Using the subgoal induction method of Theorem 9.11 there are two conditions to prove.

Induction basis   For all $\sigma \in \Sigma$, if $\mathscr{I}(x > 0)(\sigma) = $ false, then $\varphi(\sigma, \sigma) = $ true. This follows immediately, since $\mathscr{I}(x > 0)(\sigma) = $ false implies $\sigma(x) = 0$ and so $\sigma(y) = \sigma(x)! * \sigma(y)$.

Induction step   It must be proved that for all $\sigma, \sigma' \in \Sigma$, if $\mathscr{I}(x > 0)(\sigma) = $ true, $\mathscr{M}(S_1)(\sigma)$ is defined and $\varphi(\mathscr{M}(S_1)(\sigma), \sigma') = $ true, then $\varphi(\sigma, \sigma') = $ true, where S_1 is the while-program

$$y := y * x; x := x - 1.$$

Now $\mathscr{M}(S_1)(\sigma) = \sigma[y/\sigma(y) * \sigma(x)][x/\sigma(x) - 1]$. So $\varphi(\mathscr{M}(S_1)(\sigma), \sigma') = $ true yields

$\sigma'(y) = (\sigma(x) - 1)! * \sigma(y) * \sigma(x)$. Since $\sigma(x) > 0$, one obtains $\sigma'(y) = \sigma(x)! * \sigma(y)$, which is exactly $\varphi(\sigma, \sigma') = \text{true}$. This ends the proof that φ is an invariant.

To complete the proof of partial correctness one must consider the effect of the initial assignment statement $y := 1$. Now for all $\sigma \in \Sigma$

$$\mathcal{M}^\omega(S)(\sigma) = \mathcal{M}^\omega(S')(\mathcal{M}^\omega(y := 1)(\sigma))$$
$$= \mathcal{M}^\omega(S')(\sigma[y/1]).$$

So if $\mathcal{M}(S)(\sigma)$ is defined, then

$$\mathcal{M}(S)(\sigma)(y) = \mathcal{M}(S')(\sigma[y/1])(y) = \sigma(x)! * 1 = \sigma(x)!. \qquad \Box$$

EXAMPLE 9.13 (Partial Correctness)   Let S be the while-program from Examples 3.10 and 8.4:

$$y_1 := 0; \; y_2 := 1; \; y_3 := 1;$$
$$\textit{while } y_3 \leq x \textit{ do } y_1 := y_1 + 1;$$
$$y_2 := y_2 + 2;$$
$$y_3 := y_3 + y_2$$
$$\textit{od.}$$

If one wishes to prove that the program is partially correct with respect to the formulas $\textit{true}$ and $y_1^2 \leq x < (y_1 + 1)^2$, one first shows that the predicate φ defined by

$$\varphi(\sigma, \sigma') = \text{true} \quad \text{iff } (\sigma(y_1)^2 \leq \sigma(x) \wedge \sigma(y_3) = (\sigma(y_1) + 1)^2 \wedge$$
$$\sigma(y_2) = 2 * \sigma(y_1) + 1) \supset (\sigma'(y_1)^2 \leq \sigma(x) < (\sigma'(y_1) + 1)^2)$$

is an invariant of the subgoal induction method for the while-statement of S.

$\textit{Induction basis}$ It must be proved that if $\sigma(y_3) > \sigma(x)$, then

$$(\sigma(y_1)^2 \leq \sigma(x) \wedge \sigma(y_3) = (\sigma(y_1) + 1)^2 \wedge \sigma(y_2) = 2 * \sigma(y_1) + 1)$$
$$\supset (\sigma(y_1)^2 \leq \sigma(x) < (\sigma(y_1) + 1)^2).$$

That $\sigma(y_1)^2 \leq \sigma(x)$, follows directly from the left-hand side of the implication. That $\sigma(x) < (\sigma(y_1) + 1)^2$, follows from $\sigma(x) < \sigma(y_3)$ and from $\sigma(y_3) = (\sigma(y_1) + 1)^2$.

$\textit{Induction step}$ It must be proved that if

$$\sigma(y_3) \leq \sigma(x) \qquad (1)$$

and

$$((\sigma(y_1) + 1)^2 \leq \sigma(x) \wedge \sigma(y_2) + \sigma(y_3) + 2 = (\sigma(y_1) + 2)^2 \wedge$$
$$\sigma(y_2) + 2 = 2 * (\sigma(y_1) + 1) + 1) \supset (\sigma'(y_1)^2 \leq \sigma(x) < (\sigma'(y_1) + 1)^2), \qquad (2)$$

then

$$(\sigma(y_1)^2 \leq \sigma(x) \wedge \sigma(y_3) = (\sigma(y_1) + 1)^2 \wedge \sigma(y_2) = 2 * \sigma(y_1) + 1)$$
$$\supset (\sigma'(y_1)^2 \leq \sigma(x) < (\sigma'(y_1) + 1)^2) \qquad (3)$$

Notice that (2) and (3) are in the form

$$H_1 \supset C$$
$$H_2 \supset C$$

respectively. Hence to prove $(H_1 \supset C) \supset (H_2 \supset C)$ it is sufficient to show $H_2 \supset H_1$. Translated back this is: if

$$\sigma(y_1)^2 \le \sigma(x) \wedge \sigma(y_3) = (\sigma(y_1) + 1)^2 \wedge \sigma(y_2) = 2 * \sigma(y_1) + 1 \qquad (4)$$

then

$$(\sigma(y_1) + 1)^2 \le \sigma(x) \wedge \sigma(y_3) + \sigma(y_2) + 2 = (\sigma(y_1) + 2)^2$$
$$\wedge \sigma(y_2) + 2 = 2 * (\sigma(y_1) + 1) + 1. \qquad (5)$$

The equalities in (5) follow directly from (4); the inequality in (5) follows from (1) and (4). This ends the proof that φ is an invariant.

Analogously to the previous example one can derive: for every $\sigma \in \Sigma$, if $\mathscr{M}(S)(\sigma)$ is defined, then

$$(0 \le \sigma(x) \wedge 1 = (0 + 1)^2 \wedge 1 = 2 * 0 + 1)$$
$$\supset (\mathscr{M}(S)(\sigma)(y_1))^2 \le \sigma(x) < (\mathscr{M}(S)(\sigma)(y_1) + 1)^2.$$

Therefore, S is partially correct with respect to $x = a$ and $y_1 = \sqrt{a}$. □

9.2.1 Subgoal Induction and Hoare Logic

The while-rule of the Hoare calculus introduced in Chapter 8 reflects the idea behind the inductive assertions method of Chapter 7. An alternative while-rule will now be established which reflects the idea behind the subgoal induction method.

At first sight the construction of such a while-rule may seem impossible for the following reason: while a formula of predicate logic is always interpreted as a one-place predicate (from Σ to *Bool*), the subgoal induction method makes use of an invariant which is a two-place predicate (from Σ^2 to *Bool*). Actually, this difficulty can be surmounted by the following technique. Consider a while-program of the form

$$while\ e\ do\ S\ od.$$

Let $x_1, x_2, \ldots, x_n$ be the variables occurring in this program. Let $x'_1, x'_2, \ldots, x'_n$ be a corresponding list of new variables. A subgoal invariant

$$\varphi \colon \Sigma^2 \to Bool$$

of this while-program may then be defined by a formula r of predicate logic in which these new variables may also occur. More precisely, if $\mathscr{I}$ is the interpretation under consideration, the formula r defines the two-place predicate φ by

$$\varphi(\sigma, \sigma') = \mathscr{I}(r)(\sigma[x'_1/\sigma'(x_n)] \ldots [x'_n/\sigma'(x_n)]) \qquad \text{for all } \sigma, \sigma' \in \Sigma.$$

Informally speaking, the values assigned by σ are those of the variables $x_1, \ldots, x_n$

and the values assigned by σ' are those of the corresponding variables $x_1', \ldots, x_n'$. 'Translating' all conditions for the subgoal invariant into Hoare logic leads to the alternative while-rule.

Subgoal induction while-rule

$$\frac{\neg e \supset r_{x_1, \ldots, x_n}^{x_1, \ldots, x_p}, \quad \{e \wedge \neg r\} S \{\neg r\}, \quad (p \wedge r) \supset q_{x_1, \ldots, x_n}^{x_1', \ldots, x_n'}}{\{p\} \ while \ e \ do \ S \ od \ \{q\}}$$

where $x_1, \ldots, x_n, x_1', \ldots, x_n'$ are defined as above. Note in particular that the second premise of this rule is an 'indirect' version of condition (ii) of Theorem 9.11, a 'direct' version of this condition being not translatable into a Hoare formula. Soundness and completeness questions for this rule are treated in Exercises 9.2–2 and 9.2–3.

The two following examples illustrate the use of the subgoal induction rule.

EXAMPLE 9.14 (Subgoal Induction Rule)   Let S be as in Example 9.12. It is again proved that S is partially correct with respect to the formulas $x = a$ and $y = a!$ To this end it is sufficient to prove the validity of the Hoare formula

$$\{x = a \wedge y = 1\} \ while \ x > 0 \ do \ y := y * x; \ x := x - 1 \ od \ \{y = a!\}.$$

Note that the variables occurring in this while-program are x and y. Let x' and y' be the corresponding new variables. The invariant φ of Example 9.12 is then expressed by the formula

$$y' = x! * y.$$

Taking this formula for the formula r of the subgoal induction while-rule, one obtains for the three premises of this rule:

(a) $\neg x > 0 \supset y = x! * y$

(b) $\{x > 0 \wedge \neg y' = x! * y\} \ y := y * x; \ x := x - 1 \ \{\neg y' = x! * y\}$

(c) $(x = a \wedge y = 1 \wedge y' = x! * y) \supset y' = a!$

The validity of these formulas is evident.   □

EXAMPLE 9.15 (Subgoal Induction While-rule)   Consider the while-program S:

$$while \ x \neq y \ do$$
$$if \ x > y \ then \ while \ x \geq y \ do \ x := x - y \ od$$
$$else \ while \ y \geq x \ do \ y := y - x \ od \ fi$$
$$od.$$

In order to prove

$$\{x = a \wedge y = b\} S \{x = \gcd(a, b)\}$$

one can choose the formula

$$x' = \gcd(x, y)$$

for the subgoal invariant. Then it remains to be proved:

(a) $x = y \supset x = \gcd(x, y)$
(b) $\{x \ne y \land \neg x' = \gcd(x, y)\}$ if $\ldots fi$ $\{\neg x' = \gcd(x, y)\}$
(c) $(x = a \land y = b \land x' = \gcd(x, y)) \supset x' = \gcd(a, b)$

While the validity of (a) and (c) is evident, (b) must be split into two Hoare formulas with the aid of the conditional rule, namely:

$\{x > y \land \neg x' = \gcd(x, y)\}$ *while* $x \ge y$ *do* $x := x - y$ *od* $\{\neg x' = \gcd(x, y)\}$
$\{y > x \land \neg x' = \gcd(x, y)\}$ *while* $y \ge x$ *do* $y := y - x$ *od* $\{\neg x' = \gcd(x, y)\}$

The validity of these two Hoare formulas can again be proved with the help of the subgoal induction while-rule. This is illustrated here for the former of these Hoare formulas.

A 'natural' subgoal invariant for

$$\text{while } x \ge y \text{ do } x := x - y \text{ od}$$

is the formula

$$x'' = \mathrm{rem}(x, y) \land y'' = y$$

where 'rem' denotes the remainder of integer division and x'', y'' are the new variables. (Note that these new variables also must be different from the variable x' occurring in the Hoare formula.) This invariant leads to the premises:

(a) $x < y \supset (x = \mathrm{rem}(x, y) \land y = y)$
(b) $\{x \ge y \land \neg(x'' = \mathrm{rem}(x, y) \land y'' = y)\}$ $x := x - y$
$$\{\neg(x'' = \mathrm{rem}(x, y) \land y'' = y)\}$$
(c) $(x > y \land \neg x' = \gcd(x, y) \land x'' = \mathrm{rem}(x, y) \land y'' = y) \supset (\neg x' = \gcd(x'', y''))$

the validity of which can be proved easily. $\qquad\Box$

The subgoal induction method can of course also be derived out of the operational semantics for while-programs. What is interesting about this derivation is the following. Let $(S_1, \sigma_1), (S_2, \sigma_2), \ldots, (S_n, \sigma_n)$ be a computation of a while-program in the sense of Section 3.2. Essentially the inductive assertions method is derived by induction over the index i of the configurations (S_i, σ_i). The induction basis corresponds to $i = 1$. The induction step corresponds to a step from i to $i + 1$. The subgoal induction method can also—as a little thinking can convince one—be derived from such an induction. The induction basis now corresponds to $i = n$ and the induction step is from $i + 1$ to i. Hence the inductive assertions method corresponds to 'forward' induction, the subgoal induction method to 'backward' induction.

Experience shows that invariants of the inductive assertions method are often more easy to find than those of the subgoal induction method. The reason is that the invariants of the inductive assertions method can take the initial values 'into account', while the invariants of the subgoal induction method cannot, because of the backward character of the induction. Subgoal induction invariants are therefore more 'general'.

192

From Exercise 9.2–3, it is possible to deduce an invariant of the inductive assertions method from an invariant of the subgoal induction method, and— under certain conditions—vice versa. It should be noted that the invariants thus obtained are not necessarily the most natural ones.

9.3 Structural Induction

When the values of the variables in a program are from a well-founded set, it is possible, in principle, to prove properties about the program with the help of Noetherian induction. This program verification method is known, somewhat confusingly, under the name *structural induction* method. Notice that this Noetherian induction is to be made over the domain D of values which the variables can take on, *not* over the extended domain D_ω.

The structural induction method is simple and powerful, especially in the case of recursive programs (Examples 9.16 to 9.20 and 9.22). The case of while-programs is illustrated in Example 9.21.

In most examples use is made of the fact that the least fixpoint is a fixpoint; an exception is Example 9.22.

EXAMPLE 9.16 (Total Correctness) Let S be the familiar recursive program

$$F(x) \Leftarrow if \ x = 0 \ then \ 1 \ else \ x * F(x - 1) \ fi.$$

To prove that, for all $n \in Nat$, $\mathcal{M}(S)(n) = n!$ it is sufficient to prove that

$$\mathcal{M}^\omega(S)(n) = n! \qquad \text{for all } n \in Nat.$$

The proof is by the structural induction method with the well-founded set of the natural numbers $(Nat, \leq)$.

Induction basis For this well-founded set there is only one minimal element, namely 0. One has

$$\mathcal{M}^\omega(S)(0) = if \ 0 = 0 \ then \ 1 \ else \ x * \mathcal{M}^\omega(S)(0) \ fi \qquad \text{(because } \mathcal{M}^\omega(S) \text{ is a fixpoint)}$$
$$= 0!$$

Induction step Let $n \in Nat$ with $n \neq 0$:

$$\mathcal{M}^\omega(S)(n) = if \ n = 0 \ then \ 1 \ else \ n * \mathcal{M}^\omega(S)(n - 1) \ fi$$
$$= n * \mathcal{M}^\omega(S)(n - 1)$$
$$= n * ((n - 1)!) \qquad \text{(by induction hypothesis)}$$
$$= n! \qquad \qquad \Box$$

EXAMPLE 9.17 (Total Correctness) Let S be the recursive program of Example 9.2:

$$F_1(x) \Leftarrow F_2(0, 1, 0, x)$$
$$F_2(y_1, y_2, y_3, x) \Leftarrow if \ y_2 + y_3 \leq x \ then \ F_2(y_1 + 1, y_2 + 2, y_2 + y_3, x) \ else \ y_1 \ fi,$$

where F_1 is the main function symbol. To prove that, for all $m \in Nat$, $\mathcal{M}^\omega(S)(m) = \sqrt{m}$ one first proves that the recursive program formed by the second recursive equation, call this program S', satisfies the following property:

for all $n_1, n_2, n_3, m \in Nat$,

$$\text{if } n_1^2 \leq m \wedge n_2 = 2n_1 + 1 \wedge n_3 = n_1^2 \tag{1}$$

$$\text{then } (\mathcal{M}^\omega(S')(n_1, n_2, n_3, m))^2 \leq m < (\mathcal{M}^\omega(S')(n_1, n_2, n_3, m) + 1)^2 \tag{2}$$

$$(\text{and } \mathcal{M}^\omega(S')(n_1, n_2, n_3, m) \neq \omega)$$

The proof is by the structural induction method with the well-founded set $(Nat^4, \sqsubseteq)$, where the irreflexive partial order '$\sqsubseteq$' is defined by

$$(n_1, n_2, n_3, m) \sqsubseteq (n_1', n_2', n_3', m') \qquad \text{iff } (m + 1 - n_2 - n_3) < (m' + 1 - n_2' - n_3').$$

That $(Nat^4, \sqsubseteq)$ is a well-founded set follows from the fact that it has no infinite descending sequences (Theorem 1.11).

Induction basis Let $(n_1, n_2, n_3, m) \in Nat^4$ be an arbitrary minimal element. So

$$m + 1 - n_2 - n_3 = 0$$

or, equivalently

$$m + 1 \leq n_2 + n_3$$

or, equivalently

$$m < n_2 + n_3 \tag{3}$$

Assume that (n_1, n_2, n_3, m) satisfies (1) (otherwise there is nothing to prove). But

$$\mathcal{M}^\omega(S')(n_1, n_2, n_3, m) = \text{if } n_2 + n_3 \leq m \text{ then} \ldots \text{else } n_1 \ fi$$
$$\text{(because } \mathcal{M}^\omega(S') \text{ is a fixpoint)}$$
$$= n_1 \qquad \text{(by (3))}$$

But $n_1^2 \leq m$ holds by (1). Moreover, $m < (n_1 + 1)^2$ holds, because of (3) and because $n_2 + n_3 = (n_1 + 1)^2$ by (1). Hence (2) holds.

Induction step Let $(n_1, n_2, n_3, m) \in Nat^4$ be an element that is not a minimal element, hence

$$m + 1 - n_2 - n_3 > 0$$

or

$$m \geq n_2 + n_3 \tag{4}$$

Again (1) is assumed. Now

$$\mathcal{M}^\omega(S')(n_1, n_2, n_3, m) = \text{if } n_2 + n_3 \leq m \text{ then } \mathcal{M}^\omega(S')(n_1 + 1, n_2 + 2, n_2 + n_3, m)$$
$$\text{else} \ldots fi$$
$$= \mathcal{M}^\omega(S')(n_1 + 1, n_2 + 2, n_2 + n_3, m) \qquad \text{(by (4))} \tag{5}$$

But

$$(n_1 + 1, n_2 + 2, n_2 + n_3, m) \sqsubseteq (n_1, n_2, n_3, m)$$

194

because

$$m + 1 - 2n_2 - n_3 - 2 < m + 1 - n_2 - n_3$$

(this holds in particular because of (4)). Hence the induction assumption is valid and so

if $(n_1 + 1)^2 \leq m \land n_2 = 2n_1 + 1 \land n_2 + n_3 = (n_1 + 1)^2$,   (6)
then (2) holds.

(6) holds because of (4) and because (1) was assumed. This ends the proof of the property (2).

But, for all $m \in Nat$,

$$\mathcal{M}^\omega(S)(m) = \mathcal{M}^\omega(S')(0, 1, 0, m)$$

since the pair $(\mathcal{M}^\omega(S), \mathcal{M}^\omega(S'))$ is a fixpoint of $\Phi(S)$. The property of S which was to be proved follows immediately.   □

EXAMPLE 9.18 (Total Correctness)   Let S be the recursive program

$$F(x,y) \Leftarrow \textit{if } x = y \textit{ then } 1 \textit{ else } (y + 2) * (y + 1) * F(x, y + 2) \textit{ fi}$$

from Examples 9.6 and 9.9. It is now proved by the structural induction method that for all $m, n \in Nat$ with $m \geq n$ and $(m - n)$ even,

$$\mathcal{M}^\omega(S)(m, n) = m!/n!.$$

One considers the well-founded set defined by the set

$$W = \{(m, n) \in Nat^2 \mid m \geq n \text{ and } (m - n) \text{ even}\}$$

and the partial order '$\sqsubseteq$' defined by

$$(m, n) \sqsubseteq (m', n') \qquad \text{iff } m = m' \text{ and } n \geq n'.$$

Induction basis   An element (m, n) from W is a minimal element exactly when $m = n$. But then

$$\mathcal{M}^\omega(S)(m, n) = 1, \text{ so } \mathcal{M}^\omega(S)(m, n) = m!/n!.$$

Induction step   If $(m, n) \in W$ is not a minimal element, then $m \geq n + 2$. But then

$$\mathcal{M}^\omega(S)(m, n) = (n + 2) * (n + 1) * \mathcal{M}^\omega(S)(m, n + 2).$$

Since $(m, n + 2)$ is an element of W and since $(m, n + 2) \sqsubseteq (m, n)$, the induction hypothesis can be applied, yielding

$$\mathcal{M}^\omega(S)(m, n) = (n + 2) * (n + 1) * m!/(n + 2)!.$$

Hence, $\mathcal{M}^\omega(S)(m, n) = m!/n!.$ □

EXAMPLE 9.19 (A Proof Method for Termination)   Let S be the recursive program

$$F(\bar{x}) \Leftarrow if \ e(\bar{x}) \ then \ g(\bar{x}) \ else \ h(\bar{x}, F(l(\bar{x}))) \ fi,$$

where $\bar{x}$ is a vector of variables $x_1, \ldots, x_n$, $n \geq 1$, e is interpreted as a predicate from $(D^n \to Bool)$, g, l as functions from $(D^n \to D)$ and h as a function from $(D^{n+1} \to D)$. (As in Example 9.4, S is a program scheme rather than a program.) Let φ be some n-place predicate and define the set W by

$$W = \{d \in D^n \mid \varphi(d) = \text{true}\}$$

Then $\mathcal{M}(S)(d)$ is defined for any $d \in D^n$ with $\varphi(d) = \text{true}$ if there is a partial order '$\sqsubseteq$' on W such that

(1) $(W, \sqsubseteq)$ is a well-founded set;
(2) For each $d \in W$, d is a minimal element of W iff $e(d) = \text{true}$;
(3) For each $d \in W$, if $e(d) = \text{false}$ then $l(d) \in W$ and $l(d) \sqsubset d$.

The proof is by the structural induction method.

Induction basis If $d \in W$ is a minimal element of W, then $\mathcal{M}^\omega(S)(d) = g(d) \neq \omega$, so $\mathcal{M}(S)(d)$ is defined.

Induction step Suppose $d \in W$ is not a minimal element of W. Then $\mathcal{M}^\omega(S)(d) = h(d, \mathcal{M}^\omega(S)(l(d)))$. By induction hypothesis $\mathcal{M}^\omega(S)(l(d)) \neq \omega$, so $\mathcal{M}^\omega(S)(d) \neq \omega$. $\qquad\square$

EXAMPLE 9.20 (Termination)   Let S be the recursive program

$$F(x, y) \Leftarrow if \ x = 0 \ then \ y + 1$$
$$else \ if \ y = 0 \ then \ F(x - 1, 1)$$
$$else \ F(x - 1, F(x, y - 1)) \ fi \ fi.$$

This program computes the famous Ackermann function, but here it will just be shown that it terminates for all input values. The greatest difficulty is finding the proper well-founded set. Consider $(Nat^2, \sqsubseteq)$ with the lexicographical ordering (see Example 1.12(3)); that is,

$$(m_1, m_2) \sqsubseteq (n_1, n_2) \qquad \text{iff } m_1 < n_1, \text{ or } m_1 = n_1 \text{ and } m_2 \leq n_2.$$

The proof proceeds along the structural induction method the details of which are entrusted to the reader. $\qquad\square$

Notice that the previous proof could not be carried out by 'ordinary' induction over the natural numbers (called structural induction in Section 1.2): as was remarked in Example 1.12 the (Noetherian) induction used to carry out the proof is more 'powerful'.

The next example uses the structural induction method to prove the total correctness of a while-program.

EXAMPLE 9.21 (Total Correctness of a while-Program)   Let S be the while-program from Example 9.10:

$$y := 1;$$
$$\textit{while } x > 0 \textit{ do } y := y * x; x := x - 1 \textit{ od}.$$

It is proved that S is totally correct with respect to the formulas $x = a$ and $y = a!$
One first proves by the structural induction method that for all states $\sigma \in \Sigma$,

$$\mathcal{M}^\omega(\textit{while } x > 0 \textit{ do } x := y * x; x := x - 1 \textit{ od})(\sigma)(y) = \sigma(x)! * \sigma(y). \quad (1)$$

This is done by choosing the well-founded set $(\Sigma, \sqsubseteq)$ where '$\sqsubseteq$' is defined by

$$\sigma \sqsubseteq \sigma' \qquad \text{iff } \sigma(x) < \sigma'(x) \text{ or } \sigma = \sigma!$$

Induction basis Let σ be any minimal element of Σ. Then $\sigma(x) = 0$, and

$$\mathcal{M}^\omega(\textit{while} \ldots \textit{od})(\sigma)(y) = \sigma(y) \qquad \text{(by the semantics of while-programs)}$$
$$= \sigma(x)! * \sigma(y) \qquad \text{(since } \sigma(x)! = 1).$$

Induction step Suppose σ is not a minimal element of Σ, hence $\sigma(x) > 0$

$$\mathcal{M}^\omega(\textit{while} \ldots \textit{od})(\sigma)(y) = \mathcal{M}^\omega(\textit{while} \ldots \textit{od})(\mathcal{M}^\omega(y := y * x; x := x - 1)(\sigma))(y)$$
$$\text{(by the semantics of while-programs)}$$
$$= \mathcal{M}^\omega(\textit{while} \ldots \textit{od})(\sigma[x/\sigma(x) - 1][y/\sigma(y) * \sigma(x)])(y).$$

Since

$$\sigma[x/\sigma(x) - 1][y/\sigma(y) * \sigma(x)] \sqsubseteq \sigma$$

the induction hypothesis applies yielding

$$\mathcal{M}^\omega(\textit{while} \ldots \textit{od})(\sigma[x/\sigma(x) - 1][y/\sigma(y) * \sigma(x)])(y) = (\sigma(x) - 1)! * \sigma(y) * \sigma(x)$$
$$= \sigma(x)! * \sigma(y).$$

This completes the proof of (1).
As usual one shows that for all $\sigma \in \Sigma$,

$$\mathcal{M}^\omega(S)(\sigma)(y) = \mathcal{M}^\omega(\textit{while} \ldots \textit{od})(\sigma[y/1])(y)$$
$$= \sigma(x)! \qquad \qquad \qquad \square$$

In the previous examples, except for properties of a well-founded set, the only fact used was that the least fixpoint is a fixpoint. So all properties proved in this section hold for any fixpoint, not just the least fixpoint. Hence it is not possible to prove in this way any property which is specific to the least fixpoint (see also Exercise 9.3–3). For example, it is not possible to prove in this way that the recursive program

$$F(x) \Leftarrow F(x)$$

does not terminate for any input value. Nevertheless, the structural induction method may also be useful in a proof of a property which is specific to the least fixpoint, provided an extra fact (characterizing the least fixpoint) may be called upon. This is illustrated in the next example.

EXAMPLE 9.22 (Proof of Non-Termination) Let S be the program from Examples 9.6, 9.9, and 9.18. It will be proved that for all $m, n \in Nat$, $\mathcal{M}^{\omega}(S)(m, n) = \omega$, whenever $m \geq n$ and $(m - n)$ is odd. Notice that this property does not hold for every fixpoint of $\Phi(S)$. In particular, it does not hold for the function $[\lambda m, n \cdot m!/n!]$ which, as can easily be checked, is a fixpoint of $\Phi(S)$.

Consider the well-founded set $(W, \sqsubseteq)$, where

$$W = \{(m, n) \in Nat^2 \mid m \geq n \text{ and } (m - n) \text{ odd}\}$$

and '$\sqsubset$' is defined as in Example 9.18.

Induction basis   Let (m, n) be a minimal element of W. Then $m = n + 1$ and

$$\mathcal{M}^{\omega}(S)(m, n) = (m + 1) * m * \mathcal{M}^{\omega}(S)(m, m + 1). \tag{1}$$

Suppose one has already proved that for all $(i, j) \in Nat^2$ with $i < j$, $\mathcal{M}^{\omega}(S)(i, j) = \omega$. This can be done, for instance, quite easily with fixpoint induction, as illustrated in Example 9.6. Then (1) becomes $\mathcal{M}^{\omega}(S)(m, n) = \omega$.

Induction step   Suppose $(m, n) \in W$ is not a minimal element. Then $m \geq n + 3$ and

$$\mathcal{M}^{\omega}(S)(m, n) = (n + 2) * (n + 1) * \mathcal{M}^{\omega}(S)(m, n + 2).$$

Since $(m, n + 2)$ is also an element of W and $(m, n + 2) \sqsubset (m, n)$, the induction hypothesis is applicable, and one obtains

$$\mathcal{M}^{\omega}(S)(m, n) = \omega. \qquad \square$$

EXERCISES

9.1–1 Complete the proof of Example 9.2.
9.1–2 Find out to which programs the method of Example 9.3 is applicable.
9.1–3 Consider the program (scheme) S defined by the recursive equation

$$F(x) \Leftarrow \text{ if } p(x) \text{ then } x \text{ else } F(F(h(x))) \text{ } fi$$

in which p and h stand for a strict predicate and a strict function respectively. Prove that $\mathcal{M}(S) = \mathcal{M}(S) \circ \mathcal{M}(S)$. (*Hint*: Apply fixpoint induction to the predicate φ defined by

$$\varphi(f) = \text{true} \qquad \text{iff } \mathcal{M}(S) \circ f = f.)$$

9.2–1 Prove again the result of Exercise 8.1–1 but now with the aid of the subgoal induction while-rule instead of the (classical) while-rule.
9.2–2 Prove for an arbitrary interpretation $\mathcal{I}$ that the conclusion of the subgoal induction while-rule is valid in $\mathcal{I}$, whenever its premises are. (*Hint*: Prove first that $\mathcal{I}(r)(\sigma[\bar{y}/\sigma'(\bar{x})]) = \text{true}$ for all $\sigma, \sigma' \in \Sigma$ for which $\sigma' = \mathcal{M}_{\mathcal{I}}(\text{while } e \text{ do } S \text{ od})(\sigma)$.)
*9.2–3 Prove that every application of the subgoal induction while-rule can be replaced by an application of the (classical) while-rule and vice versa. (*Hint*: Show that the formula $\forall \bar{y} . (r \supset q_{\bar{x}}^{\bar{y}})$ is an inductive assertions invariant, if r is a subgoal invariant; try to find a similar construction for the other direction.) Together with the result of Exercise 9.2–2 this means that the Hoare calculus obtained by replacing the classical while-rule by the subgoal induction while-rule is sound *and* relatively complete.

198

9.2–4 Is the subgoal induction while-rule a 'derived rule' (in the sense of Chapter 8) or is it a completely new rule?

9.3–1 In Example 9.17 the set Nat^4 was made into a well-founded set by the definition

$$(n_1, n_2, n_3, m) \sqsubseteq (n'_1, n'_2, n'_3, m') \qquad \text{iff } (m + 1 - n_2 - n_3) < (m' + 1 - n'_2 - n'_3)$$

(i) Prove that for any $k \in Nat, k \geq 1, Nat^k$ can be made into a well-founded set with the aid of any function $g: Nat^k \to Nat$ by defining

$$(n_1, \ldots, n_k) \sqsubseteq (n'_1, \ldots, n'_k) \qquad \text{iff } g(n_1, \ldots, n_k) < g(n'_1, \ldots, n'_k)$$

(ii) Use the same notations as in (i). Can the well-founded set also be defined by

$$(n_1, \ldots, n_k) \sqsubseteq (n'_1, \ldots, n'_k) \qquad \text{iff } g(n_1, \ldots, n_k) \leq g(n'_1, \ldots, n'_k)?$$

9.3–2
(i) Complete the proof of termination of the Ackermann function (Example 9.20).
(ii) Replace the term $F(x, y - 1)$ in the program of Example 9.20 by $F(x, y)$ and try to find out for which input values the new program terminates (and for which it does not). Prove your result.

9.3–3 In most of the examples of Section 9.3 use was made of the property that the meaning of a program is a fixpoint. The property that the meaning of a program is the *least* fixpoint was not made use of. Show that proofs of termination or total correctness (according to the structural induction method) may always do without making use of this latter property.

HISTORICAL AND BIBLIOGRAPHICAL REMARKS

Proof methods based on the use of properties of cpo's trace back to a large number of papers among which are de Bakker and Scott (1969), Park (1969), Manna, Ness, and Vuillemin (1973). Subgoal induction was introduced in Morris and Wegbreit (1977). The first paper explicitly devoted to the structural induction method is Burstall (1969).

The use of properties of cpo's for program verification is discussed to some extent in Manna (1974) and Bird (1976). More on subgoal induction may be found in Yeh and Reynolds (1976) and King (1980). An extensive and precise study of structural induction is in Aubin (1979).

10
LCF, A Logic for Computable Functions

LCF consists of a logic for cpo's and continuous functions, and of a corresponding calculus allowing in particular the formal verification of programs. It differs from the Hoare logic and calculus in the following points. First, the Hoare calculus was developed for a particular programming language, namely the while-programming language. LCF was developed for cpo's and is applicable to any programming language whose semantics is denotationally described. Second, it is possible to formulate and prove total correctness in LCF as well as partial correctness. Properties like those in Examples 9.4 and 9.5 are also provable. Third, LCF does not build on the predicate logic, but instead starts from scratch. The reason is that it is necessary to consider the ω-extensions of predicates, that is, those predicates with range $Bool_\omega$ and not the 'usual' predicates with range $Bool$. For a similar reason it was not possible in Section 3.3 to build the (operational) semantics of recursive programs on the predicate logic.

10.1 The Logic

Essentially terms in LCF are defined as λ-terms of a λ-notation with two distinguished function symbols interpreted as the if-then-else function and the least fixpoint operator respectively.

10.1.1 Syntax

A *basis* for LCF is a basis for the λ-notation (Section 5.1) which satisfies the following five conditions:

(1) There is a distinguished basis type *bool*.
(2) There are two function symbols TT and FF of type *bool*. (TT and FF stand for 'true' and 'false'.)
(3) There is a function symbol UU_τ (or UU for short) of type τ, for every type τ. (UU_τ stands for the 'undefined value' of type τ.)

199

(4) There is a function symbol *if-then-else*$_\tau$ (or *if-then-else* for short) of type $(bool, \tau, \tau \rightarrow \tau)$, for every type τ.

(5) There is a function symbol MM$_\tau$ (or MM for short) of type $((\tau \rightarrow \tau) \rightarrow \tau)$, for every type τ. (MM$_\tau$ stands for the least fixpoint operator of Theorem 4.32.)

An *LCF-term* (and its *type*) for a given basis is a λ-term (and its type) for this basis.

Formulas are constructed using the (logical) symbol '$\sqsubseteq$' which is intended to be interpreted as the partial order 'is less or equally defined than'. An *atomic LCF-formula* has the form

$$t_1 \sqsubseteq t_2$$

where t_1 and t_2 are LCF-terms of the same type. An *LCF-formula* has the form $P_1, \ldots, P_n$, where the $P_i, i = 1, \ldots, n$, are all atomic LCF-formulas. The case that $n = 0$ is also allowed, so that the 'empty formula' is also a formula. Finally, an *LCF-sentence* has the form $P \Rightarrow Q$, where P and Q are LCF-formulas and '$\Rightarrow$' is one more logic symbol.

10.1.2 Semantics

An *interpretation* $\mathscr{I}$ of a basis for LCF is an interpretation according to Definition 5.2 which satisfies the following five conditions:

(1) The set D_{bool} is taken to be the set $Bool_\omega$ ($= \{\text{true}, \text{false}, \omega\}$).

(2) $\mathscr{I}_0(\text{TT}) = \text{true}$ and $\mathscr{I}_0(\text{FF}) = \text{false}$.

(3) For every type τ, $\mathscr{I}_0(\text{UU}_\tau) = \bot_\tau$ ($=$ the least element of D_τ). So in particular, $\mathscr{I}_0(\text{UU}_{bool}) = \omega$.

(4) For every type τ, $\mathscr{I}_0(\textit{if-then-else}_\tau)$ is taken to be the usual ω-extension if-then-else: $Bool_\omega \times D_\tau \times D_\tau \rightarrow D_\tau$ defined by

$$\text{if-then-else}(b, d_1, d_2) = \begin{cases} d_1 & \text{if } b = \text{true} \\ d_2 & \text{if } b = \text{false} \\ \bot_\tau & \text{if } b = \omega. \end{cases}$$

(5) For every type τ, $\mathscr{I}_0(\text{MM}_\tau)$ is taken to be the fixpoint operator $\mu: [D_\tau \rightarrow D_\tau] \rightarrow D_\tau$ as described in Theorem 4.32.

Notice that an interpretation fulfilling these requirements has the property that $\mathscr{I}_0(f) \in D_\tau$ for every function symbol f of type τ. In particular, the if-then-else function is continuous for every type τ (this was proved in Section 4.2), so

$$\mathscr{I}_0(\textit{if-then-else}_\tau) \in [Bool_\omega \times D_\tau \times D_\tau \rightarrow D_\tau] = D_{(bool, \tau, \tau \rightarrow \tau)}.$$

As for every function $f \in [D_\tau \rightarrow D_\tau]$, $\mu(f) \in D_\tau$ (by definition of μ) and as moreover the fixpoint operator μ is continuous (see Theorem 4.32),

$$\mathscr{I}_0(\text{MM}_\tau) \in [[D_\tau \rightarrow D_\tau] \rightarrow D_\tau] = D_{((\tau \rightarrow \tau) \rightarrow \tau)}.$$

Armed now with an interpretation, the semantics of LCF-terms, LCF-formulas, and LCF-sentences can be given. As usual $\mathscr{I}$ will also denote the semantic functional.

The semantics of LCF-terms is defined as in Definition 5.3. Hence $\mathscr{I}$ maps an LCF-term t to a function $\mathscr{I}(t)\colon \Gamma \to D_\tau$, where Γ is the set of all assignments (for the basis and the interpretation under consideration).

The semantics of an atomic LCF-formula $t_1 \sqsubseteq t_2$ are defined—as usual—by an extension of the semantic functional $\mathscr{I}$:

$$\mathscr{I}(t_1 \sqsubseteq t_2)(\gamma) = \begin{cases} \text{true} & \text{if } \mathscr{I}(t_1)(\gamma) \sqsubseteq \mathscr{I}(t_2)(\gamma) \\ \text{false} & \text{otherwise,} \end{cases}$$

for all assignments $\gamma \in \Gamma$. The symbol '$\sqsubseteq$' on the right-hand side of this equation stands for the partial order of the appropriate cpo.

Similarly for an LCF-formula consisting of the atomic LCF-formulas $P_1, P_2, \ldots, P_n$:

$$\mathscr{I}(P_1, P_2, \ldots, P_n)(\gamma) = \begin{cases} \text{true} & \text{if } \mathscr{I}(P_i)(\gamma) = \text{true, for every } i, i = 1, \ldots, n; \\ \text{false} & \text{otherwise,} \end{cases}$$

for all assignments $\gamma \in \Gamma$. In particular for $n = 0$, $\mathscr{I}(\ )(\gamma) = \text{true}$.

Finally, for an LCF-sentence $P \Rightarrow Q$ one defines

$$\mathscr{I}(P \Rightarrow Q)(\gamma) = \begin{cases} \text{true} & \text{if } \mathscr{I}(P)(\gamma) = \text{true implies } \mathscr{I}(Q)(\gamma) = \text{true} \\ \text{false} & \text{otherwise,} \end{cases}$$

for all assignments $\gamma \in \Gamma$.

If $\mathscr{I}(P \Rightarrow Q)(\gamma) = \text{true}$ for every interpretation $\mathscr{I}$ and every assignment γ, then $P \Rightarrow Q$ is said to be a *logically valid* LCF-sentence; if P is empty, then Q is said to be a *logically valid* LCF-formula.

Notice that for an LCF-term t of type τ (and an assignment γ) $\mathscr{I}(t)(\gamma) \in D_\tau$, so in the case that $\tau = bool$, $\mathscr{I}(t)(\gamma) \in \{\text{true, false, } \omega\}$. On the other hand, for an LCF-formula P, $\mathscr{I}(P)(\gamma) \in \{\text{true, false}\}$. So on the level of LCF-terms (of type $bool$) one works with a three-valued logic (namely true, false, and ω), while on the level of LCF-formulas one works with the usual two-valued logic. This reflects the fact that LCF-terms represent objects under discussion, in particular non-terminating programs, while LCF-formulas represent statements about these objects.

Now follow some examples of logically valid LCF-formulas and LCF-sentences.

EXAMPLE 10.1   Let s, t, and u be LCF-terms of type τ, and x a variable of type σ. The formulas

$$s \sqsubseteq s \quad \text{and} \quad UU_\tau \sqsubseteq s$$

are logically valid due to the obvious properties of the partial order '$\sqsubseteq$'. The following are logically valid LCF-sentences:

$$s \sqsubseteq t, t \sqsubseteq u \Rightarrow s \sqsubseteq u$$
$$[\lambda x . s] \sqsubseteq UU_{(\sigma \to \tau)} \Rightarrow s \sqsubseteq UU_{\tau}$$
$$TT \sqsubseteq UU_{bool} \Rightarrow s \sqsubseteq UU_{\tau}.$$

Notice that this last LCF-sentence trivially holds, since $\mathscr{I}(TT \sqsubseteq UU_{bool})(\gamma) =$ false for every interpretation $\mathscr{I}$ and every assignment γ. $\square$

In comparison with predicate logic, LCF contains '$\sqsubseteq$' and '$\Rightarrow$' as the only logical symbols. Hence, in LCF the atomic formulas cannot be joined by any connectives such as '$\neg$' or '$\vee$', even if these are available as function symbols in the basis. One may very well want to write

$$\Rightarrow \neg(TT \sqsubseteq UU_{bool})$$

but this is not a legal LCF-sentence, because the function symbol '$\neg$' may be 'applied' on LCF-terms only, not on atomic formulas. A further difference with predicate logic is the lack of quantifiers. Additionally, LCF can make statements about continuous (that is, 'computable') functions only. On the other hand LCF is provided with function variables—something that first-order predicate logic is not. All these differences make it difficult to compare the expressive power of predicate logic and LCF.

In the treatment of the semantics of LCF the fact that the fixpoint operator is continuous was used for the first time in this book. The reason this is necessary is because LCF allows more 'complicated' expressions than those used above in the denotational semantics of Chapter 5. LCF allows in particular terms with 'nested' fixpoint operators. An example of such a term is

$$\dots [\lambda F. \dots . MM([\lambda G. \dots . F \dots]) \dots] \dots$$

10.1.3 Syntactic Simplifications

In order to simplify the calculus to be described four simplifications are introduced.

Instead of

$$\textit{if-then-else}_{\tau}(e, t_1, t_2)$$

where e, t_1, t_2 are LCF-terms of type $bool$, τ, and τ respectively, one writes simply

$$(e \to t_1, t_2)$$

The second simplification is a more fundamental one. It consists in requiring $n = 1$ for each type

$$(\tau_1, \dots, \tau_n \to \tau);$$

informally, this means that one considers only functions with one argument. Syntactically, this simplification has as a consequence that application leads to LCF-terms

$$u(t)$$

rather than

$$u(t_1, \ldots, t_n)$$

and λ-abstraction to

$$[\lambda x . t]$$

rather than

$$[\lambda x_1, \ldots, x_n . t]$$

(see Definition 5.1). Semantically this simplification does not constitute a restriction since by currying it is possible to replace any n-place continuous function by a 1-ary continuous function (see Section 4.2 and, in particular, Theorem 4.23).

The next two simplifications are again purely notational ones. An LCF-term

$$MM_\tau([\lambda x . t])$$

with x a variable of type τ and t an LCF-term of type τ is written as

$$[\alpha x . t]$$

Note that this notational convention allows one to eliminate any occurrence of the function symbol MM_τ as any LCF-term u of type $(\tau \rightarrow \tau)$ may be written as

$$[\lambda x . u(x)]$$

where x is a variable of type τ not occurring free in u; in other words, $MM_\tau(u)$ may be written as

$$[\alpha x . u(x)].$$

Finally,

$$t_1 \equiv t_2$$

is allowed as an abbreviation for the LCF-formula

$$t_1 \sqsubseteq t_2, \, t_2 \sqsubseteq t_1$$

where t_1, t_2 are LCF-terms of the same type. Note that, semantically, '$\equiv$' expresses the equality in D_τ, τ being the type of t_1 and t_2.

Notice the difference between '$\equiv$' and the function symbol '$=$' with type $(\tau, \tau \rightarrow bool)$ or, more precisely, $(\tau \rightarrow (\tau \rightarrow bool))$. The interpretation of the LCF-term $t_1 = t_2$ leads to a value from $\{true, false, \omega\}$. On the other hand, $t_1 \equiv t_2$ is an LCF-formula and hence when interpreted leads to a value from $\{true, false\}$. By the way, when considered as a function, '$\equiv$' is not only not continuous, it is not monotonic, since '$\bot \equiv \bot$' has the value true, and '$\bot \equiv true$' has the value false (see also the remark preceding Example 10.1).

10.2 The Calculus

The LCF-calculus is a calculus over (the set of all) LCF- sentences. Its goal is to derive the logically valid LCF-sentences and, in particular, the logically valid LCF-formulas. Notice the interest here is only in deriving sentences from the empty set although the abstract notion of a calculus permits the derivation of LCF-sentences from an arbitrarily given set of LCF-sentences (see Section 2.3).

Before the calculus can be presented, the definition of substitution in λ-terms (hence also in LCF-terms) given in Section 5.1 (see Theorem 5.9) must first be generalized to LCF-formulas. The first step is to define the substitution for atomic LCF-formulas. Let x be a variable and t an LCF-term of the same type. Then t substituted for x in the atomic formula $t_1 \sqsubseteq t_2$ is written $(t_1 \sqsubseteq t_2)_x^t$ and is defined to stand for $(t_1)_x^t \sqsubseteq (t_2)_x^t$. Since t_1 and t_2 are LCF-terms, the substitution of t for x is already understood. For an LCF-formula which consists of the atomic formulas $P_1, \ldots, P_n$, $(P_1, \ldots, P_n)_x^t$ stands for the LCF-formula $(P_1)_x^t, \ldots, (P_n)_x^t$.

Furthermore the following convention will be used. If P and Q are LCF-formulas which consist of the atomic LCF-formulas $P_1, \ldots, P_n$ and $Q_1, \ldots, Q_m$ respectively, then P, Q stands for the LCF-formula

$$P_1, \ldots, P_n, Q_1, \ldots, Q_m.$$

This convention holds also for $n = 0$ or $m = 0$.

The eleven axiom schemes and seven inference rules of the LCF-calculus now follow. The axioms and rules are labelled with an identifier like INCL or FIXP. They are grouped in seven parts corresponding to their 'meaning'. In the axioms and rules P, Q, R and S stand for LCF-formulas, s, t and u stand for terms, f stands for a 1-ary function symbol, x stands for a variable and τ and σ are types. All LCF-terms and LCF-formulas are assumed to be correctly typed.

(i) '$\Rightarrow$'-Definition

$$P, Q \Rightarrow P \qquad \qquad \text{INCL1}$$

$$P, Q \Rightarrow Q \qquad \qquad \text{INCL2}$$

$$\frac{P \Rightarrow Q \quad Q \Rightarrow R}{P \Rightarrow R} \qquad \qquad \text{CUT}$$

$$\frac{P \Rightarrow Q \quad P \Rightarrow R}{P \Rightarrow Q, R} \qquad \qquad \text{CONJ}$$

(ii) '$\sqsubseteq$'-Definition

$$\frac{P \Rightarrow s \sqsubseteq t}{P \Rightarrow u(s) \sqsubseteq u(t)} \qquad \qquad \text{APPL}$$

$$\Rightarrow s \sqsubseteq s \qquad \qquad \text{REFL}$$

$$\frac{P \Rightarrow s \sqsubseteq t \quad P \Rightarrow t \sqsubseteq u}{P \Rightarrow s \sqsubseteq u} \qquad \qquad \text{TRANS}$$

(iii) 'UU'-Definition

$$\Rightarrow UU_\tau \sqsubseteq s \qquad \qquad \text{MIN1}$$

$$\Rightarrow UU_{(\tau \to \sigma)}(s) \sqsubseteq UU_\sigma \qquad \qquad \text{MIN2}$$

(iv)   'if-then-else'-Definition

$\Rightarrow (TT \rightarrow s, t) \equiv s$ CONDT

$\Rightarrow (FF \rightarrow s, t) \equiv t$ CONDF

$\Rightarrow (UU_{bool} \rightarrow s, t) \equiv UU_{\tau}$ CONDU

(v)   'λ'-Definition

$$\frac{P \Rightarrow s \sqsubseteq t}{P \Rightarrow [\lambda x . s] \sqsubseteq [\lambda x . t]} \quad (x \text{ not free in P}) \qquad \text{ABSTR}$$

$\Rightarrow [\lambda x . s](t) \equiv s_x^t$ CONV

$\Rightarrow [\lambda x . f(x)] \equiv f$ FUNC

(vi)   Case Distinction

$$\frac{P, s \equiv TT \Rightarrow Q \quad P, s \equiv FF \Rightarrow Q \quad P, s \equiv UU_{bool} \Rightarrow Q}{P \Rightarrow Q} \qquad \text{CASES}$$

(vii)   'α'-Definition

$\Rightarrow [\alpha x . s] \equiv s_x^{[\alpha x . s]}$ FIXP

$$\frac{P \Rightarrow Q_x^{UU} \quad P, Q \Rightarrow Q_x^t}{P \Rightarrow Q_x^{[\alpha x . t]}} \quad (x \text{ not free in P}) \qquad \text{INDUCT}$$

These axioms and rules capture formally what one would expect to be true. INCL1, INCL2, CUT, and CONJ express the semantics of LCF-sentences and LCF-formulas. In particular they imply that the order of occurrence of the atomic LCF-formulas in an LCF-formula is immaterial. APPL captures the monotonicity of an LCF-term u. REFL and TRANS express the reflexivity and transitivity of the partial order '$\sqsubseteq$'. MIN1 and MIN2 characterize the least element of each type. CONDT, CONDF, CONDU axiomatically define the function if-then-else. ABSTR is the familiar way of extending (by 'λ-abstraction') a cpo of a domain to a cpo of functions to that domain. CONV and FUNC make sure that functions obtained by λ-abstraction behave correctly. CASES corresponds to the proof method based on case distinction. FIXP expresses that the least fixpoint $[\alpha x . s]$ of the function $[\lambda x . s]$ is a fixpoint of this function, that is,

$$[\alpha x . s] \equiv [\lambda x . s]([\alpha x . s]).$$

INDUCT is the fixpoint induction principle; the proof of Theorem 10.7 sheds some light on this rule.

Before the soundness of the calculus is proved some simple deductions in the LCF-calculus are given. It appears that, as in the predicate calculus, the formal deduction of 'obviously' correct theorems is not necessarily trivial. In these example deductions P, Q and R stand for LCF-formulas, s, t and u stand for LCF-terms, and x and y for variables. All LCF-terms and LCF-formulas are assumed to be correctly typed. The first three examples establish derived rules (in the sense of Section 8.1).

EXAMPLE 10.2   It is to prove that the LCF-sentence $P \Rightarrow R$ is derivable from the LCF-sentence $P \Rightarrow Q, R, S$ or, more formally, that

$$\frac{P \Rightarrow Q, R, S}{P \Rightarrow R} \quad \text{is a derived rule.}$$

Here is the deduction proving this statement:

$P \Rightarrow Q, R, S$	assumption	(1)
$Q, R, S \Rightarrow Q, R$	INCL1	(2)
$P \Rightarrow Q, R$	CUT on (1), (2)	(3)
$Q, R \Rightarrow R$	INCL2	(4)
$P \Rightarrow R$	CUT on (3), (4)	□

EXAMPLE 10.3   That

$$\frac{R \Rightarrow P}{Q, R, S \Rightarrow P}$$

is a derived rule is proved by the following deduction:

$R \Rightarrow P$	assumption	(1)
$R, S \Rightarrow R$	INCL1	(2)
$R, S \Rightarrow P$	CUT on (2), (1)	(3)
$Q, R, S \Rightarrow R, S$	INCL2	(4)
$Q, R, S \Rightarrow P$	CUT on (4), (3)	□

EXAMPLE 10.4

$$\frac{P \Rightarrow s \sqsubseteq t \quad Q \Rightarrow t \sqsubseteq u}{P, Q \Rightarrow s \sqsubseteq u} \quad \text{is a derived rule:}$$

$P \Rightarrow s \sqsubseteq t$	assumption	(1)
$Q \Rightarrow t \sqsubseteq u$	assumption	(2)
$P, Q \Rightarrow s \sqsubseteq t$	Example 10.3 on (1)	(3)
$P, Q \Rightarrow t \sqsubseteq u$	Example 10.3 on (2)	(4)
$P, Q \Rightarrow s \sqsubseteq u$	TRANS on (3), (4)	□

The previous three examples established a derived rule; the next two each establish a 'theorem' or, equivalently, a 'derived axiom'.

EXAMPLE 10.5   If the variable x does not occur free in the LCF-terms s and t, the LCF-sentence

$$s(t) \sqsubseteq t \Rightarrow [\alpha x . s(x)] \sqsubseteq t$$

is derivable (from the empty set). This theorem expresses Park's Theorem (Corollary 4.31).

Here is the deduction:

$\Rightarrow UU \sqsubseteq t$	MIN1	(1)
$s(t) \sqsubseteq t \Rightarrow UU \sqsubseteq t$	Example 10.3 on (1)	(2)
$x \sqsubseteq t \Rightarrow x \sqsubseteq t$	INCL1	(3)
$x \sqsubseteq t \Rightarrow s(x) \sqsubseteq s(t)$	APPL on (3)	(4)
$s(t) \sqsubseteq t, x \sqsubseteq t \Rightarrow s(x) \sqsubseteq s(t)$	Example 10.3 on (4)	(5)
$s(t) \sqsubseteq t, x \sqsubseteq t \Rightarrow s(t) \sqsubseteq t$	INCL1	(6)
$s(t) \sqsubseteq t, x \sqsubseteq t \Rightarrow s(x) \sqsubseteq t$	TRANS on (5), (6)	(7)
$s(t) \sqsubseteq t \Rightarrow [\alpha x . s(x)] \sqsubseteq t$	INDUCT on (2), (7)	
	(remember that x does not occur free in s and t)	□

EXAMPLE 10.6 If the variable y does not occur free in the LCF-term s, then the LCF-sentence

$$\Rightarrow [\alpha x . s] \sqsubseteq [\alpha y . s_x^y]$$

is derivable. One can also derive the LCF-sentence with '$\equiv$' instead of '$\sqsubseteq$' in which case the theorem expresses the obvious semantical property, that the name of the variable bound by α is irrelevant.

$\Rightarrow UU \sqsubseteq [\alpha y . s_x^y]$	MIN1	(1)
$x \sqsubseteq [\alpha y . s_x^y] \Rightarrow x \sqsubseteq [\alpha y . s_x^y]$	INCL1	(2)
$x \sqsubseteq [\alpha y . s_x^y] \Rightarrow [\lambda x . s](x)$		
$\qquad \sqsubseteq [\lambda x . s]([\alpha y . s_x^y])$	APPL on (2)	(3)
$\Rightarrow [\lambda x . s](x) \equiv s_x^x$	CONV	
$\qquad \equiv s$		(4)
$\Rightarrow s \sqsubseteq [\lambda x . s](x)$	Example 10.2 on (4)	(5)
$x \sqsubseteq [\alpha y . s_x^y] \Rightarrow s \sqsubseteq [\lambda x . s]([\alpha y . s_x^y])$	Example 10.4 on (5), (3)	(6)
$\Rightarrow [\lambda x . s]([\alpha y . s_x^y]) \equiv s_x^{[\alpha y . s_x^y]}$	CONV	
$\qquad \equiv (s_x^y)_y^{[\alpha y . s_x^y]}$	since y is not free in s	(7)
$\Rightarrow [\lambda x . s]([\alpha y . s_x^y]) \sqsubseteq (s_x^y)_y^{[\alpha y . s_x^y]}$	Example 10.2 on (7)	(8)
$\Rightarrow [\alpha y . s_x^y] \equiv (s_x^y)_y^{[\alpha y . s_x^y]}$	FIXP	(9)
$\Rightarrow (s_x^y)_y^{[\alpha y . s_x^y]} \sqsubseteq [\alpha y . s_x^y]$	Example 10.2 on (9)	(10)
$\Rightarrow [\lambda x . s]([\alpha y . s_x^y]) \sqsubseteq [\alpha y . s_x^y]$	TRANS on (8), (10)	(11)
$x \sqsubseteq [\alpha y . s_x^y] \Rightarrow s \sqsubseteq [\alpha y . s_x^y]$	Example 10.4 on (6), (11)	(12)
$\Rightarrow [\alpha x . s] \sqsubseteq [\alpha y . s_x^y]$	INDUCT on (1), (12)	□

10.3 Soundness and Completeness Problems

THEOREM 10.7 (Soundness of the LCF-calculus) An LCF-sentence $P \Rightarrow Q$ which is derivable in the calculus from the empty set, is logically valid.

Proof. The proof proceeds by showing that every axiom is a logically valid LCF-sentence, and that for every inference rule if the premises are logically valid, then the conclusion is too.

By way of example the axiom INCL1 and the inference rule INDUCT will be treated. The remaining cases are left to the reader.

(1) To show that the axiom $P, Q \Rightarrow P$ is logically valid, one must show for every interpretation $\mathscr{I}$ and every assignment γ that

$$\mathscr{I}(P, Q)(\gamma) = \text{true} \quad \text{implies} \quad \mathscr{I}(P)(\gamma) = \text{true}.$$

Recalling the notational convention about P, Q it is clear that $\mathscr{I}(P, Q)(\gamma)$ is true iff $\mathscr{I}(P)(\gamma) = \text{true}$ and $\mathscr{I}(Q)(\gamma) = \text{true}$, so the proof is immediate.

(2) Now the proof for INDUCT. By assumption the premises are logically valid. So for all interpretations $\mathscr{I}$ and all assignments γ

$$\mathscr{I}(P)(\gamma) = \text{true} \quad \text{implies} \quad \mathscr{I}(Q_x^{UU})(\gamma) = \text{true} \tag{1}$$

and

$$\mathscr{I}(P)(\gamma) = \text{true and } \mathscr{I}(Q)(\gamma) = \text{true} \quad \text{imply} \quad \mathscr{I}(Q_x^t)(\gamma) = \text{true}. \tag{2}$$

It must be proved that for all interpretations $\mathscr{I}$ and assignments γ

$$\mathscr{I}(P)(\gamma) = \text{true} \quad \text{implies} \quad \mathscr{I}(Q_x^{[\alpha x . t]})(\gamma) = \text{true}.$$

Let $\mathscr{I}$ be an interpretation and γ an assignment such that $\mathscr{I}(P)(\gamma) = \text{true}$. Define the predicate $\Phi: D_\tau \to Bool$ by

$$\Phi(d) = \text{true} \quad \text{iff } \mathscr{I}(Q)(\gamma[x/d]) = \text{true},$$

where τ is the type of the variable x. It is now proved that

$$\Phi(\mu f) = \text{true} \tag{3}$$

where f is defined to be

$$f = \mathscr{I}([\lambda x . t])(\gamma).$$

Notice that Q has the form

$$t_1 \sqsubseteq t_1', \ldots, t_n \sqsubseteq t_n'$$

where t_i and t_i' are LCF-terms, $i = 1, \ldots, n$ and $n \geq 0$. Therefore for all $d \in D_\tau$

$$\Phi(d) = \text{true} \quad \text{iff } \mathscr{I}(t_1)(\gamma[x/d]) \sqsubseteq \mathscr{I}(t_1')(\gamma[x/d]) \text{ and} \ldots$$
$$\text{and } \mathscr{I}(t_n)(\gamma[x/d]) \sqsubseteq \mathscr{I}(t_n')(\gamma[x/d]);$$

so Φ is an admissible predicate and the property (3) may be proved by fixpoint induction.

The first step is to show that $\Phi(\bot) = \text{true}$:

$$\mathscr{I}(Q_x^{UU})(\gamma) = \mathscr{I}(Q)(\gamma[x/\bot]) \quad \text{(by a straightforward generalization to} $$
$$\text{LCF-formulas of the Substitution Theorem 5.9)}$$
$$= \Phi(\bot).$$

By assumption (1), $\Phi(\bot) = \text{true}$.

Now comes the harder part. Let d be an arbitrary element of D_τ. It must be shown that

$$\Phi(d) = \text{true} \quad \text{implies} \quad \Phi(f(d)) = \text{true}.$$

Suppose $\Phi(d) = \text{true}$, then $\mathscr{I}(Q)(\gamma[x/d]) = \text{true}$. And hence,

$$\mathscr{I}(P)(\gamma[x/d]) = \mathscr{I}(P)(\gamma) \qquad \text{(by the Coincidence Theorem 5.7 since } x \text{ is not}$$
$$\text{free in P)}$$
$$= \text{true} \qquad \text{(by choice of } \mathscr{I} \text{ and } \gamma)$$

This means the hypothesis of assumption (2) is true (with $\gamma[x/d]$ for γ), so one may conclude $\mathscr{I}(Q_x^t)(\gamma[x/d]) = \text{true}$. Now

$$\mathscr{I}(Q_x^t)(\gamma[x/d]) = \mathscr{I}(Q)((\gamma[x/d])[x/\mathscr{I}(t)(\gamma[x/d])]) \qquad \text{(by the Substitution Theorem)}$$
$$= \mathscr{I}(Q)(\gamma[x/\mathscr{I}(t)(\gamma[x/d])])$$
$$= \Phi(\mathscr{I}(t)(\gamma[x/d])) \qquad \text{(by the definition of } \Phi)$$
$$= \Phi(\mathscr{I}([\lambda x . t])(\gamma)(d)) \qquad \text{(by the semantics of the } \lambda\text{-notation)}$$
$$= \Phi(f(d)).$$

So $\Phi(f(d)) = \text{true}$, too. This completes the proof of (3). Now

$$\mu f = \mu \mathscr{I}([\lambda x . t])(\gamma) \qquad \text{(by definition of } f)$$
$$= \mathscr{I}(MM([\lambda x . t]))(\gamma) \quad \text{(by definition of } \mathscr{I}_0(MM))$$
$$= \mathscr{I}([\alpha x . t])(\gamma) \qquad \text{(by definition of the notation } \alpha)$$

Hence, by (3)

$$\Phi(\mathscr{I}([\alpha x . t])(\gamma)) = \text{true}$$

which means that

$$\mathscr{I}(Q)(\gamma[x/\mathscr{I}([\alpha x . t])(\gamma)]) = \text{true}$$

and so, by the Substitution Theorem,

$$\mathscr{I}(Q_x^{[\alpha x . t]})(\gamma) = \text{true}. \qquad \square$$

The LCF-calculus is not complete; moreover, there can be no complete calculus for LCF. A proof of this assertion will not be given here, instead a sketch of it is given which is based on the following facts (which will not be proved here either):

(i) The Peano axioms can be formulated as LCF-formulas. (See also Section 10.4.)

(ii) The principle of induction over the natural numbers can be formulated as an LCF-formula. (This fact is directly related to the availability of function variables in LCF; see Newey (1973).)

(iii) The LCF-terms which may be constructed from the function symbols of Peano arithmetic represent exactly the computable functions in the standard model of Peano arithmetic. In other words, starting from the functions (contained in the basis) of Peano arithmetic, the operations of composition, λ-abstraction, and least fixpoint operation lead to exactly the computable functions.

From (i) and (ii) it is possible to deduce that Peano arithmetic or, more precisely, the Peano axioms *and* the principle of induction can be expressed as an LCF-formula, say PA. Now for this LCF-formula there can only be one model— up to isomorphism—namely, the natural numbers model (see Section 2.4). So consider the LCF-sentences of the form

$$PA \Rightarrow t_1 \equiv t_2,$$

where t_1 and t_2 are LCF-terms which are interpreted (in the standard interpretation of Peano arithmetic) as functions over the natural numbers. From computation theory it is known that this set of LCF-sentences cannot be recursively enumerable. Therefore, there can be no complete calculus for LCF.

10.4 Application to Program Verification

To prove something about a program it is necessary to be able to use properties about the underlying data or, more precisely, about the domain of the interpretation. As in Hoare calculus these properties must be introduced as formulas. These formulas may be the formulas of the theory $Th(\mathscr{I})$ where $\mathscr{I}$ is the interpretation under consideration. Alternatively, these formulas may be axioms for this theory, for instance the Peano axioms in the case of programs dealing with natural numbers. Clearly, in the LCF calculus these axioms must first be rewritten as LCF-formulas. In this rewriting process at least two problems arise.

(1) There is no universal quantifier in LCF. This problem can be circumvented by using λ-abstraction. For example, the Peano axiom (A1) in Section 2.4

$$\forall x . x + 0 = x$$

becomes

$$[\lambda x . x + 0] \equiv [\lambda x . x]$$

in LCF.

(2) One must take care of the undefined value in LCF. For example, the Peano axiom (M1)

$$\forall x . x * 0 = 0$$

cannot be written

$$[\lambda x . x * 0] \equiv [\lambda x . 0]$$

if the intended interpretation of '*' is to be the strict ω-extension of multiplication. One solution consists in testing for ω with the help of the (strict ω-extension of the) equality:

$$[\lambda x . ((x = x) \rightarrow x * 0, 0)] \equiv [\lambda x . ((x = x) \rightarrow 0, 0)].$$

This requires the additional axiom

$$UU * 0 \equiv UU$$

for the undefined value. Actually this only shifts the problem, as now the properties of the equality '=' must be axiomatized. This can be done by the following four LCF-formulas:

$$[\lambda x.\,((x = x) \to x, \mathrm{UU})] \equiv [\lambda x.\,x]$$
$$[\lambda x.\,[\lambda y.\,((x = y) \to x, \mathrm{UU})]] \equiv [\lambda x.\,[\lambda y.\,((x = y)$$
$$\to y, \mathrm{UU})]]$$
$$[\lambda x.\,[\lambda y.\,((x = x) \to ((y = y) \to \mathrm{TT}, \mathrm{UU}), \mathrm{UU})]] \equiv [\lambda x.\,[\lambda y.\,((x = y)$$
$$\to \mathrm{TT}, \mathrm{TT})]]$$
$$(\mathrm{UU} = \mathrm{UU}) \equiv \mathrm{UU}.$$

That these four axioms are correct is easy to check, but that they are enough to fully define equality is not trivial. For a complete treatment of the axiomatization of Peano arithmetic in LCF the interested reader is referred to Newey (1973).

The problems involved with the properties of the underlying data will now be ignored, and the 'real' problems of proving properties of programs will be addressed. As should be apparent LCF is readily adapted to proofs about the recursive programs. The next example concerns such a program. Subsequently, the case of the while-programming language will be discussed.

EXAMPLE 10.8   Let S be again the recursive program

$$F(x, y) \Leftarrow if \ x = y \ then \ 1 \ else \ (y + 1) * F(x, y + 1) \ fi.$$

In Example 9.1 it was proved that $\mu\Phi(S) \sqsubseteq [\lambda x, y.\,x!/y!]$. In LCF this is formulated as

$$\mathrm{PA} \Rightarrow [\alpha\mathrm{F}.\,[\lambda x.\,[\lambda y.\,((x = y) \to 1, (y + 1) * F(x)(y + 1))]]]$$
$$\sqsubseteq [\lambda x.\,[\lambda y.\,x!/y!]], \tag{1}$$

where PA is the LCF-formula that expresses all the necessary properties of arithmetic.

A deduction in the LCF-calculus in the style of Example 10.2 through Example 10.6 would be very long, not to mention obscure. So a sketch of the proof is given.

LCF-sentence (1) is derived by INDUCT from

$$\mathrm{PA} \Rightarrow \mathrm{UU} \sqsubseteq [\lambda x.\,[\lambda y.\,x!/y!]] \tag{2}$$

and

$$\mathrm{PA}, f \sqsubseteq [\lambda x.\,[\lambda y.\,x!/y!]] \Rightarrow$$
$$[\lambda x.\,[\lambda y.\,((x = y) \to 1, (y + 1) * f(x)(y + 1))]] \sqsubseteq [\lambda x.\,[\lambda y.\,x!/y!]] \tag{3}$$

LCF-sentence (2) is obtained by MIN1. LCF-sentence (3) is derived by ABSTR from:

$$\mathrm{PA}, f \sqsubseteq [\lambda x.\,[\lambda y.\,x!/y!]] \Rightarrow ((x = y) \to 1, (y + 1) * f(x)(y + 1)) \sqsubseteq (x!/y!) \tag{4}$$

LCF-sentence (4) is derived by CASES from:

$$\mathrm{PA}, f \sqsubseteq [\lambda x.\,[\lambda y.\,x!/y!]], (x = y) \equiv \mathrm{UU} \Rightarrow$$
$$((x = y) \to 1, (y + 1) * f(x)(y + 1)) \sqsubseteq (x!/y!) \tag{5a}$$

$$\mathrm{PA}, f \sqsubseteq [\ldots], (x = y) \equiv \mathrm{TT} \Rightarrow ((x = y) \to 1, \ldots) \sqsubseteq (x!/y!) \tag{5b}$$

$$\mathrm{PA}, f \sqsubseteq [\ldots], (x = y) \equiv \mathrm{FF} \Rightarrow ((x = y) \to 1, \ldots) \sqsubseteq (x!/y!) \tag{5c}$$

LCF-sentence (5a) is derived by (among others) TRANS and MIN1 from:

$$(x = y) \equiv UU \Rightarrow ((x = y) \rightarrow 1, \ldots) \sqsubseteq UU \qquad (6a)$$

LCF-sentences (5b) and (5c) are derived from similar LCF-sentences (6b) and (6c). To the proof of (6a):

$(x = y) \equiv UU \Rightarrow (x = y) \sqsubseteq UU$ by INCL1   (7)

$(x = y) \equiv UU \Rightarrow [\lambda b.(b \rightarrow 1, \ldots)](x = y)$

$\qquad\qquad \sqsubseteq [\lambda b.(b \rightarrow 1, \ldots)](UU)$ by APPL   (8)

$\Rightarrow ((x = y) \rightarrow 1, \ldots) \sqsubseteq [\lambda b.(b \rightarrow 1, \ldots)](x = y)$ by CONV   (9)

$\Rightarrow [\lambda b.(b \rightarrow 1, \ldots)](UU) \sqsubseteq (UU \rightarrow 1, \ldots)$ by CONV   (10)

$\Rightarrow (UU \rightarrow 1, \ldots) \sqsubseteq UU$ by CONDU   (11)

LCF-sentence (6a) is then derived by several applications of TRANS applied to (8) through (11) (among other things).

    The LCF-sentences (6b) and (6c) are derived similarly. In the case of (6c) it is advantageous to use the derived rule of inference

$$\frac{P \Rightarrow f \sqsubseteq g}{P \Rightarrow f(s) \sqsubseteq g(s)}$$

proved in Exercise 10.2–2(i) together with Exercise 10.2–1(i)—when using the 'induction hypothesis' $f \sqsubseteq [\lambda x.[\lambda y.x!/y!]]$. $\square$

    Examples from the while-programming language can in principle be handled the same way. But as is clear from Example 9.21, the function $\mathcal{M}^\omega$ appears in the LCF-sentence to be proved. In order to be able to use the properties of $\mathcal{M}^\omega$ in the proof, they must be available as LCF-formulas. Now the domain of $\mathcal{M}^\omega$ (considered as a function) is L_2^B, the set of while-programs for the given basis B. These programs are introduced as an additional basis type. Furthermore, some basic predicates and functions on L_2^B must also be axiomatized (just like '<' and '+' for the natural numbers in Peano arithmetic). One such predicate distinguishes between an assignment statement and a conditional statement and one such function extracts the quantifier-free formula from a conditional statement (in view of its evaluation). For a complete treatment of the subject the interested reader is referred to Milner (1979).

EXERCISES

10.2–1 Let Q and R be LCF-formulas.

(i) Prove that the LCF-sentence

$$Q \Rightarrow R$$

can be derived in the LCF-calculus (from the empty set), iff

$$\frac{P \Rightarrow Q}{P \Rightarrow R} \quad \text{for all LCF-formulas P}$$

is a derived inference rule.

(ii) Give an example where

$$\frac{Q}{R}$$

is a derived inference rule, but

$$Q \Rightarrow R$$

is not a logically valid LCF-sentence.

10.2–2 Let s, t, u be LCF-terms (of the appropriate types).

(i) Prove that the LCF-sentence

$$s \sqsubseteq t \Rightarrow s(u) \sqsubseteq t(u)$$

is derivable in the LCF-calculus (from the empty set). (*Hint:* The LCF-sentence expresses the 'monotonicity of application to the argument u'. Try to express this 'application operator' as an LCF-term.)

(ii) Prove that the LCF-sentence

$$[\lambda x. s] \sqsubseteq [\lambda x. t] \Rightarrow [\alpha x. s] \sqsubseteq [\alpha x. t]$$

is derivable in the LCF-calculus (from the empty set).

10.3–1 Prove the soundness of the inference rules 'APPL' and 'ABSTR' of the LCF-calculus. Show that 'ABSTR' would not be sound, if x was allowed to occur free in P.

10.4–1 In Section 10.4 four 'axioms' for the strict equality were presented.

(i) Prove that these axioms hold for the strict equality.
(ii) Prove that these axioms are sufficient to characterize the strict equality. (*Hint:* First try to find out what the first two and the fourth formula say about the interpretation of '=' and use this information to 'interpret' the third one.)
(iii) Prove that the four axioms are independent of each other in the sense that none of them follows from the others. (*Hint:* Show that for any three of them there exists an interpretation of '=', which is different from the strict equality.)

*10.4–2 'Axiomatize' the domain Nat_ω with LCF-formulas in the following way:

(i) As indicated in Section 10.4 use the strict equality to write the (first-order) Peano axioms of Chapter 2 as LCF-formulas.
(ii) Write the induction principle for the natural numbers as an LCF-formula by using a variable of type $(nat \rightarrow bool)$. Note that, as in (i), the undefined element must be 'excluded'.
(iii) Add axioms which express that (the interpretations of) all function symbols are strict.

Note that an axiomatization of Nat_ω with LCF-*formulas* (rather than LCF-*sentences*) is presupposed in the incompleteness proof of the calculus in Section 10.3.

10.4–3 Let S be the recursive program

$$F(x, y) \Leftarrow \textit{if } x = y \textit{ then } x$$
$$\textit{else if } x > y \textit{ then } F(x - y, y)$$
$$\textit{else } F(x, y - x) \textit{ fi}$$
$$\textit{fi}$$

Prove—in the style of Example 10.8—that

$$\mu\Phi(S) \sqsubseteq [\lambda x, y. \gcd(x, y)]$$

HISTORICAL AND BIBLIOGRAPHICAL REMARKS

LCF is due to D. Scott and R. Milner; the basic paper on LCF is Milner (1972).

There are a relatively large number of publications on LCF, most of which are referenced in the bibliography of Gordon, Milner, and Wadsworth (1979). For a better and broader insight in LCF the reader may, for instance, consult Milner (1979), Aiello, Aiello, and Weyhrauch (1977), and Newey (1973).

PART D

Prospects

11
An Overview of Further Developments

The aim of this chapter is to present an overview of further developments of the topics treated so far, of other approaches to these topics and of some related ones. Bibliographic hints should allow the interested reader to introduce himself to the subject.

11.1 Including Further Program Constructs

The program constructs examined so far are essentially the assignment, the if-then-else statement, the while-statement (in the language of while-programs), the jump (in the flowchart programming language) and the (possibly recursive) procedure with a parameter mechanism passing values (in the language of recursive programs). Important program constructs such as the block structure, the parameter mechanism passing names and the parallelism as well as data types, such as arrays, records, or pointers have not been considered.

Extending the operational semantics for these program constructs and data types is in principle easy. Unfortunately the description may lose its transparency, as is illustrated by the description of the programming language PL/I in Lucas and Walk (1971).

The description of jumps in denotational semantics is classically solved by introducing *continuations*. A continuation is defined as a function mapping states into states. The meaning of a program construct is then defined as a function mapping continuations into continuations (rather than states into states); the argument of this function represents the meaning (in the usual sense) of the piece of program following the program construct, and its value represents the meaning (in the usual sense) of the program construct together with the piece of program following it. The interested reader may consult Gordon (1979) for an informal introduction and de Bruin (1981) for a formal one. The treatment of blocks and the parameter mechanism passing names leads, among other things, to the problem of *aliasing* and can only be tackled with some additional sophistication. For the denotational semantics of 'real-life' programming languages the reader may consult de Bakker (1980) which treats the subject in some detail; Aiello, Aiello, and Weyhrauch (1977) contains a commented description of denotational semantics for (nearly full) Algol-60. The extension of the techniques of denotational semantics to non-determinism, which seems an indispensable requisite in the study of concurrency, has recently been the subject of a large number of publications. Basic work on *power domains* is described in Plotkin (1976) and Smyth (1978). These works were followed by attempts to give denotational semantics to communicating concurrent systems (Milner, 1980) using for instance combinations of complete partial orders (Broy, 1982) or metric topology (de Bakker and Zucker, 1982).

The extension of semi-formalized proof methods such as the inductive assertions method or the subgoal induction method is possible at the price of some sophistication. An illustrative example is the generalization of the inductive assertions and the well-founded sets methods for arrays in Manna (1974).

The extension of the Hoare calculus has been the subject of a large number of publications (see Apt, 1981 for an excellent overview). Examples of such extensions may be found in de Bakker (1980), Olderog (1981) and Sieber (1984). The study of the verification of parallel programs leads to several additional notions such as *deadlock* or *fairness*. The extension of proof methods to include these features is still at an experimental stage. For an introduction to the subject the reader may consult Owicki and Gries (1976), Flon and Suzuki (1981), Apt and Plotkin (1981), or Berg *et al.* (1982). See also Section 11.3.

As a consequence the extension of the proof methods described in this book to 'real-life' programming languages appears to be possible, but except for small programs the verification rapidly becomes infeasible. A solution may be found in the use of programming methods in which the development of modularized programs and their verification go hand in hand (Sections 11.5 and 11.6), and in the use of verification systems (Section 11.7).

11.2 Other Semantics Descriptions

Apart from operational and denotational semantics several other descriptions have been proposed in the literature. Some of them are discussed in Donahue (1976) and Greif and Meyer (1981).

Attribute grammar semantics are based on the use of attributed context-free grammars (Knuth, 1968). They are useful for the construction of compilers rather than for verification purposes.

Algebraic semantics are similar to denotational semantics but use notions from universal algebra and category theory rather than from predicate logic. In particular one speaks of free algebras instead of syntax and uses homomorphisms instead of interpretations. Classical papers are, for instance, Goguen *et al.* (1977) and Courcelle and Nivat (1978). For a good and detailed introduction the reader should consult Guessarian (1981).

Hoare semantics are merely constituted by the axioms and the deduction rules of the Hoare calculus. In fact, these axioms and deduction rules completely define the semantics of the underlying programming language up to termination; a discussion of this limitation may be found in Halpern and Meyer (1981) and Bergstra, Tiuryn, and Tucker (1982). A description of the programming language PASCAL along these lines is in Hoare and Wirth (1973).

Weakest-precondition semantics (or: *predicate transformer semantics*) is based on the notion of the weakest precondition. It is similar to the Hoare semantics but has the advantage that it can be expressed in predicate logic. More on these semantics may be found in Basu and Yeh (1975), Hoare (1978), or de Bakker (1980).

11.3 Other Logics and Related Programming Languages

In this book three logics have been used: predicate logic, Hoare logic, and LCF. Several other logics have been proposed in the literature. Most of them may be seen as particular cases of modal logic (Hughes and Cresswell, 1968): programs are considered as modal operators operating on logic formulas. A particular example is *dynamic logic* introduced by Pratt (1976). For a good and detailed introduction to dynamic logic the reader may consult Harel (1979); for an overview Harel (1980). Another example is *temporal logic* which has been introduced for reasoning about parallel programs via assertions. The basic paper on temporal logic is Pnueli (1977), a good introduction is Manna and Pnueli (1981), a detailed treatment is in Hailpern (1982). Similar to dynamic logic are the *algorithmic logic* of Salwicki (1970) and the *programming logic* of Constable, Johnson, and Eichenlaub (1982).

An alternative approach to the development of new logics consists in the development of formalisms which allow one to write programs as well as to express properties of these programs. *LUCID* is an example of such a formalism. A program in LUCID is a set of formulas ('axioms') from which other formulas expressing properties of this program may be deduced as theorems. Correctness proofs in LUCID are often very simple but as a programming language LUCID has a relatively poor structure. An introduction to LUCID may be found in Ashcroft and Wadge (1976); the philosophy behind it is explained in Ashcroft and Wadge (1982). Another example of such a formalism is *PROLOG* which may be considered as first-order predicate logic turned into a programming language. As for LUCID a program in PROLOG is a set of formulas. The 'computation' is now performed by the resolution algorithm (Robinson, 1979) and delivers as output values the results of the unifications performed by this algorithm. A PROLOG-program being its own specification, its correctness needs not be proved. As with LUCID, the structure of PROLOG as a programming language is rather poor in spite of some 'efficiency increasing' constructs added to the predicate logic. One of the basic papers on PROLOG is Colmerauer (1975); programming techniques in PROLOG are described in Clocksin and Mellish (1981); theoretical foundations may be found in Kowalski (1979).

11.4 Other Proof Methods

A large number of proof methods have been described in the literature. They generally appear to be slight variants, particular cases, or mild generalizations of the methods described in this book.

The *intermittent assertions method* uses invariants which do not hold 'each time' the cutpoint is reached but only 'sometimes'; more precisely the invariant has to hold 'eventually'. A description of the method which allows proof of total correctness, is in Manna and Waldinger (1978); a criticism is in Gries (1979).

The *multiset ordering method* is a particular case of the well-founded sets method. It is based on an ordering on multisets rather than sets (Dershowitz and Manna, 1979).

Further methods for proving termination and total correctness may be found in Katz and Manna (1975) and Wang (1976). Further verification methods based on denotational semantics may be found in Manna (1974).

11.5 The Development of Correct Programs

The fundamental idea consists in developing (well-structured) programs together with their correctness proofs. Classically such a program is interspersed with predicate logic formulas using, for instance, the Hoare logic notation. The correctness is then proved for each program part enclosed by a pair of formulas using well-known methods such as the inductive assertions method or the Hoare calculus. Books illustrating this method are, for instance, Dijkstra (1976), Alagić and Arbib (1978), and Gries (1981). A somewhat more formal method based on the same idea may be found in Blikle (1981).

A related idea is that of *program transformations* 'translating' programs into 'equivalent' more efficient or 'lower-level' ones (see, for instance, Gerhart (1976)). Basically program transformations allow one to consider the process of program construction as a formal activity applying verified rules from some calculus. Thus an efficient program is to be deduced from some formal specification (see, for example, Bauer and Wössner (1982) or Broy and Pepper (1981)).

Still on a very experimental stage are the works on *program synthesis* which automatically constructs programs with techniques of artificial intelligence (see, for example, Manna and Waldinger (1980)).

11.6 Abstract Data Types

The purpose of *abstract data types* is the same as in Section 11.5 but the modularization of programs is now on the basis of the data (= objects + functions) rather than on the basis of program parts (= procedures) (see, for example, Liskov *et al.* (1977) or Guttag, Horowitz, and Musser (1978)). The topic is relatively new and at the present time (1982) relevant practical experience in the use of abstract data types as a programming method is still lacking (see, for example, Guttag, Horning, and Wing (1982)).

There exist essentially two different approaches. The first leads to an imperative (i.e. $\mathscr{L}_2$-type) programming style (see, for example, Liskov (1981)), the second to a functional (i.e. $\mathscr{L}_3$-type) one (see, for example, Goguen, Thatcher, and Wagner (1978), Broy *et al.* (1979), and Loeckx (1981)). The latter has the advantage that the powerful proof method of structural induction (Section 9.3) is applicable in correctness proofs.

11.7 Mechanical Verification Systems

Several mostly experimental verification systems have been constructed and described in the literature. All are dialog systems: essentially, the user specifies the invariants and the different steps in the proof and the computer merely cares for the formula manipulation and bookkeeping.

The *Boyer–Moore System* is a verification system for programs written in LISP (Boyer and Moore, 1979). The *LCF-System* is, as its name indicates, based on LCF; it is provided with a language allowing the user to build proof strategies out of elementary proof steps (Gordon, Milner, and Wadsworth, 1979). The *Stanford Verifier* is described in Stanford Verification Group (1979) and is essentially based on a Hoare calculus for the programming language PASCAL. The basic ideas of such a system were already in Igarashi, London, and Luckham (1975). The treatment of a non-trivial example with this verification system is described in Polak (1981). The *PL/CV2 Proof Checker* (Constable, Johnson, and Eichenlaub, 1982) is a system in which one can prove the total correctness of PL/C programs. The ability to reason about common programming objects like integers, arrays, and procedures is supplied. Unlike the Stanford Verifier logical inferences which are not immediate are proved directly in the program. The *AFFIRM-System* (Thomson, 1979) and the *IOTA Programming System* (Nakajima and Yuasa, 1983) are verification systems for abstract data types.

Bibliography

Aiello, L., Aiello, M., and Weyhrauch, R.: PASCAL in LCF: semantics and examples of a proof, *Theor. Comp. Sc.*, **5**, pp. 135–177, 1977.

Alagić, S. and Arbib, M. A.: *The Design of Well-Structured and Correct Programs*, Springer-Verlag, 1978.

Anderson, R. B.: *Proving Programs Correct*, John Wiley, 1979.

Apt, K. R.: Ten years of Hoare's logic: a survey, *TOPLAS*, **3**, pp. 431–483, 1981.

Apt, K. R. and Plotkin, G. D.: A Cook's tour of countable nondeterminism, *Proc. 8th ICALP (Acre)*, Lect. Notes in Comp. Sc., **115**, pp. 479–494, 1981.

Ashcroft, E. A. and Wadge, W. W.: LUCID, a formal system for writing and proving programs, *SIAM Journ. on Comp.*, **5**, pp. 336–354, 1976.

Ashcroft, E. A. and Wadge, W. W.: R for semantics, *TOPLAS*, **4**, pp. 283–294, 1982.

Aubin, R.: Mechanizing structural induction (Part I), *Theor. Comp. Sc.*, **9**, pp. 329–345, 1979.

de Bakker, J. W. and Scott, D.: A theory of programs, IBM Seminar, unpublished notes, 1969.

de Bakker, J. W. and Meertens, L. G. L. T.: On the completeness of the inductive assertion method, *J. of Comp. and Syst. Sc.*, **11**, pp. 323–357, 1975.

de Bakker, J. W.: *Mathematical Theory of Program Correctness*, Prentice-Hall, 1980.

de Bakker, J. W. and Zucker, J. I.: Denotational semantics of concurrency, *Proc. 14th ACM Symp. on Theory of Comp.*, pp. 153–158, 1982.

Barendregt, H. P.: *The Lambda Calculus: Its Syntax and Semantics*, North-Holland, 1981.

Basu, S. K. and Yeh, R. T.: Strong verification of programs, *IEEE Trans. on Softw. Eng.*, **1**, pp. 339–345, 1975.

Bauer, F. L. and Wössner, H.: *Algorithmic Language and Program Development*, Springer-Verlag, 1982.

Bell, J. L. and Machover, M.: *A Course in Mathematical Logic*, North-Holland, 1977.

Berg, H. K., Boebert, W. E., Franta, W. R., and Moher, T. G.: *Formal Methods of Program Verification and Specification*, Prentice-Hall, 1982.

Bergmann, E. and Noll, H.: *Mathematische Logik mit Informatik-Anwendungen*, Heidelberger Taschenbücher, Band 187, Springer-Verlag, 1977.

Bergstra, J. A., Tiuryn, J., and Tucker, J. V.: Floyd's principle, correctness theories and program equivalence, *Theor. Comp. Sc.*, **17**, pp. 113–149, 1982.

Bird, R.: *Programs and Machines*, John Wiley, 1976.

Blikle, A. J.: On the development of correct specified programs, *IEEE Trans. on Softw. Eng.*, **7**, pp. 519–527, 1981.

Boyer, R. S. and Moore, J. S.: *A Computational Logic*, Academic Press, 1979.

Brainerd, W. S. and Landweber, L. H.: *Theory of Computation*, John Wiley, 1974.

Broy, M., Dotsch, W., Partsch, H., Pepper, P., and Wirsing, M.: Existential quantifiers in abstract data types, *Proc. 6th ICALP (Graz)*, Lect. Notes in Comp. Sc., **71**, pp. 71–87, Springer-Verlag, 1979.

Broy, M. and Pepper, P.: Programming as a formal activity, *IEEE Trans. on Softw. Eng.*, **7**, pp. 14–22, 1981.

Broy, M.: Fixed point theory for communication and concurrency, *Formal Description of Programming Concepts II* (ed. D. Bjørner), North-Holland, 1982.

de Bruin, A.: Goto statement: semantics and deduction systems, *Acta Inform.*, **15**, pp. 385–424, 1981.

Burstall, R. M.: Proving properties of programs by structural induction, *Comp. J.*, **12**, pp. 41–48, 1969.

Burstall, R. M.: Program proving as hand simulation with a little induction, *Proc. IFIP Congress 74*, North-Holland, pp. 308–312, 1974.

Cadiou, J. M.: Recursive definitions of partial functions and their computations, Ph.D. Thesis, Stanford Univ., 1972.

Clarke, E. M.: Programming language constructs for which it is impossible to obtain good Hoare-like axioms, *Journ. ACM*, **26**, pp. 129–147, 1979.

Clarke, E. M., German, S. M., and Halpern, J. Y.: On effective axiomatizations of Hoare logics, *Proc. 9th POPL Conf.*, pp. 309–321, 1982.

Clocksin, W. F. and Mellish, C. S.: *Programming in PROLOG*, Springer-Verlag, 1981.

Cohn, P. M.: *Universal Algebra*, Harper and Row, 1965.

Colmerauer, A.: *Les grammaires de méthamorphose*, Rapport interne, Groupe d'Intelligence Artificielle, U.E.R. Scientif. de Luminy, 1975.

Constable, R. L. and Johnson, S. D.: A PL/CV precis, *Proc. 6th POPL Conf.*, ACM, New York, 1979.

Constable, R. L., Johnson, S. D., and Eichenlaub, C. D.: *An Introduction to the PL/CV 2 Programming Logic*, Lect. Notes in Comp. Sc., **135**, Springer-Verlag, 1983.

Cook, S. A.: Soundness and completeness of an axiom system for program verification, *SIAM Journ. on Comp.*, **7**, pp. 70–90, 1978.

Courcelle, B. and Nivat, M.: The algebraic semantics of recursive program schemes, *Proc. 7th Symp. on Math. Found. Comp. Sc. (Zakopane)*, Lect. Notes in Comp. Sc., **64**, pp. 16–30, 1978.

Cutland, N.: *Computability: An Introduction to Recursive Function Theory*, Cambridge University Press, Cambridge, 1980.

Dershowitz, N. and Manna, Z.: Proving termination with multiset orderings, *Comm. ACM*, **22**, pp. 465–476, 1979.

Dijkstra, E. W.: *A Discipline of Programming*, Prentice-Hall, 1976.

Donahue, J. E.: *Complementary Definitions of Programming Language Semantics*, Lect. Notes in Comp. Sc., **42**, Springer-Verlag, 1976.

Ebbinghaus, H. D., Flum, J., and Thomas, W.: *An Introduction into Mathematical Logic*, Springer-Verlag, 1983.

Enderton, H. B.: *A Mathematical Introduction to Logic*, Academic Press, 1972.

Flon, L. and Suzuki, N.: The total correctness of parallel programs, *SIAM Journ. on Comp.*, **10**, pp. 227–246, 1981.

Floyd, R. W.: Assigning meanings to programs, *Proc. Symp. on Appl. Math.*, **19** (Math. Aspects of Comp. Sc.), American Math. Society, New York, 1967.

Gerhart, S. L.: Proof theory of partial correctness verification systems, *SIAM Journ. on Comp.*, **5**, pp. 355–377, 1976.

Goguen, J. A., Thatcher, J. W., Wagner, E. G., and Wright, J. B.: Initial algebra semantics and continuous algebras, *Journ. ACM*, **24**, pp. 68–95, 1977.

Goguen, J. A., Thatcher, J. W., and Wagner, E. G.: An initial algebra approach to the specification, correctness and implementation of abstract data types, *Current Trends in Programming Methodology IV* (ed. R. Yeh), pp. 80–149, Prentice-Hall, 1978.

Gordon, M. J. C.: *The Denotational Description of Programming Languages*, Springer-Verlag, 1979.

Gordon, M. J., Milner, A. J., and Wadsworth, C. P.: *Edinburgh LCF*, Lect. Notes in Comp. Sc., **78**, Springer-Verlag, 1979.

Greibach, S. A.: *Theory of Program Structures: Schemes, Semantics, Verification*, Lect. Notes in Comp. Sc., **36**, Springer-Verlag, 1975.

Greif, I. and Meyer, A. R.: Specifying the semantics of while-programs: a tutorial and critique of a paper by Hoare and Lauer, *TOPLAS*, **3**, pp. 484–507, 1981.

Gries, D.: Is Sometime ever better than Alway? *TOPLAS*, **1**, 258–265, 1979.

Gries, D.: *The Science of Programming*, Springer-Verlag, 1981.

Guessarian, I.: *Algebraic Semantics*, Lect. Notes in Comp. Sc., **99**, Springer-Verlag, 1981.

Guttag, J. V., Horowitz, E., and Musser, D. R.: Abstract data types and software validation, *Comm. ACM*, **21**, pp. 1048–1063, 1978.

Guttag, J. V., Horning, J., and Wing, J.: Some notes on putting formal specifications to productive use, *Sc. of Comp. Programming*, **2**, pp. 53–68, 1982.

Hailpern, B. T.: *Verifying Concurrent Processes Using Temporal Logic*, Lect. Notes in Comp. Sc., **129**, Springer-Verlag, 1982.

Halpern, J. Y. and Meyer, A. R.: Axiomatic definitions of programming languages II, *Proc. 8th POPL Conf.*, pp. 139–148, 1981.

Harel, D.: *First-Order Dynamic Logic*, Lect. Notes in Comp. Sc., **68**, Springer-Verlag, 1979.

Harel, D.: Proving the correctness of regular deterministic programs: a unifying survey, *Theor. Comp. Sc.*, **12**, pp. 61–81, 1980.

Hoare, C. A. R.: An axiomatic basis of computer programming, *Comm. ACM*, **12**, pp. 576–583, 1969.

Hoare, C. A. R. and Wirth, N.: An axiomatic definition of the programming language PASCAL, *Acta Inform.*, **2**, pp. 335–355, 1973.

Hoare, C. A. R.: Some properties of predicate transformers, *Journ. ACM*, **25**, pp. 461–480, 1978.

Hughes, G. E. and Cresswell, M. J.: *An Introduction to Modal Logic*, Methuen and Co. (London), 1968.

Igarashi, S., London, R. L., and Luckham, D. C.: Automatic program verification I: logical basis and its implementation, *Acta Inform.*, **4**, pp. 145–182, 1975.

Katz, S. M. and Manna, Z.: A closer look at termination, *Acta Inform.*, **5**, pp. 333–352, 1975.

Katz, S. and Manna, Z.: Logical analysis of programs, *Studies in Automatic Programming Logic* (ed. Z. Manna and R. Waldinger), pp. 93–140, North-Holland, 1977.

King, J. C.: Program correctness: on inductive assertion methods, *IEEE Trans. on Softw. Eng.*, **6**, pp. 465–479, 1980.

Kleene, S. C.: *Introduction to Metamathematics*, North-Holland, 1952.

Kleene, S. C.: *Mathematical Logic*, John Wiley, 1967.

Knuth, D.: Semantics of context-free languages, *Math. Syst. Theory*, **2**, pp. 127–145, 1968.

Kowalski, R.: *Logic Problem Solving*, North-Holland, 1979.

Lipton, R. J.: A necessary and sufficient condition for the existence of Hoare logics, *Proc. 18th IEEE Symp. on Found. Comp. Sc.*, pp. 1–6, 1977.

Liskov, B., Snyder, A., Atkinson, R., and Schaffert, C.: Abstraction mechanisms in CLU, *Comm. ACM*, **20**, pp. 564–576, 1977.

Liskov, B.: *CLU: Reference Manual*, Lect. Notes in Comp. Sc., **114**, Springer-Verlag, 1981.

Livercy, C.: *Théorie des Programmes*, Dunod, 1978.

Loeckx, J.: *Algorithmentheorie*, Springer-Verlag, 1976.

Loeckx, J.: Algorithmic specifications of abstract data types, *Proc. 8th ICALP (Acre)*, Lect. Notes in Comp. Sc., **115**, pp. 129–147, Springer-Verlag, 1981.

Lucas, P. and Walk, K.: On the formal description of PL/I, *Annual Review in Autom. Progr.*, **6**, pp. 105–182, 1971.

Manna, Z., Ness, S., and Vuillemin, J.: Inductive methods for proving properties of programs, *Comm. ACM*, **16**, pp. 491–502, 1973.

Manna, Z.: *Mathematical Theory of Computation*, McGraw-Hill, 1974.

Manna, Z. and Pnueli, A.: Axiomatic approach to total correctness of programs, *Acta Inform.*, **3**, pp. 243–264, 1974.

Manna, Z. and Waldinger, R.: Is 'sometime' sometimes better than 'always'? Intermittent assertions in proving program correctness, *Comm. ACM*, **21**, 2, pp. 159–172, 1978.

Manna, Z. and Pnueli, A.: Verification of concurrent programs: the temporal framework, *The Correctness Problem in Computer Science* (ed. R. S. Boyer and J. S. Moore), pp. 215–273, Academic Press, 1981.

Manna, Z. and Waldinger, R.: A deductive approach to program synthesis, *TOPLAS*, **2**, pp. 90–121, 1980.

McCarthy, J.: Towards a mathematical science of computation, *Proc. IFIP Congress 62*, pp. 21–28, North-Holland, 1963.

De Millo, R. A., Lipton, R. J., and Perlis, A. J.: Social processes and proofs of theorems and programs, *Comm. ACM*, **22**, pp. 271–280, 1979.

Milne, R. and Strachey, C.: *A Theory of Programming Language Semantics*, Chapman and Hall, 1976.

Milner, R.: Logic for computable functions: description of a machine implementation, *SIGPLAN NOTICES*, 7, pp. 1–6, 1972.

Milner, R.: LCF: a way of doing proofs with a machine, *Proc. 8th MFCS Symp. (Olomouc)*, pp. 146–159, Lect. Notes in Comp. Sc., **74**, Springer-Verlag, 1979.

Milner, R.: *A Calculus of Communicating Systems*, Lect. Notes in Comp. Sc., **92**, Springer-Verlag, 1980.

Morris, J. H. and Wegbreit, B.: Subgoal induction, *Comm. ACM*, **20**, pp. 209–222, 1977.

Nakajima, R. and Yuasa, T.: *The IOTA Programming System*, Lect. Notes in Comp. Sc., **160**, Springer-Verlag, 1983.

Naur, P.: Proofs of algorithms by general snapshots, *BIT*, **6**, pp. 310–316, 1966.

Newey, M.: Axioms and theorems for integers, lists and finite sets, *Memo AIM—184*, Stanford Univ., 1973.

Olderog, E.-R.: Sound and complete Hoare-like calculi based on copy rules, *Acta Inform.*, **16**, pp. 161–197, 1981.

Owicki, S. and Gries, D.: Verifying properties of parallel programs: an axiomatic approach, *Comm. ACM*, **19**, pp. 279–286, 1976.

Park, D.: Fixpoint induction and proofs of program properties, *Machine Intelligence*, **5** (ed. B. Meltzer and D. Michie), pp. 59–78, Edinburgh Univ. Press, 1969.

Plotkin, G.: A power domain construction, *SIAM Journ. on Com.*, **5**, pp. 452–487, 1976.

Pnueli, A.: The temporal logic of programs, *Proc. 18th FOCS*, pp. 46–57, 1977.

Polak, W.: *Compiler Specification and Verification*, Lect. Notes in Comp. Sc., **124**, Springer-Verlag, 1981.

Pratt, V. R.: Semantical considerations on Floyd–Hoare logic, *Proc. 17th IEEE Symp. on Found. of Comp. Sc.*, pp. 109–121, 1976.

Robinson, J. A.: *Logic: Form and Function*, University Press, Edinburgh, 1979.

Salwicki, A.: Formalized algorithmic languages, *Bull. Acad. Pol. Sc., Ser. Sc. Math. Astr. Phys.*, **18**, No. 5, 1970.

Scott, D.: Outline of a mathematical theory of computation, *4th Annual Princeton Conf. Inform. Sc. and Systems*, pp. 169–176, 1970.

Sieber, K.: Weakest expressible preconditions: a new tool for proving completeness results about Hoare-calculi, *Proc. 6th GI Conf. on Theor. Comp. Sc.*, Lect. Notes in Comp. Sc., **145**, Springer-Verlag, 1982.

Sieber, K.: *Die "Modale Logik der Prozeduren", eine Erweiterung der Hoare-Logik für Korrektheitsbeweise im Sinne des "stepwise refinement"*, Dissertation, Universität des Saarlandes, Saarbrücken, 1984.

Smyth, M. B.: Power domains, *J. of Comp. Syst. Sc.*, **16**, pp. 23–36, 1978.

Stanford Verification Group: *Stanford Pascal Verifier User Manual*, Stanford Verification Group Report No. 11, 1979.

Steel, T. B. Jr. (Editor): *Formal Language Description Languages for Computer Programming*, North-Holland, 1966.

Stoy, J. E.: *Denotational Semantics: The Scott–Strachey Approach to Programming Language Theory*, M.I.T. Press, 1977.

Tennent, R. D.: The denotational semantics of programming languages, *Comm. ACM*, **19**, pp. 437–453, 1976.

Thompson, D. H. (Editor): *AFFIRM Reference Manual*, USC Information Sciences Institute, Marina del Rey, 1979.

Vuillemin, J.: Correct and optimal implementations of recursion in a simple programming language, *J. of Comp. Syst. Sc.*, **9**, pp. 332–354, 1976.

Wand, M.: A new incompleteness result for Hoare's system, *Journ. ACM*, **25**, pp. 168–175, 1978.

Wand, M.: *Induction, Recursion and Programming*, North-Holland, 1980.

Wang, A.: An axiomatic basis for proving total correctness of goto programs, *BIT*, **16**, pp. 88–102, 1976.

Yeh, R. and Reynolds, C.: Induction as the basis for program verification, *IEEE Trans. on Softw. Eng.*, **SE-2**, pp. 244–252, 1976.

Index

227